HISTORY OF CIVILISATION

Russia under the Old Regime

Russia under the Old Regime

RICHARD PIPES

Charles Scribner's Sons
New York

1 3 5 7 9 11 13 15 17 19 C/C   20 18 16 14 12 10 8 6 4 2
1 3 5 7 9 11 13 15 17 19 C/P   20 18 16 14 12 10 8 6 4 2

Printed in the United States of America
Library of Congress Catalog Card Number 74-32567

ISBN 0-684—14225-2 (paper)
ISBN 0-684—14041-1 (cloth)

To
Daniel and Steven

CONTENTS

ILLUSTRATIONS

* Geissler's full name was Christian Gottfried Heinrich Geissler, but he also published under the initials 'J.G.' and 'J.G.H.', as noted below.

MAPS

FOREWORD

The theme of this book is the political system of Russia. It traces the growth of the Russian state from its beginnings in the ninth century to the end of the nineteenth, and the parallel development of the principal social orders: peasantry, nobility, middle class and clergy. The question which it poses is why in Russia – unlike the rest of Europe to which Russia belongs by virtue of her location, race and religion – society has proven unable to impose on political authority any kind of effective restraints. After suggesting some answers to this problem, I go on to show how in Russia the opposition to absolutism tended to assume the form of a struggle for ideals rather than for class interests, and how the imperial government, challenged in this manner, responded by devising administrative practices that clearly anticipate those of the modern police state. Unlike most historians who seek the roots of twentieth-century totalitarianism in western ideas, I look for them in Russian institutions. Although I do make occasional allusions to later events, my narrative largely terminates in the 1880s because, as the concluding chapter points out, the *ancien régime* in the traditionally understood sense died a quiet death in Russia at that time, yielding to a bureaucratic-police regime which in effect has been in power there ever since.

In my analysis, I lay heavy stress on the relationship between property and political power. This emphasis may appear odd to readers raised on western history and accustomed to regard the two as distinct entities. (Except, of course, for economic determinists, for whom, however, this relationship everywhere follows a rigid and preordained pattern of development.) Anyone who studies the political systems of non-western societies quickly discovers that there the lines separating ownership from sovereignty either do not exist, or are so vague as to be meaningless, and that the absence of this distinction marks a cardinal point of difference between western and non-western types of government. One may say that the existence of private property as a realm over which public authority normally exercises no jurisdiction is the thing which distinguishes western political experience from all the rest. Under primitive conditions, authority over people and over objects is combined, and it required an extraordinarily complex evolution of law and institutions which began in ancient Rome for it to be split into authority exercised as sovereignty and authority exercised as ownership. It is my central thesis that in Russia this separation occurred very late and very imperfectly. Russia belongs *par excellence* to that category of states which in the political and sociological literature it has become customary to refer to as 'patrimonial'. In such states political authority is conceived and exercised as an extension of the rights of ownership, the ruler (or rulers) being both sovereigns of the realm and its proprietors. The difficulty of maintaining this type of regime in the face of steadily increased contact and rivalry with a differently governed west has brought about in Russia a condition of permanent internal tension that has not been resolved to this day.

The format of this book precludes thorough documentation. By and large, I confine my references to direct quotations and statistical facts. But any specialist will readily recognize how deep is my debt to other, uncited historians.

I should like to express my appreciation to Professor Leonard Schapiro who has read the manuscript and given me the benefit of his advice.

Richard Pipes

London, 6 March 1974.

CHAPTER 1

THE ENVIRONMENT AND ITS CONSEQUENCES

Patriotic Russian historians notwithstanding, when the Lord created mankind He did not place the Russians where they happen to be today. In the earliest times for which we have any evidence, the heartland of Russia – the forest zone in the middle of which lies the city of Moscow – was populated by peoples of Finnic and Lithuanian stock, while areas adjoining to the east and south were inhabited by Turks. The Russians first migrated into this territory towards the end of the first millennium of the Christian era. Until then, together with the rest of the Slavs, they had inhabited a region whose boundaries cannot be determined even with approximate precision but which is believed to have lain north of the Carpathian mountains between the Vistula or Oder to the west and what is today Belorussia in the east. Little is known of Slav prehistory. Archaeological artefacts, which cannot be attributed to any specific ethnic or even racial group, linguistic fossils and ethnic names of long defunct nations such as are found in early histories and travellers' accounts, have generated a great deal of theory but concrete evidence is flimsy in the extreme. All that can be said with reasonable certainty is that the early Slavs were nomadic cattle grazers organized into clans and tribes, and that they had neither political nor military forms of organization. Their neighbours to the west and south were the Goths; in the north and north-east they touched on Lithuanian territories. The Venedi or Veneti mentioned by Pliny the Elder and Tacitus were apparently Slavs. This old name is preserved in the German 'Wenden', a now extinct nation of Western Slavs, and 'Venäjä', the modern Finnish word for Russia. Other names applied to them by foreign writers were Antae and Sclaveni. The Slavs seem to have called themselves Slovene or Sloviane, which most likely derives from *slovo*, 'the word', to signify people with the gift of speech, in contrast to Nemtsy, the 'dumb ones', the name given by Slavs to all the other Europeans, and, more specifically, their German neighbours.

In the age of the Roman Empire, the Slavs lived in central Europe in an homogeneous, ethnically undifferentiated mass. This homogeneity began to break down after the Empire's collapse as a result of their being caught up in the vast population shifts caused by the influx of Asiatic barbarians. The Slav migratory movement seems to have begun towards the end of the fourth century, following the Hun invasion of Europe which led to the destruction of the neighbouring Gothic kingdoms, but it assumed major dimensions only in the sixth century after the onslaught of a fresh wave of Asians, the Avars. Following the Avar invasion, one group of Slavs spread south, into the Balkan peninsula, stopping only when they came up against the borders of Byzantium. Others moved east. Here there was no political or military power to stop them, and they fanned out in small pockets all the way from the Black Sea to the Baltic, subjugating the exceedingly primitive Finns and Lithuanians and settling in their midst. It is during this time of migrations, i.e. between the sixth and tenth centuries, that the Slavic proto-nation fell apart. The Slavs initially split into three major territorial units (western, southern and eastern); in the second millennium of the Christian era they kept on splitting further into separate nationalities, a process which in some parts of the Slav world is still not fully completed.

Before one can begin to discuss the historic evolution of the eastern Slavs, from whom the Russians descend, it is necessary to describe in some detail the physical environment into which their migrations had carried them. The contemporary western reader has little patience for physical geography, and understandably so, because science and technology have to an unprecedented degree liberated him from dependence on nature. But even that relative freedom from vagaries of the environment which modern western people have come to enjoy is an event of very recent date and narrowly confined in scope. As far as conditions of pre-modern life are concerned, the notion of independence from nature is irrelevant. To understand human life prior to the Scientific and Industrial Revolutions as well as outside the relatively limited part of the world directly affected by them, it is necessary to allow the natural environment a role much greater than that of decorative backdrop. Men living in the pre-scientific and pre-industrial phases of history hd and continue to have no choice but to adapt themselves to that nature which provides them with all they need to sustain life. And since adaptation implies dependence, it is not surprising that the natural environment, the subject-matter of geography, should have had a decisive influence on the mind and habits of pre-modern man as well as on his social and political institutions. It is only when he began to feel emancipated from total subordination to nature that man could fantasize about being master of his own fate.

In the case of Russia the geographic element is particularly important because (as will be pointed out below), the country is inherently so poor that it affords at best a precarious existence. This poverty gives the inhabitants little latitude for action; it compels them to operate within a very narrow band of options.

In terms of *vegetation*, Russia can be divided into three main zones, which run, in belt-like shape, from east to west:[1]

1. the tundra: this region, north of the Arctic Circle, is covered with lichens and cannot support organized human life;

2. south of the tundra lies an immense forest, the largest in the world, which occupies much of the northern half of Eurasia from the Arctic Circle to between 45 and 50 degrees northern latitude. This forest can be further subdivided into three parts: A. The needle-leaved taiga in the northern regions, composed mainly of spruce and pine; B. The mixed forest, partly needle-leaved, partly broad-leaved: this is the central area of Russia, where stands Moscow and where the modern Russian state had its beginning; and, C. The wooded steppe, a transitional region separating forest from grassland;

3. the steppe, an immense plain stretching from Hungary to Mongolia: here no trees grow unless planted and cultivated; of itself, nature yields only grass and brush.

As concerns cultivable *soil*, Russia can be divided into two principal zones, the border between which roughly coincides with the line separating forest from steppe:

In the forest zone, the predominant type of earth is *podzol*, a soil short of natural plant food; what there is of the latter lies in the subsoil and requires deep ploughing to be of use. In this region there are numerous bogs and marshes, as well as large stretches of sand and clay. In part of the wooded steppe and through much of the steppe proper the prevailing soil is the fertile black earth (*chernozem*), which owes both its colour and fertility to humus, the product of decayed grass and brush. The black earth has from 2 to 16 per cent humus spread in a layer two to six feet deep. Its surface covers approximately a quarter of a billion acres, which are the centre of Russian agriculture (Map 1).

The *climate* of Russia is of the so-called Continental type, that is, hot in the summer and very cold in the winter. The winter weather grows colder as one proceeds in an easterly direction. The coldest regions of Russia are to be found not in its most northern but in its most eastern parts: Verkhoiansk, the Siberian city with the lowest recorded temperature in the world has a less northerly latitude than Narvik, the ice-free port in Norway. The reason for this peculiarity of the Russian climate is that the warm air produced by the Gulf Stream, which warms western Europe, cools as it moves inland and away from the Atlantic coast. One of the consequences of this fact is that Siberia, potentially an inexhaustible

3

reservoir of agricultural land, is in its major part unsuited for farming; in its eastern regions, lands located at the same latitude as England cannot be tilled at all.

Precipitation follows a pattern different from that prevailing in the distribution of the vegetation and soil. It is heaviest in the north-west, along the coast of the Baltic Sea, where it is brought in by the warm winds, and decreases as one moves in the opposite direction, towards the south-east. In other words, it is the most generous where the soil is the poorest. Another peculiarity of precipitation in Russia is that the rain tends to fall heaviest in the second half of the summer. In the Moscow region, the two rainiest months of the year are July and August, when nearly a quarter of the entire annual precipitation occurs. A small shift in the timetable of rain distribution can mean a drought in the spring and early summer, followed by disastrous downpours during the harvest. In western Europe the rainfall distributes itself much more evenly throughout the year.

Finally, the *waterways*. Russia's rivers run in a north-south direction; none of the major rivers runs east-west. However, the lateral branches of the great rivers do just that; and because Russia is flat (no point in its European part exceeds 1,400 feet) and its rivers originate not in moun-

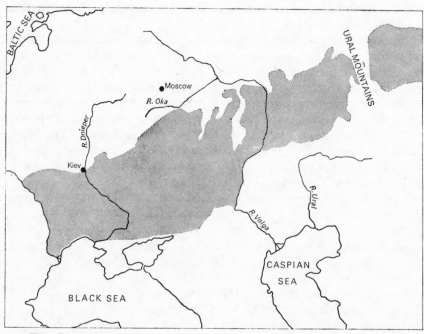

1. The Black Earth Belt

tains but in swamps and lakes formed by swamps they have gentle gradients. As a result, Russia possesses a unique network of navigable waterways, composed of large rivers and their numerous branches linked with one another by means of easy portages. Even with primitive modes of transport it is possible to navigate across Russia from the Baltic to the Caspian seas, and to reach by water a high proportion of the land lying in between. In Siberia, the water network happens to be so excellently meshed that in the seventeenth century Russian fur trappers succeeded in traversing in a very short time thousands of miles to the Pacific and inaugurating regular commerce between Siberia and the home country by means of river transport. Were it not for these waterways, life in Russia would have been hardly feasible above the mere subsistence level until the advent of railways. The distances are so great and the costs of maintaining roads under the prevailing extremes of temperature so high that land transport was practicable only in the winter, when snow provided a smooth surface for sleighs. This fact accounts for the great reliance of Russians on water transport. Until the second half of the nineteenth century the bulk of merchandise moved on boats and barges.

Like the other Slavs, the ancient Russians were primarily a pastoral people; and like them, upon settling down in their new territories, they slowly made the transition to agriculture. Unfortunately for them, the area which the Eastern Slavs penetrated and colonized happens to be uniquely ill suited for farming. The indigenous Finns and Turks treated farming as a supplementary occupation, concentrating in the forest zone on hunting and fishing, and in the steppe on livestock breeding. The Russians chose otherwise. Their heavy reliance on farming under adverse natural conditions is perhaps the single most basic cause of the problems underlying Russian history.

Some of these difficulties have been alluded to already: the indifferent quality of the soil in the north, and the vagaries of the rainfall, which is heaviest where it does the least good, and has a tendency to come down too late in the agricultural season. The peculiar topographical and seasonal distribution of the rainfall is a major reason why, over the course of its recorded history, Russia has averaged one bad harvest out of every three.

But the gravest and least soluble problems derive from the extreme northern location of the country. Together with Canada, Russia is the northernmost state in the world. It is true that modern Russia controls large territories with semi-tropical climates (the Crimea, the Caucasus and Turkestan), but these were acquired late, mostly in the mid-nineteenth century, in the course of imperial expansion. The cradle of the Russian state, that which Brandenburg is to Germany or the Île is to

5

France, lies in the zone of mixed forests. Until the middle of the sixteenth century, Russians had been virtually confined to this area, because the steppe with its coveted black earth was under the control of hostile Turkic tribes. Russians began to penetrate the steppe in the second half of the sixteenth century, but they became masters of it only towards the end of the eighteenth when they at long last conclusively defeated Turkish power. During the formative period of their statehood they had to live between 50 and 60 degrees of northern latitude. This is approximately the latitude of Canada. In drawing comparisons between the two countries, however, several differences must be kept in mind. The bulk of the Canadian population has always resided in the southernmost part of the country, along the Great Lakes and the St Lawrence River, i.e. at 45 degrees, which in Russia corresponds to the latitudes of the Crimea and the central Asian steppe. Nine-tenths of the Canadian population lives within two hundred miles of the United States border. North of the 52nd parallel Canada has little population and hardly any agriculture. Secondly, throughout its history Canada has enjoyed friendly relations with its richer southern neighbour, with which it has maintained close economic relations. (It remains to this day the largest single recipient of US capital investments.) And finally, Canada has never had to support a large population; those of its people whom the economy could not employ have been in the habit of moving, seasonally or permanently, to the United States. None of these advantages exists in the case of Russia: its neighbours have been neither rich nor friendly, and the country has had to rely on its own resources to support a population which already in the middle of the eighteenth century was larger than Canada's is today.

The principal consequence of Russia's location is an exceedingly short farming season. In the taiga, around Novgorod and St Petersburg, it lasts a mere four months in the year (from mid-May to mid-September). In the central regions, near Moscow, it stretches to five and a half months (mid-April to end of September). In the steppe, it lasts six months. The remainder of the Russian year is altogether unsuitable for agricultural work, because the soil is as hard as rock and the land is covered by a deep blanket of snow.

In western Europe, by contrast, the growing season lasts eight to nine months. In other words, the western farmer has at his disposal anywhere from 50 to 100 per cent more time for field work than the Russian. Furthermore, in parts of Europe where the winter is mild, the winter months can be employed for occupations other than field work. The economic and social consequences of this simple climatic fact will be elucidated below.

The brief growing season, and its corollary, a long and hard winter,

6

create an additional difficulty for the Russian peasant. He must confine his livestock indoors two months longer than the western farmer. His cattle thus misses out on the early spring grazing, and when finally set free in the meadow it is in a thoroughly emaciated condition. Russian livestock has always been of an inferior quality, notwithstanding attempts by the government and enlightened landlords to improve it; imported western breeds have promptly degenerated to the point where they became indistinguishable from the miserable domestic variety. The difficulties in raising livestock have discouraged efficient meat and dairy farming in the forest zone. They have affected adversely the quality of the draught animals and caused perennial shortages of manure, especially in the north, where it is most needed.

The consequence of Russia's poor soil, unreliable rainfall and brief growing season have been low yields.

Agricultural yields are most meaningfully measured in terms which indicate how many times the seed reproduces itself: when, for example, one grain cast at sowing time gives five grains at harvest, we speak of a yield ratio 1:5. The typical yield ratio in medieval Europe was 1:3 or at best 1:4, the minimum yields which make agriculture worth while and create conditions capable of sustaining life. A 1:3 ratio, it must be noted, means an annual doubling rather than tripling of the sown seed, because each year one of every three grains harvested must be set aside for seed. It also means that one acre of arable out of every three has to be devoted to seed production. In the second half of the thirteenth century, west European yields began to experience a significant rise. The principal cause of this phenomenon was the growth of cities, whose trading and manufacturing population had given up growing food, buying it from farmers instead. The emergence of a rich urban market for cereals and other produce encouraged western landlords and peasants to raise a surplus by more intensive use of labour and heavier manuring. In the late Middle Ages, western yields rose to 1:5, and then, in the course of the sixteenth and seventeenth centuries, they improved further to 1:6 and 1:7. By the middle of the nineteenth century, countries with advanced farming, headed by England, regularly obtained yields of 1:10. Such a dramatic improvement had an even greater economic significance than might appear at first glance. Where the soil can be depended upon regularly to return ten grains for each grain sown, the farmer needs to set aside for seed only a tenth of the land and a tenth of the harvest, instead of a third of each, as he must do under a 1:3 yield. The net return on a 1:10 yield is $4\frac{1}{2}$ times what it is on a 1:3 yield, making it theoretically possible to sustain in a given area that many more inhabitants. The cumulative effect of such a surplus over a number of years can be readily appreciated. It may be said that civilization begins only where one grain of seed multiplies itself at least five times; it is this minimum surplus which determines (assuming no food imports) whether a significant proportion of the population can be released from the necessity of raising food to pursue other occupations. 'In a country with rather low yield ratios highly developed industry, commerce and transport are impossible'.[2] And so, one may add, is highly developed political life.

Like the rest of Europe, Russia averaged in the Middle Ages ratios of 1:3, but unlike the west, it did not experience any improvement in yield ratios during the centuries that followed. In the nineteenth century, Russian yields remained substantially the same as they had been in the fifteenth, declining in bad years to 1:2, going up in good ones to 1:4 and even 1:5, but averaging over the centuries 1:3 (slightly below this figure in the north and slightly above it in the south). Such a ratio generally sufficed to support life. The picture of the Russian peasant as a creature for ever groaning under oppression and grubbing to eke out a miserable living is simply untenable. A Russian agrarian historian has recently challenged the prevailing view in these words:

We confront a paradox. A scholar investigates the condition of peasants in the period of early feudalism. Their condition is already so bad it cannot deteriorate further. They are perishing completely. But then, later on, they turn out to be worse off yet; in the fifteenth century still worse, in the sixteenth, seventeenth, eighteenth, nineteenth centuries, all the time worse, worse and worse. And so it goes until the Great October Socialist Revolution. It has already been pointed out, very correctly ... that the living standard of peasants is elastic and capable of shrinking. Still, it cannot shrink *ad infinitum*. How did they survive?[3]

The answer, of course, is that the traditional view of the living conditions and living standards of Russian peasants must be wrong. Recent computations of the incomes of Novgorod peasants in the fifteenth century, and of the Belorussian–Lithuanian peasants in the sixteenth (both inhabitants of northern regions with the inferior, *podzol*, soil) do indeed indicate that these groups had managed to feed themselves quite adequately.[4] The trouble with Russian agriculture was not that it could not feed its cultivators but that it never could produce a significant surplus. The productivity lag of Russia behind western Europe widened with each century. By the end of the nineteenth century, when good German farms regularly obtained in excess of one ton of cereals from an acre of land, Russian farms could barely manage to reach six hundred pounds. In Russia of the late nineteenth century, an acre of land under wheat yielded only a seventh of the English crop, and less than a half of the French, Prussian or Austrian.[5] Russian agricultural productivity, whether calculated in grain yields or yields per acre, was by then the lowest in Europe.

The low productivity of the Russian soil, however, cannot be blamed entirely on the climate. Scandinavia, despite its northern location, attained already by the eighteenth century yield ratios of 1:6, while the Baltic provinces of the Russian Empire, where the land was in the hands of German barons, in the first half of the nineteenth century had yields from 1:4·3 to 1:5·1, that is, of a kind which made it possible to begin accumulating a surplus.[6]

The other cause of low agricultural productivity in Russia, besides the natural factors already enumerated, was the absence of markets. Here, as is the case with most historical phenomena, cause and effect confronted each other in reciprocal fashion: the cause produced the effect but then the effect became a force of its own which in turn influenced and transformed its original cause. Unfavourable natural conditions made for low yields; low yields resulted in poverty; poverty meant that there were no buyers for agricultural produce; the lack of buyers discouraged yield improvements. The net effect was the absence of incentives. A vicious circle of this kind could be broken only by the intervention of some external force, in this case the opening of commercial contacts with other countries or major scientific or technical innovations.

Clearly, an agricultural surplus must be disposed of not to other farmers but to people who themselves do not grow food, and this means, in effect, the inhabitants of cities. Where an urban market is absent, little can be done with the excess grain except to distil it into spirits. As noted above, the improvement in the yield ratios of medieval Europe was originally associated with the growth of cities; the emergence of sizeable trading and artisan groups both encouraged improvements in farming and was made possible by them. Now in Russia cities have never played a significant role in the nation's economy; and paradoxically, over the centuries, their role tended to decline rather than grow. As late as the eighteenth century, Russia's urban inhabitants comprised only 3 per cent of the total population, and even this figure is deceptive because the majority of Russian city dwellers traditionally have consisted of landlords and peasants who grew their own food. Nor could Russia dispose of its grain abroad because there were for it no foreign markets until the middle of the nineteenth century at which time countries with advanced industrial economies decided it was cheaper for them to import food than to grow it. Russia is too remote from the great routes of international trade to have developed a significant urban civilization on the basis of foreign commerce. Three times in its history she was pulled into the mainstream of international trade; each time the result was the sprouting of cities; but each time, too, the urban flowering proved short-lived. The first occasion occurred between the ninth and eleventh centuries, when, following Muslim expansion and the closing of the eastern Mediterranean to Christian trade, Russia offered a convenient shortcut from northern Europe to the Near East. A great proportion of the major cities of old Russia were founded at that time. This commerce came to an end around 1200 when Turkic nomads cut the route to Byzantium. The second period of Russia's involvement in international trade took place between the thirteenth and fifteenth centuries, when Novgorod was a leading member of the Hanseatic League. This connection was forcefully severed by Moscow at the end of the fifteenth century; less than a hundred years later Moscow razed Novgorod. The third period began in 1553 when English merchants discovered a maritime route to Russia by way of the North Sea. Once again, the international trade which ensued led to a lively growth of cities, this time along the roads and rivers connecting Moscow with the North Sea. But this commerce came to a halt in the latter part of the seventeenth century, partly because the Russian government, under pressure from its own merchants, withdrew the privileges which it had granted foreign traders, partly because the demand for Russia's goods in the west had diminished. Russia's cities, few in number and, except for Moscow, small in population, came to serve primarily military and administrative purposes, and as such would not provide a significant market for food.

There were thus no economic incentives present to try to overcome nature's handicaps. The Russian landlord and peasant looked upon the soil primarily as a means of subsistence, not of enrichment. Indeed, no major fortunes in Russia were ever made from agriculture. Little money was invested in it, because the yields were meagre and the market exceedingly narrow. Well into the nineteenth century, the basic instrument of the Russian farmer was a primitive plough called *sokha*, which scratched the soil instead of turning it over (its maximum depth of penetration was 10 centimetres) but which had the advantage of requiring little pulling power and being ten times as fast as the plough. The basic crop was rye. It was chosen because of its hardiness and adaptability to the northern climate and poor soil. It also happens to be the cereal crop with the lowest yields. The prevalent pattern of cultivation from the sixteenth to the nineteenth centuries was the three-field system which required that one third of the land always lie fallow to regain its fertility. The system was so uneconomical that in countries with advanced agriculture like England it had been abandoned in the late Middle Ages. The whole stress in Russia was on getting the most out of the land with the least possible investment of time, effort and money. Every Russian sought to extricate himself from the land: the peasant desired nothing better than to abandon the fields and become a pedlar, artisan or usurer; the rural merchant, to join the nobility; the noble to move into the city or make a career in the state service. The proverbial rootlessness of Russians, their 'nomadic' proclivities so often noted by western travellers accustomed to people seeking roots, whether in the soil or in social status, have their main source in the marginal quality of Russian farming, i.e. in the inability of the land, the chief source of national wealth, to furnish much beyond sustenance.

Just how unprofitable farming was in Russia, especially in the forest zone, may be gathered from the calculations of August Haxthausen, a Prussian agrarian expert who visited the country in the 1840s. Haxthausen compared the income produced by two hypothetical farms of equal size, 1,000 hectares of arable and meadow each, one located on the Rhine, near Mainz, the other on the upper Volga, in the vicinity of Iaroslavl. A German farm of this size, in his estimation, would require the regular attention of 8 male and 6 female peasants, 1,500 man-days of seasonal hired labour and 4 teams of horses. The total operating expenses would come to 3,500 thalers. With an estimated gross income of 8,500 thalers, it would return annually a net profit of 5,000 thalers. In Iaroslavl, only because the short farming season demands a heavier concentration of labour, it would take 14 male and 10 female peasants, 2,100 man-days of hired labour, and 7 teams of horses to accomplish the same work. The resulting expenses would reduce the profit by nearly a half, down to 2,600 thalers. These calculations rest on the premises that the soil in the two cases is of equal quality, and the price obtained for the produce is the same which, of course, would not be the case. If one then adds to the disadvantages on the Russian side of the ledger the severe winters which prevent the peasant from engaging in any field work at least six months out of twelve; the high costs of transport due to great distances, poor roads and low population density; the lesser productivity of the Russian peasant as compared with the German; and, last but not least, the low prices fetched by agricultural produce – it becomes apparent that farming in northern Russia was not a paying proposition and made sense only when no alternative sources of income were available. Haxthausen concluded with the advice that anyone given the present of an estate in northern Russia on condition that he run it like a central European farm would do well to decline the gift because he would be adding year after year money to its operations. According to him, estate farming in Russia could be made profitable only on two conditions: if performed with serf labour (to free the landlord from the cost of supporting peasants and animals) or combined with manufacture (to employ idle labour during the winter months).[7] A Russian land expert in 1866 independently confirmed Haxthausen's opinion, stating that in Russia capital invested in government bonds brought better returns than that invested in agriculture; state service, too, was more remunerative than farming.[8] We can now understand why a German observer of the early nineteenth century could conclude that there was no country in Europe where 'agriculture was practised so negligently'.[9] The history of Russian agriculture is the tale of a land being mercilessly exploited without being given much if anything to nourish it and thus being driven into exhaustion. V.O.Kliuchevskii had this phenomenon in mind when he spoke of the old Russian peasants' unique talent for 'ravaging the land'.[10]

It is because the soil offered so little and dependence on it was so precarious, that Russians of all classes have learned from the earliest to supplement agricultural income with all kinds of 'industries' or *promysly*. In its virgin state, the Russian forest zone teemed with what appeared an inexhaustible supply of wildlife: deer and elk, bears, and an immense variety of fur-bearing rodents. These were hunted and trapped by peasants working for princes, landlords, monasteries as well as for themselves. Honey was plentiful; it was not even necessary to build hives, because the bees deposited honey in the trunks of dead trees. The waters abounded in fish, including sturgeon which made its way upstream from the Caspian. This abundance of wildlife allowed early Russian settlers to raise their standards of life above the bare subsistence level. How important such forest commodities were in the Russian budget may be seen from the fact that in the seventeenth century income derived from the sale of furs (mostly to foreign merchants) constituted the single largest item in the revenues of the imperial treasury. As the forests were cleared to make way for agricultural land and pastures, and overhunting and overtrapping depleted the supply of wildlife, especially the more valuable varieties of fur-bearing animals, Russians increasingly shifted their attention from the exploitation of natural resources to manufacture. In the middle of the eighteenth century there emerged in Russia a peculiar form of cottage industry (*kustarnaia promyshlennost'*), employing both free and serf labour, and working for the local market. This industry supplied Russia with a high proportion of its farming and household needs, simple cloth, silver, ikons, musical instruments and so forth. Much of the relative prosperity of both landlord and peasants between the middle of the eighteenth and middle of the nineteenth centuries derived from such manufacture. Towards the end of the nineteenth century, the growth of factory industry undercut the market for the unsophisticated products of cottage industry, and deprived peasants, especially in the northern provinces, of vital supplementary income.

Promysly, however, vital as they were, could not of themselves support the national economy: the latter, in the end, depended on farming. The rapid exhaustion of the soil under conditions of Russian agriculture compelled the peasant to be continually on the move in search of virgin land or land which had regained its fertility from a long rest. Even had the population of the country remained constant, Russia would have always experienced an unusual amount of peasant movement. The rapid growth of population in modern times gave this tendency a powerful added stimulus.

In so far as imperfect demographic records allow one to judge, until the middle of the eighteenth century the population of Russia remained relatively small. The most generous estimates place it at 9–10 million in the middle of the sixteenth century, and 11–12 million towards its end; other, more conservative estimates, put it at 6 and 8 million, respectively. These figures compare with a sixteenth-century population of 20 million in Austria, 19 in France, and 11 in Spain; Poland in the seventeenth century had some 11 million inhabitants. In Russia, as in the rest of Europe, the demographic spurt began around 1750. Between 1750 and 1850, the population of the Russian Empire quadrupled (from 17–18 to 68 million). Some of this growth, perhaps as much as 10 million, can be accounted for by conquest; but even when allowance has been made for expansion, the natural growth remains impressive. After 1850, when territorial expansion virtually ceased (the only major area conquered after that date, Turkestan, did not have many inhabitants), the population of Russia increased at a staggering rate: from 68 million in 1850 to 124 million in 1897 and 170 million in 1914. If during the second half of the sixteenth century, Russia's population had increased perhaps by 20 per cent, in the second half of the nineteenth it doubled. Russia's rate of population growth during the second half of the nineteenth century was the highest in Europe – and this at the very time when its grain yields were Europe's lowest.[11]

Unless the population were to perish from mass starvation – which until the Communist regime it did not, despite recurrent harvest failures and occasional regional famines – the food to feed these additional mouths had to come from somewhere. Imports were out of the question, for Russia had little to sell abroad with the proceeds of which to buy food; and those who did the selling – the tsar and the richest landlords – preferred to import luxuries. Indeed, cereals constituted Russia's own largest export item: Russia kept on exporting cereals in the nineteenth century even when she had not enough for her own people. Intensification of productivity through heavier manuring, use of machinery, and other methods conducive to rationalization was not feasible either, partly because the returns were too meagre to justify the necessary investments, partly because the rigid social organization of the peasantry resisted innovation. Capital was invested in land mainly on those southern farms which grew food for export to England and Germany; but on this land improvements of production did not benefit the peasant. The solution therefore was to put more and more fresh land under cultivation, that is, to practise extensive, in lieu of intensive, agriculture.

Statistical records indicate that the acreage under cultivation in Russia expanded steadily in response to this need, increasing between 1809 and 1887 by 60 per cent (from 197 to 317 million acres).[12] The availability of virgin land discouraged efforts to raise productivity; it was cheaper and easier to put new land to use than to improve the old. But even this steady expansion of the sown area did not suffice, for rapid as it was the population grew faster while yields remained constant. In the 1880s, there was virtually no virgin land left in central and southern Russia, and agricultural rents rose spectacularly. At the same time (as noted) the growth of modern industry deprived the peasants of the main source of supplementary income by preempting the market for the simple products of his cottage industry. Here, in a nutshell, is the root of the celebrated 'agrarian crisis' which so convulsed Russia during the late imperial period and contributed so greatly to its collapse.

However, so long as the frontier remained infinitely expandable, the Russian peasant pressed outward, leaving behind him the exhausted soil and seeking soil that no human hand had touched. Colonization is so fundamental a feature of Russian life that Kliuchevskii considered it to be its very essence: 'The history of Russia', he wrote at the beginning of his celebrated *Course*, 'is the history of a country which colonizes itself.'[13]

Until the middle of the sixteenth century, Russian colonization had to be confined to the western portion of the forest zone. Attempts to gain a foothold in the black earth belt were invariably beaten back. The steppe, where the black earth lay, provided ideal conditions for livestock grazing, the principal occupation of the nomadic Turks, and they annihilated any agricultural settlements which tried to establish themselves on it. The road leading to the east, to Siberia, was barred first by the Golden Horde, and then, after its dissolution in the fifteenth century, by its successor states, the khanates of Kazan and Astrakhan. The only area open to Russian colonization in the first six or seven centuries of Russian history was the far north. Some colonists, spearheaded by monasteries, did indeed venture beyond the upper Volga, but this inhospitable area could not absorb much population.

A dramatic change in the history of Russian colonization occurred after the conquest in 1552–6 of the khanates of Kazan and Astrakhan. Russian settlers immediately began to pour towards the mid-Volga, ejecting the indigenous Turks from the best lands; others pushed beyond, crossing 'the Rock', as they called the Urals, into southern Siberia where lay large stretches of pure, virgin black earth. But the main migratory push then and subsequently proceeded in the southern and southeastern direction, towards the so-called Central Black Earth Zone. In the 1570s the government constructed a chain of stockades facing the steppe from the Donets to the Irtysh rivers, and under its protection, peasants ventured into what had been always a nomad preserve. The movement, once inaugurated, progressed with an elemental force. Each major economic or political upheaval in the centre of Russia produced migratory outpourings. In this colonist expansion sometimes the peasant preceded the government, sometimes the government led the way; sooner or later, however, the two elements were certain to meet and fuse. One of the basic reasons for the tenacity with which Russians have managed to hold on to conquered territories lies in the fact that their political absorption was and to this day continues to be accompanied by colonization.

It is estimated that in the seventeenth and eighteenth centuries more than two million settlers migrated southward from Russia's central regions, penetrating first the wooded steppe and then the steppe proper. During these two centuries, some 400,000 settlers also migrated into Siberia. The greatest migratory wave struck the black earth belt after 1783, the year the Russians annexed the Crimea and subjugated the raiders who from its territory for centuries had harassed their settlements. In the nineteenth and early twentieth centuries 12–13 million migrants, most of them natives of the central provinces, moved south, with another four and a half or five million migrating into southern Siberia and the steppes of central Asia. The latter movement involved a wholesale dispossession and ejection of the Asian natives from their ancestral grazing lands.

In the earlier period (1552–1861), the mass of Russian migrants consisted either of free peasants or of runaway serfs, or else serfs forcibly transferred from the centre to work on the estates of military men serving on the frontier. After the emancipation of the serfs in 1861, the migrants were free peasants, now sometimes resettling with the assistance of the government which was eager to ease rural overpopulation in the central provinces. Over the centuries, the geographic pattern of Russian population distribution assumed the shape of a wedge, whose base has come to rest in the western part of the forest zone and the tip of which points south-east. This demographic wedge has continued to elongate over time, its changing shape reflecting a steady shift of the centre of the Russian population from its original homeland in the forest towards the steppe. In modern times, the heaviest concentration of the Russian population is in the black earth belt. The Revolution changed nothing in this respect. Between 1926 and 1939 over four million persons migrated eastward, mostly into the Kazakh steppe. The census of 1970 indicates that the movement has not ceased, the central regions continuing to lose population to the borderlands. A major secular process in progress for four hundred years has been carrying the Russian population outward from the central forest zone, mostly towards the east and south, causing them to inundate areas inhabited by nations of other races and cultures, and producing serious demographic dislocations in the path of their movement.*

Having surveyed the economic and demographic consequences produced by Russia's environment, we can now turn to the consequences of a social character.

The first fact to note is that the geography of Russia discourages individual farming. A general rule seems to exist which holds that northern climates are conducive to collective farm work: 'Everything indicates that fields lying in the north have been cultivated by people who conceive agricultural exploitation as collective labour, and those in the south by people determined to safeguard the independence and the freedom of initiative of each cultivator on his land.'[14] There are many reasons why this should be so, but in the ultimate analysis all of them have to do with the brevity of the agricultural season. Any job that requires x workers y days of full-time work to complete, will – if it must be done in $1/2\ y$ time – require $2x$ workers; and the same applies to the draught animals and agricultural implements used by these workers. The unalterable fact that all the field work in Russia must be completed between four and six months (instead of the eight to nine months available to the western farmer) calls for work being performed with great intensity, and induces the pooling of resources, human as well as animal and material. An individual Russian peasant, farming with his wife and minor children and a horse or two simply cannot manage under the climatic conditions prevailing in the forest zone; he needs help from his married children and neighbours. In the southern zone of Russia the pressure to work collectively diminishes somewhat, which explains why in pre-Revolutionary Russia most of the individual farmsteads, called *khutora*, were to be found in the Ukraine and the Cossack regions.

The collective character of farming in Russia influenced the structure of the peasant family and the village.

The traditional type of peasant family in Russia, prevalent until a century ago, was of the so-called joint type; it consisted of father, mother, minor children and married sons with their wives and offspring. The head of this group was called *bol'shak* ('the big one' or 'boss'). He was most commonly the father. Upon his death the family usually broke up; but sometimes it happened that after the father had died or become

* Since the end of the Second World War, there has been significant Russian migration westward as well, into areas originally populated by Poles, Jews, Germans and the Baltic nationalities. This colonization, in contrast with those of the past, is heavily urban. It is occasionally accompanied by mass expulsions and deportations of the indigenous peoples on charges of 'nationalism'.

incapacitated the joint family continued together under one of the brothers whom it elected to serve as bolshak. The bolshak, a kind of pater-familias, had final say in all family matters; he also set the schedule for field work and performed the sowing. His authority, originally derived from customary law, was given legal status in the 1860s by the rural courts which recognized his verdict as binding in disputes occurring within the family. All the property was held in common. The joint family was economically very advantageous. It was widely acknow-ledged by persons with expertise in rural life that field work in Russia was best done by large family teams, and that the quality of the peasants' performance depended in large measure on the bolshak's intelligence and authority. Both the government and landlords did all in their power to preserve this institution, not only because of its demonstrable influ-ence on productivity but also because of its political and social benefits to them. Officials and landlords alike preferred to deal with the head of the household rather than with its individual members. Furthermore, they liked the asssurance that a peasant who for some reason (illness or alcoholism, for example) could not work would be taken care of by his relatives. The peasants themselves had more ambivalent feelings. They undoubtedly recognized the economic advantages of the joint family since they had developed it spontaneously. But they disliked the tensions which were bound to arise where several married couples lived under the same roof; they also preferred to hold property individually. After gaining personal freedom in 1861, the one-time serfs broke up the joint families into their constituent units with precipitous speed, much to the detriment of Russian agriculture and their own well-being.

The basic social unit of the ancient Slavs was a tribal community, estimated to have consisted of some fifty or sixty people, all related by blood and working as a team. In time, the communities based on blood relationship dissolved, giving way to a type of communal organization based on joint ownership of arable and meadow, called in Russian *mir* or *obshchina*. The origin of this famous institution has been a subject of intense debate for more than a century. The debate began in the 1840s when a group of romantic nationalists known as Slavophiles became aware of the peasant commune as an institution confined to Russia, and extolled it as proof that the Russian people, allegedly lacking in the acquisitive 'bourgeois' impulses of western Europeans, were destined to solve mankind's social problems. Haxthausen popularized this view in his book, published in 1847. In the second half of the nineteenth cen-tury, the Russian mir became in Western Europe the starting-point of several theories concerning communal land-tenure of primitive societies. In 1854, however, this whole interpretation was challenged by Boris Chicherin, a leading spokesman of the so-called Westerner camp, who argued that the peasant commune as then known was neither ancient nor autochthonous in origin, but had been introduced by the Russian monarchy in the middle of the eighteenth century as a means of assuring the collection of taxes. Until then, according to Chicherin, Russian peasants had held their land by individual households. Subsequent researches blurred the lines of the controversy. Contemporary opinion holds that the commune of the imperial period was indeed a modern institution, as Chicherin claimed, there being no solid evidence of its existence before the eighteenth century. It is also widely agreed that pressure by the state and landlord played a major part in its formation. At the same time, economic factors seem also to have affected its evolution to the extent that there exists a demonstrable connection between the availability of land and communal tenure: where land is scarce, the communal form of tenure tends to prevail, but where it is abundant it is replaced by household or even family tenure.

Whatever the merits of the case, in the imperial period the vast majority of the Russian peasants held their land communally; in the central provinces the commune was virtually universal. The arable was divided into sections corresponding to the quality of the soil and distance from the village. Each household had the right to claim in every such section one or more strips corresponding to the number of its adult members; the latter were typically defined as all men between the ages of 15 or 17 and 60–65, and all married women under the age of 48. The strips were extremely narrow, measuring between nine and twelve feet in width and several hundred yards in length. A household might have had thirty to fifty or more such strips scattered in a dozen different locations around the village. The principal purpose of this arrangement was to enable every peasant to pay his share of rents and taxes. Since households grew or diminished over time, every so often (e.g. at nine-, twelve-, or fifteen-year intervals) the commune took its own census, on the basis of which it carried out a 'black repartition' (*chernyi peredel*), resulting in a re-allotment of the strips. The system was meant to guarantee every peasant an equitable share of the land, and every household enough land to support itself and to meet its responsibilities to the landlord and state. In reality, peasants were loath to part with the strips in which they had invested time and effort, especially if from an increase of the village population the repartition caused their allotments to be diminished. The authorities therefore had to step in repeatedly to enforce redistribution by decree.

One occasionally hears analogies drawn between the pre-revolutionary communes and the collective farms (*kolkhozy*) introduced in 1928–32 by the communist regime. The analogy has little to recommend it, except for a negative factor common to both institutions, i.e. the absence of private ownership in land. The differences are quite basic. The mir was not a collective; farming in it was carried out privately, by households. Even more significantly, the peasant living in the mir owned the product of his labour, whereas in the *kolkhoz* it belongs to the state which compensates the farmer for his work. The Soviet kolkhoz corresponds most closely to an institution encountered in Russia under serfdom under the name *mesiachina*. Under this system the landlord enclosed his land and placed the peasants on full-time labour on his own behalf, paying them a wage to support themselves.

Unlike the joint family, imposed on them by a combination of economic necessity and pressure from above, the commune enjoyed peasant loyalty. It provided a high degree of security without seriously inhibiting freedom of movement. It also allowed common access to meadow as well as co-ordination of field work which was highly desirable under the prevailing climatic conditions and the open field system. The latter was done by a council of the mir, composed of all the bolshaks (Plate 5). The peasants ignored the criticism levied at the commune by economists, who saw it as a millstone around the neck of the more enterprising among them, and tenaciously clung to it. In November 1906, the imperial government introduced easy procedures for the consolidation of strips into individual farmsteads. The legislation had a limited measure of success in the borderlands of the empire; in central Russia, the peasants simply ignored it.*

In so far as the political system of Russia is the main theme of this book, at this point the influence of the natural environment upon Russia's constitution need only be delineated in the most general terms.

On the face of it, nature intended Russia to be a decentralized country formed of a multitude of self-contained and self-governing communities. Everything here militates against statehood: the poverty of the soil, remoteness from the main routes of international trade, the sparsity and mobility of the population. And Russia might well have remained a decentralized society, with many scattered centres of localized power, were it not for geopolitical factors which urgently demanded firm political authority. The extensive, highly wasteful nature of Russian rural economy and the need for ever fresh land to replace that exhausted by overcultivation and undermanuring compelled Russians at all times to push outward. As long as their colonization had been confined to the taiga, the process could unroll spontaneously and without military protection. But the rich and desirable soil lay in the steppe, under the

---

* By 1913, only 17·7 per cent of peasant households availed themselves of the right to consolidate their strips and leave the commune, and most of these were in the Ukraine and Belorussia: A.N.Chelintsev, *Sel'sko-khoziaistvennaia geografiia Rossii* (Berlin 1923), p. 117, and Lazar Volin, *A century of Russian agriculture* (Cambridge, Mass. 1970), p. 107.

control of nomadic Turkic and Mongol tribes which not only did not tolerate any agricultural settlements on their grazing territories, but themselves frequently carried out raids into the forest in search of slaves and loot. Until the end of the eighteenth century, when their superior political and military organization gave them an upper hand, the Russians were unable to penetrate the black earth zone in any significant numbers, and indeed were often themselves victims of aggression on the part of their steppe neighbours. In the sixteenth and seventeenth centuries there was scarcely a year when Russians did not fight along their southern and south-eastern frontiers. Although Russian historians tend to depict these wars as defensive in nature, they were as often as not instigated by Russian colonist pressure. In the western parts, where Russians bordered on Poles, Lithuanians, Swedes and Germans, the situation was somewhat calmer, but even here, during this period, there was war approximately one year out of every two. Sometimes it was the westerners who pushed eastward; sometimes it was the Russians who took the initiative in their quest for access to ports or to the rich lands of the Polish–Lithuanian Commonwealth. Military organization thus was a necessity, for without it Russian colonization, so essential to its economic survival, could not have been carried out.

This being the case, one might have expected Russia to develop early in its history something akin to the bureaucratic regime of the 'despotic' or 'Asiatic' kind. The logic of things, indeed, impelled Russia in this direction, but for a variety of reasons its political development took a somewhat different route. The typical regime of the 'Oriental Despotic' kind seems to have come into being not to meet military exigencies but from the need for effective central management capable of organizing the collection and distribution of water for irrigation. Thus arose what Karl Wittfogel calls the 'agro-despotism' common to much of Asia and Central America.[15] Now in Russia there was no need for authority to assist in the extraction of wealth from the land. Russia was traditionally a country of widely scattered small farms, not one of latifundia, and it knew nothing of central economic management until the imposition of War Communism in 1918. But even if such management had been required, the county's natural conditions would have prevented its introduction. One need only consider the difficulties of transport and communication in Russia before the advent of railroads and telegraphs to realize that the kind of control and surveillance essential to an 'Oriental Despotism' was entirely out of the question here. The immense distances and the climate with its severe winters and spring floods precluded in pre-modern Russia the construction of a regular road network. In Persia of the fifth century BC a messenger of King Darius travelled along the Royal Road at a rate of 380 kilometres in 24 hours; in Mongol

Persia of the thirteenth century government couriers covered some 335 kilometres in the same period of time. In Russia, *after* regular postal services had been introduced by Swedish and German experts in the second half of the seventeenth century, messengers crawled at an average rate of 6–7 kilometres an hour; and since they travelled only by daytime, with luck and in the right season they might have made 80 or so kilometres in a 24-hour period. It required approximately 8 to 12 days for a dispatch from Moscow to reach one of the principal border towns of the empire, such as Archangelsk, Pskov and Kiev. For an inquiry to be answered, therefore, 3 weeks were needed.[16] Towns and villages lying at some distance from the principal roads, especially those along the eastern frontier, were for all practical purposes incommunicable. This factor alone made it impossible to institute in Russia a tightly organized bureaucratic regime before the 1860s when railways and telecommunications were introduced.

The resultant situation presented an antinomy: its economic conditions and external situation required Russia to organize militarily and therefore politically in a highly efficient manner, and yet its economy inhibited such organization. There was a basic incompatibility between the country's possibilities and its needs.

The manner in which this predicament was resolved provides the key to Russia's constitutional development. The state neither grew out of the society, nor was imposed on it from above. Rather it grew up side by side with society and bit by bit swallowed it. The locus of original political authority was the private domain of the prince or tsar, his *oikos* or *dvor*. Within this domain the prince reigned absolute, exercising authority in the double capacity as sovereign and proprietor. Here he was in full command, a counterpart of the Greek *despotes*, the Roman *dominus*, and the Russian *gosudar'*, that is lord, master, outright owner of all men and things. Initially, the population of the princely domain consisted mainly of slaves and other persons bonded in one form or another to the proprietor. Outside his domains, where the population was free and exceedingly mobile, the Russian ruler exercised very little authority at first, his power being confined largely to the collection of tribute. This kind of dyarchy established itself in the forest zone during the twelfth and thirteenth centuries, at the same time when in England, France and Spain the modern western state was beginning to take shape as an entity separate from the ruler. From the solid base of authority furnished by their private domains, the Russian princes – gradually and only after having overcome massive resistance – spread their personal power over the free population living outside these domains. The princely dynasty of Moscow–Vladimir, which emerged as the country's leader, transferred the institutions and practices which it had initially worked out in

21

the closed world of its oikos to the realm at large, transforming Russia (in theory, at any rate) into a giant royal estate. However, even after it had laid formal claim to all Russia being its private domain or *votchina* (sixteenth to seventeenth centuries), the Russian government lacked the means to make the claim good. It had no alternative, therefore, but to continue the old dyarchic arrangement, farming out the bulk of the country to the landed gentry, clergy and bureaucracy in return for fixed quotas of taxes and services. But the principle that Russia belonged to its sovereign, that he was its *dominus* was firmly established; all that was lacking to enforce it were the financial and technical means, and these were bound to become available in due course.

Since Aristotle, political thinkers have distinguished a special variant of 'despotic' or 'tyrannical' governments characterized by a proprietary manner of treating the realm, although no one seems to have worked out a theory of such a system. In Book III of his *Politics*, Aristotle devotes a brief paragraph to what he calls 'paternal government' under which the king rules the state the way a father does his household; but he does not develop the theme. The French theorist, Jean Bodin, in the late sixteenth century spoke of a 'seigneural' monarchy under which the ruler owned his subjects and their properties (see below, p. 65). In Hobbes's *Elements of Law*, governments are divided into two basic types, the Commonwealth, formed by mutual consent for the purpose of protection from external enemies, and Dominium or 'Patrimonial Monarchy' created as a result of conquest and submission 'to an assailant for fear of death'.[17] But Hobbes, too, having stated the issue, let the matter drop. The term 'patrimonial regime' was revived and introduced into current usage by Max Weber. In his threefold division of types of political authority, distinguished mainly by their administrative character, Weber defined the 'patrimonial system' as a variant of personal authority based on tradition (the other variant being 'charismatic'). 'Where authority is primarily oriented to tradition but in its exercise makes the claim of full personal powers, it will be called "patrimonial authority".'[18] In its extreme form, 'Sultanism', it entails complete ownership of land and mastery over the population. Under a patrimonial regime, the economic element absorbs, as it were, the political. 'Where the prince organizes his political power – that is, his non-domainial, physical power of compulsion *vis-à-vis* his subjects outside his patrimonial territories and people, his political subjects – in the same essential manner as he does his authority over his household, there we speak of a *patrimonial state* structure.' 'In such cases, the political structure becomes essentially identical with that of a gigantic landed estate of the prince.'[19]

There is considerable advantage in retaining the term 'patrimonial' to define a regime where the rights of sovereignty and those of ownership

22

blend to the point of becoming indistinguishable, and political power is exercised in the same manner as economic power. 'Despotism', whose root is the Greek *despotes*, has much the same etymological origins, but over time it has acquired the meaning of a deviation or corruption of genuine kingship, the latter being understood to respect the property rights of subjects. The patrimonial regime, on the other hand, is a regime in its own right, not a corruption of something else. Here conflicts between sovereignty and property do not and cannot arise because, as in the case of a primitive family run by a paterfamilias they are one and the same thing. A despot violates his subjects' property rights; a patrimonial ruler does not even acknowledge their existence. By inference, under a patrimonial system there can be no clear distinction between state and society in so far as such a distinction postulates the right of persons other than the sovereign to exercise control over things and (where there is slavery) over persons. In a patrimonial state there exist no formal limitations on political authority, nor rule of law, nor individual liberties. There can be, however, a highly efficient system of political, economic and military organization derived from the fact that the same man or men – kings or bureaucracies – dispose of the country's entire human and material resources.

Classic examples of patrimonial regimes are to be found among the Hellenistic states which emerged from the dissolution of the empire of Alexander the Great, such as Egypt of the Ptolomies (305–30 BC) and the Attalid state in Pergamum (*c.* 283–133 BC). In these kingdoms, founded by Macedonian conquerors, the ruler controlled all or nearly all the productive wealth. In particular, he owned the entire cultivated land which he exploited partly directly, through his personal staff using his own labour force, and partly indirectly, by distributing estates on service tenure to his nobility. The Hellenistic king was often also the country's principal industrialist and merchant. The primary purpose of this kind of arrangement was to enrich its sovereign proprietor. Rather than seeking to maximize resources, the emphasis lay on stabilizing income, and to this purpose the government often set fixed quotas of goods which it expected to receive, leaving the remainder to the inhabitants. In extreme cases, such as Hellenistic Pergamum, something close to a planned economy seems to have come into being. Because there was no free market, social classes in the customary sense of the word could not arise; instead there were social estates organized hierarchically to serve the king and tending to ossify into castes. There was no nobility with defined rights and privileges, but only ranks of servitors, whose status depended wholly on royal grace. The bureaucracy was powerful but it was not permitted to become hereditary. Like the nobility, it owed its status and privileges to the king.[20]

The patrimonial system best defines the type of regime which emerged in Russia between the twelfth and seventeenth centuries and which, with certain lapses and modifications, has survived until the present. One can find no better description of the Muscovite system of government at the height of its development during the seventeenth century than that given by Julius Kaerst for the Hellenistic world:

[The Hellenistic state represents] a personal-dynastic regime which does not grow out of a specific land or people but is imposed from above upon a specific political realm [*Herrschaftsbezirk*]. Accordingly, it has at its side special, technically trained instruments of rule which originally also have not grown up along with the land but have become tied to the ruler of the dynasty by a purely personal relationship. They form the principal support of the new monarchical authority in the form of a bureaucracy, subordinate to the king's will, and of a body of battle-ready warriors ... Political life not only concentrates itself in the persons of the rulers; it is actually rooted in them. A citizenry (*demos*) ... as such does not exist at all ... The people is the *object* of the ruling authority, not an independent bearer of some national mission.[21]

The history of the patrimonial system of government in Russia is the principal theme of this book. It rests on the contention that the essential quality of Russian politics derives from the identification of sovereignty and ownership, that is, of a 'proprietary' way of looking at political authority on the part of those who happen to be in power. Part I will trace the growth and evolution of the patrimonial regime in Russia. Part II will deal with the principal social estates and inquire why they failed to transform themselves from an object of public authority into a subject of public rights. Part III will describe the conflict between the state and that articulate element of society known as the intelligentsia as it unfolded during the imperial period and which led in the 1880s to the modernization of patrimonial institutions in which unmistakable germs of totalitarianism can be discerned.

I
THE STATE

CHAPTER 2

THE GENESIS OF THE PATRIMONIAL
STATE IN RUSSIA

In the middle of the seventh century, when the Slavs were in the course of penetrating the Russian forest on their eastward migration, the Black Sea steppe fell under the control of the Khazars, a Turkic nation from Inner Asia. Unlike the other Turkic groups of the time the Khazars did not pursue an exclusively nomadic mode of life centred on cattle breeding, but settled down to cultivate the soil and to trade. The main artery of their commerce was the Volga, which they controlled as far north as it was navigable. Using this route, they shipped luxury goods obtained from the Levant to trading posts in the forest populated by Ugro-Finnic peoples where they exchanged them for slaves, furs and various primary and semi-finished raw materials. By the end of the eighth century, the Khazars established a powerful state or *kaganate* extending from the Crimea to the Caspian and northward to the mid-Volga. At this time, the ruling élite, probably under the influence of Jewish colonists from the Crimea, were converted to Judaism. The kaganate's military power shielded the Black Sea steppe from Asiatic nomads, and enabled the early Slavic migrants to gain a precarious foothold in the black earth region. During the eighth and ninth centuries, the Slavs in the steppe and adjoining forest paid tribute to the Khazars and lived under their protection.

The little that is known of Eastern Slavs during this period (the seventh to ninth centuries) suggests that they were organized into tribal communities. The prevailing agricultural technique in the forest zone, where most of them resided, was 'slash-burn', a primitive method well suited to the conditions under which they then lived. (Plate 2) Having made a clearing in the woods and hauled away the logs the peasants set the stumps and brush on fire. The ashes deposited after the flames had died down were so rich in potash and lime that seeds could be sown directly on the ground with a minimum of soil preparation. The soil treated in this manner yielded a few good harvests; as soon as it became exhausted, the peasants moved on to repeat the procedure in another part of the endless forest. This method of cultivation demanded constant movement and undoubtedly helps explain the remarkable rapidity with which the Slavs spread throughout Russia. 'Slash-burn' remained the prevalent technique of farming in Russia until the sixteenth century, when under the combined pressure of the state and its landed servitors the peasants had to settle down and go over to the three-field system. It continued, however, to be practised in the remoter areas of the north well into the present century.

A characteristic feature of early Slav settlements was the construction of stockades. In the steppe, these were built of earth, in the forest of wood alone or in combination with earth. Such primitively fortified places served the members of the communities scattered in near-by clearings as common defensive centres. There were hundreds of such tribal stockades all over early Russia. The tribal communities combined to form larger social units, known by a variety of names, such as *mir*, whose connecting link was the worship of common gods.* An agglomeration of *miry* formed the largest socio-territorial entity known to early Eastern Slavs, *plemia*, of which the chronicles identify by name a dozen or so. As in tribal groupings elsewhere, authority rested in the patriarch, who enjoyed virtually unlimited power over the other members of the tribe and their belongings. At this stage in their history, the Eastern Slavs had neither institutions nor officials charged with the performance of judiciary or military functions, and therefore nothing approximating statehood even in its most rudimentary form.

In the ninth century, the Volga trade plied by the Khazars attracted the attention of the Normans. The ninth century was for the Normans a period of extraordinary expansion. Scattering far and wide from Scandinavia, they roamed with impunity in central and western Europe, conquering in the process, Ireland (820), Iceland (874), and Normandy (911). During this initial phase of their expansion, some of the Normans turned east and founded settlements on territory of what later became Russia. The first Norse colony on Russian soil was Aldeigjuborg, a fortress on the shores of lake Ladoga. This was an excellent base from which to launch exploration of the water routes leading south, towards the great centres of Levantine wealth and civilization. Routes connecting northern Europe with the Near East by way of Russia acquired special value at this particular time, because Muslim conquests of the eighth century had closed the Mediterranean to Christian trade. From Aldeigjuborg and other fortresses built near by and to the south, the Normans explored in their flat, capacious boats the rivers leading to the Near East.

---

* This early *mir* must not be confused with the repartitional commune, known by the same name, but created much later, (see above, p. 17).

They soon discovered what medieval Russian sources call 'the Saracen route', the network of rivers and portages connecting the Baltic Sea with the Caspian by way of the Volga, and entered into commercial relations with the Khazars. Hoards of Arabic coins dating from the ninth and tenth centuries discovered throughout Russia and Sweden attest to the wide reach and intensity of these commercial activities of the Normans. The Arab traveller Ibn Fadlan left a vivid description of a ship burial of a Norman ('Russian') chieftain which he had witnessed on the Volga early in the tenth century.

In the long run, however, the 'Saracen route' proved to the Normans of lesser importance than the 'Greek route' leading down the Dnieper to the Black Sea and Constantinople. Utilizing this road, they carried out several raids against the capital of the Byzantine Empire, compelling the Byzantines to grant them commercial privileges. The texts of the treaties in which these privileges are enumerated, recorded complete in the Primary Chronicle, are the oldest documents bearing on Norman rule in Russia. In the ninth and tenth centuries, regular commercial relations developed between the Russian forest and Byzantium, the management of which was in the hands of Norman merchant-soldiers.

In most of Europe under their control, the Normans settled down and assumed the role of territorial sovereigns. In Russia they behaved differently. For reasons enumerated before, they had little inducement to bother with agriculture and territorial claims, preferring to concentrate on foreign trade. They gradually gained control of all the principal riverways leading to the Black Sea, along which they built fortresses. From these bases they extracted as tribute from the Slavs, Finns and Lithuanians commodities most in demand in Byzantium and the Arab world: slaves, furs and wax. It is precisely in the ninth century that there began to appear in Russia populated centres of a new type; no longer the tiny earthern or wooden stockades of the Slavic settlers, but regular fortress-cities. These served as habitations for the Norman chieftains, their families and retainers. Around them there often grew up suburbs populated by native artisans and shopkeepers. Each of these fortress-cities had near by its burial grounds. Normans and Slavs were often buried in the same mounds, but the tombs of the two were quite different, the Norman ones containing weapons, jewels and home implements of a distinctly Scandinavian type, and on occasion entire boats. Judging by archaeological evidence, the Normans maintained in Russia four major settlement areas: one along the Gulf of Riga; a second around lake Ladoga and the Volkhov river; a third to the east of Smolensk; and a fourth in the mesopotamia between the upper Volga and the Oka. In addition, they had isolated settlements, of which Könugard (Kiev) was by far the largest. All four of the major Norman settlement areas lay along the trade routes connecting the Baltic with the Caspian and Black seas. In their sagas, the Normans called Russia 'Gardariki', 'the country of strongholds'.

Since only a part of the tribute levied on the native population was required for support of the garrisons, and its most valuable portion was intended for export to distant markets reached by a route full of hazards, the Norman fortress-cities had to organize. This process, begun around 800 CE when the first Norse settlements were formed around lake Ladoga, was completed around 882 when Prince Helgi (Oleg) united under his authority the two terminal points of the 'Greek Route', Holmgard (Novgorod) and Kiev. Kiev became the headquarters of the central trade organization. The choice of Kiev was dictated by the fact that the Normans experienced no difficulty shipping the goods collected as tribute all over Russia and destined for Constantinople as far south as that city, being in full control of western Russia to that point. It was the next leg of the journey, from Kiev to the Black Sea, that presented the greatest problems, because here the merchandise had to traverse a steppe infested with nomad freebooters. Every spring, as soon as the ice on the rivers had broken, the tribute was floated from its scattered collection points to Kiev. May was devoted to the task of outfitting the great annual flotilla. In June, the ships laden with slaves and produce sailed under heavy guard from Kiev down the Dnieper. The most dangerous segment of the journey was a stretch of granite rapids twenty-five to sixty-five miles south of Kiev. As Emperor Constantine VII Porphyrogenitus describes it, the Normans learned how to navigate the first three of the cataracts, but upon reaching the fourth they had to unload the merchandise and proceed on foot. The boats were partly dragged, partly carried. Some of the Normans helped bear the merchandise, others guarded the slaves, others yet were on the look-out for the enemy and, if attacked, beat him off. The flotilla was reasonably safe only after it had passed the last cataract, and the personnel with the goods could be reloaded on the boats. The importance of Kiev and the reason why it was chosen as the capital of the Norman trade organization in Russia thus becomes apparent. Kiev functioned in a double capacity: as the main depot of the tribute collected in all parts of Russia, and as the port from where it was transhipped under guard to its ultimate destination.

It is in this manner, almost as a by-product of international trade between two alien peoples, Normans and Greeks, that the first East Slav state came into being. Sovereign power over the fortress-cities and the territories adjoining them was assumed by a dynasty claiming descent from the semi-legendary Norse prince Hroerekr or Roderick (the Riurik of Russian chronicles). The head of the dynasty, the Great Prince, officiated in Kiev, while his sons, relatives, and leading retainers manned the provincial towns. Lest, however, the name 'Kiev state' evoke the image of a territorial entity familiar from Norman history of France, England or Sicily, it most be stressed that it was nothing of the kind. The Norman state in Russia rather resembled the great merchant enterprises of seventeenth- and eighteenth-century Europe, such as the East India or Hudson's Bay companies, founded to make money but compelled by the absence of any administration in the area of their operations to assume quasi-governmental responsibilities. The Great Prince was a merchant *par excellence*, and his realm was essentially a commercial enterprise, composed of loosely affiliated towns whose garrisons collected the tribute and maintained, in a rough sort of way, public order. The princes were quite independent of one another. Together with their retainers (*druzhiny*) the Norman rulers of Russia formed a distinct caste. They lived apart from the rest of the population, they judged their own members by special laws, and preferred to have their remains buried in separate tombs. Norman administration was carried out in a most casual fashion. During the winter months, the princes accompanied by their druzhiny travelled in the countryside arranging for the delivery of the tribute and dispensing justice. It is only in the eleventh century, when the Kievan state already showed symptoms of decline, that in the larger cities there appeared popular assemblies called *veche*. Composed of all the adult males, these assemblies gave the prince advice on important policy questions. In Novgorod and Pskov, the veche even succeeded in arrogating to itself legislative authority and forcing the princes to execute its will. But these two cases apart, the prince–veche relationship tended to be informal and unstructured. Certainly one cannot speak of the populace of Kievan Russia exerting any institutional pressure on the ruling élite, least of all in the ninth and tenth centuries, when the veche did not as yet even exist. In the heyday of Kievan statehood, authority was exercised on the model of a pre-modern commercial enterprise, subject to restraint neither by law nor popular will.

Nothing reflects better the relationship of the Normans towards their Russian realm than their failure to work out an orderly system of princely succession. In the ninth and tenth centuries the problem seems to have been solved by force: on the death of the Kievan ruler, prince fell upon prince, and all semblance of national unity vanished until the victor made good his claim to the Kievan throne. Later various attempts were made – none of them successful – to assure a regular procedure of succession. Before his death in 1054, Great Prince Iaroslav apportioned the main cities among his five sons, urging them 'to heed' the eldest, to whom he entrusted Kiev. This device did not work, however, and conflicts persisted. Subsequently, Kievan princes held conferences at which they discussed and sometimes settled their disagreements, including conflicts over cities. Scholars have long debated whether Kievan Russia in fact had any system of succession and, if so, what were its guiding principles. Those writing in the nineteenth century, when Hegel's influence on historical thinking was paramount, assumed that the early Russian state was at the pre-governmental stage of social development, under which the kingdom and its constituent cities belonged to the entire dynastic clan. In their view, succession followed the principle of clan seniority, according to which the princes 'rotated' the cities among them in a kind of game of musical chairs, with the eldest taking Kiev, and the younger ones settling down in order in the provincial cities. This traditional interpretation was challenged in the early years of the present century by the historian A.E.Presniakov who maintained that the Kievan princes treated the state as an entity, and fought among themselves for control not of the individual cities but of the state as a whole. Some modern scholars adhere to a modified version of the old clan theory which holds that the Kievan princes adopted the practices of the nomadic Turkic tribes like the Pechenegs, with whom they were in constant contact, for whom seniority descended along lateral lines, i.e. from brother to brother rather than from father to son. However, no matter which system the Russian Normans and their successors may have adopted in theory, they adhered to none in practice, with the result that the Kievan state was constantly shaken by internal conflicts of a kind which later were to destroy the empire of Genghis Khan. As Henry Maine has shown, the absence of primogeniture is a characteristic quality of authority and ownership in the pre-individualistic and pre-public phase of society's development. The fact that the Normans considered Russia their common dynastic property, rather than that of a single member or branch of the family, howsoever they thought proper to apportion it, suggests that they lacked any clear notion of political authority and viewed their power not so much in public as in private terms.

The Normans nowhere displayed much resistance to assimilation, and at least in this one respect their Russian branch was no exception. A nation of crude freebooters, originating in a backward region on the periphery of the civilized world, they tended everywhere to succumb to the culture of the people whom they subjugated by force of arms. The Kievan Normans were Slavicized by the middle of the eleventh century, which is about the same time that the Normans in France became Gallic. An important factor in their assimilation was conversion to Orthodox Christianity. One of the consequences of this act was the adoption of Church Slavonic, a literary language devised by Byzantine missionaries. The use of this language in all written documents, lay and clerical, undoubtedly contributed greatly to the loss by the Norman élite of their ethnic identity. Another factor promoting assimilation was intermarriage with Slavic women and the gradual infiltration of indigenous warriors into the ranks of the once solidly Scandinavian druzhiny. In the treaty concluded between Kievan princes and Byzantium in 912, all the Kievan signatories bore Scandinavian names (e.g. Ingjald, Farulf, Vermund, Gunnar). Subsequently, these names were either Slavicized or replaced by Slavic names, and in the chronicle narratives (the earliest complete text of which dates from 1116), the Norman names appear already in their Slavic form; thus Helgi becomes Oleg, Helga turns into Olga, Ingwarr into Igor, and Waldemar into Vladimir.

By a related linguistic process, the ethnic name which the Normans of eastern Europe had originally applied to themselves was transferred on to the Eastern Slavs and their land. In Byzantine, western and Arabic sources of the ninth and tenth centuries, *Rus'* – the root of *'Rossiia'* and 'Russia' – always referred to people of Scandinavian ancestry. Thus, Constantine Porphyrogenitus in *De Administrando Imperio* provides two parallel sets of names for the Dnieper cataracts, one of which, that labelled 'Russian', turns out to be Scandinavian, while the other is Slavic. According to the Bertinian Annals, a Byzantine delegation which came in 839 to the court of Emperor Louis the Pious at Ingelheim brought along a body of men called 'Rhos'; on being questioned about their nationality, they identified themselves as Swedes. *'Quos alios nos nomine Nordmannos appellamus'* ('whom by another name we call Northmen') is how the tenth-century historian, Liutprand of Cremona, defines 'Rusios'. We have mentioned already the description of the burial of a 'Russian' prince by Ibn Fadlan, which fully conforms to what is known of Norse practices, the contents of tombs, and the signatures of Kievans on treaties with Byzantium. All these facts require emphasis because in the past two hundred years hyper-patriotic Russian historians have often thought it incumbent on them to deny what to third parties seems incontrovertible, namely that the founders of the Kievan state and the first bearers of the name 'Russians' were men of Scandinavian origin. The source of the name Rus' is by no means certain, however. One possibility is Roslagen, the Swedish coast north of Stockholm, whose inhabitants to this day are known as Rospiggar (pronounced Ruspiggar). Another is the Nordic 'Ropsmenn' or 'Ropskarlar', meaning 'men of the rudder'. The Finns, with whom the Norman settlers at Ladoga first came in contact, called them Ruōtsi – a name which survives in the modern Finnish for Sweden. (As noted above, the Finnish word for Russia is Venäjä.) Following the standard linguistic rule by which the Slavs assimilate Finnic ethnic names, Ruōtsi became Rus'. Originally, Rus' designated the Normans and their country. Ibn Rusta, an Arab geographer writing around the year 900, spoke of Rus' (which he distinguished from Slavs) as living in a country of lakes and forests, probably meaning the region

Ladoga-Novgorod. But as the Normans assimilated and the ranks of their retainers filled with Slavs, Rus' lost its ethnic connotation and came to designate all the people manning the fortress-cities and involved in the annual expeditions to Constantinople. From such usage, it required only a minor shift for 'Rus' ' to be extended to the country where these people lived, and, finally, to all of this country's inhabitants, regardless of ancestry and occupation. Examples of such name transfers from conqueror to the conquered are not uncommon, the case of France, a name adopted for Gaul from the invading German Franks, being the one that most readily comes to mind.

The Normans gave the Eastern Slavs several elements essential to forging out of their disparate tribes and tribal associations a national entity: a rudimentary state organization headed by one dynasty, a common religion and an ethnic name. How much national unity the East Slavs actually perceived during the tenth and eleventh centuries no one knows, because the only indigenous documents bearing on this period, the chronicles, are of a later provenance.

One more legacy bequeathed by the Normans to the Eastern Slavs deserves mention – it is a legacy of a negative kind to which allusion has been made already and will continue to be made on the pages of this book. The Kievan state which they had founded and which their Slavicized and Slavic descendants had inherited did not emerge out of the society over which it ruled. Neither the princes nor their retainers, the raw material of a future nobility, issued from the Slavic communities. The same, of course, holds true of England after the Norman Conquest. But in England, where land is fertile and valuable, the Norman élite promptly divided it among themselves and turned into a landowning aristocracy. In Russia, the Norman élite retained all along a semicolonial character: its principal interest lay not in exploiting land but in extracting tribute. Its local roots were extremely shallow. We have here a type of political formation characterized by an unusually sharp gulf between rulers and ruled. The Kievan state and Kievan society lacked a common interest capable of binding them: state and society coexisted, retaining their separate identities and barely conscious of a sense of commitment to one another.*

* Just how little the Normans cared for their Russian kingdom may be gathered from an incident in the life of Great Prince Sviatoslav. Having in 968 seized the Bulgarian city of Pereieslavets (the Roman Martianopol) he announced the following year to his mother and boyars: 'I do not care to remain in Kiev, but should prefer to live in Pereieslavets on the Danube, since that is the centre of my realm, where all riches are concentrated; gold, silks, wine, and various fruits from Greece, silver and horses from Hungary and Bohemia, and from Rus' furs, wax, honey, and slaves' (*The Russian Primary Chronicle; Laurentian Text*, edited by S.H. Cross and O.P. Sherbowitz-Wetzor, Cambridge, Mass. [1953], p. 86). The intention was frustrated by a Pecheneg attack on Kiev; but the sentiments speak for themselves.

The Kievan state distintegrated in the twelfth century. Its collapse can be explained by the combined action of internal and external factors.

The internal factor was the inability of the ruling dynasty to resolve the issue of succession. Because there existed no orderly system by which Kiev and the provincial cities with their adjoining tributary territories, the *volosti*, passed from hand to hand upon the death of their rulers, the princes tended to develop a proprietary interest in whatever areas happened to have come under their control. Thus, what had been intended as a temporary and conditional right to exploit a given city and region transformed itself into outright ownership. The princely custom of bequeathing their sons cities and volosti in perpetuity must have been well established by 1097 when a conference of Kievan princes held at Liubech acknowledged the right of each prince to retain as property territories inherited from his father. This principle implied that princes were also at liberty to bequeath cities and volosti to their sons. The common dynastic ownership of Russia, though never formally abjured, thus ceased to be observed in practice.

The centrifugal force inherent in this process was aggravated by a concurrent external development, namely the decline of Russia's trade with Byzantium. In 966-7 the impetuous Prince Sviatoslav, in an argument over control of the only remaining Slavic group still paying tribute to the Khazars, attacked and destroyed the capital of the Khazar kaganate. By this foolhardy act he helped open the flood-gates through which at once poured into the Black Sea steppe belligerent Turkic tribes, until then kept in check by the Khazars. First came the Pechenegs. They were followed in the eleventh century by the Cumans (Polovtsy), an exceptionally aggressive nation who carried out such vicious attacks on the flotillas sailing from Kiev to Constantinople as eventually to bring this traffic to a standstill. Expeditions to dislodge the Cumans had little success; one such disastrous campaign, launched in 1185, is commemorated in the Song of the Host of Igor, the medieval Russian epic. In the middle of the twelfth century, Russian princes ceased to mint coins, which suggests they were in serious financial difficulty and that the economic unity of the country was distintegrating. To compound Kiev's calamities, in 1204 the Fourth Crusade captured and sacked Constantinople, at the same time opening up the eastern Mediterranean to Christian navigation. In other words, around 1200 there disappeared those particular circumstances which in the preceding four centuries had brought the territories inhabited by Eastern Slavs under a single authority.

The internal and external tendencies working independently but towards the same end unleashed powerful destructive forces, and caused the country to fall apart into self-contained and virtually sovereign

35

principalities. The pull, of course, was not all in one direction. The country as before, continued to be ruled by members of a single dynasty and to profess one and the same faith – a faith which sharply separated it from its Catholic and Muslim neighbours. These centripetal forces eventually enabled Russia to reunite. But this occurred several centuries later. In the meantime, the dominant force was centrifugal. The impetus was towards the creation of regions composed of economically self-sufficient principalities, each of which, by virtue of an inner logic, tended to divide and subdivide without end.

In the initial stage of its disintegration, the Kievan state broke up into three major regions: one in the north, centred on Novgorod; a second one in the west and south-west, which Lithuania and Poland soon took over; and a third one in the north-east, in the area between the Oka and Volga, where power was eventually assumed by the principality of Moscow.

The most affluent and culturally advanced of these regions lay in the north-west. After Byzantium had collapsed, what was left of Russia's foreign commerce shifted to the Baltic, and Novgorod, with its dependency Pskov, replaced Kiev as the business capital of the country. Like the Khazars and the Normans before them, the merchants of Novgorod sold raw materials and imported luxuries. Owing to its extreme northern location, Novgorod could not grow enough food for its needs and had to buy cereals in Germany and the Volga–Oka mesopotamia. The slaves, traditionally Russia's major export commodity had no market in western Europe, where human bondage had become virtually extinct by this time; slaves, therefore, were left in Russia, with important economic and social consequences which will be noted later. The prosperity of Novgorod rested on close collaboration with the Hanseatic League of which it became an active member. German merchants established permanent settlements in Novgorod, Pskov and several other Russian cities. They had to pledge to deal with the producers only through the intermediacy of Russian agents; in return, they obtained full control of the entire foreign side of the business, including shipping and marketing. In search of commodities to trade with the Germans, the Novgorodians explored and colonized much of the north, extending the frontier of their state all the way to the Urals.

Politically, Novgorod began to detach itself from the other Kievan principalities around the middle of the twelfth century. Even at the height of Kievan statehood, it had enjoyed a somewhat privileged position, possibly because it was the senior of the Norman cities and because proximity to Scandinavia enabled it somewhat better to resist Slavization. The system of government evolved in Novgorod resembled in all essentials that familiar from the history of medieval city-states of western

Europe. The bulk of the wealth was in the hands not of princes but powerful merchant and landowning families. The task of expanding the territories of the principality, elsewhere assumed by the princes, was in Novgorod carried out by business entrepreneurs and peasants. Because they played a secondary role in the growth of Novgorod's wealth and territory, its princes enjoyed relatively little power. Their main task was to dispense justice and command the city-state's armed forces. All other political functions were concentrated in the *veche* which after 1200 became the locus of Novgorod's sovereignty. The veche elected the prince and laid down the rules which he was obliged to follow. The oldest of such contractual charters dates from 1265. The rules were strict, especially as concerned fiscal matters. The prince received in usufruct certain properties, but both he and his retainers were explicitly forbidden to accumulate estates or slaves on the territory of Novgorod, or even to exploit promysly without the veche's permission. The prince could not raise taxes, declare war or peace, or interfere in any manner with the institutions or policies of Novgorod. Sometimes he was specifically prohibited from entering into direct relations with the German merchants. These limitations were by no means empty formalities, as evidenced by the frequent expulsions from Novgorod of princes accused of violating their mandate; in one particularly turbulent 102-year period, Novgorod had 38 successive princes. The veche also controlled the civil administration of the city and of its provinces, and elected the head of its ecclesiastical establishment. Effective power in the veche lay in the hands of Novgorod boyars, a patriciate descended from the old druzhiny and composed of forty leading families, each organized into a corporation around a patron saint and his church. These families monopolized all the high offices and in large measure determined the course of the veche's deliberations. Their sense of self-confidence could not be duplicated in any other Russian city, then or later. Despite its civic pride, however, the Great Sovereign City of Novgorod (*Gospodin Velikii Novgorod*) lacked strong national ambitions. Content to trade and to lead undisturbed its own kind of existence, it made no attempt to replace Kiev as the centre of the country's political life. Economic exigencies which in the case of the Byzantine trade called for national unification, made no such demands in regard to the trade with the Hanseatic cities.

The situation in the western and south-western regions of the defunct Kievan state was different. By their constant raids, the Pechenegs and Cumans had made unbearable the life of the Slav settlers in the black earth region and the forest zone adjoining it: the latter had to abandon the steppe and withdraw into the safety of the forest. How insignificant the city of Kiev had become, long before its destruction by the Mongols in 1241, may be judged from the refusal of Prince Andrei Bogoliubskii of

Suzdal in 1169 to move to Kiev, which he had conquered, to assume the title of Great Prince; he preferred to turn Kiev over to a younger brother and himself stay in his domain deep in the forest.

In the course of the thirteenth and fourteenth centuries the main territory of what had been the Kievan state – the basin of the Dnieper and its tributaries – fell under the control of Lithuanians. Moving into the vacuum created by the disintegration of the Kievan state, they encountered little resistance and soon made themselves masters of western and south-western Russia. The Lithuanian Great Prince did not interfere with the internal life of the conquered principalities, allowing local institutions and traditions to function. The petty princes became his vassals, paying him tribute and serving him in time of war, but in other respects they were not molested. The Great Prince had less landed property than the princes and their retainers combined. This unfavourable distribution of wealth compelled him to pay close attention to the wishes of the Council (*Rada*), composed of his major vassals. If in Novgorod the prince resembled an elected chief executive, the Great Prince of Lithuanian Rus' was not unlike a constitutional king.

In 1386 Lithuania and Poland entered into a dynastic union, after which the territories of Lithuania and Lithuanian Rus' gradually merged. A certain degree of administrative centralization followed and the old Lithuanian institutions disappeared; still, the government of the bi-national monarchy was anything but centralized. The upper classes in the eastern provinces profited from the steady decline of the Polish monarchy to extract for themselves all manner of liberties and privileges, such as title to their landed estates, easing of terms of state service, access to administrative offices, and participation in the elections of the kings of Poland. The Lithuanian nobility, partly Catholic, partly Orthodox, became a genuine aristocracy. Lithuania–Poland might well have absorbed most of the Russian population and obviated the necessity of creating a distinct Russian state were it not for the religious issue. In the early sixteenth century, Poland hovered on the brink of Protestantism. Its defection from Rome was ultimately prevented by a prodigious effort of the Catholic Church and its Jesuit arm. The danger averted, Rome determined not only to extirpate in the Lithuanian–Polish monarchy the remnants of Protestant influence, but also to pressure the Orthodox population living there to acknowledge its authority. The effort brought partial success in 1596 when a segment of the Orthodox hierarchy on Lithuanian territory formed the Uniate Church, Orthodox in ritual but subject to Rome's control. However, the majority of the Orthodox inhabitants refused to follow suit, and began to look east for support. The religious division, exacerbated by the Counter Reformation, caused a great deal of bitterness between Poles and

Russians, and eliminated the Lithuanian–Polish state as a potential focus of Russian national aspirations.

Thus neither Novgorod nor Lithuania–Poland, notwithstanding their wealth and high level of civilization, were in a position to reunify the Eastern Slavs: the one because of its narrow, essentially commercial outlook, the other because of the divisive religious question. The task devolved by default on the poorest and most backward area of Russia, the so-called 'lowland' located in the north-east, at the confluence of the Oka and Volga.

When the Kievan state had stood at its zenith, the Volga–Oka region was a frontier area of minor importance. Its population then was still predominantly Finnish; to this day nearly all the rivers and lakes here bear Finnic names. Its rise began early in the twelfth century, when the main city of the region, Rostov the Great, became the hereditary property of the cadet branch of the family of Kiev's Great Prince, Vladimir Monomakh. Monomakh's younger son, Prince Iurii Dolgorukii (c. 1090–1157) the first independent ruler of Rostov, turned out to be a very enterprising colonizer. He built numerous cities, villages, churches and monasteries, and by generous offers of land and exemptions from taxes lured to his domain settlers from other principalities. This policy was continued by his son, Andrei Bogoliubskii (c. 1110–74). Careful analysis of the historical geography of the Rostov area carried out by M.K.Liubavskii revealed that already by the end of the twelfth century this was the most densely populated region in all Russia.[1] Colonists streamed here from all directions – Novgorod, the western territories and the steppe – attracted by exemptions from taxes, security from nomad harassment and the relatively good quality of the soil. (The Volga–Oka region straddles a belt of marginal black earth with a 0·5 to 2·0 per cent humus content.) The colonists behaved here exactly as they had done several centuries earlier on entering Russia, first building stockades and then scattering around them in small settlements composed of one or two households. The Slavs inundated the indigenous Finns, ultimately assimilating them by intermarriage. The mixture of the two nationalities resulted in a new racial type, the Great Russian, in which, from the infusion of Finno–Ugric blood, certain oriental characteristics (e.g. high cheekbones and small eyes), absent among other Slavs, made their appearance.

The principality of Rostov became in time the cradle of a new Russian state, the Muscovite. Russian historiography traditionally has taken it for granted that the Muscovite state stands in linear succession to the Kievan, and that the sovereignty once exercised by the Great Princes of Kiev passed intact from their hands into those of Muscovite rulers.

Western scholars, too, for the major part accept the Kiev–Moscow line of succession. The issue, however, is by no means self-evident. Kliuchevskii was the first to stress the fundamental differences between the north-eastern principalities and the Kievan state. Subsequently, Miliukov showed that the traditional scheme had its origin in the writings of Muscovite publicists of the late fifteenth and early sixteenth centuries who wished to demonstrate Moscow's claim to all Russia, particularly to the territories then under Lithuanian suzereignty; from them it was uncritically adopted by historians of the imperial period.[2] The Ukrainian scholar, Michael Hrushevsky, taking Kliuchevskii's and Miliukov's critique as his starting-point, went a step further, arguing that the legitimate successors to Kiev are to be found in the western principalities, Galich and Volhynia, subsequently taken over by Lithuania, for it was here that Kievan traditions and institutions had been best preserved. Moscow, in his view, was a new political formation.[3]

Without attempting to resolve the dispute between historians as to which nationality, Great Russian or Ukrainian, has the better claim to Kievan heritage, one cannot ignore an important issue raised by the critics of the Kiev–Moscow succession line. The Muscovite state did in fact introduce basic political innovations which gave it a constitution very different from Kiev's. The root of many of these innovations can be traced to the way the Muscovite state was formed. In Kievan Rus' and in all but its north-eastern successor states, the population antedated the princes; settlement came first and political authority followed. The north-east, by contrast, had been largely colonized on the initiative and under the auspices of the princes; here authority preceded settlement. As a result, the north-eastern princes enjoyed a degree of power and prestige which their counterparts in Novgorod and Lithuania could never aspire to. The land, they believed and claimed, belonged to them: the cities, forests, arable, meadows and waterways were their property because it was they who had caused them to be built, cleared or exploited. By an extension of this thought, the people living on this land were either their slaves or their tenants; in either event, they had no claim to the land and no inherent personal 'rights'. A kind of proprietary attitude thus surfaced on the north-eastern frontier. Penetrating all the institutions of political authority it gave them a character fundamentally different from that found in any other part of Russia, or, for that matter, Europe at large.

The term for property in medieval Russia was *votchina* (plural, *votchiny*). It is frequently met with in medieval chronicles, testaments and treaties between princes. Its root, *ot*, is the same as that of the Russian word for father (*otets*). Votchina is indeed the exact equivalent of the Latin *patrimonium* and, like it, denotes goods and powers inherited from one's father. At a time when there were no firm legal definitions of property or courts to enforce one's claim to it, acquisition by inheritance was regarded if not as the only then certainly as the best proof of ownership. 'This thing my father left me' meant 'this is incontrovertibly mine'. The language was readily understood in a society in which the patriarchal order was still very much alive, especially among the lower classes. No distinction was drawn between the various forms of property; an estate was votchina, so were slaves, and valuables, and fishing or mining rights and even one's very ancestry or pedigree. But so too, more significantly, was political authority which was treated as if it were a commodity. This is not in the least surprising if one considers that political authority in early Russia was essentially the right to levy tribute exercised by a body of foreign conquerors, that is, that it was an economic prerogative and little else. Quite naturally, therefore, the testaments of the north-eastern princes, many of which have survived, read like ordinary business inventories in which cities and volosti are indiscriminately lumped with valuables, orchards, mills, apiaries or herds of horses. Ivan I of Moscow in his last will referred to the principality as his votchina, and as such felt free to bequeath it to his sons. Ivan's grandson, Dmitry Donskoi, in his will (1389) defined as votchina not only the principality of Moscow but also the title of Great Prince. The testaments of the Russian princes fully conformed in their formal, legal aspect to ordinary civil documents, even to the extent of being witnessed by third parties.

As private property, the principalities in the north-east (and in the north-east only) were bequeathed in accord with the provisions of Russian customary law pertaining to property, that is after provisions had been set aside for the women and usually also for clerical establishments, they were divided into shares of approximately equal value for distribution among the male heirs. This practice may appear odd to the modern mind, accustomed as it is to regard the state as indivisible and the monarchy as subject to succession by primogeniture. But primogeniture is a relatively modern phenomenon. Although occasionally practised by primitive societies, it was unknown to antiquity; neither the Romans nor the German barbarians knew of it, and it also remained uncommon among Islamic cultures. It first appeared where property was intended to do more than merely furnish the personal support of the owner, i.e. where its function – to enable him to render military or other services – meant that it could not be reduced below a certain effective minimum. The popularity of primogeniture dates back to the grants of benefices made by Charlemagne. With the spread of feudalism and conditional land tenure it gained wide acceptance in Europe. The connection between conditional tenure and primogeniture is quite striking in the case of England, where alodial property was the least developed and primogeniture the most. Primogeniture survived feudalism in western Europe for two reasons. One was the growing familiarity with Roman law; Roman law knew no conditional ownership and tended to sweep aside the many restraints imposed by feudal custom on the eldest heir, transforming what had been intended as a kind of trusteeship into outright ownership. The other was the growth of capitalism which enabled the younger sons to earn a living without necessarily inheriting a share of the parental estate. Primogeniture, however, never struck root in Russia because here all the necessary conditions for it were missing, including knowledge of Roman law and opportunities in manufacture or trade. It has been a firm principle of Russian customary law to divide all property in equal shares among male heirs, and all attempts to change this tradition by the government have met with failure.

Upon the death of a north-eastern prince, the realm was apportioned among his sons, each of whom received his share or *udel*. Exactly the same practice was followed on private estates. Udel is customarily rendered in English as appanage, a term borrowed from the vocabulary of French feudalism. Alexander Eck, a Belgian medievalist, is quite correct in criticizing this usage on the grounds that while the terms udel and appanage both refer to provisions or 'livings' made by the sovereign for his sons, the French institution was only a lifelong grant which reverted to the treasury on the holder's death, whereas the udel was hereditary property, held in perpetuity[4]. Unfortunately, 'appanage' has become so deeply entrenched that it does not seem feasible to try to replace it.

The appanage which a Russian prince inherited from his father became his patrimony or votchina which, once the time came to draw up his last will, he in turn subdivided together with any acquisitions he himself might have made among his own sons. The practice led to a relentless diminution of the north-eastern principalities, some of which, in the end, were reduced to the size of small estates. The age when such subdividing took place – from the mid-twelfth to the mid-fifteenth century – is known in the historical literature as the 'appanage period' (*udel 'nyi period*).

One of the recurrent hazards of historical study is the difficulty of distinguishing theory from practice, and this is nowhere truer than in the case of Russia, where ambition always tends to run far ahead of the available means. Although in theory the principality belonged to the prince, in reality no appanage ruler had either the money or the administration to enforce a proprietary claim. In medieval Russia, effective ownership over land and any other natural resource (as distinct from theoretical ownership) was established exactly as Locke and other classical theorists imagined it, namely by 'removing' objects from the 'state of nature' and 'mixing' with them one's labour. Nine-tenths of the typical principality was wilderness and therefore *res nullius*. Kliuchevskii describes as follows the procedure by which ownership was asserted in appanage Russia other than by inheritance:

This land is *mine*, because it is my *men* who cultivate it, whom I have attached to it: such was the dialectical process by which the first Russian landowners assimilated the idea of private property in land. Such juridical dialectic was natural at a time when the prevailing method of acquiring landed property in Russia was the occupation of wild expanses belonging to no one.[5]

Unable to colonize the empty land by themselves, but eager to have it populated because colonists enriched the area and brought income, princes solicited well-to-do military men, monasteries and peasant families to come and settle down. In this manner there emerged in each appanage principality three principal types of land tenure: 1. the private domains of the prince directly exploited by him; 2. the estates of the landowners and monastic establishments; and, 3. the so-called 'black lands', cultivated by free peasants. Economically, the three types did not differ much from each other except in size. Appanage Russia knew no large latifundia. Even the biggest properties consisted of numerous tiny units – villages of one or two households, fisheries, apiaries, orchards, mills, mines – all scattered pell-mell along river banks and in isolated forest clearings.

The prince was the principality's largest landowner. The lion's share of his revenues came from the exploitation of his private domains; the prince's economic power rested on the *oikos*, his household properties. This was worked and administered by a labour force composed mostly and in some principalities almost exclusively of slaves, called *kholopy*. The slaves came from two principal sources. One was war; many kholopy were captives and descendants of captives taken in raids on neighbouring principalities, so common during the appanage period, or in forays into the forest wilderness. The other source was the poor who had been either forced into bondage because they could not pay their debts, or else entered into bondage voluntarily in search of aid and protection. Historical experience suggests that in the case of economies based on slave labour the decisive factor may often be the supply rather than the demand: i.e. that slave economies can come into being because of the availability of a massive supply of slaves for whom work must be found.* The rupture of trade with Byzantium, where slaves had been in great demand, created in Russia of the twelfth and thirteenth centuries a glut of human merchandise. There are recorded instances when, following successful military campaigns, five slaves were sold for the price

---

* The slave economies of the Americas are an exception to this rule.

of one goat. This oversupply must have provided a very strong inducement for the appange princes and landlords to turn to the exploitation
of land.

The main emphasis of the household economy of the appanage prince
was not on growing cereals. The need for cereals of the princely household was easily satisfied, and the surplus was not of much use; Novgorod
bought some, but its requirements, too, were limited, and as for distilling,
the Russians learned that art from the Tatars only in the sixteenth century. The main energy went into promysly, preoccupation with which
transformed some princely households into bustling business undertakings. The following description applies to a later age, but in its main
outlines it is valid for the appanage period as well:

> The prince's residence ... was not only the political centre of the state: it
> was also the centre of a large princely business enterprise ... In the testaments
> of the princes of Moscow, Moscow – the farmstead often even overshadows
> Moscow – the capital. In the fifteenth century, Moscow is surrounded by a
> chain of large and small villages and by clearings, scattered along the basins
> of the Moskva and Iauza rivers, the property of the Great Prince and appan-
> age princes. In the commercial settlements (*posady*) and in the towns stand
> their manors, orchards and kennels, along with whole communities of the
> princes' artisans and gardeners. Strung out along the Iauza, Neglinnaia and
> Kliazma rivers are the princes' mills. Along the low banks of the Moskva and
> the Khodynka spread out far-flung meadows, their property, some of them
> submerged under water. The environs of Moscow are settled with rent-paying
> peasants and slaves of the prince, his beaver-trappers, falconers, dog-keepers
> and stable boys. Beyond the Moskva river stretch apiaries (the so-called
> Dobranitskii Bee Forest) where, scattered in their villages, live the bee-
> keepers. In the midst of all these hamlets, orchards, gardens, kennels and
> mills, stands the Kremlin, half-covered with princes' manors, their servants'
> quarters, warehouses, granaries, their falconers and the cottages of their
> tailors and artisans. This whole kaleidoscopic picture of the princely economy
> bears the unmistakable imprint of a large farming establishment. And the
> same holds true of the residences of the other princes. In Pereiaslavl, the capi-
> tal of the principality of Riazan, we find the same rows of the princes' manor
> houses; in the city's environs, princely mills, fields, pastures; in the commer-
> cial settlements, fishermen and falconers, the property of the prince; and
> further away, their suburban bee-keepers.[6]

The management of these complex domains was entrusted to the
domestic staff of the prince's household (*dvor*). It, too, consisted mostly
of slaves; but even the freemen holding these posts were in a semi-
bonded condition in the sense that they could not leave their employer
without permission. The top official of the household was the *dvoretskii* or
dvorskii, a kind of major-domo or head steward. Under him served
diverse functionaries, each responsible for supervising a specific source

of income; one official assumed charge of the apiaries, another of the orchards, another yet of the falcons (which were used not for amusement but for hunting). An income-producing property was called *put'* and the officer in charge of it, *putnyi boiarin* or *putnik*. A *putnyi boiarin* had assigned to him villages and promysly, revenues from which he used to support himself and his staff. Administrative functions of the dvor were organized along economic lines: that is, the *putnyi boiarin* administered and judged the slaves and other peasants employed in his particular branch of the economy. He enjoyed the same authority over the inhabitants of the villages and promysly assigned to him for his personal support.

Outside the princely domain, administrative responsibilities were held to a minimum. Lay and ecclesiastical landowners enjoyed extensive immunities which allowed them to tax and to judge the population of their estates, while the black peasants governed themselves through their communal organizations. In so far, however, as it was necessary to perform certain public functions (e.g. tax gathering and later, after Mongol conquest, collection of the tribute), these were entrusted to the dvoretskii and his staff. The prince's household administration thus served in a double capacity; its principal task, managing the princely domain, was supplemented, when so required, by responsibilities over the principality at large – an essential characteristic of all regimes of the patrimonial type.

As one might expect, the slaves entrusted with administrative duties soon differentiated themselves from those employed in manual labour and formed a caste placed somewhere between freemen and bondmen. In some documents the two categories are distinguished as *prikaznye liudi* (commissioned men) and *stradnye liudi* (labouring men). By virtue of their responsibilities and the power that it gave them, the former constituted a kind of lower order of the nobility. At the same time, they had no confirmed rights whatever and their freedom of movement was subject to severe restrictions. In treaties between appanage princes it was customary to insert clauses pledging the parties not to lure away members of their respective household staffs, referred to by such names as *slugi pod dvorskim* (servants under the steward), *dvornye liudi* (household men), or, for short, *dvoriane* ('householders'). This group later became the nucleus of the basic service class of Muscovite and imperial Russia.

So much for the personal domain of the appanage prince. Outside his domain the appanage prince enjoyed precious little authority. The inhabitants at large owed him nothing but taxes, and could move from one principality to another with perfect ease. The right of freemen to roam about the land of Rus' was firmly rooted in customary law and formally acknowledged in treaties between princes. Its existence, of course, represented an anomaly; for whereas, after approximately 1150, the Russian princes turned into territorial rulers with a strongly developed proprietary sense, their military retainers and the commoners living on their land continued to behave as if Russia were still the common property of the whole dynasty. The former enrolled in the service and the latter rented land wherever they found conditions most attractive. The resolution of this contradiction constitutes one of the main themes of Russia's early modern history. It was accomplished only in the middle of the seventeenth century, when the rulers of Muscovy – by then, tsars of Russia – succeeded at long last in compelling both the military retainers and commoners to stay put. Until then, Russia had sedentary rulers and a floating population. The appanage prince could tax those living in his principality at large but he could not tell his taxpayers what to do; he had no subjects and therefore no public authority.

Princes apart, the only landowners in medieval north-eastern Russia were the clergy and the *boyars*. We shall postpone discussion of clerical holdings to the chapter on the church (Chapter 9), and here touch only on lay properties. During the appanage period, the term boyar meant a secular landowner or *seigneur*.* The ancestors of these boyars had served in the druzhiny of the princes of the Kievan state. Like them, finding fewer and fewer opportunities to make money from international trade and robbing expeditions, they turned in the eleventh and twelfth centuries to the exploitation of land. The princes, unable to offer them incomes or loot, now distributed to them land from among their large reserves of wild, uncultivated territory. This land was held as votchina, which meant that the holder could bequeath it to his heirs. Article 91 of the Russian law code (*Russkaia Pravda, Prostrannaia Redaktsiia*), dating from the early twelfth century, states that if a boyar died without sons, his estate, instead of reverting to the Treasury, went to his daughters; a provision which indicates that by this time the boyars were absolute owners of their properties. The boyars apparently relied less than the princes on slave labour. Most of their land was rented out to tenant farmers with a smaller segment being sometimes retained by them for direct exploitation as demesne by domestic slaves or tenant farmers in payment of rent (*boiarshchina*, or as later contracted, *barshchina*). Large estates duplicated the princely domains and like them were administered by staffs of domestics organized according to *puti*. Rich boyars were virtual sovereigns. The administrators of the prince's household rarely interfered with their people, and sometimes were formally forbidden to do so by immunity charters.

---

* In the early seventeenth century, it came to designate an honorary rank or *chin*, bestowed on the tsar's leading servitors, at most thirty in number, possession of which entitled the holder to serve on the tsarist Council (*Duma*). Here boyar will be used throughout in its original sense.

Secular votchiny were alodial property. On the death of the owner, they were divided in equal shares among the male heirs, after provisions had been set aside for the widow and daughters of the deceased. Votchiny could be freely sold. Later, in the mid-sixteenth century, the Muscovite monarchy introduced legislation which authorized members of the votchina-owner's clan to repurchase over a stated period (forty years) properties which he had sold to outsiders. In the appanage period no such restrictions existed. Although boyars almost invariably performed military service (in large measure because income from their estates was inadequate), their land being alod they were not required to serve the prince on whose territory their estate happened to lie. In Kievan Rus', members of the druzhiny were freemen, who chose their own leaders and served them at their own pleasure. This tradition went back to ancient Germanic practices according to which chieftains gathered around themselves temporary bands of volunteers (*comites*). The freedom to choose one's chief had been prevalent among Germanic peoples, Normans included, until restricted by the bonds of vassalage. In Russia, the custom of free service outlived the dissolution of the Kievan state, persisting throughout the appanage period. The situation of the boyars was not unlike that of the citizen of a modern state who pays real estate taxes to the community or state in which he happens to hold property, but is free to establish legal residence and find employment elsewhere. Customary law guaranteed boyars the right to enrol in the service of the Russian prince of their choice; they could even serve a foreign ruler, such as the Great Prince of Lithuania. Treaties among princes commonly contained articles affirming this right, usually employing a standard formula: 'the boyars and free servitors are free [to choose] among us' (*a boiaram i slugam nashim mezhi nas vol'nym volia*). A servitor could leave his prince at a moment's notice by exercising his right of 'renunciation' or 'disavowal' (*otkaz*). This fact explains why, in administering their private domains, the appanage princes preferred to rely on slaves and semi-dependent personnel.

The cultivated land exploited neither by the prince nor by the lay and clerical votchinniki, was 'black land', that is, land subject to taxation (in contrast to 'white' clerical and service land, exempt from it). It consisted mostly of arable which the peasants cleared on their own initiative in the forest, but towns and trading posts were often included in this category. The peasants were organized into self-governing communities, whose members did much of the field work in common, and distributed among themselves their tax obligations. The legal status of black land was ambiguous. The peasants behaved as if it were their property, selling and bequeathing it. But that it did not legally belong to them can be seen from the fact that land of peasants who died without male issue was incorporated into the prince's domains, and not, as was the case with boyar land, turned over to female descendants. The black peasants were in every respect freemen, able to move anywhere; in the lovely phrase of the time, they had open to them throughout Russia 'a clean road, without boundaries'. The taxes they paid the prince were essentially a form of rent. Occasionally visited by a servant of the prince's household, they lived in their self-contained and self-sufficient communities. Like the boyars they were not the subjects of the prince but his tenants, and their relationship to him was of a private (economic) rather than public (political) nature.

From all that has been said about the appanage principality, it should be apparent that the public authority of the medieval Russian prince, his *imperium* or *iurisdictio*, was extraordinarily feeble. He had no way of compelling anyone except slaves and domestics to do his will; anyone else – soldier, peasant and tradesman – could abandon him and move from his principality to someone else's. Immunity charters originally issued to attract colonists had the ultimate effect of removing from the princes' jurisdiction a large part of the population living on lay and clerical votchiny. Whatever effective authority an appanage prince enjoyed, derived from his ownership of landed property and slaves, that is from the position which Roman law would have defined as that of *dominus*. It is for this reason that one can speak of Russian statehood acquiring from the earliest a decidedly patrimonial character; its roots lie not in relations between sovereign and subjects, but in those between seigneur and the bonded and semi-bonded working force of his domains.

North-eastern Russia of the appanage period in many respects resembled feudal western Europe. We see here the same disintegration of the state into small and inward-oriented, quasi-sovereign entities, and the replacement of a public order by personal arrangements. We also find some familiar feudal institutions, such as immunities and manorial justice. Impressed by these similarities, N. P. Pavlov-Silvanskii argued that between the twelfth and sixteenth centuries Russia lived under a system which, minor differences notwithstanding, was feudal in the fullest sense of the word.[7] This view has become mandatory for communist historians, but it is not shared by the great majority of contemporary scholars unfettered by the bonds of censorship. As in so many controversies, the issue depends in large measure on one's definition of the critical word; and this, in turn, depends in the case at hand on whether one happens to be interested in finding similarities or differences. In recent decades it has become common practice to assign historical terms the broadest possible meaning so as to fit under a common rubric phenomena from

48

the histories of the most diverse peoples and periods. Where the purpose is historical sociology, or the typology of historical institutions, it may indeed be quite useful to employ 'feudalism' loosely to mean any system characterized by political decentralization, private law and a natural economy employing unfree labour. Defined in this sense, 'feudalism' is a widespread historic phenomenon, and many societies may be said, at one time or another, to have gone through it. If, however, one wishes to determine what accounts for the immense variety of political and social formations in the modern world, then such broad usage is of little use. In particular, in order to learn why western Europe has developed a set of institutions found nowhere else (unless implanted by its immigrants) it is necessary to isolate those features which distinguish feudal western Europe from all other 'feudal' systems. Once this is done, it becomes apparent that certain elements of feudalism as practised in the west cannot be found elsewhere, even in countries like Japan, India and Russia, all of which had experienced long periods of collapse of central authority, the triumph of private law and the absence of a market economy.

The western feudal system can be reduced to three essential elements: 1. political decentralization; 2. vassalage; and 3. conditional land tenure. If we bear these elements in mind, we will find that they either were unknown in Russia or, if known, appeared in an entirely different historical context, producing diametrically opposite results.

After Charlemagne, political authority in the West, theoretically vested in the king, was usurped by counts, margraves, dukes, bishops and other powerful feudatories. *De jure*, the status of the medieval western king as the sole anointed ruler remained unchallenged, even when feudal particularism attained its zenith; it was his ability to use the nominal power at his disposal that eroded. 'Theoretically, feudalism never abolished royal power: in practice, if one may say so, the great seigneurs placed royal power between parentheses.'[8]

The same cannot be said of Russia, and this for two reasons. In the first place, the Kievan state, unlike the Carolingian, had had no experience with centralized authority. Appanage Russia, therefore, could have no single figurehead king with an authentic claim to the monopoly of political power; instead, it had a whole dynasty of princes, petty and grand, each of whom had an equal right to the royal title. There was nothing here to place 'between parentheses'. Secondly, no boyar or churchman in medieval Russia succeeded in usurping princely authority; decentralization occurred from the multiplication of princes, not from the appropriation of princely prerogatives by powerful subjects. As will be noted in Chapter 3, these two related facts had profound bearing on the process of building royal power in Russia and on the character of Russian absolutism.

Vassalage represented the personal side of western feudalism (as conditional land tenure represented the material). It was a contractual relationship by virtue of which the lord pledged sustenance and protection, and the vassal reciprocated with promises of loyalty and service. This mutual obligation, formalized in the ceremony of commendation, was taken very seriously by the parties concerned and society at large. Violation of its terms by either party nullified the contract. From the vantage point of the development of western institutions, four aspects of vassalage require emphasis. First, it was a personal contract between two individuals, valid only in the course of their lifetime; on the death of either it lapsed. Implied in it was personal consent; one did not inherit the obligations of a vassal. Hereditary vassalage appeared only towards the end of the feudal era and it is considered to have been a powerful factor in feudalism's decline. Secondly, although originally an arrangement between two individuals, through the practice of subinfeudation vassalage produced a whole network of human dependencies. Its by-product was a strong social bond linking society with government. Thirdly, the obligations of vassalage were as binding on the stronger party, the lord, as on the weaker, the vassal. The lord's failure to keep his part of the bargain, released the vassal from his duties. 'The originality [of western feudalism]', writes Marc Bloch, contrasting it with its Japanese namesake, 'consisted in the emphasis it placed on the idea of an agreement capable of binding the rulers; and in this way, oppressive as it may have been to the poor, it has in truth bequeathed to our western civilization something with which we still desire to live.'[9] That something, of course, was law – an idea which in due time led to the establishment of courts, first as a means of adjudicating disputes between the parties involved in the lord–vassal relationship, and eventually as a regular feature of public life. Constitutions which are at bottom only generalized forms of feudal contract, descend from the institution of vassalage. Fourthly, the feudal contract, beside its legal aspect had also a moral side : in addition to their specific obligations, the lord and vassal pledged one another good faith. This good faith, imponderable as it may be, is an important source of the western notion of citizenship. Countries which had no vassalage or where vassalage entailed only a one-sided commitment of the weak towards the strong, have experienced great difficulties inculcating in their officials and citizens that sense of common interest from which western states have always drawn much inner strength.

What do we find in Russia? Of vassalage, in its proper sense, nothing.* The Russian landowning class, the boyars, were expected to bear arms but they were not required to do so on behalf of any particular prince. There was no trace of mutual responsibility in the prince–boyar relationship. In the western ceremony of commendation the vassal knelt before his lord who cupped his hands in a symbolic gesture of protection, lifting him to his feet and embracing him. In medieval Russia, the corresponding ceremony involved an oath ('kissing the cross') and the kowtowing of the servitor to the prince. Although some historians claim that the relations between princes and boyars were regulated by a contract, the fact that not a single document of this kind has come down to us from Russian (as distinct from Lithuanian) territories raises grave doubts whether they ever existed. There is no evidence in medieval Russia of mutual obligations binding prince and his servitor, and, therefore, also nothing resembling legal and moral 'rights' of subjects, and little need for law and courts. A disaffected boyar had no place to turn to obtain satisfaction; the only recourse open to him was to exercise the right of renunciation and leave for another lord. Admittedly, free departure – the one 'right' a boyar may be said to have enjoyed – was an ultimate form of personal liberty, which, on the face of it, should have promoted in Russia the emergence of a free society. But liberty not grounded in law is incapable of evolution and tends to turn upon itself; it is an act of bare negation which implicitly denies any mutual obligation or even a lasting relationship between human beings.† The ability of boyars arbitrarily to abandon their princes forced the princes to behave arbitrarily as well; and since, in the long run, it was the princes' power that grew, the boyars had much occasion to regret their prized 'right'. Once Moscow had conquered all of Russia and there were no more independent appanage princes to whom to transfer one's loyalty, the boyars found that they had no rights left at all. They then had to assume very heavy service obligations without obtaining any reciprocity. The endemic lawlessness of Russia, especially in the relations between those in authority and those subject to it, undoubtedly has one of its principal

* Vassalage did exist in Lithuanian Russia. Sometimes princes and boyars from the Volga-Oka region, making use of the right to choose their lord, placed themselves under the protection of the Lithuanian Great Prince, and entered with him into contracts which made them vassals. An example of such a contract between Great Prince Ivan Fedorovich of Riazan, and Witold, the Great Prince of Lithuania, from *c.* 1430, can be found in A.L. Cherepnin, ed., *Dukhovnye i dogovornye gramoty velikikh i udel'nykh kniazei XIV–XVI vv* (Moscow-Leningrad 1950), pp. 67–68. In north-eastern Russia, such contracts seem to have been unknown.

† This the Russians and their subject peoples found out at great cost to themselves after 1917. The generous promises made by Lenin to the peasants, workers and national minorities, allowing them to seize control of the land and industries and to exercise the unlimited right of national self-determination – promises utterly extreme in their libertarian scope but undefined in law and unprotected by courts – in the end produced the very opposite result.

sources in the absence of the whole tradition of contract, implanted in western Europe by vassalage.

Noteworthy also was the ignorance in Russia of subinfeudation. Boyars engaged themselves to serve princes only; and although well-to-do boyars sometimes had their own retainers, there were no complex ties of fealty linking prince, boyar and boyar's retainer, and therefore no network of mutual dependence so characteristic of western feudalism and so important for the political development of the west.

The material side of western feudalism was the fief, that is property, either land or office, provisionally given to the vassal as reward for service. While modern scholars no longer adhere to the view that nearly all land in feudal Europe was held conditionally, no one questions that the fief was then the dominant form of land tenure. Property given servitors conditionally is known elsewhere; but the combination of the fief with vassalage is unique to western Europe.

Until recently it was widely believed that some kind of conditional land tenure had been known in appanage Russia at least since the 1330s, when Ivan I Kalita, the Great Prince of Moscow, had inserted in his testament a passage which seemed to allude to it. But the great authority on medieval landholding in Russia, S.B. Veselovskii, has shown that this belief rested on a misreading of the texts, and that, in fact, the first Russian fiefs (*pomest'ia*) were introduced only in the 1470s in conquered Novgorod.[10] Until then, alod (*votchina*), which did not require service, was the only form of land tenure known in Russia. The absence in appanage Russia of any formal link between the ownership of land and the rendering of service signifies the absence of a fundamental feature of feudalism as practised in the west. Conditional land tenure, when it came to Russia in the 1470s, was not a feudal but an anti-feudal institution, introduced by the absolute monarchy for the purpose of destroying the class of 'feudal' princes and boyars (see below, Chapter 3). 'When [freemen in Russia] were vassals, they did not as yet receive compensation from the sovereign, or, at any rate, they did not have *fiefs-terre*, i.e. they lived, for the major part, on their alodial properties (*votchiny*)', writes Peter Struve, 'And when they began to receive *fiefs-terre* in the form of *pomest'ia*, they ceased to be vassals, i.e. contractual servants.'[11]

Appanage Russia did have an institution corresponding to fief-office in the so-called *kormleniia*, as provincial administrative posts were known. Appointments of this sort, however, were always made for limited periods (two years at the most), and they were not allowed to become the hereditary property of their holders, as was often the case with the western fief-office. They represented, in effect, bonuses given to trusted servants in lieu of money of which the Russian princes were always desperately short.

The absence in medieval Russia of feudal institutions of the western European kind has had profound bearing on the deviation of Russia's political development from the course followed by western Europe. Feudalism is commonly regarded as an order antithetical to statehood; in ordinary speech 'feudal' signifies as much as inward-oriented, disorganized, lacking in public spirit. This usage, made popular by the French Revolution and liberal publicists of the nineteenth century, is not shared by modern historians. The latter are impressed by the hidden centripetal impulses inherent in western feudalism, and by the critical contributions it has made to the growth of modern statehood. Vassalage proved an excellent surrogate for public authority after that authority had declined and in places disappeared following the collapse of the Carolingian Empire. The authority which western kings could no longer exercise in their public capacity, as territorial rulers, they were able at least partly to enforce through personal liens over vassals. At first, feudal authority extended only to the vassals who had personally sworn fealty to the king (*vassi dominici*); but in some western countries it was eventually extended to embrace also the vassals' vassals. In this manner through subinfeudation, a chain of command was forged which, though private and contractual in origin, functioned in a manner similar to the public and obligatory. It is from feudal institutions, too, that some of the most important political institutions of the modern state emerged. The feudal *curia regis*, originally a convocation of royal vassals assembled to give the king the advice which, as lord, he had a right to demand, became in thirteenth-century France a central organ of royal government employing salaried officials. The Estates General of thirteenth-century France and England transformed themselves from *ad hoc* gatherings, convoked in periods of national emergency, into parliaments which claimed as a right what had once been their obligation. The court systems of England and France likewise grew out of feudal institutions, namely the right of the vassal to an open trial, administered by persons other than his lord. Thus, for all its apparent anarchist tendencies, feudalism furnished western monarchs with a superb set of instruments with which to consolidate their power and organize centralized states. Sovereignty over the persons of the vassals and control of their fiefs could be and in places actually became a means for the establishment of sovereignty over all the people and the territory which they inhabited. The rulers of Germany and Italy proved unable to make proper use of this instrument; those of England, France and Spain succeeded, and from 1300 onwards laid the foundation work of powerful, centralized states. In these three countries, feudalism provided the womb within which gestated the modern state.[12]

The Russian appanage prince, lacking vassalage and conditional land tenure, was at a great disadvantage compared to the western king. It was only on his private domains that he was master. It is, therefore, quite natural that he had an obsession with accumulating real estate. He bought land, traded it, married into it and seized it by force. This preoccupation had the consequence of transforming the more ambitious of the appanage princes into ordinary businessmen, strengthening in their mind the already well-developed proprietary instincts.

Because of this background, once the ideas of 'state' and 'sovereignty' finally came to Russia (this occurred in the seventeenth century) they were instinctively perceived through the patrimonial prism. The tsars of Muscovy looked upon their empire extending from Poland to China with the eyes of landlords, much as their ancestors had once viewed their minuscule appanages. The proprietary manner of regarding the realm and its inhabitants impressed itself very deeply on the mind of Russian rulers and of their service class. When nineteenth-century emperors, men thoroughly western in their upbringing, adamantly refused to grant their country a constitution, they were behaving not unlike ordinary property owners afraid to jeopardize their title by some legal precedent. Nicholas II, Russia's last tsar, was by temperament ideally suited to serve as a constitutional monarch. Yet he could not bring himself to grant a constitution, or, after having been forced to do so, to respect it, because he conceived absolute authority as some kind of a property trust which he was duty-bound to pass intact to his heir. The patrimonial mentality constitutes the intellectual and psychological basis of that authoritarianism, common to most of Russia's rulers, whose essence lies in the refusal to grant the 'land', the patrimony, the right to exist apart from its owner, the ruler and his 'state'.

The qualities characteristic of the internal development of early Russian statehood – an unusually wide gulf separating those in political authority from society, and a proprietary, patrimonial manner of exercising sovereignty – were intensified by a shattering external event, the Mongol conquest of 1237–41.

From the time they had first settled in eastern Europe, the Slavs had learned to treat nomad harassment as an inescapable fact of life. Indeed, by the early thirteenth century they had even managed to establish a *modus vivendi* with the once dreaded Cumans, with whom they now married and joined in common military ventures. But then they always had the forest where they could retreat in case of an emergency. The nomads rarely ventured into it for any length of time, and the Slavic settlers cultivating land in the Oka–Volga region, not to speak of those on distant Novgorodian territories, were reasonably safe from them. The appearance in the winter of 1236–7 of Mongol horsemen deep in the forest zone caused, therefore, a shock that has never been quite erased from the collective consciousness of the Russian people. These were forward patrols of a large army headed by Baty, the grandson of Genghis Khan, who had received in inheritance as his share of the global Mongol empire all territories lying in the direction of the setting sun. Baty's men were no mere band of marauders engaged in a hit-and-run raid; they were a superb military force come to conquer and stay. Their main army penetrated the Russian forest in the spring of 1237 'like a darkness chased by a cloud', in the words of an Arab who saw them strike elsewhere. In 1237–8 and then again in 1239–41 they ravaged Russian cities and villages, massacring all who dared to resist them. Of the major cities only Novgorod escaped destruction thanks to the spring floods which made impassable to the Mongol cavalry the swampy approaches to it. Having burned Kiev to the ground, the invaders moved westward. They would probably have conquered western Europe as well, were it not that in the summer of 1242, while encamped in Hungary, news reached them of the Great Khan's death, whereupon they headed back to Mongolia never to return.

North-east Russia and Novgorod now became tributary states of one branch of the Mongol empire, the so-called Golden Horde, whose centre was at Sarai on the Lower Volga. (Lithuania with its sizeable Russian population escaped this fate.)* The Mongols were not interested in land, least of all in forest; they wanted money and recruits. Rather than occupy Russia, as they had done in the richer and more civilized China and Iran, they imposed on it a tribute. In 1257, using imported Chinese experts, they conducted the first general census of the Russian population, on the basis of which they apportioned the tribute obligations. The basic taxable unit, as in China, was the household. In addition, a turnover tax (*tamga*) was imposed on all commodities exchanged in trade. Each city had to accommodate Mongol officials and their armed guards whose job it was to collect the tribute, turn over taxes and recruits (mostly children) and to keep an eye on their master's interests. There was nothing to restrain these consuls and their guards from abusing the population. Russian chronicles are filled with accounts of barbarities perpetrated by them. The population sometimes rebelled (e.g. 1257–9 in Novgorod and 1262 in several of the cities), but such

---

* The force which subjugated Russia was led by Mongols but its rank and file consisted mostly of Turkic peoples commonly known as Tatars. The Golden Horde gradually became Turkicized or 'Tatarized', and for this reason one often speaks of the 'Tatar yoke'.

disobedience was invariably punished in a most brutal fashion.*

The Mongol khan became the country's first undisputed personal sovereign. In post-1240 Russian documents he is customarily referred to as the *tsar* or Caesar (*tsezar'*), titles previously reserved for the Emperor of Byzantium. No prince could assume authority without first obtaining from him an investiture charter called *iarlyk*. To secure it, appanage princes had to make pilgrimages to Sarai and sometimes even to Karakorum in Mongolia. There, dressed in Mongol clothes they were required to undergo a ritualistic passage between two flames, and then kneel before the sovereign to beg for title to their votchiny. On occasion, terrible indignities were inflicted on them, and some princes lost their lives at Sarai. *Iarlyki* were disposed of by means of virtual auctions, the prizes going to them who promised the most money and men, and gave the best assurance of keeping the restless population under control. In effect, behaviour contrary to what may be called national interest became the prerequisite to princely authority. Closely watched by agents of the khan dispersed throughout Russia (they still kept permanent missions in Moscow in the late fifteenth century), the princes had to keep on squeezing tribute and recruits without being allowed to consider the effects of these measures on the population. Any false step, any arrears, could mean a summons to Sarai, the loss of the charter to a more compliant rival, and possibly execution. Princes who under an impulse sided with the people against the Mongol tribute-collectors – and there were such – suffered prompt retribution. In these circumstances something like a process of natural selection began to operate under which the most opportunistic and ruthless survived, and the rest went under. Collaboration, or what Karamzin called 'the base cunning of slavery', became the highest political virtue for Russians. The veche, never strong in the north-east, declined drastically after a short period of ascendancy in the twelfth century. The Mongols did not like it, seeing in the veche a troublesome focus of popular discontent, and they prodded the princes to liquidate it. By the middle of the fourteenth century little remained of the veche except in Novgorod and Pskov. With it vanished the only institution in some measure capable of restraining political authority.

There is considerable disagreement among historians as to the effect which Mongol rule produced on Russia; some regard it as paramount,

---

* I do not mean to imply that the Mongols and Turks of the Golden Horde were nothing but savage barbarians. At the time, they were in almost every respect culturally superior to the Russians: as late as 1591 the English traveller Giles Fletcher described them in these terms. But as the Germans and Japanese amply demonstrated during the Second World War, people with a high level of culture at home can behave on conquered territory in an odious manner. The greater the cultural difference separating conqueror from the vanquished, the more likely is the former to regard his victim as subhuman, and to treat him as such. In the words of a Japanese proverb: 'A man away from home has no neighbours.'

others treat it as a mere backdrop to internal developments occurring within the appanage or 'feudal' systems. There can be scarcely any doubt, however, that domination by a foreign power, which in its worst form lasted for a century and a half, had a very debilitating effect on the political climate of Russia. It tended to isolate the princes from the population further than they were already inclined to be by the workings of the appanage system, to make them less conscious of political responsibilities, and yet more eager to use power to accumulate private properties. It also accustomed them to regard authority as by its very nature arbitrary. A prince confronted with popular dissatisfaction had merely to threaten with calling in the Mongols to secure obedience – a practice that easily grew into habit. Russian life became terribly brutalized, as witnessed by the Mongol or Turco-Tatar derivation of so many Russian words having to do with repression, such as *kandaly* and *kaidaly* (chains), *nagaika* (a kind of whip) and *kabala* (a form of slavery). The death penalty, unknown to the law codes of Kievan Rus', came in with the Mongols. During these years, the population at large first learned what the state was; that it was arbitrary and violent, that it took what it could lay its hands on and gave nothing in return, and that one had to obey it because it was strong. All of which set the stage for the peculiar type of political authority, blending native and Mongol elements, which arose in Moscow once the Golden Horde began to loosen its grip on Russia.

CHAPTER 3

THE TRIUMPH OF PATRIMONIALISM

The amalgamation of a welter of small, semi-sovereign political entities into a unitary state governed by an absolute king was accomplished in Russia by methods different from those made familiar by western history. As has been noted before, the appanage system differed from western feudalism in a number of respects, two of which had direct bearing on the course of Russia's political unification. For one, Russia had never had a single national sovereign (if one excepts, as one must, the Mongol khan); instead, it had a single royal dynasty divided into many competing branches. Secondly, the distintegration of national political authority occurred here not from its usurpation by feudatories, but from its apportionment among the princes themselves. For these related reasons, the establishment of a unitary state in Russia proved more complicated than in the west. There, it involved one basic task: cutting down to size the feudal usurpers and reclaiming from them on the monarch's behalf his theoretical but unexercisable powers. In Russia, two steps were required to attain the same end. First, it was necessary to settle in an unequivocal manner which of the numerous princes descended from the House of Riurik would become the exclusive possessor of royal authority – who would be Russia's 'monocrat' (*edinorzhets*). After this issue had been resolved – and it had to be done by force because customary law offered no guidelines – then and only then could the victor turn his attention to the more familiar task of suppressing internal competitors and acquiring the status of 'autocrat' (*samoderzhets*) as well. In other words, in Russia the process leading from 'feudal' decentralization to unitary statehood required not one but two stages, the first of which pitted prince against prince, and the second, the triumphant 'Great Prince' against nobles and (to a lesser extent) ecclesiastics. In practice, of course, the establishment of 'monocracy' and 'autocracy' was by no means as neatly separated as these words might suggest. For the purposes of historical analysis, however, it makes sense to keep them distinct, because the striving for 'monocratic' authority, peculiar to Russia, provides important clues to that country's subsequent constitutional development.

Russia's national unification began around 1300, that is, concurrently with analogous developments in England, France and Spain. At the time, it was by no means a foregone conclusion that there would be a unitary Russian state or that its centre would lie in Moscow. Nothing is easier than to demonstrate that whatever happened had to happen. It is also a very satisfying exercise because it seems to confirm that all is always for the best, which cheers the common man and also suits his betters. However, the trouble with the concept of historical inevitability is that it works only retrospectively, i.e. for the writers of history, not for its makers. If the behaviour of the appanage princes is any indication, at the time when Russia's unification got under way, there was certainly no overwhelming sense of it being desirable, let alone inevitable. The theological and historical theories justifying the process were worked out much later. In fact, it would be difficult to prove that Russia could not have gone the way of Germany or Italy and entered the modern age thoroughly dismembered.

If, however, Russia were to be united, then, for reasons previously given, the task had to be accomplished neither by Novgorod nor by Lithuania, but by one of the north-eastern appanage principalities. Here, out of the original principality of Rostov the Great there had emerged, through the perpetual splitting of patrimonies, many appanages, large and small. After 1169, when Andrei Bogoliubskii had decided against abandoning his appanage in this area and moving to Kiev to assume the throne of Great Prince (see above, p. 37), the title of Great Prince came to be associated with his favourite city, Vladimir. His brothers and their progeny rotated control of Vladimir with Bogoliubskii's direct descendants. The Mongols respected the custom, and the person whom they invested as Great Prince assumed concurrently the title Prince of Vladimir, although he did not, as a rule, actually move there. Under the appanage system, the title of Great Prince gave the bearer very little authority over his brethren, but it did carry prestige as well as the right to collect the revenues of the city of Vladimir and its adjoining territories, for which reason it was coveted. The Mongols liked to invest with it princes whom they thought particularly accommodating.

In the competition for Vladimir and the title of Great Prince, the descendants of Prince Alexander Nevsky turned out to be the most successful contenders. A grandson of Bogoliubskii and the eldest son of the reigning prince of Vladimir, Nevsky served at the time of the Mongol invasion as prince of Novgorod and Pskov where he distinguished himself fighting the Germans, Swedes and Lithuanians. In 1242, after his father's death, he journeyed to Sarai to pay homage to the country's conqueror and most likely to request from him a *iarlyk* for Vladimir. For unknown reasons the Mongols entrusted Vladimir to Nevsky's younger brother, issuing him instead a charter for Kiev and Novgorod. But Nevsky did not give up. He bided his time and ten years later in 1252, succeeded in persuading the khan to reverse himself. With a Mongol force which the khan placed at his disposal he captured Vladimir, unseated his brother, and assumed the title of Great Prince. His subsequent behaviour fully justified the Mongols' confidence in him. In 1257–9 he stamped out popular uprisings against Mongol census-takers which had broken out in Novgorod, and a few years later he did so again in several other rebellious cities, all of which must have pleased his masters. After Nevsky's death (1263) the Mongols several times took Vladimir from his descendants, investing with it, in turn, the princes of Tver, Riazan and Nizhnii Novgorod; but his offspring always recaptured it and in the end made Vladimir and the title of Great Prince the hereditary property (*votchina*) of their house.

Nevsky and his descendants owed their success to the adoption of a shrewd political strategy *vis-à-vis* the conqueror. The Golden Horde, whose servants they were, had been formed from an association of nomadic tribes and clans which Genghis Khan had fused to wage warfare. Even after it had become a large state with a numerous sedentary population, it lacked the necessary apparatus to administer a country as vast and sparsely populated as Russia. Their tax collectors (*basqaqs*) and census-takers accompanied by military retainers were very unpopular and provoked many uprisings which, brutally as the Mongols suppressed them, kept on recurring. If Russia had been as rich and civilized as China or Persia, the Mongols undoubtedly would have occupied it and assumed over it direct rule. But since this was not the case, they had no incentive to move into the forest; they much preferred to remain in the steppe with its excellent pastures and profitable trade routes. At first they experimented with Muslim tax-farmers, but this method did not work, and eventually they concluded that the job could best be done by the Russians themselves. Nevsky and even more his successors met this need. They assumed on behalf of the Horde the principal administrative and fiscal responsibilities over Russian territories, as compensation for which they gained for their principalities relative freedom from Mongol interference and for themselves influence at Sarai; the latter proved an immensely valuable weapon with which to undermine rival princes. As long as the money kept on being accurately delivered and the country remained reasonably peaceful, the Mongols had no reason to tamper with this arrangement.

In the policy of collaboration, no one excelled the branch of Nevsky's family ensconced in what in the thirteenth century was the insignificant

Moscow appanage carved out in 1276 for Nevsky's son, Danil Aleksandrovich. Danil's son, Iurii, managed in 1317 to secure for himself the hand of the khan's sister and the title to Vladimir to go with it. Eight years later he was murdered by the son of the prince of Tver, whom the Mongols had executed at his, Iurii's, instigation, whereupon Moscow (without Vladimir and the Grand Princely title, however) passed to his younger brother, Ivan Danilovich, later designated Ivan I of Russia. The new ruler proved an extraordinarily gifted and unscrupulous political manipulator. By one scholar's estimate, he spent most of his reign either at Sarai or *en route* to or from it, which gives some idea how busy he must have been intriguing there.[1] An astute businessman (the population nicknamed him 'Kalita' or 'the Moneybag') he amassed what by the standards of the time was a sizable fortune. Much of his income came from tolls which he imposed on people and goods crossing his properties, which happened to straddle several trade routes. This money not only enabled him promptly to deliver payments of his share of the tribute, but also to make up the arrears of other princes. To the latter he lent money against the security of their appanages, which he sometimes foreclosed. The poverty of Russian agriculture and its uncertainties made the life of the average tribute-paying appanage prince very precarious, placing him at the mercy of the richest of his relatives.

Ivan's most serious rival for Mongol favour was the prince of Tver, who, after Ivan's elder brother Iurii's death, had succeeded in wresting from Moscow the title of Great Prince. In 1327, the population of Tver rose against the Mongols and massacred a high-level deputation sent from Sarai to oversee the collection of the tribute. After some hesitation, the prince of Tver sided with the rebels. As soon as this news had reached him, Ivan left for Sarai. He returned as the head of a combined Mongol–Russian punitive force which so devastated Tver and a great deal of central Russia besides that the region was not yet fully recovered half a century later. As a reward for his loyalty, the Mongols invested Ivan with the title of Great Prince, and appointed him Farmer General of the tribute throughout Russia. This was undoubtedly an expensive privilege since it made Ivan responsible for the arrears and defaults of others, but one that offered him unique opportunities for meddling in the internal affairs of rival appanages. Control of the tribute meant in effect monopoly of access to the khan's court. Taking advantage of it, Ivan and his successors forbade the other princes to enter into direct relations with any other state, the Horde included, except through the agency of Moscow. In this manner, Moscow gradually isolated its rivals, and moved to the forefront as the intermediary between the conqueror and his Russian subjects. The Mongols had no cause to regret the favours they had heaped on Ivan. In the twelve remaining years of his life, he served them no less ably than his grandfather Alexander Nevsky had done, keeping in line, with force when necessary, Novgorod, Rostov, Smolensk and any other city that dared to raise its head. Karl Marx, whom the present government of Russia regards as an authoritative historian, characterized this first prominent representative of the Moscow line as a blend of 'the characters of the Tartar's hangman, sycophant and slave-in-chief'.[2]

Moscow profited in many ways from Sarai's favour. The Mongols, who frequently raided other parts of Russia to loot and take prisoners, tended to respect the properties of their principal agent, with the result that the principality of Moscow became an island of relative security in a country torn by violence. Boyars with their retainers readily entered the service of the Moscow prince to benefit from the protection which the principal collaborator alone was able to provide. *Pax mongolica*, whatever its dark aspects, placed a good part of Asia and the Near East under the sovereignty of a single dynasty, of which Russia was a tributary. This political unity opened considerable commercial opportunities. It was under Mongol domination that Russian merchants first began to venture to the Caspian and Black seas to trade with Persians and Turks, and it is then that the north-eastern principalities began to develop a rudimentary mercantile culture.

Moscow also profited greatly from support of the church. The Metropolitan of Kiev, Russia's highest ecclesiastic, finding himself in a deserted city, transferred in 1299 his see to Vladimir. He had excellent reasons for maintaining close relations with the Horde, because under Mongol rule the church and the monasteries enjoyed exemption from the tribute and all the other obligations imposed on the Russian populace. This valuable privilege was granted by charters which every new khan had to reconfirm on his accession. To preserve its advantages, the church obviously required effective representation at Sarai. In 1299, the contest between Tver and Moscow was not yet resolved, and although the Metropolitan favoured Moscow, he preferred formally to assume a neutral stance by establishing himself in Vladimir. But after Tver's uprising in 1327 and its sacking by Ivan I the outcome could no longer remain in doubt. The very next year (1328), the Metropolitan see was moved from Vladimir to Moscow which became henceforth the centre of Russia's Orthodoxy and a 'Holy City'. In all subsequent rivalries over the title of Great Prince, the church loyally supported Moscow's claim. In gratitude, Moscow bestowed on it large landholdings backed by immunity charters.

Although all the appanage princes had a keen acquisitive spirit, the princes of Moscow seem to have inherited an outstanding business acumen, which proved a great asset at a time when political power was largely conceived and measured in terms of property. They accumulated villages, towns and promysly with the single-minded determination of modern monopolists bent on cornering some commodity. They spurned no opportunity to turn a profit, trading in oriental rugs, precious stones, furs, wax or any other merchandise which had a ready market. They continued to do so even after having laid claim to the imperial title, a fact which never ceased to astonish foreign visitors to the Kremlin. As will be shown later (Chapter 8), during the sixteenth and seventeenth centuries the tsars of Muscovy enjoyed a virtual monopoly in the country's wholesale commerce as well as in its manufacturing and mining. The penury of some of them went to extraordinary lengths: Ivan III, for example, insisted on foreign ambassadors returning to him the skins of sheep which he had sent them for food.[3] They grew rich, minded their fortunes and took every precaution to prevent their descendants from squandering what they had accumulated. Fortunately for them, the princes of Moscow tended to be long-lived; during nearly two hundred years separating the accession of Basil I (1389) from the death of Ivan IV (1584), Muscovy had only five rulers; a remarkable record of longevity for the age.

It must have been their business sense rather than any political design (for which evidence is lacking) that accounts for the skill with which the princes of Moscow succeeded in neutralizing the most pernicious feature of Russian inheritance law. They could not entirely ignore custom which demanded that each male descendant receive an equal portion of the patrimony, but they did manage quietly to circumvent it. Their testaments read like the dispositions made by a landlord, and even Moscow and the title of Great Prince are bequeathed as if they were ordinary commodities. But the wealth and power of Moscow depended so heavily on its relations with the Horde that both were certain to be dissipated in no time unless special provisions were made to maintain some kind of seniority in the Muscovite house. Hence, in dictating their last wills, the Moscow princes began early to discriminate in favour of the eldest son, increasing his share with each generation until by the early sixteenth century he emerged as the indisputable head of the house. Dmitry Donskoi, who died in 1389, divided his patrimony among five sons, leaving the eldest, Basil I, whom he designated Great Prince, about a third and making him responsible for 34·2 per cent of the Mongol tribute. Basil I happened to have had only one son, Basil II, survive him and to him he left everything. As if wishing to guarantee that his status as exclusive heir would not be assailed by his, Basil I's, brothers, he arranged to have Basil II placed on the throne while he was still alive. When death approached, Basil II assigned his eldest, Ivan III, as many towns as the other four sons combined. Ivan III continued this tradition by bequeathing his eldest, Basil III, sixty-six of the best towns of the ninety-nine towns in his possession; the remaining four sons had to divide among themselves appanages containing thirty-three of the minor towns. How much the share of the eldest son increased by these procedures may be gathered from the fact that whereas Basil I on his accession in 1389 owed 34·2 per cent of the Mongol tribute due from his father's estate, by the time his great-grandson Basil III ascended the throne in 1505 his theoretical share of the tribute (for it was no longer paid) rose to 71·7 per cent. Thus, by the beginning of the sixteenth century, the appanages allotted to the cadet heirs became mere lifelong provisions and as such no longer threatened the coherence of the family holdings. It now became customary for the appanages, as in feudal France, to revert to the Great Prince upon the holder's death. In this form, they survived until the expiration of the Riurik dynasty in 1598. A vital political reform – the introduction of a system of royal succession based on primogeniture – was accomplished quietly, almost surreptitiously, within the context of the law of property and through the institution of property inheritance. The adoption of this system gave the rulers of Moscow an immense advantage over rival princes who continued to split properties into equal shares among their heirs.

As had been said earlier, the ascendancy of Moscow to the position of unquestioned pre-eminence in Russia involved two processes; an external one, aimed at compelling all the other appanage princes, as well as Novgorod and Lithuania, to acknowledge the ruler of Moscow as their sovereign; and an internal one, whose purpose it was to make sovereignty acquire the attributes of patrimonial or domainial power, i.e. full ownership of the land and its inhabitants. Both processes had their roots in the idea of votchina.

The Great Princes of Vladimir, whether their home was in Moscow, Tver or any other appanage principality, regarded their realm as their votchina, that is outright property. Their power over it was comparable to that of the possessor of *dominium* in Roman law, a power defined as 'absolute ownership excluding all other appropriation and involving the right to use, to abuse and to destroy at will'.[4] At first, the princes' patrimonial claims were limited to the towns and volosti which they had either inherited or personally acquired. But from the middle of the fifteenth century, as the power of the Moscow princes grew and they began openly to aspire to all-Russian sovereignty, the term was broadened to include all of Rus'. 'Not only those cities and volosti which are now ours belong to our patrimony,' the legates of Ivan III once told the Lithuanians, 'all the land of Rus', Kiev and Smolensk, and the other cities which [the Lithuanian Great Prince] now holds in the Lithuanian land, they too by God's will, since the days of old, are our votchina [inherited] from our ancestors.'[5] Later on, as he invaded Livonia which had never formed part of the Kievan state, Ivan IV did not hesitate to call it his votchina as well.

The concept of the kingdom as the personal patrimony of the prince was not entirely alien to western political thought. The record exists of a conversation between Frederick II and two legal experts in the course of which the Emperor asked them 'whether an emperor was not rightly the *dominus* of everything held by his subjects'. The interlocutor who had the courage to reply rejected it out of hand: 'he was lord in the political sense, but not in the sense of an owner.'[6] Indeed it never struck root in the west, where theorists steadfastly adhered to the fundamental distinction between ownership and authority, between *dominium* and *imperium* or *iurisdictio*. The notion of political authority exercised as *dominium* carried visibly dangerous implications for the owners of private property, so numerous and influential in western Europe, and this sufficed to make the idea unacceptable. The spread of knowledge of Roman law during the twelfth century helped to give the distinction a powerful theoretical underpinning. In his *Six Books of the Commonwealth* (1576–86) Jean Bodin, the founder of the modern theory of sovereignty, isolated from the two traditional types of authority headed by one man, the monarchical and its corruption, the tyrannical, a third, which he called 'seigneural'. (The English translator of 1606 rendered it as 'lordly'.) This type of monarchy, in his view, came into being by conquest of arms. The distinguishing characteristic of *la monarchie seigneuriale* was that 'the prince is become lord of the goods and persons of his subjects ... governing them as a master of a family does his slaves'. Bodin added that in Europe there were only two such regimes, one in Turkey, the other in Muscovy, although they were common in Asia and Africa. In western Europe, he thought, the people would not tolerate this kind of government.[7]

At issue, of course, were not only ideas and labels. The patrimonial system rested on the assumption that there existed no separation between the properties of the ruler and those of the state. Western Europe insisted that this distinction be drawn. In France, beginning with approximately 1290, custom required the king to safeguard crown estates as an inviolate trust. After 1364, French kings had to swear an oath that they would not alienate any part of the royal domain as constituted on their accession; excluded were only revenues, personal properties and conquered territories. In the sixteenth century, it was further specified that the king's conquests were at his disposal for only ten years, after which they merged with the crown domains.[8] In this way, the rulers of France, western Europe's most authoritarian, had to give up proprietary

65

claim to the crown heritage; and even when violating the principle in practice, they did not challenge its general validity. A fifteenth-century Spanish jurist stated succinctly western Europe's feeling about 'seigneural' or patrimonial government: 'To the King is confided solely the administration of the kingdom, and not dominion over things, for the property and rights of the State are public, and cannot be the private patrimony of anyone.'[9] As for the sanctity of private property, it was axiomatic in western political theory and jurisprudence in the Middle Ages and afterwards; and although periodically abused, it was never seriously questioned until the spread of socialist doctrines in modern times. One of the standard criteria used in western thought for distinguishing a legitimate king from a despot was that one respected his subjects' properties while the other did not.

In Russia such objections to domainial rule were unknown. In a series of letters which he wrote to Ivan IV from his refuge in Lithuania, Prince Andrei Kurbskii, a prominent boyar, assailed the entire notion of the state as votchina. But a recent analysis of the Kurbskii–Ivan correspondence has thrown such doubts on its authenticity that it can no longer be depended on as a source.[10] Under the economic conditions prevailing in medieval and early modern Russia the institution of private property could not count on secure grounding either in custom or positive law; and the ignorance of Roman law presented formidable obstacles to its introduction from the outside. No distinction, therefore, was drawn between the king in his capacities of proprietor and sovereign. As Moscow expanded, new territorial acquisitions were at once attached to the Great Prince's private patrimony and there they stayed. In this manner the Russian monarchy emerged directly from the seigniory of the appanage principality: that is, from what had been originally an arrangement for economic exploitation, operating largely with slave labour.

The domainial origin of the Russian state is reflected in the origins of its administrative apparatus. Unfortunately, the Moscow fire of 1626 destroyed a large part of the archives of the central administration, which makes it difficult to determine when and under what circumstances it had been created. Still, enough is known strongly to suggest that it evolved directly from the offices originally charged with the management of the appanage prince's private domain. The dvor of the Moscow prince served for a long time – probably until the middle of the sixteenth century – in a double capacity as the management of the princely estates and the administration of the rest of the principality. 'Until the reforms of the 1550s–1560s,' writes a leading authority on the subject, 'general control over the whole system of local administration [of Muscovite Russia] was exercised by none other than the offices of the prince's household (dvor) ... which concentrated in their hands almost all the basic branches of the state administration then in existence.'[11]

Especially striking is the evolution of the executive bureaux of Muscovite administration, the *prikazy*. The term prikaz has its etymological roots in the language of the appanage domain: as noted, *prikaznye liudi* (men of the prikaz) (p. 45), were those domestic slaves and dependants who performed administrative functions on large domains, princely as well as private. Prikaz was the name of an office headed by such an official. With some possible minor exceptions, the earliest Muscovite prikazy seem to have been constituted only in the second half of the sixteenth century, that is a good one hundred years after Moscow had become the capital of an empire. Until that time, the administrators serving the prince – the steward (*dvoretskii*) and the *putnye boiare* – continued to carry out public administrative functions outside the prince's domain, as needed. As other appanages were conquered and annexed to Moscow, the dvory of the deposed princes were transported and reestablished in Moscow as new administrative entities: thus there appeared in Moscow special bureaux to administer Riazan, and Novgorod, and other areas. Each of these regional prikazy was a separate government, as it were, with complete authority over the territory entrusted to its charge. A similar arrangement was made in the sixteenth century for the conquered principality of Kazan, and in the seventeenth for Siberia. Thus, side by side with purely functional bureaux there appeared in Moscow bureaux formed on the territorial principle. This kind of administration prevented any region of the realm from developing organs of self-government or even a sense of local political identity. As Paul Miliukov says,

At the very inception of our institutions, we run into an immense difference from the west. There, every region constituted a compact, self-contained whole, bound together by means of special rights ... Our history has failed to work out any lasting local ties or local organization. Upon their annexation by Moscow, the annexed regions at once disintegrated into atoms out of which the government could form any shapes it desired. But to begin with it was content to isolate each atom from those surrounding it and to attach it with administrative links directly to the centre.[12]

All of which, of course, had profound bearing on the absence in tsarist and imperial Russia of any effective regional loci of power, able to stand up to central authority.

To replace the local administrations transported to Moscow, the dvor of the Moscow prince opened branches in the main cities of the conquered principalities. These exercised both private and public functions, exactly as had been the case with the prince's own dvor inside the appanage principality. Under the pressure of expanding business, resulting from Moscow's uninterrupted territorial growth, the household administration of the Prince constituted itself into the Bureau of the Large Household (*Prikaz Bol'shogo Dvortsa*), the first prikaz about which there is solid information and certainly the most important. Even so Moscow expanded at such a rapid rate that the task exceeded the capacities of the domestic staff of the Prince. In time, therefore, a rudimentary state administration began to emerge, separate from the household. The first to detach itself was the Treasury (*Kazennyi Prikaz*); subsequently, other officials formed their own bureaux as well.[13]

Through its evolution, the Muscovite administration retained strong traces of the old domainial system of administration out of which it had grown out. Like the appanage *puti* (p. 45), the Moscow prikazy were organized in accord with the sources of revenue rather than according to some principle of public responsibility. And the reason for this was that, just like the management of an estate, they were set up to extract goods and services. As before, too, each prikaz had assigned to it its own means of financial support, and each continued to dispense justice to the people within its competence. These relics of the appanage period remained embedded in the Russian system of government until the time when Peter I, following western examples, introduced the principle of administrative rationalism and created a national budget.

In the west, the machinery of state administration also grew out of the apparatus managing the royal estates. But what is striking about Russia is how late domainial institutions transformed themselves into public ones. In France, the differentiation was completed by the fourteenth century; in Russia it only began in the eighteenth. This lag assumes considerable importance if one bears in mind that these two countries began to constitute themselves into national states at approximately the same time, i.e. around 1300. Secondly, in Russia the distinction between the domainial and the public spheres always remained very vague, and this fact could not but influence the conduct of the administration. Western feudalism created a number of institutions (courts, *curia regis*, Estates General) which by the mere fact of having separate identities from the king's household administration strengthened the sense of a public order. Sir Thomas Smith, a sixteenth-century English constitutional theorist, put the matter very well when he described sovereignty as resulting from the fusion of the king and the nation occurring when Parliament was in session. In Russia, the state administration came into being not because of a recognition that prince and state were things apart, requiring separate institutional expression, but rather because the prince's household staff no longer could handle the whole job. Recognition of the separate identity of ruler and state – natural to any country with a feudal past – came to Russia only in the eighteenth century as a result of western intellectual influences; but by this time the country's political ideas and practices were fully set.

Another item of evidence in favour of the contention that the Muscovite state apparatus evolved out of the domainial administration of the Muscovite princes has to do with the way Russian officials were paid. In the appanage principality, on the relatively infrequent occasions that a member of the prince's dvor had to perform duties outside the domain, (e.g. on black lands), it was assumed that his wages would be provided for by the population. Such payments, in money and kind, were called *kormleniia* (literally, 'feedings'). The system was retained by the tsars of Moscow. Officials of the prikazy and of other offices located in the city of Moscow and serving directly under the sovereign, were paid out of the tsar's treasury. But no funds at all were allocated for the provincial administration whose members received kormleniia in the form of regular contributions as well as fees for particular services rendered. This system, too, survived until the time when Peter I introduced regular salaries for state officials; however, since financial difficulties compelled Peter's immediate successors to suspend salary payments, the post-Petrine bureaucracy once again reverted in large measure to living off the land.

Thus, both in its organization and manner of rewarding its civil service the Muscovite state followed practices of the appanage principality – a fact strongly indicative of its domainial antecedents.

Further evidence for this thesis can be found in the failure of the Russians to distinguish either in theory or in practice among three types of properties; those belonging personally to the monarch, those belonging to the state, and those belonging to private citizens. During the appanage period private property in land was recognized in the form of votchiny. But as will be shown in the next chapter, during the fifteenth and sixteenth centuries the Moscow monarchy succeeded in eliminating alodial holdings and making secular land tenure a form of possession conditional on state service. It is only in 1785 under Catherine II when Russian landholders secured clear legal title to their estates that private property in land came once again into being in Russia. Given this background it is not surprising that the kind of distinction drawn in France since the late Middle Ages between the properties of the king and those of the crown came to Russia very late:

Neither in the appanage of Moscow, nor in the Great Principality of Vladimir in which this Muscovite princely line establishes itself, nor in the Muscovite state do we find the slightest indication of the presence of state properties as something distinct from the properties of the prince. Moscow knows only the landed properties of the Great Prince, not those of the state. The properties of the Great Prince are divided into black ones and those of the royal household (*dvortsovye*); the latter are assigned to the households and carry special obligations for their support, but both belong equally to the sovereign and cannot even always be distinguished as to their duties. The Great Prince disposes of both in the same manner. Black lands can be assigned to the royal household, and those of the royal household can be transferred into black status. Both can be handed out as pomestia and votchiny, or turned over to sons, princesses, daughters, monasteries and so on. Our sources draw no distinction whatever between properties purchased by the prince, lands which he confiscated from private individuals, and his other properties, whose method of acquisition remains unknown to us. All this is called without differentiation, 'lands of the sovereign' (*gosudarevy zemli*) and is administered in accord with identical principles.[14]

The first attempt to separate royal from state lands in Russia was made by Paul I who created a Department of Appanages in charge of the Romanov family properties, income from which was used to support members of the imperial household. Under Nicholas I in 1826 this department was elevated to the status of a ministry (*Ministerstvo Imperatorskogo Dvora i Udelov*) which enjoyed the distinction of being exempt from control by the Senate and all other state organs, and responsible only to the emperor himself. In 1837 the Ministry of State Domains (*Ministerstvo Gosudarstvennykh Imushchestv*) came into being to administer state properties. Until then, revenues flowing from the two types of properties were pooled. Until then, too, Russian emperors felt perfectly at liberty to hand over or sell to private individuals vast state properties with hundreds of thousands of peasants. But even after these reforms, the distinction between crown and state properties was not strictly observed. The Ministry of State Domains had been created not to satisfy legal propriety, but because of dissatisfaction with the manner in which the millions of state peasants had been administered. Nicholas I, who established the two above-named ministries, never hesitated to shift peasants from imperial properties to state lands, and vice versa. The fact that until the early eighteenth century Russia had no national budget, and that what budget there was after 1700 remained until the 1860s a closely guarded state secret, facilitated such practices.

In his capacity as *votchinnik* or seigneur of all Russia, the ruler of Moscow treated his kingdom much as his ancestors had treated their landed estates. The idea of state was absent in Russia until the middle of the seventeenth century, and even after its introduction it remained imperfectly assimilated. And since there was no notion of state, its corollary, society, was also unknown.* That which modern Russian renders by the

* Some scholars (e.g. John Keep in the *Slavonic and East European Review*, April 1970, p. 204, and Hans Torke in *Canadian Slavic Studies*, winter 1971, p. 467) see an emergent society in Russia as early as the late seventeenth (Keep) and even mid-sixteenth centuries (Torke).

word *obshchestvo* (an eighteenth-century neologism), the language of Muscovite Russia expressed by *zemlia*. In modern Russian, this word signifies 'the land', but in medieval usage it meant income-producing property.[15] In other words, it was mainly seen not as a counterpoise to the seigneur, the tsar, but as the object of his exploitation. The purpose of the patrimonial regime in Russia as anywhere else was to extract from the country all the income and the labour it had to offer. There was no notion of reciprocity, of the monarchy owing the country something in return. Giles Fletcher, an Elizabethan poet and statesman who visited Russia in 1588–9 and left what in many respects is the finest firsthand account of Muscovy extant, relates that Ivan IV used to compare his people to a beard or to sheep in that like them, to grow well, they required frequent clipping.[16] Whether authentic or invented by English merchants, the metaphor accurately reflects the spirit behind the internal policies of the Muscovite government, or for that matter, of any government of the patrimonial or 'seigneural' type.

At a certain point in the history of Moscow, the patrimonial mentality, rooted in purely economic attitudes, became politicized; the votchinnik-landlord turned into votchinnik-tsar. The spirit remained the same but it acquired new forms of expression and a theoretical overlay. Evidence is lacking precisely when and how this transformation occurred. But there are strong indications that the critical period was the reign of Ivan III, when two concurrent events suddenly freed Muscovy and the principalities which it dominated from ties of external dependence, allowing north-east Russia for the first time to think of itself as a sovereign state.

One of these events was the dissolution of the Golden Horde. The system of succession prevailing among the 'White Bone' (descendants of Genghis Khan), with its complicated lines of seniority better suited to a nomadic nation organized into tribes than to an imperial power, caused uninterrupted internal conflicts. In the 1360s, the Horde was thrown into turmoil as packs of pretenders battled with each other for the throne; during the next twenty years, Sarai had no fewer than fourteen khans. Moscow exploited these dissensions by playing one party against the other. In 1380, Dmitry of Moscow dared even to resist the Mongols by force of arms. True, the khan he challenged was a Crimean and a usurper; true also, the victory which he won over this khan at Kulikovo

Professor Keep rests his case on evidence of restlessness of the service class, but he concludes that its attempt to gain some freedom from the state did not succeed. Professor Torke's evidence indicates mainly that the sixteenth-century Russian government realized it could use the various social estates to help it administer the country. The idea of society as I understand it, and as it has been customarily defined in the west, entails recognition by the state of the right of social groups to legal status and a legitimate sphere of free action. This recognition came to Russia only with the reign of Catherine II.

had little military significance since two years later the Mongols avenged themselves by sacking Moscow. Still, Kulikovo showed that Russians could stand up to their masters.

Already severely weakened by internal conflicts, the Golden Horde received its *coup de grâce* from Timur (Tamerlane). From his base in central Asia, this Turkic conqueror mounted between 1389 and 1395 three campaigns against the Horde, on the last of which his troops destroyed Sarai. The Horde never recovered from these blows. In the middle of the fifteenth century it broke up into several parts, the most important of which became the khanates of Kazan, Astrakhan and the Crimea. These successor states, notably the khanate of the Crimea, could still launch at will raids into Russia, but they no longer had control over it. Indeed, by the end of the fifteenth century it was Moscow that decided which candidate would occupy the throne in Kazan. During the reign of Ivan III (tradition dates the event as having occurred in 1480), Moscow ceased to pay the tribute to the Golden Horde or its successor states.

The other event which helped to politicize the seigneurs of Muscovy was the collapse of the Byzantine Empire. Russian relations to Byzantium had never been clearly defined. From the time of its conversion to Orthodoxy, the assumption undoubtedly existed that Russia stood in some kind of dependence on Constantinople. The point was pressed by the Greek hierarchy, which liked to put forward Justinian's theory of 'harmony' or *symphonia* according to which the church and imperial authority could not exist without one another. But the implied claim that the Russian Orthodox were subjects of the emperors of Byzantium could never be enforced, and during the Mongol rule became quite meaningless in any event, since Russia's emperor then was the very un-Christian khan. Whatever control Byzantium exercised over Russia was channelled through the clergy, that is through appointments to high ecclesiastical offices made or endorsed in Constantinople. But even this link snapped after 1439 when the Russian church rejected Byzantium's union with the Catholics concluded at the Council of Florence. Henceforth, proceeding on the assumption that Constantinople had committed at Florence an act of apostasy, the Great Princes of Moscow began to appoint their own metropolitans, no longer bothering to secure the approval of the Greek hierarchy. Whatever authority over Russia the Byzantine emperors and the Byzantine church may have laid claim to disappeared in 1453 when Constantinople fell to the Turks and the imperial line ceased.

After the fall of the Byzantine Empire, the Orthodox church had vital reasons for building up in Russia powerful imperial authority. The subject will be treated in greater detail in the chapter devoted to the relations between church and state (Chapter 9). Here only the main point needs emphasis. Overwhelmed by Muslims, challenged by Catholics, and undermined by heretical reform movements within its own establishment, the Orthodox church was fighting for its very life. With the fall of Constantinople, the ruler of Moscow emerged as the only Orthodox prince in the world able to protect the Orthodox church from its many external and internal enemies. It became therefore a matter of sheer survival to support the Muscovite rulers, and to imbue these land-grabbers and profiteers with a political consciousness that would help raise their eyes beyond the horizon of their landed properties. After 1453, the Greek and Russian ecclesiastical establishments did all in their power to transform the prince of Moscow into a *fidei defensor*, responsible for the welfare of all Orthodox Christians. The process had one of its culminating points at the church Synod of 1561, which appended to its resolutions an epistle from the Patriarch of Constantinople acclaiming Ivan iv 'emperor and seigneur [*Tsar' i Gosudar'*, i.e. *imperator et dominus*] of Orthodox Christians in the entire universe'.[17]

The collapse of the Golden Horde and the Byzantine Empire freed Moscow from subservience to the two imperial powers which had claimed over it some form of suzerainty. It is therefore at this time, too – the second half of the fifteenth century – that the Great Princes of Moscow began in a tentative manner to claim the imperial title. Ivan iii was the first Russian ruler occasionally to call himself tsar, a title originally applied to the Byzantine emperor and, since 1265 reserved for the khan of the Golden Horde. After marrying the niece of the last Byzantine emperor, he also adopted the imperial double-headed eagle. His son, Basil iii, called himself tsar more often, and his grandson, Ivan iv formalized the practice in 1547 by making 'Tsar of all Russia' (*Tsar vseia Rossii*) the title of Russia's rulers. Heady ideas now began to circulate in the towns and villages of north-eastern Russia. Princes, whose ancestors had to crawl on all fours for the amusement of the khan and his court, now traced their family descent to Emperor Augustus and their crown to an alleged Byzantine investiture. Talk was heard of Moscow being the 'Third Rome', destined for all time to replace the corrupted and fallen Romes of Peter and Constantine. Fantastic legends began to circulate among the illiterate people, linking the largely wooden city on the Moskva river with dimly understood events from biblical and classical history.

Such were the circumstances under which the patrimonial outlook became politicized. Next arises the question what model the princes of Moscow took to emulate in their quest for autocratic and imperial status. The two with which they were familiar were Byzantine and Mongol: the *basileus* and the khan. Western kings could not have served for the purpose, in part because of their Catholicism, in part because,

73

nominally at least, they were vassals of the Roman Emperor, and therefore not true sovereigns in the sense in which Moscow understood the term. In 1488 a legate sent by the Emperor Frederick III arrived in Moscow to seek help against the Turk. As an inducement he offered Ivan III help in obtaining the royal crown. The answer given to this offer not only revealed the high opinion the Muscovite prince had of himself, but also, indirectly, what he thought of ordinary European royalty: 'We are, by the grace of God, masters (*gosudari*) on our land from the very beginning, from our first ancestors, and we have our investiture from God, like our ancestors ... And as for investure, as we did not want it before from anyone, so we do not want it now.'[18]

The Byzantine model reached Russia almost exclusively through the clergy and ecclesiastical literature. Moscow had no direct links with Constantinople, either diplomatic or commercial, and therefore no way of learning from it what a king was or did. The church, for reasons stated above, was much interested in a strong Russian monarchy. It encouraged its ambitions, it helped it formulate a doctrine of absolutism, it devised an elaborate coronation ceremonial. But it is difficult to see how the church could have taught the princes of Moscow the craft of politics.

If we wish to find where Moscow learned about kingship not as an ideal but as a working institution, then we must turn to the Golden Horde. The subject of Mongol influence is a very sensitive one for Russians, who are quick to take offence at the suggestion that their cultural heritage has been shaped in any way by the orient, and especially by the oriental power best remembered for its appalling atrocities and the destruction of great centres of civilization. Still, the issue cannot be skirted; and with a few exceptions, Russian historians have been willing to assign a major and even decisive role in the formation of Muscovite statehood to Mongol influence. The spiritual and moral impact of Mongol rule on Russian politics has been touched upon in the preceding chapter; here we will deal with institutional influences.

The Golden Horde was the first centralized political authority which the Russian princes met face to face. For a century and a half, the khan was the absolute master of their fate. His power and majesty all but erased from memory the image of the Byzantine basileus. The latter was a distant thing, a legend: not one appanage prince had ever set foot in Constantinople; the road to Sarai was only too familiar to them. It was at Sarai that they had an opportunity of observing at close hand the operations of absolute monarchy, of 'authority with which one cannot enter into agreements but must unconditionally obey'.[19] Here they learned how to impose taxes on households and commercial transactions, how to conduct diplomatic relations, how to operate a courier service, and how to deal with insubordinate subjects. The Russian vocabulary retains unmistakable traces of this influence. Its word for treasury – *kazna* – derives from its exact Mongol–Tatar equivalent, and so do the cognate terms designating money and customs (*denga* and *tamozhnia*), both of which are adapted from *tamga*, which under the Mongols meant a government seal placed on merchandise as proof that taxes on it have been paid. The postal service linking Moscow with the provinces (*iamskaia sluzhba*) was nothing but the Mongol *yam* under new management. The Mongol–Tatar influence on the Russian vocabulary of repression has been mentioned previously (p. 57). Most importantly, perhaps, the Russians learned from the Mongols a conception of politics which limited the functions of the state to the collection of tribute (or taxes), maintenance of order, and preservation of security, but was entirely devoid of any sense of responsibility for public well-being.

During the time it served as the Horde's agent in Russia, Moscow had to build up an administrative apparatus geared to that which it served. Given the innate conservatism of political institutions, it is not surprising that much of this structure remained intact even after Muscovy had become a sovereign state. Thus the tribute which the Moscow Great Prince had collected for the khan was not done away with after the Russians emancipated themselves from the Mongols; instead, it became a tax levied on behalf of the Great Prince. Similarly, responsibility for the maintenance of the Mongol courier service was made into an obligation due to the Great Prince.[20] In this manner, almost imperceptibly, Moscow took over many Mongol institutions. Because of the economic orientation of the appanage principality out of which the Muscovite state emerged, and the corresponding underdevelopment of political institutions, the Russians naturally tended to borrow from the Mongols that which they themselves lacked, that is central fiscal institutions, communications, and means of repression.

There are some indications that the early tsars viewed themselves as heirs of the Mongol khans. Although under ecclesiastical influence they sometimes alluded to Byzantine precedent, in assuming the imperial title they did not claim they were successors to the Byzantine emperors. V. Savva found that in seeking international recognition for their tsarsist or imperial title, the rulers of Russia did not trace their authority back to Byzantium.[21] On the other hand, there is no shortage of evidence that they attached critical importance to the conquest of the successor states of the Golden Horde, Kazan and Astrakhan. Already at the time of the final assault on Kazan and Astrakhan, Ivan called them his votchina — a claim which could only have meant that he saw himself as heir to the khan of the Golden Horde. Grigorii Kotoshikhin, an official of the Muscovite Office of Ambassadors who fled to Sweden and there in

1666–7 wrote an invaluable account of Moscow's government, began his narrative with the assertion that Ivan IV became 'tsar and Great Prince of all Rus' ' from the instant he had conquered Kazan, Astrakhan and Siberia.[22] The title 'White Tsar' (*Belyi Tsar*), occasionally used by Russian rulers in the sixteenth century, in all probability refers to 'White Bone', the clan of the descendants of Genghis Khan, and may represent another attempt to link up with the Mongol ruling dynasty.

Authentic documentation on the political *theory* of Russian kingship during its formative phase is very scarce. But there is enough authenticated evidence about the political *attitudes* of the Moscow court to permit some generalizations on the subject. Westerners who visited Russia in the sixteenth and seventeenth centuries were struck by the arrogance they encountered in Moscow. Possevino, a Jesuit ambassador sent by the Pope to Ivan IV, found the tsar convinced that he was the strongest and wisest ruler in the world. When, in response to these boasts, Possevino delicately reminded him of other illustrious Christian princes, Ivan asked – contemptuously rather than incredulously – 'How many of them are there in this world?' (*Quinam isti sunt in mundo?*). The people of Moscow, Possevino found, shared their ruler's view of himself, for he heard them say:

God alone and our Great Master [*Magnus Dominus*] (that is, our Prince) know this. This our Great Master knows all. With one word he can unravel all the knots and solve all the difficulties. There exists no religion whose rites and dogmas he is not familiar with. Whatever we have, whether we ride properly, or are in good health, all this we owe to the clemency of our Great Master.

Possevino adds that the tsar assiduously cultivated this faith among his people.[23]

Toward foreign ambassadors, especially if they came from the west, the Moscow court liked to display deliberate rudeness, as if to show that in its eyes they represented rulers of inferior rank. As Moscow perceived it, a true sovereign had to meet three tests: he had to be of ancient lineage, he had to have come to the throne by hereditary right, and he had to be independent of any other power, external as well as internal.[24] Moscow was exceedingly proud of its ancient lineage, which it considerably extended by connecting itself to the Roman imperial house of Augustus. From the heights of this spurious genealogical tree it could look down on almost all contemporary royal houses. As concerns the manner of accession, here too the principle of inheritance was greatly stressed; a true king had to be patrimonial (*votchinnyi*) not elected (*posazhennyi*). As long as the Polish throne was occupied by a hereditary monarch, Sigismund Augustus, Ivan IV addressed the king of Poland as 'brother'. But he refused to address Sigismund's successor, Stephan

Bathory, in the same manner because this king had been elected to office. The greatest importance of all was attached to the criterion of independence. A ruler was a true sovereign or *samoderzhets* (*autokrator*) only if he could do with his realm as he pleased. Limitation on royal authority was called *urok* (instruction) and a limited monarch was an *uriadnik* ('man under contract' or 'on commission'). Whenever the question of establishing relations with a new foreign power confronted tsarist Moscow it made careful inquiries to determine whether its ruler was indeed in every way his own master – not only in respect to other states, which was standard procedure in western diplomacy as well, but also within his own realm. An early example of such practice occurred in 1532 when the Emperor Babur of the newly founded Moghul dynasty of India sent an embassy to Moscow to establish 'amicable and brotherly' relations with the Great Prince of Moscow, Basil III. Moscow's response to this overture was negative. The Great Prince 'did not order to be brothers with him [Babur] because he was not familiar with his state, and it was not known whether he was a sovereign or under contract'.[25] These assumptions were also spelled out in a letter which Ivan IV sent in 1570 to Queen Elizabeth:

> We thought that you lord it over your domain, and rule by yourself, and seek honour for yourself and profit for your realm. And it is for these reasons that we wanted to engage in these affairs with you. But [now we see that] there are men who rule beside you, and not only men [*liudi*] but trading boors [*muzhiki torgovye*] [who] concern themselves not with our sovereign safety, and honours and income from our lands. but seek their own merchant profit.*

Ultimately, only two sovereigns met the high standards set by Moscow: the Turkish Sultan and its own Great Prince – the very two rulers Bodin had singled out as Europe's 'seigneural' monarchs. We can now understand Ivan IV's scornful reaction to Possevino's mention of other 'illustrious' Christian kings.

To conclude the discussion of patrimonial kingship in early modern Russia, attention must be drawn to an interesting etymological fact. Among early Slavs two words were used interchangeably to designate the paterfamilias with full authority over the family's possessions as well as the lives of its minor members (whom he could sell into slavery). These words were *gospodin* (or *gospod*) and *gosudar'* (or *gospodar*). These

---

* Iurii V.Tolstoi, *Pervye sorok let snoshenii mezhdu Rossiieiu i Anglieiu, 1553–1593* (St Petersburg 1875), p. 109. The opening sentence of this passage reads in Russian: 'I my chaiali togo chto ty na svoem gosudarstve gosudarynia i sama vladeesh i svoei gosudar'skoi chesti smotrish i svoemu gosudarstvu pribytka.' The contemporary English translator did not know what to make of this, so strange was the patrimonial language to his ears. He omitted the phrase 'and rule by yourself' ('i sama vladeesh') and translated 'gosudarstvo' and its derivatives variously as 'rule', 'land', and 'country' (ibid., p. 114) which, as we shall shortly see, these words did not mean at all.

words have a common root, *gos*, derived from the Indo–European *ghes*, 'to strike', from which developed also many words in the European vocabulary having to do with the home and its antithesis, the outsider, such as the Latin *hostis* (stranger, enemy) and *hostia* (sacrificial victim), and the English opposites, 'host' and 'guest'.[26] In documents of the Kievan and early appanage periods, *gospodin* and *gosudar'* were used indiscriminately to describe both ruler and proprietor, which is not surprising given the absence of any significant distinction between authority and ownership at that stage of Russia's historical development. There was one important exception to this rule, namely that the slave owner was invariably called gosudar. Towards the end of the appanage period a distinction developed; gospodin came to be applied to authority in the public sphere and gosudar in the private. The appanage prince was normally addressed by freemen as gospodin. Novgorod, too, called itself *Gospodin Velikii Novgorod*, meaning 'The Great Sovereign [City–State of] Novgorod'. Gosudar, on the other hand, came to be restricted to what in classical Greek would have been called *despotes*, and in Latin, *dominus*. The prince was gospodin of the freemen living in his appanage, whereas he was gosudar of his slaves. On their estates, ordinary votchina-owners were also addressed as gosudar even as late as the seventeenth century.

Such was the prevailing practice until Moscow rose to a position of national pre-eminence. It is a reflection of the proprietary character of princely authority in Russia that its tsars did away with that distinction and insisted on being addressed exclusively as gosudar. This custom was introduced in the early fifteenth century, and possibly represented a deliberate imitation of Mongol practices. Ivan III stamped his coins and seals with the title gosudar and demanded to be thus addressed. Upon the accession of Ivan IV gosudar became part of the formal title of the sovereigns of Russia, used in all official documents. It is obviously significant that the term for 'sovereign' in modern Russian should derive from the vocabulary of private law, from a word which had meant owner and particularly owner of slaves. Although we translate *gosudarstvo* as 'state' a more accurate equivalent would be 'domain'. The word 'state' implies a distinction between private and public, between *dominium* and *imperium*. *Gosudarstvo* carries no such connotation; it is *dominium*, pure and simple, signifying as has been noted, 'absolute ownership excluding all other appropriation and involving the right to use, to abuse and to destroy at will'.*

Like other historians, in tracing the evolution of Russian monarchy

* As Leonard Schapiro indicates (*Totalitarianism*, London 1972, p. 129) the English 'state' and its counterparts derive etymologically from the Latin *status* which conveys the sense of ranking, order, establishment – in other words, a concept which implies law. These implications are missing from the concept *gosudar*'.

we have concentrated on Moscow, because Moscow became the capital of a Russian empire and its history is the best known of all the principalities. But the patrimonial mentality and institutions were not confined to Muscovy; they were rooted in the appanage system and the whole geopolitical situation of north-eastern Russia. A literary work composed in 1446–53 in Tver (*Slovo inoka Fomy*) extols the prince of Tver in much the same language that the publicistic literature of Moscow later applied to its ruler. It calls him tsar, gosudar, autocrat (*samoderzhets*) and a successor to the imperial title, and refers to Tver as the new capital of the Orthodox faith.[27] This fragment suggests that if events had gone otherwise historians might well have talked of Tver as the fountainhead of the patrimonial regime in Russia.

It is in a mood of great confidence that in the middle of the fifteenth century Moscow began to gather the vast 'patrimony' to which it laid claim. In theory, Moscow expansionist drive had as its objective the assembly of all the land of Rus'; hence, most of Lithuania was included. But, as we have noted, so were Kazan, Astrakhan and Livonia, none of which had ever been part of the Kievan state. Given the absence of natural frontiers in this part of the world it would have been impossible even with the best of will to draw a boundary separating the land of Rus' from territories inhabited by other races and religions. There were Finns and Turks under Russian rule when the national state was only beginning to take shape. Later, other nationalities joined them. As a result, the building of the national state and the forging of an empire, processes which in the west were clearly separated both in time and space, proceeded in Russia concurrently and contiguously and became virtually indistinguishable. Once an area had been annexed to Moscow, whether or not it had ever formed part of Kiev, and whatever the ethnic and religious affiliation of its indigenous population, it immediately joined the 'patrimony' of the ruling house, and all succeeding monarchs treated it as a sacred trust which was not under any circumstances to be given up. The tenacity with which Russian governments, whatever their professed ideology, have held on to every square inch of land that has ever belonged to any of them is embedded in the patrimonial mentality. It is a territorial expression of the same principle by virtue of which Russia's rulers have refused voluntarily to concede to their subjects one iota of political power.*

* Amusing examples of this mentality can be found in communist histories which treat the absorption of any territory by the Russian state in the past thousand years as an act of 'unification' (*prisoedinenie*). An identical act by another country becomes 'seizure' (*zakhvat*). Thus, for example, the Russian imperial government (which the same communist government had declared illegitimate in 1917) 'united' Turkestan with Russia, whereas Victorian England 'seized' Egypt.

In 1300, the principality of Moscow covered approximately 20,000 square kilometres; it was then one of the minor appanages. During the next century and a half, most of its growth took place at the expense of its neighbours to the east and north-east. Of great value to it was the acquisition in 1392 of the principality of Nizhnii Novgorod, which the khan of the Golden Horde presented in return for assistance against one of his rivals. Possession of this strategic area at the confluence of the Oka and Volga gave Moscow an excellent base for further expansion. On his accession in 1462, Ivan III inherited 430,000 square kilometres, an area slightly larger than post-Versailles Germany. Much of this land had been acquired by purchase and foreclosure for debts. Ivan III made his last purchase in 1474, when he bought that part of the principality of Rostov which he still lacked. From then on, Moscow grew by conquest; freed from subjection to the Horde, it began to behave as the Horde had taught it befitted a sovereign power.

Ivan's most important acquisition was Novgorod, a city-state whose territory covered most of northern Russia. Rich and cultivated as it was, militarily it could not stand up to Moscow; its extreme northern location and the prevalence on its territory of bogs made for very poor agricultural returns. Recent calculations indicate that in the mid-fifteenth century 77·8 per cent of Novgorod's landowners did not earn enough from their estates to equip themselves for war.[28] Moscow began to exert political pressure on Novgorod already at the end of the fourteenth century, when it acquired Beloozero, possession of which brought its holdings almost to the shores of lake Onega, and placed it in a position to cut Novgorod's territory in half.

Moscow's conquest of Novgorod began in 1471. That year a conflict broke out between the two principalities. Although Moscow handily defeated Novgorod's inferior forces, Ivan III chose not to interfere in the city-state's internal affairs, content, for the time being, to have it acknowledge its status as his votchina. Six years later this formal sovereignty was transformed into actual control. As the chronicles tell it, in March 1477 a delegation from Novgorod arrived in Moscow for an audience with the Great Prince. In the course of the talks, the Novgorodians, apparently inadvertently, addressed Ivan as *gospodar* (a variant of gosudar), instead of *gospodin*, as had been their custom. Ivan promptly seized on this formula and the following month dispatched his officials to Novgorod to inquire, 'What kind of *gosudarstvo* does it, his patrimony, want?' The panic-stricken Novgorodians replied that they had authorized no one to address the Great Prince as *gospodar*. In response, Ivan assembled his army and in November, when the marshes barring access to the city had hardened, appeared outside Novgorod's walls. Bowing to the inevitable, the Novgorodians tried to salvage what they could by

Arctic Circle

SWEDEN

SWEDEN

WHITE SEA

NOVGOROD PRINCIPALITY

URAL MOUNTAINS

Stockholm

LIVONIA

R.Volkhov Ladoga

Novgorod

MOSCOW PRINCIPALITY

BALTIC SEA

Pskov

Iaroslavl

Tver

Rostov
Suzdal
Vladimir
Moscow

Nizhnii
Novgorod

Kazan

KAZAN
KHANATE

PRUSSIA

Vilno

GREAT
PRINCIPALITY OF
LITHUANIA

WILD FIELD

ASTRAKHAN
KHANATE

Warsaw

POLAND

Kiev

R.Dnieper

R.Volga

Astrakhan

schematic line. separating
forest zone from steppe
black soil.

CRIMEAN
KHANATE

BLACK SEA

CAUCASIAN
MOUNTAINS

CASPIAN SEA

OTTOMAN

EMPIRE

2. Eastern Europe on the Accession of Ivan III to the Moscow
Throne (1462)

asking for assurances that recognition of him as *gospodin gosudar'* would not mean the end of their traditional liberties. They requested that the deputy whom the tsar would assign Novgorod should dispense justice jointly with a local official, that the amount of tribute due from Novgorod be fixed, that the citizens of Novgorod neither suffer deportations or confiscations, nor be required to serve the tsar outside the boundaries of their land. Ivan impatiently rejected these terms: 'You were told that we desire the same *gosudarstvo* in Novgorod as [we have] in the Low Country, on the Moskva [river]; and now you tell me how I should rule you? [Literally: 'You give me an *urok* (instruction) how our *gosudarstvo* is to be?'] What kind of a *gosudarstvo* will I have then?'[29]

In the end, Novgorod had to capitulate and surrender all its liberties. It agreed to abolish all institutions of self-rule, including the veche: the bell which had been sounded for centuries to assemble the people for deliberations was taken down and shipped to Moscow. In his insistence on the elimination of the veche, Ivan behaved exactly as the Mongols had done when they had conquered Russia two centuries earlier. The only concession the Novgorodians managed to extract from their new ruler was the promise that they would not be obliged to serve outside Novgorodian territory. A gracious gift, not a right, it was soon revoked.

In his new acquisition, Ivan proceeded to practise the kind of systematic elimination of potential opponents which Stalin's proconsul in Hungary five hundred years later called 'salami tactics'. Upon assuming office, the Muscovite viceroy ordered piecemeal deportations of families whose social status and anti-Muscovite reputation seemed to endanger Moscow's hold on the conquered city-state. In 1484, alleging that the Novgorodians were conspiring against him, Ivan had ordered his troops to occupy the city. Over seven thousand citizens, a major part of the patriciate, were now arrested. Some of the prisoners were executed; the remainder, accompanied by their families, were deported and resettled on territories near Moscow where they had neither ancestral roots nor personal influence. Their votchiny were confiscated in the Great Prince's name. In 1489 this procedure was repeated. Such mass deportation, called *vyvody*, were subsequently carried out also in other conquered cities, for example in Pskov after it had been conquered in 1510 by Ivan's son, Basil III. In these instances, the patrimonial principle empowered the prince to shunt subjects from one part of the kingdom to another as he would slaves within the boundaries of his estate.

Thus, one by one, Novgorod's liberties were whittled away and the families responsible for its greatness executed or scattered. In 1494, using as a pretext the murder of a Russian merchant in the Hanseatic city of Revel, Moscow shut down the Hansa's depot in Novgorod, arrested its members and confiscated their goods. This measure had a catastrophic effect not only on the prosperity of Novgorod but on that of the Hanseatic League as well.* So it went on, until 1570 when Ivan IV, in a spell of madness, had Novgorod razed to the ground; the massacre of its inhabitants went on for weeks on end. After this savage act, Novgorod was once and for all reduced to the status of a provincial town.

Graphic evidence of the absorption of Novgorod by Moscow is provided by the evolution of the city-state's seal. Originally, it showed a flight of steps, representing the veche tribune, and a long T-shaped pole, apparently symbolic of the city's sovereignty. In the hands of Muscovite designers, the steps gradually assumed the shape of the tsarist throne and the pole, shrunk and suitably embellished, turned into the tsarist sceptre (Plate 52).

Ivan's successors kept on accumulating territories lying to the west and south-west of Muscovy, stopping only when they came up against the frontier of the formidable Polish–Lithuanian Commonwealth. Between the accession of Ivan III in 1462 and the death of Basil III, his son, in 1533, the territory of Moscow multiplied more than sixfold (from 430,000 to 2,800,000 square kilometres). But the greatest conquests were still to come. In 1552, Ivan IV, assisted by German military engineers, captured Kazan and thereby eliminated the main barrier to Russian expansion eastward. From Ivan's accession (1533) to the end of the sixteenth century, the realm of Moscow doubled, increasing from 2·8 to 5·4 million square kilometres. In all the conquered territories massive land confiscations were carried out. During the first half of the seventeenth century, Russian fur trappers moved virtually unopposed across the whole length of Siberia, reaching in remarkably short time the borders of China and the shores of the Pacific. Government officials, following on their heels, claimed these territories on behalf of the tsar. In some fifty years Russia thus added another ten million square kilometres to its holdings.

Already by the middle of the seventeenth century the tsars of Russia ruled over the largest state in the world. Their possessions grew at a rate unparalleled in history. Suffice it to say that between the middle of the sixteenth century and the end of the seventeenth, Moscow acquired on the average 35,000 square kilometres – an area equivalent to modern Holland – *every year* for 150 consecutive years. In 1600, Muscovy was as large as the rest of Europe. Siberia, conquered in the first half of the seventeenth, was twice again Europe's size. The population of this immense realm was small even by standards of the time. In the most

* At a meeting of the Hanseatic League held in 1628 it was said that all of its great European commercial establishments were based on the trade with Novgorod: Ivan Andreevskii, *O Dogovore Novagoroda s Nemetskimi gorodami i Gotlandom* (St Petersburg 1855), p. 4.

heavily populated areas – Novgorod, Pskov and the Volga–Oka region – the population density in the sixteenth century averaged at most three persons per square kilometre, and it may have been as low as one; in the west, the corresponding figure was twenty to thirty. Most of Russia was virgin forest, and large stretches of it were complete wilderness. Between the Urals and Tobolsk, the capital of Siberia, over a distance of 750 kilometres, lived an estimated 10,000 inhabitants. Such low population density goes far to explain the poverty of the Muscovite state and its limited manoeuvrability.

But such considerations did not trouble the country's sovereigns. They were conscious of the unlimited power they held and pleased to learn from westerners that their patrimony exceeded in size the surface of the full moon. Having been eminently successful in acquiring power through the accumulation of real estate, they tended to identify political power with the growth of territory, and the growth of territory with absolute, domainial authority. The idea of an international state system with its corollary, balance of power, formulated in the west in the seventeenth century, remained foreign to their way of thinking. So did the idea of reciprocal relations between state and society. Success, as they then understood it, bred in the Muscovite government a remarkably conservative frame of mind.

CHAPTER 4

THE ANATOMY OF THE PATRIMONIAL
REGIME

> All the people consider themselves to be
> *kholops*, that is slaves of their Prince.
>> *Sigismund Herberstein, a*
>> *sixteenth-century German*
>> *traveller to Russia*[1]

How was Moscow's extraordinary expansion achieved? The answer is best sought in the internal structure of the Moscow state and particularly in the tie connecting its sovereign with his 'land'. After prodigious effort and at great cost to all concerned, the tsars eventually succeeded in transforming Russia into a gigantic royal domain. The system of management which had once prevailed on their private properties was politicized and gradually imposed on the rest of the country, until it came to embrace the whole empire. In this spacious kingdom, the tsar became seigneur, the population his *kholopy*, the land and all else that yielded profit his property. The arrangement was not without serious shortcomings. But it did give the rulers of Moscow a mechanism for mobilizing manpower and resources which no government of Europe or Asia could duplicate.

The transformation of Russia into its ruler's patrimony required two centuries to accomplish. The process began in the middle of the fifteenth century and was completed by the middle of the seventeenth. Between these dates lies an age of civil turbulence unprecedented even for Russia, when state and society engaged in ceaseless conflict, as the former sought to impose its will and the latter made desperate efforts to elude it.

The domain of an appanage prince represented an arrangement for economic exploitation utilizing slave labour – this was its most characteristic feature. The population was assigned tasks; it worked not for itself but for its prince and owner. It was divided into two basic categories: slaves who did menial labour and slaves who administered and held other positions of trust. Outside the princely domain, the social structure was very different. Here the inhabitants were largely free: boyar and commoner could move anywhere they wished in search of better service conditions, virgin land or profitable promysly. For all practical purposes their obligations to the prince were limited to the payment of taxes.

Now in order to fashion their empire on the model of an appanage domain – to make all Russia their votchina in fact as well as in name – the tsars had to accomplish several tasks. They had to put an end to the traditional right of the free population to circulate: all landowners had to be compelled to serve the ruler of Moscow, which meant converting their votchiny into fiefs; all commoners had to be fixed to their places of work, i.e. enserfed. This done, the population had to be divided into occupational or functional groups, each with its stated obligations. An expanded administrative apparatus, modelled on the appanage dvor, had to be created to assure that the social estates in fact fulfilled their various duties. These tasks proved exceedingly difficult to carry out, so contrary were they to the country's habits and traditions. Where there had been unlimited freedom of movement in space and a certain amount of social mobility there was to be none of either. Outright property in land, whether obtained by inheritance or by the clearing of wilderness, was to give way to tenure conditional on royal favour. A country which had been virtually ungoverned, was to come under the watchful eye of a bureaucracy. The extension of the domainial order on the country at large was nothing short of a social revolution imposed from above. The resistance was commensurate.

Following the domainial practice, the rulers of Moscow divided the empire's population into two main estates. Those who served them in a military or administrative capacity comprised the service estate (*sluzhiloe soslovie*). The others – farmers, artisans, traders, trappers, fishermen and sundry manual workers – formed the estate of '*tiaglo*-bearers', the word *tiaglo* designating the load of taxes and labour which the commoners owed the tsar. The two groups were sometimes distinguished as 'big men' (*muzhi* or *liudi*) and 'little men' (*muzhiki*). As during the appanage period, the clergy formed a separate social order, parallel to the secular one. It neither paid taxes nor served.*

The distinction between servitors and commoners was of fundamental importance for the social history of Muscovite and imperial Russia. On the one side of the dividing line stood those working directly for the sovereign, men who (figuratively speaking) formed part of his household. They were not a nobility in the western sense because they lacked the corporate privileges which in the west distinguished nobles from ordinary mortals. Even the most eminent Muscovite servitor could be deprived of life and property at his sovereign's whim. Collectively,

---

* Moscow also retained the class of slaves (*kholopy*), inherited from the past, whose members lived entirely outside the social structure. They will be referred to later in this chapter.

however, the service estate enjoyed very real material benefits. The most valuable of these was monopoly on land and serfs; until 1861, only those registered on the rolls of the service class could hold landed estates and employ serf labour (the clergy, as always, forming an exception to the rule). On the other side, stood the little men or muzhiki who enjoyed neither personal rights nor economic benefits, except such as they managed to acquire in defiance of the law. Their job it was to produce the goods and contribute the labour necessary to sustain the monarchy and its servitors.

The gulf separating the two estates was virtually impassable. Early Moscow tolerated a certain amount of social mobility and in its own interest even encouraged some of it; but the historic tendency pointed unmistakably in the direction of caste formation. The Muscovite state, being interested only in service and incomes, wanted everything to be in its proper place. The bureaucracy was structured to match the society which it administered; it too wanted maximum social rigidity, that is, the least possible movement of people from one category of tax or service obligation to another, since each such shift confused its account books. In the sixteenth and seventeenth centuries, laws were passed prohibiting peasants from leaving their farms and tradesmen from changing their places of residence. Clergymen were forbidden to abandon the priesthood; priests' sons had to follow their fathers' vocation. Commoners were not to enter the ranks of the service class under the threat of heavy penalties. Sons of service personnel upon reaching adolescence had to register in the office that supervised such matters. The cumulative effect of these measures was to make social status in Muscovite Russia hereditary.

We will now take up in turn the history of Muscovite servitors and commoners and show how each became bonded to the monarchy.

In general historical surveys it is sometimes said that Russian boyars lost the right of free departure because in time Moscow had gobbled up all the appanage principalities and they no longer had anywhere to go. In fact, however, this right had been effectively subverted before Moscow absorbed the rest of appanage Russia. The practice had never been a popular one with the appanage princes. What made it particularly noxious was that sometimes disaffected boyars quit their prince *en masse*, leaving him on the eve of battle without troops – a situation Basil 1 of Moscow confronted twice, once in 1433 and then again in 1446. Novgorod is believed, as early as the thirteenth century, to have taken measures to prevent boyars holding votchiny on its territory from enrolling in the service of princes outside its boundaries. Moscow began to interfere with the right of free departure already in the 1370s.[2] At first, the Muscovite princes tried to intimidate would-be defectors by harassing them personally and looting their estates. These measures, however, did not have the desired effect, and much stronger devices were introduced under Ivan III. In 1474, suspecting the loyalty of Daniel Kholmskii, a powerful appanage prince from Tver, Ivan exacted from him an oath that neither he nor his children would ever abandon Muscovite service. The tsar had the metropolitan and another boyar witness the oath; and then, for good measure, he required eight boyars to put up bail of eight thousand rubles which they were to forfeit in the event Kholmskii or his offspring violated the oath. This procedure was repeated on subsequent occasions, the number of guarantors sometimes exceeding one hundred. A kind of collective responsibility binding the higher echelons of the service class thus came into being. With lesser servitors, cruder methods were employed. Upon departing from a prince a boyar required a document certifying the nature of his service and his rank. If Moscow wished to prevent his departure, the chancery in charge of service records could refuse to issue such a certificate, or else it would issue one but deliberately lower the recipient's position and rank: in either event, his career was damaged. Moscow also applied pressure on appanage princes to return to it departed boyars, sometimes using force. As the territory of Moscow grew, safety from the long arm of its prince could be found only in Lithuania. But after 1386 whoever went there automatically became an apostate, because in that year Lithuania was converted to Catholicism – which meant that the tsar felt free to confiscate not only the properties of the defector himself but also those of his family and clan. Curiously, in treaties with other appanage princes, Moscow insisted on the inclusion of the traditional formulas affirming the right of boyars to choose their prince which it no longer observed itself. This was a ploy, designed to assure the unimpeded flow to Moscow of servitors from the independent principalities. Whenever the flow happened to proceed in the opposite direction, Moscow knew how to stop it, treaties or no.

The right of free departure was honoured in name as late as the 1530s, but in reality it had been abrogated several decades earlier. As is the case with nearly all landmarks of Russian social history, the legal record reflects very inadequately the process by which this change was carried out. No general statute exists forbidding free movement of boyars any more than there is one enserfing the peasantry. The practice resulted from a combination of concrete measures taken to frustrate boyar departures, and of occasional ordinances, such as that contained in the testament of Ivan III in regard to the principality of Iaroslavl: 'the boyars and boyar sons of Iaroslavl ... with their votchiny and purchased lands must not leave my son, Basil [III] for anyone anywhere; and from him who leaves, take his land for my son.' By the time this testament was written it had become accepted practice that he who held land on the territory of Moscow had to render service within its borders – if not to the tsar himself, then to one of his servitors. Failure to serve meant, in theory at least, forfeiture of the land. In practice, many landlords managed to evade service, and pass their days quietly on secluded estates. This is evidenced by a stream of decrees threatening dire punishment for failure to respond to a call to arms or desertion from the ranks. An accidentally preserved document from the Tver region indicates that in the second half of the sixteenth century more than one of every four votchina owners living there served no one.[3] But the principle of compulsory service was established; the rest was a matter of enforcement. Ownership of land and rendering of service, traditionally separated in Russia, were made interdependent. A country which had had only alodial land ownership henceforth had only conditional land tenure. The fief, unknown in medieval, 'feudal' Russia, came to it under the auspices of the absolute monarchy.

The imposition of compulsory service on all land owners represented a major triumph for the Russian monarchy: 'in no other European land was the sovereign able to make all non-clerical landholding conditional upon the performance of service for him'.[4] But the battle was only half won. Although boyars no longer could refuse to serve their prince, they still had many ways of frustrating his will. Behind the façade of monocratic and autocratic monarchy survived powerful vestiges of the appanage era. Even though their principalities had been annexed to Moscow and they themselves enrolled in the ranks of the tsar's servitors, the richer among the one-time princes continued to behave on their properties like petty sovereigns. Annexation was often a mere formality; Moscow might take charge of the main town or towns, installing there its agents, but leave the countryside in the hands of the local prince and his boyars. Some of the deposed princes maintained household staffs with a quasi-governmental structure, dispensed immunity charters to monasteries and lay landlords, and marched into battle at the head of private regiments. And some, as we noted, refused to serve. Such landlords took great pride in their ancestry and consciously separated themselves from upstart service families. In the middle of the fifteenth century they began to keep books in which their ancestries were recorded in great detail. The most prestigious of these was the 'Sovereign's Book of Pedigrees' (*Gosudarev Rodoslovets*) compiled in 1555–6. This book opened with the genealogy of the tsarist family, which it traced all the way back to the emperors of ancient Rome, then continued with the rest of the house of Riurik, the 'tsarist' dynasties of Kazan, Astrakhan and the Crimea, the appanage princes, and concluded with the most illustrious boyar houses. The families and clans included in this and similar lists were regarded as 'pedigreed' (*rodoslovnye*). They formed a self-conscious and powerful body with the sensitivities of which the most wilful tsars had to reckon.

The pedigreed families and clans established something like a closed shop; they and they alone qualified for the highest ranks or *chiny* in the tsarist service, those of *boiar, okol'nichii* and *dumnyi dvorianin*. At the beginning of the seventeenth century nineteen clans, considered the most eminent, enjoyed special privileges enabling their senior representatives to reach the top of the rank hierarchy more or less automatically. Writing in the mid-seventeenth century, Kotoshikhin (p. 75 above), speaks of thirty clans enjoying the exclusive right to the highest posts, including membership in the tsarist council, top administrative offices in the principal towns, judgeships in the major prikazy and important diplomatic assignments. Servitors not inscribed in the genealogical books had to be content with service in the ranks of the cavalry and lesser administrative posts. The monarchy had to honour the system or risk the united opposition of the leading houses of the realm. The tsar could do anything but change the genealogical status of a boyar family; this was regarded as 'patrimony', beyond the competence even of royal power.

The pedigreed boyars not only restricted to themselves the pool of servitors available for high office; they also had a great deal to say about who among them would fill these posts. This they did through the institution of *mestnichestvo* or 'placement', introduced sometime early in the fifteenth century and formally abolished in 1682. The Muscovite service class, even in its upper ranks, was an amalgam of people of very different background and status; descendants of the Riurikides, whose lineage was as distinguished as that of the reigning house itself and who, had fortune's wheel turned otherwise, could well have sat on the imperial throne; heirs of baptized khans and Tatar princes; boyars whose ancestors had served the Moscow house; boyars of dispossessed appanage princes; a group known as 'boyars' sons' (*deti boiarskie*), like the Spanish hidalgos usually penniless and landless soldiers. Even among those considered pedigreed, there were great social distinctions. To avoid loss of status and dissolution in a grey mass, the pedigreed families and clans established a ranking system of extreme complexity and refinement which they compelled the monarchy to take into account in making higher service appointments and arranging ceremonial functions at the court or in church.

Each pedigreed clan had its own, internal order of precedence based on seniority. A father was one 'place' ahead of his sons, and two ahead of his grandsons. Seniority among brothers, uncles, nephews, cousins and in-laws as well as among the component families of the clan was regulated by elaborate codes. Whenever members of a given clan were due for a service appointment, great care was exercised to assure that those with lower 'placement' status did not get ahead of those with a higher one.

More important yet were 'placement' accounts regulating relations among the families and clans. The service records of all servitors (consisting, in the seventeenth century, of approximately 3,000 clans divided into 15,000 families) were kept in the rolls of the *Razriadnyi Prikaz*, or, as it was known for short, *Razriad*. Preserved to this day, they run into thousands of volumes – a monument to the industry of the Muscovite civil service. From these records it was possible to ascertain what service appointments or what places at ceremonial functions one's ancestors and relatives had ever held, as well who had been above and who below them. These were entered into special mestnichestvo books. The boyars used the records to assure that in making appointments the tsar respected the relative ranking of the clans and of their individual members *vis-à-vis* one another. Clan honour required that a servitor should refuse any post which would have caused him to serve in a position subordinate to or even equal with anyone whose ancestors or relatives had been subordinate to his ancestors or relatives. To do otherwise debased for ever one's clan and lowered the service status of all its members, living and those yet unborn.* In this reckoning, the nature of the assignment or its intrinsic importance did not matter; all that counted was who served under whom. On the eve of every battle the tsar was besieged with petitions from servitors who objected to being put in command positions below their rightful 'places' (*mesta*). Were it not for the device of declaring certain military campaigns 'outside places' (i.e. exempt from being recorded and used in future mestnichestvo accounts) it is difficult to see how Moscow could have waged war. But in the civil service, and even more at court ceremonials, petitions and litigations of the most childish kind were commonplace. The following, reputed to be the last instance of a mestnichestvo squabble, may serve as an illustration:

In 1691, on 15 April, the boyars Lev Kirillovich Naryshkin, Prince Grigorii Afanasevich Kozlovskii ... Fedor Timofeevich Zykov, and ... Emelian Ignatovich Ukraintsev were told to dine with the Patriarch Adrian. Prince Kozlovskii, for some reasons connected with mestnichestvo reckonings, deemed it improper to attend this dinner and refused on grounds of sickness. But at the court, in the tsar's entourage, they probably knew the reason for Kozlovskii's refusal, and messengers were sent to him to tell him that if he was ill he should, without fail, come in a carriage. Kozlovskii still would not come. Orders were given to inform him that if he did not come in a carriage he would be brought to the palace by force in a cart. Even after this threat, Kozlovskii did not appear. He was then forcibly brought in a cart to the

---

* This is the reason why the practice of the deliberate lowering of a boyar's service record, used by Moscow to discourage boyar departure, was such an effective deterrent.

Beautiful Stair. As he would not step out of the cart, he was forcibly carried to the Patriarch's Chamber and placed behind the table. Kozlovskii intentionally fell to the floor and lay there a long time. Orders were then given to place him at the table against his will; but as he would not sit up but constantly fell to the side, clerks were ordered to support him. After dinner, on the square of the Beautiful Stair Kozlovskii was informed of a decree that 'for his disobedience he was deprived of honour and the boyar title, and inscribed on the rolls of the city Serpeisk, so that, from this example, others would not find it advantageous to act in a similar manner'.[5]

Special boyar committees were set up to adjudicate mestnichestvo disputes. They usually decided against petitioners, and to discourage others often ordered them to be subjected to beating by the knout or some form of humiliation.

Now clearly mestnichestvo was never strictly enforced; had it been, Muscovite government would have had to grind to a halt. It was essentially a nuisance and an irritant, which served to remind the monarch that he was not full master in his house. Although strong tsars managed to keep the boyars in hand, whenever the monarchy was in difficulty – in times of regency or during interregna, for example – conflicts among the boyar clans threatened to destroy the unity of the state. All these considerations impelled the monarchy to build up alongside the ancient clans another body of servitors, less clannish, more dependent and pliable, a class which had never known free departure or ownership of votchiny.

It will be recalled (pp. 44–5) that appanage princes employed domestic servitors called dvoriane who performed on their domains all kinds of administrative responsibilities. Most of these people were slaves; but even freemen among them were constrained from leaving. These people closely resembled the *ministeriales* of feudal Germany and Austria. Their ranks were steadily swollen by the accretion of 'boyars' sons' who lacked land and therefore liked to attach themselves to the prince's household to serve for whatever remuneration they could get. At the beginning of the sixteenth century, Moscow had at its disposal a sizeable reservoir of such low-grade servitors. Because of their total dependence on him, they were well suited to serve the tsar as a counterbalance to the pedigreed families and clans.

A basic difference between boyars and dvoriane was that the former owned votchiny whereas the latter did not. It was the ownership of votchina land which determined whether a servitor enjoyed – even if in theory only – the right to free departure. With the expansion of Moscow, the land reserves of the tsar increased greatly, but so did the need for servitors because there were not enough boyars to man the garrison cities constructed to defend the country's long frontier. The idea therefore arose of giving some of that land to dvoriane as fief, or, as it came to be known in the 1470s, *pomest'e*. After he had conquered Novgorod and massacred or deported its leading citizens, Ivan III carried out a major land reform there. He confiscated on his own behalf 81·7 per cent of the cultivated land. Of this, more than half he turned over to the royal household for direct exploitation; most of the remainder he distributed among dvoriane as pomestia.[6] The Novgorod patricians whom he deported and resettled in the central regions of Muscovy he also gave their new estates as pomestia. Unlike a votchina, a pomestie was the legal property of the tsar. It was turned over to servitors for exploitation on the understanding that they and their descendants could retain it but only for as long as they continued to render satisfactory service.

In so far as from the reign of Ivan III onward a votchina could not be held either unless its owner served the tsar, the question arises what distinguished the two forms of land tenure.* First and foremost, votchina property could be divided among one's heirs or sold, whereas a pomestie could not. Secondly, the votchina of a servitor who died without sons remained within the clan; a pomestie reverted to the royal treasury. Thirdly, from the middle of the sixteenth century the clan had the right to repurchase within a forty-year period votchiny which its members had sold to outsiders. For these reasons, votchina was regarded as a superior type of conditional land tenure and preferred to pomestie. Well-to-do servitors usually had some of both.

The monarchy had different preferences. All the features which made votchiny attractive to servitors tainted them in its eyes. On the territories which they conquered, Ivan III and Basil III carried out systematic confiscations of votchiny, the way it was first done in Novgorod, transferring title to themselves and distributing them wholly or in part as pomestie. From this policy, the quantity of votchina land steadily diminished. On the death of Basil III (1533) it still predominated in the central regions of Muscovy where the dynasty had its original home and where it had made acquisitions before pomestia were invented. On the periphery of the Muscovite homeland – in Novgorod, Pskov, Smolensk, Riazan and other territories conquered after 1477 – the bulk of the service land was held as pomestie.

The imposition of service obligations on all holders of land had profound implications for the future course of Russian history. It meant nothing less than the elimination of private property in land; and since land was and remained the main source of wealth in Russia, the net result was that private property of the means of production became

---

* Without wishing to complicate the issue further we may add that in later Muscovy the term votchina covered not only properties inherited from one's father; there were also votchiny which one bought and those which one received for outstanding service.

virtually extinct. This occurred at the very time when western Europe was moving in the opposite direction. With the decline of vassalage after 1300, western fiefs passed into outright ownership, while the development of trade and manufacture produced an additional source of wealth in the form of capital. In the early modern west, the bulk of the wealth gradually accumulated in the hands of society, giving it powerful leverage against the crown; in Russia, it is the crown that, as it were, expropriated society. It was the combination of absolute political power with nearly complete control of the country's productive resources that made the Muscovite monarchy so formidable an institution.

In order to bring the process of expropriation to its conclusion it was still necessary to uproot boyars holding large votchina estates in the central regions of Muscovy. This was done by Ivan IV. This tsar undoubtedly suffered from mental derangement, and it would be a mistake to assign to all his policies rational aims. He killed and tortured to exorcise the spirits tormenting him, not to change the course of his country's history. But it so happened that the people who stood in his way, those who most frustrated his will and sent him into fits of blind rage, belonged to the pedigreed clans holding votchiny in and around Moscow. By destroying so many of them, Ivan inadvertently altered the balance of forces in Russian society and profoundly influenced its future.

In 1550, Ivan took the unprecedented step of allotting pomestia in the vicinity of Moscow to 1,064 'boyars' sons', the majority of them impoverished dvoriane and not a few descendants of slaves. By this act, he bestowed upon these parvenus the respected title of 'Moscow Dvoriane', previously reserved for the pedigreed boyars. This was a clear warning to the great clans. In the years that followed, Ivan was too preoccupied with administrative reforms and foreign policy to dare challenge the boyars. But once he decided to do so, it was with a ferocity and sadism that can only be compared with that displayed by Stalin in the 1930s.

In 1564, Ivan split the country in two parts. One half, called *zemshchina*, 'the land', constituted the kingdom proper, the public part as it were. The other, which he took under his personal management, he designated *oprichnina*. The virtual absence of records from the time when Russia was subjected to this formalized dyarchy (1564–72) makes it very difficult to know exactly what had happened. But the political implications of the oprichnina are reasonably clear. Ivan temporarily reversed the procedure used by his ancestors, who appear to have attempted too much too quickly. He withdrew from the realm at large those areas in which royal power still had to contend with powerful entrenched interests, where the process of 'domainialization' had not yet been successfully carried out. These areas he now assigned directly to his personal household; that is, he incorporated them in his private domain. By so doing he was free at last to extirpate the large pockets of boyar votchina left over from the appanage period. Individual Moscow streets, small towns, or market places and particularly large votchiny, upon being designated by tsarist order as part of the oprichnina, became the personal property of the tsar, and as such were turned over to a special corps of *oprichniki*. This crew of native and foreign riffraff were permitted with impunity to abuse or kill the inhabitants of areas under their control and to loot their properties. Boyars fortunate enough to survive the terror, received, as compensation for their votchiny, pomestia in other parts of the country. The method used was basically not different from that first employed by Ivan III on the territory of conquered Novgorod, only this time it was applied to the ancient homeland of the Muscovite state and its earliest territorial acquisitions. Researches by S.Platonov have shown that the areas taken under the oprichnina were located primarily in the central regions of the state, whereas zemshchina was concentrated on the periphery conquered by Ivan III and Basil III.

The oprichnina was officially abolished in 1572 and the two halves merged once again. After that date it was forbidden to mention the once-dreaded word under the penalty of death. Some oprichniki were punished; here and there tracts of confiscated land were returned to their rightful owners. But the job was done. The centre of boyar power was destroyed. For at least another century, and in some respects for a few decades beyond it, the boyars belonging to the pedigreed clans continued to exert powerful influence at the court. Indeed, mestnichestvo blossomed most luxuriantly in the seventeenth century, that is after the reign of Ivan IV. Still, most of their economic power and their local roots had been undercut. The future belonged not to the boyars but to the dvoriane. At the end of the sixteenth century, after the oprichnina had been lifted, this once-despised class of low-grade servitors began to take precedence at court ceremonies over ordinary boyars, yielding only to representatives of the most eminent clans.

After the oprichnina, private property in land no longer played any significant role in Muscovite Russia; with the elimination of the patrimonial nests of the old families, votchina became fief held at more advantageous terms than pomestie, but it was still only a fief.*

Gosudarevy sluzhilye liudi – the Sovereign's Serving People – received their main compensation in the form of votchiny and pomestia. But offices and salaries were also used for this purpose.

Distinguished soldiers and civil servants had opportunities to amass

---

* One of the by-products of the massive expropriations carried out between 1477 and 1572 was the virtual disappearance of privately-owned cities in Russia. In appanage and early Muscovite Russia, many towns – essentially market-places – were built on private votchiny and belonged to boyars. They too were now confiscated on behalf of the crown.

fortunes by securing appointments to provincial posts. As noted, in Muscovy the costs of local administration and justice were borne by the population, and took the form of 'feeding' (*kormleniia*). Resourcefully exploited, such appointments could enrich in no time. The principal Muscovite provincial officer, *voevoda*, was a kind of satrap who combined administrative, fiscal, military and judiciary functions, each of which enabled him to extort money. The monarchy was not concerned what uses a voevoda made of his powers, as long as he maintained order and accurately delivered his quotas of servitors and taxes – an attitude essentially not different from that once adopted by the Mongols towards conquered Russia. Unlike the Mongols, however, Moscow was very careful not to allow any voevoda to ensconce himself in power. Offices were assigned on a strictly temporary basis, one year being the norm, one and a half years a sign of exceptional favour, and two the utmost limit. Voevody were never assigned to localities where they owned estates. The political implications of this practice did not escape Giles Fletcher who noted in 1591 that the 'dukes and diaks [secretaries] are ... changed ordinarily at every year's end ... They are men of themselves of no credit nor favour with the people where they govern, being neither born nor brought up among them, nor yet having inheritance of their own there or elsewhere.'[7]

High civil servants employed in the city of Moscow were paid regular salaries. Heads of prikazy received as much as one thousand rubles a year (the equivalent of $30,000–$40,000 in US currency of 1900). Secretaries and scribes received proportionately less. At the opposite end of the spectrum, ordinary dvoriane were given at most a few rubles on the eve of important campaigns to help defray the costs of a horse and weapons, and even for that sum they had to petition.

Service for holders of votchiny and pomestia began at the age of fifteen. It was lifelong, terminating only with physical disability or old age. The great majority served in the cavalry. Military servitors usually spent the winter months on their estates, and reported for duty in the spring. In 1555 or 1556 an attempt was made to set precise norms for service obligations: each 125 acres of cultivated land was to supply one fully equipped horseman, and each additional 125 acres one armed retainer. Apparently this system proved impossible to enforce, because in the seventeenth century it was abandoned and new norms were set based on the number of peasant households which the servitor had in his possession. Adolescents served from their father's land; if this was inadequate, they received a pomestie of their own. Competition over pomestia which had fallen vacant occupied a great deal of the time of dvoriane, who were for ever petitioning for supplementary allotments.

Service also could take civilian forms, especially for the pedigreed families and clans, whose senior representatives attended the tsar's Council (*Duma*). This body sat in permanent session at the Moscow Kremlin, and its members were expected to be on call twenty-four hours a day. Clerks holding executive positions also belonged to the service class, as did diplomats. As a rule, the top civil servants owned large landed properties.

To ensure that the service class did not shirk its duties, two offices were established in Moscow in the second half of the sixteenth century. One, the Razriad, has been mentioned already. It seems that at first the Razriad kept track of both personnel records and the estate holdings of servitors, but that later the second task was entrusted to a special Bureau of Pomestia (*Pomestnyi Prikaz*). Using data from the Razriad, this bureau made certain that all the land held by members of the service class yielded the proper quantity of state service. The efficiency of these establishments must have been of a very high order. It is estimated that in the 1560s, the Razriad maintained records of at least 22,000 servitors, scattered over an immense territory. Occasionally, as in the second half of Ivan IV's reign when control over it fell into the hands of one family (the brothers, Andrei and Vassilii Shchelkalov), the Razriad provided a unique personal power base within the bureaucracy.

Now that its ingredients have been enumerated, one can appreciate the complexity of the Muscovite service structure in the seventeenth century, when the system was fully formed. All appointments of any distinction required that account be taken of three disparate factors in the candidate's background: his pedigree (*rodoslovnost'*), his service rank (*chinovnost'*) and the previous posts he has held (*razriadnost'*).[8]

In the mid-sixteenth century, Russia had an estimated 22,000–23,000 servitors. Of this number, 2,000 or 3,000 were inscribed in the service rolls of the city of Moscow, and composed the élite of the pedigreed. They held large properties, sometimes running into thousands of acres. The remainder, some 20,000 strong, were inscribed in the rolls of the provincial cities. The majority of these were exceedingly poor, with average holdings of 100–200 acres. At the end of the sixteenth century, there was one servitor for each 300 taxpayers and clergy. The ratio rose only slightly in the seventeenth century; in 1651, with an estimated population of 13 million, Russia had 39,000 servitors, or one per 333 inhabitants. Apparently this figure represented the maximum that the economy of the time could support.

The Muscovite service class, from which, in direct line of succession, descend the dvorianstvo of imperial Russia and the communist apparatus of Soviet Russia, represents a unique phenomenon in the history of social institutions. No term borrowed from western history, such as 'nobility' or 'gentry' satisfactorily defines it. It was a pool of skilled manpower used by the state to perform any and all functions which it required: soldiering, administration, legislation, justice, diplomacy, commerce and manufacture. The fact that its living derived almost exclusively from the exploitation of land and (after the 1590s) bonded labour, was an accident of Russian history, namely the shortage of cash. Later on, in the eighteenth and nineteenth centuries, the civil branch of the service class was put on salary without its character or function being thereby significantly altered. The roots of this class were not in the land, as was the case with nobilities the world over, but in the royal service. In some respects, the Russian service class was a very modern institution, a kind of proto-meritocracy. Its members enjoyed superior status but by virtue of their usefulness to their employer. Whatever their advantages *vis-à-vis* the rest of the population, with regard to the crown their position was utterly precarious.

So much for the service class. The 99·7 per cent of Russians who did not belong to it, unless they were men of the cloth, owed the state a variety of obligations in money and labour called collectively *tiaglo*. Like the French *taille* with which it has much in common, the term is of domainial origin. It derives from the verb *tianut'*, 'to pull'. In the appanage period villages were said to be 'pulled' towards the manor or town to which they owed taxes or rents. Later, the term acquired a generalized fiscal meaning. In Muscovite Russia, the non-service people were called *tiagloe naselenie*, 'the pulling population', and their burdens, tiaglo, 'the pull'. But as late as the nineteenth century, after it had ceased to be used by the state, tiaglo was still current on private domains to designate a unit of serf labour, normally consisting of a peasant and his wife and one horse.

Taxes due under tiaglo were set in Moscow on the basis of registers (*pistsovye knigi*). In the rural areas, the taxable unit was sometimes an area of cultivated land, sometimes a household, sometimes a combination of the two. The trading and artisan population living in towns and settlements was taxed by households. The local authorities enjoyed the additional right of imposing various labour obligations as part of tiaglo. Responsibility for the distribution of moneys and services was placed on the tax-payers themselves. The bureaucracy in Moscow having determined the global sum required by the state, apportioned it among the various regions and tax-paying groups. It was then up to the provincial officials and landlords to see to it that the tiaglo-bearers distributed the burdens equitably among themselves. In the colourful phrase of Miliukov, the government 'largely left it up to the tax to locate the payer'.[9] Implied in this system was collective responsibility. All tiaglo-bearers formed communities, whose members were jointly accountable for the moneys and services imposed on their group. The system inhibited the development in Russia of individual farming and large-scale private business.

The quantity of moneys and services due under tiaglo was not fixed. The government adjusted taxes in accord with its needs and its estimate of what the population could pay. After foreign invasions or severe droughts, they were lowered; in times of prosperity, they were raised. The system was unpredictable in the extreme. Whenever the state required additional revenue, it devised a new tax to pile on top of the existing ones. Special taxes were imposed to redeem Russian prisoners from Tatar captivity, to equip newly-formed musketeer units (*strel'tsy*), to maintain the courier service. Moscow's tax practices give the impression that by skimming it at once with new imposts the government wanted to prevent any surplus from accumulating in the hands of the population.

A particularly arbitrary feature of tiaglo was the requisition of labour services on behalf of the state. Voevody could demand from the population help in construction of fortifications, on road and bridge repairs, and in the billeting and feeding of troops. Since it was not compensated, work performed in fulfilment of tiaglo represented a form of forced labour. When at the end of the seventeenth century the government needed workers for the manufactures and mines which it had licensed foreign entrepreneurs to open, it had little difficulty finding them; it simply impressed muzhiki unattached to any tiaglo community, or exempted a certain number of households in neighbouring villages from monetary payments and put their able-bodied men on full-time labour tiaglo. As will be seen (Chapter 8), the working class employed in the manufacturing and mining establishments founded by Peter I was assembled in the same manner. When early in the seventeenth century Moscow decided to form infantry regiments under western officers to supplement the regular army composed of cavalry of dvoriane, it had no need for novel recruiting measures. Already at the end of the fifteenth century thousands of conscripts served in the armed forces. In 1631 a decree was issued that lands which did not furnish servitors – i.e. possessions of the church, widows, minors, retired servitors and the 'black lands' of independent peasants – were to furnish regularly one foot soldier for each five hundred acres of arable. These *datochnye liudi* were the earliest regular recruits in Europe. Sometimes tiaglo-bearers living on state lands were transferred *en masse* to distant parts of the country; for example, in the seventeenth century entire villages of black peasants were shipped to Siberia to help feed garrisons staffed by dvoriane. In the institution of tiaglo the Muscovite government disposed of an infinitely flexible device for harnessing ordinary manpower, much as in compulsory state service it had a ready mechanism for recruiting higher skills.

The bulk of tiaglo-bearers consisted of peasants, shopkeepers and artisans. But there was also a small category of military personnel which rendered full-time service and yet did not belong to the service estate, among them, the musketeers (streltsy), Cossacks and artillery gunners. These people formed a hereditary caste, in the sense that their sons had to follow their occupations, but they were not privileged; their ranks were wide open to newcomers and they lacked access to land. They supported themselves largely from trade carried out between campaigns.

Free movement proved more difficult to terminate among commoners than among servitors. A landowner could be discouraged from going into someone else's service by any of the methods enumerated above; and there was always his landed estate or that of his clan to provide collateral. But it was a different matter to try to keep in place farmers or tradesmen who had no title to the land which they tilled, no career status to worry about, and for whom nothing was easier than to disappear without trace in the endless forest. The only solution to the problem was to attach the commoners permanently to their localities and to their tiaglo communities; in other words, to enserf them.

We have noted in connection with the Russian fief that it came into being not during the age of 'feudal' decentralization, as had been the case in western Europe, but at the height of monarchical centralization. The same can be said of serfdom. Serfdom emerged in western Europe in the wake of the collapse in the early Middle Ages of public authority. In the thirteenth and fourteenth centuries, with the liquidation of the feudal order, serfdom also disappeared in most of western Europe, as one-time serfs became tenants. In Russia, on the contrary, the bulk of the rural population ceased to be tenants and turned into serfs between approximately 1550 and 1650, that is at the very time when the monarchy, freed from the last vestiges of appanage particularism, emerged as the absolute master of the country. Like compulsory service for the landowning class, peasant serfdom represented a stage in the transformation of Russia into a royal domain.

Russia's non-service population was not enserfed overnight. It was once believed that in 1592 Moscow had issued a general edict forbidding peasant movement, but this view is no longer held. Bondage is now seen as a gradual process, extending over a century or more. One type of procedure was used to tie to the land peasants of black and trading communities, another to bond peasants on private estates. Sometimes economic factors were decisive, sometimes political.

Until the middle of the sixteenth century, the peasant's right to move was rarely interfered with. The few recorded instances of such interference were made in response to complaints by influential monasteries or boyars; in 1455 and 1462, for example, the Great Prince authorized the Troitse–Sergeev monastery to prohibit peasants of several of its villages, specified by name, from moving elsewhere. These measures were exceptional. However, as early as the middle of the fifteenth century, Moscow began to circumscribe the time of the year when peasants were authorized to exercise the right of departure. Responding to complaints of landlords that peasants were quitting them at the height of the agricultural season, the crown issued edicts limiting the period when departures could take place; this was set usually at one week before and one week after the autumn St George's Day (26 November Old Style or 4–7 December New Style), by which time all farm work would have been completed. The Law Code of 1497 extended the applicability of this date to all the territories under Moscow's rule.

Two events in the third quarter of the sixteenth century compelled the government to take drastic measures to stop further peasant movement. One was the conquest of Kazan and Astrakhan, which opened up to Russian colonization much of the black earth belt, previously controlled by nomads. The peasants immediately seized the opportunity and abandoning the forest in droves, poured on to the virgin soil to the east, south-east and south. The depopulation of the central areas of Muscovy was already well under way, when in 1564 Ivan IV introduced the oprichnina. Although it was directed at the boyars, the majority of the victims of this – as of any other – terror, were ordinary people, in this case, peasants living on estates confiscated from boyars and turned over to the oprichniki. To escape their clutches, more peasants fled to the newly conquered lands. The exodus continued for three decades with the result that large stretches of central and north-western Russia, traditionally the most densely populated, were left half-deserted. Land cadasters conducted between 1581 and 1592 recorded many villages deserted and reverting to forest, arable converted into pasture, churches which once had reverberated with chant standing empty and silent. Depopulation on this vast scale created a major crisis for the state and its servitors. Uninhabited villages neither paid taxes to the treasury, nor provided the labour necessary to release the service class for war. Particularly affected were the rank-and-file dvoriane, the monarchy's favoured class. In the competition for working hands which grew keener the more peasants fled from the central provinces, dvoriane usually lost out to monasteries and boyars who attracted peasants with better terms. The monarchy could not stand by idly and watch the foundations of its wealth and power erode, and so it began to issue decrees designed to prevent further peasant departures.

The first to be fixed to the land were the black people. Beginning with the 1550s decrees were passed forbidding peasants in this category to move. The trading peasants and artisans – also considered black – were bonded concurrently. As will be described in the chapter on the middle class, in Muscovite Russia commerce was carried on primarily in places set aside for the purpose, called posady. These were sometimes separate town quarters, sometimes suburbs, and occasionally rural settlements. Persons authorized to trade or produce articles for sale were united in communities called *posadskie obshchiny*, which bore collective responsibility for the tiaglo of its members. A succession of edicts, the first issued in the middle of the sixteenth century, forbade members of posad communities to leave.

The bonding of the black peasants, traders and artisans was largely motivated by the desire to protect the interests of the treasury. In bonding peasants living on votchiny and pomestia, the government had uppermost in mind the well-being of its service class. These peasants were enserfed gradually, by a combination of economic pressures and legislative ordinances. Which of the two causes played the decisive role is a matter of dispute among Russian historians.

Except in the northernmost regions, where he lived in isolation, the Russian peasant never had legal title to the land he tilled; land was monopolized by the crown, church and service class. Traditionally, the Russian farmer was a tenant. As a tenant in a country where natural conditions were unfavourable to agriculture, he was in an economically precarious condition. Upon settling down on a private estate, he customarily entered into an agreement with the landlord (oral in early Muscovy, later usually written down) which specified the payments and services he owed as rent. It was common for the landlord, as part of such an agreement, to offer his tenant assistance in the form of a loan (at 20 per cent interest or higher), seed, livestock and implements. Before he could quit the farm and move elsewhere, the peasant was required to return the cost of this assistance, as well as pay rent for the living quarters he and his family had inhabited, compensation for the losses suffered by the landlord from the peasant's inability to perform winter chores, and sometimes a 'departure fee'. A peasant who left without having settled his accounts was liable to be treated by the authority as a defaulted debtor and if caught to be turned over to the creditor as his slave. Heavily indebted peasants became in effect immobilized. The longer they remained in debt the less opportunity had they of extricating themselves because their debts kept on increasing from the relentless compounding of interest while their incomes stayed more or less stationary. Such indebted peasants, although theoretically free to leave around St George's Day, could rarely take advantage of the opportunity. To make matters worse, in 1580 the government temporarily suspended the right of departures around St George's Day; in 1603, the suspension became permanent. Henceforth, there were no more periods left during the year when a peasant could assert the right of departure if his land-lord did not wish to grant it to him. At about the same time (late six-teenth century), Moscow offices began to keep track of the debts owed by peasants to their landlords.

Rich landlords in need of working hands would sometimes redeem the obligations of indebted peasants and settle them on their own properties. Many peasants were shifted about in this fashion, the flow occurring usually from small pomestia to large votchiny and monasteries. But a peasant relieved of his debts in this way gained little, for he soon fell in debt to his new landlord. The redemption of debtors resembled more traffic in human beings than the exercise of the right of free movement.

For the indebted peasant, the only way out of his predicament was flight. He could escape to landlords powerful enough to shield him from pursuers, or to the steppe areas newly opened to colonization, or to the self-governing communities of so-called 'Cossacks' formed by run-aways from Russia and Poland on the Don and Dnieper. To impede such flights, the government carried out between 1581 and 1592 a cadaster which became an official record of peasant residence. From these lists it was possible to establish where a runaway peasant had his home. In 1597 the government decreed that peasants who had run away since 1592, if caught, were to be sent back to their landlords; those who had managed to make good their escape before 1592 were safe. No distinction was drawn between indebted peasants and others; the as-sumption was that residence, as recorded in the 1581–92 cadasters, was proof of attachment to the given locality. (It was this decree, since lost, which misled early historians into believing that in 1592 a general law had been passed fixing peasants to the land.) At the beginning of the seventeenth century, the statute of limitations on the return of runaways was periodically renewed, always going back to the base year of 1592. Finally the Code of 1649 did away with any time limit on the retrieval of runaway peasants. It forbade anyone to harbour them, decreeing that runaways were to be sent back to their villages no matter when they had departed and that those who had concealed them owed compensations to their landlords for any losses they might have incurred. It is cus-tomary to date full-scale serfdom in Russia from this date, although it was a fact of life a good fifty years earlier.

Strictly speaking, the peasants fixed to the land did not belong to their landlords; they were *glebae adscripti*. In documents of the Muscovite period, serfs, called *krepostnye*, were always distinguished from slaves, *kholopy*. From the government's point of view, the distinction made sense; a slave did not pay taxes, he was not liable to any of the obliga-tions subsumed under tiaglo, and he was member of no community.

Slavery was inconvenient to the government, and it issued many decrees forbidding subjects to pledge themselves as slaves, as a consequence of which the number of kholopy in Muscovy declined steadily. But from the serf's point of view, the distinction between himself and a kholop was not all that significant. Because the Russian monarchy had no apparatus of provincial administration to speak of, Russian landlords traditionally enjoyed very broad prerogatives over the population of their estates. S.B. Veselovskii, who first called attention to the historical role of manorial justice in medieval Russia as a prelude to serfdom, showed that even during the appanage period it had been generally recognized that what a landlord did with his tenants was his private business.[10] The attitude, of course, remained. Although it no longer issued immunity charters, the Muscovite monarchy of the sixteenth and seventeenth centuries was content to leave peasants on private estates to the mercy of their landlords. Once the peasants became fixed to the land, landlords were held liable for their serfs' taxes: a responsibility which inevitably enhanced their manorial authority.

This trend had ominous consequences for the peasantry, because the monarchy kept on transferring large quantities of court and black land to its servitors. In the 1560s and 1570s, it handed over to the service class as pomestia much of the black earth on the southern and south-eastern frontier conquered from Kazan and Astrakhan. Upon its accession to the throne in 1613, the Romanov dynasty, wishing to solidify its position, also generously distributed land. By the early seventeenth century black lands had almost disappeared from the heartland of the Moscow state, and with them vanished most of the independent peasants living in self-governing communities. Kliuchevskii estimated that in the second half of the seventeenth century, of the 888,000 households subject to tiaglo in Russia, 67 per cent stood on land held by boyars and dvoriane (10 and 57 per cent, respectively), and 13·3 per cent on that held by the church. In other words, 80·3 per cent of the tiaglo households were under private control. The crown owned outright only 9·3 per cent. The remainder consisted partly of households of black peasants (about 50,000, most of them in the north, a small remnant of what had once been the major class of Russian peasants), and of trading (posad) communities (about 43,000).[11] For all practical purposes then, by the end of the seventeenth century four out of every five Russians had ceased to be subjects of the state, in the sense that the state had relinquished to their landlords nearly all authority over them. This condition was formalized in the Code of 1649. Among the hundreds of articles defining the power of landlords over their peasants there is not one which sets on it any limits. The 1649 code recognizes peasants as chattel, by making them personally liable for debts of bankrupt landlords, forbidding them to lodge complaints against landlords unless state security was involved (when they were required to do so) and depriving them of the right to testify in court in civil disputes.

From all that had been said earlier about compulsory service of landlords, it should be apparent that peasant serfdom in Russia was not an exceptional condition, but an integral aspect of an all-embracing system binding the entire population to the state. Unlike the slave of the ancient world or the Americas, the Muscovite serf was not an unfree being living in the midst of freemen, a helot among citizens. He was a member of a social system which allowed no one to dispose of his time or belongings. The hereditary nature of social status in Muscovite Russia, and the absence of charters guaranteeing members of social groups any rights and privileges meant that – from the western European point of view – all Russians lived in a servile condition.* Michael Speranskii, surveying Russia of his time from the perspective of his western education, concluded that it had only two estates: 'slaves of the sovereign, and slaves of the landlords. The former are called free only in regard to the latter.'[12] These words were written in 1805, when the legal condition of dvoriane was vastly improved compared to what it had been in the sixteenth and seventeenth centuries.

To be sure the peasant was at the bottom of the social pyramid and in some respects (though not all) he was the worst off; but he belonged to a universal system, and his bondage must be viewed as an intrinsic part of it: 'The peasant was enserfed neither to the land nor to the person [of the landlord]: he was enserfed, if one may say so, to the state; he was made a state worker through the intermediacy of the landlord.'[13] In at least one respect Muscovite servitors were at a disadvantage compared to their serfs, and that was that unlike them they could not live year round in their own houses, in the midst of their families. How onerous was the status of a servitor may be gathered from clauses in the Law Codes of 1497 and 1550, enjoining landlords from binding themselves as slaves (*kholopy*) to evade state service. The trading and artisan population, too, was fixed to their occupations and places of residence. In other words, peasant serfdom was only the most widespread and most visible form of bondage which pervaded every layer of Muscovite society creating an interlocking system without room for personal freedom.

* According to Marc Bloch, in feudal France and Burgundy 'the notion arose that freedom was lost when free choice could not be exercised at least once in a lifetime. In other words, every hereditary tie was regarded as being marked by a servile character.' (*Feudal Society*, London, 1961, p. 261). As concerns the second point, in western practice it was established that only those belonging to groups given royal charters constituted social estates – the peasants who lacked such charters were for that reason not considered to form an estate. (Jacques Ellul, *Histoire des Institutions* (Paris 1956), II, p. 224).

The administrative apparatus of Muscovite Russia was remarkably simple.

The tsar had a council, called either *Duma* or *Boiare* ('boyars'). (The familiar 'Boyar Duma' is a neologism, introduced by nineteenth-century historians.) Its antecedents recede to the Norman period, when it was customary for princes to hold consultations with the elder members of their druzhiny. During the appanage period, such councils were mostly staffed by the servitors charged with administering the princely domains and collection of taxes, and known as *putnye boiare*. With the growth of the monarchy, the Council of the Great Prince of Moscow was expanded to include, in addition to his close relatives and chief officials, also representatives of the leading pedigreed clans. In the fourteenth, fifteenth and first half of the sixteenth century, the Duma was pronouncedly aristocratic, but as the power of the great clans waned, their representatives were gradually replaced by ordinary service personnel. In the seventeenth century, merit rather than ancestry tended to decide who was asked to sit in the Duma.

Russian historians have spilled much ink over the question whether the Duma enjoyed legislative and administrative power, or whether it merely ratified decisions taken by others. The evidence seems to support the latter view. The Duma lacked some of the most important characteristics of institutions known to wield effective political power. Its composition was unstable in the extreme; not only did its membership turn over with great rapidity, but the numbers varied wildly, sometimes rising as high as 167, sometimes sinking as low as 2. There was no regular calendar of sessions. No records were kept of the debates and the main evidence of the Duma's participation in decision-making is the formula attached to many decrees: 'the tsar ordered and the boyars affirmed' (*tsar'ukazal a boiare prigovorili*). The Duma had no prescribed sphere of activity. The quiet, almost unnoticed way in which it went out of existence in 1711 indicates that it failed to develop a corporate spirit and did not greatly matter to the service élite. For all these reasons, the Duma is best regarded not as a counterweight to royal authority but as its instrumentality; a proto-cabinet rather than a proto-parliament. Its main importance lay in the opportunity it afforded high officials to participate in the formulation of policies which they were obliged to carry out. It was particularly active whenever the government confronted major foreign policy decisions, and the country's leading diplomats issued from its ranks. Towards the end of its existence, in the late seventeenth century, it increasingly assumed responsibility over the prikazy and over questions of justice. (The Code of 1649 was drafted by a Duma subcommittee.) It thus moved toward the functions of the Senate, which in 1711 replaced it.

On certain occasions, usually during periods of national crisis when the monarchy needed the support of the 'land', the Duma was enlarged and turned into an Assembly (*Sobor*). (Like 'Boyar Duma', the common name, 'Land Assembly' or *Zemskii Sobor*, is a nineteenth-century invention.) When that happened, all the members of the Duma received personal invitations to attend (a characteristic detail, indicative of the Duma's lack of corporate status); and so, too, did the high clergy. In addition, invitations were dispatched to the provinces to have the service class and tiaglo-bearers send their representatives. No election procedures or quotas were established; sometimes the instructions requested that as many representatives as desired should come. The first known Assembly met in 1549. In 1566, Ivan IV convoked one to help him out with fiscal and other difficulties occasioned by his unsuccessful war in Livonia. The golden age of the Assembly followed the Time of Troubles (1598–1613). In 1613, an Assembly with a particularly broad representation (it included black peasants) elected to the throne Michael, the first of the Romanovs. It then sat in almost continuous session until 1622, helping the bureaucracy re-establish order in the war-ravaged country. As the new dynasty consolidated its position, Assemblies were convened less frequently. In 1648–9, at a time of serious urban disorders, an Assembly was asked to ratify the new Code. The last Assembly met in 1653, after which that institution vanished from Russian life.

There are so many superficial similarities between the Muscovite Assemblies and the Estates General of early modern Europe (including the time of their suspension) that analogies are inevitable. Nevertheless, if there is disagreement among Russian historians as to the historic function of the Duma, there is little debate over the Assemblies. Even Kliuchevskii, who regarded the Duma as Russia's effective government between the tenth and eighteenth centuries, regarded the Assemblies as a tool of absolutism. His view of the Assembly of 1566 – that it was a 'consultation of the government with its own agents'[14] – applies to all the other Assemblies as well. The principal difference between western Estates General and the Russian Assemblies derives from the fact that Russia had nothing comparable to the three western 'estates', which were legally recognized corporate entities, all of whose members enjoyed rights and privileges appropriate to their status. Russia had only 'ranks' (*chiny*), and these of course defined one's position *vis-à-vis* the tsar. The Russian Assemblies were gatherings of 'all the ranks of the Muscovite state' (*vse chiny moskovskogo gosudarstva*). Participants in them were considered to be performing state service and received pay from the treasury; attendance was a duty, not a right. As in the case of the Duma, there were no rules of procedure, no systems for selecting participants (representatives), no schedules; some Assemblies met for several hours, some for a few days, some sat in session for months or even years.

In sum, the Duma and the Assemblies may best be viewed as expedients necessary to the state until such time as it could afford an adequate bureaucratic apparatus. The Duma provided a link between the crown and the central administration, the Assembly a link between the crown and the provinces. As the bureaucratic apparatus improved, both institutions were quietly dropped.

The bureaucracy was still surprisingly small. Recent estimates put the total staff of the central administrative apparatus at the end of the seventeenth century (exclusive of scribes) at around two thousand. Over half of this number served in the four major bureaux: the Prikaz of Pomestia, the two prikazy handling government revenue (Bolshogo Dvortsa and Bolshoi Kazny) and the Razriad.[15] The prikazy divided the country among themselves partly along functional, partly along geographic lines. Examples of the former kind were the four principal prikazy mentioned above; of the latter, those in charge of Siberia, Smolensk and Little Russia (the Ukraine). The administration of the countryside was entrusted to voevody (see above, p. 96). Justice independent of administration did not exist. On certain occasions – notably in the middle of the sixteenth century – the government encouraged the formation of organs of local self-government. But a closer analysis of these organs reveals that their primary function was to provide an adjunct to the rudimentary state bureaucracy, not to serve the interests of the populations, as evidenced by the fact that they owed responsibility to Moscow.[16]

An indispensable concomitant of a political system which made such extreme demands on society was an apparatus of control. Someone had to see to it that throughout the millions of square kilometres belonging to Muscovy the servitors turned up to do their duty, commoners stayed put in their communities, merchants paid the turnover tax. The more the state asked of it, the more society practised evasion, and the state, in Soloviev's phrase, had to engage in systematic manhunts:

The chase after human beings, after working hands, was carried out throughout the Muscovite state on a vast scale. Hunted were city people who ran away from tiaglo wherever they only could, by concealing themselves, bonding themselves [as slaves to private persons], enrolling in the ranks of lower grade clerks. Hunted were peasants who, burdened with heavy taxes, roamed individually and in droves migrated beyond 'the Rock' (the Urals). Landlords hunted for their peasants who scattered, sought concealment among other landlords, run away to the Ukraine, to the Cossacks.[17]

Ideally, the Muscovite state required a modern police force with all its technical resources. But since it lacked the means to maintain over its domain even the most rudimentary apparatus of surveillance, it had to have recourse to cruder methods.

Of these, the most effective and most widely used was denunciation. It had been noted above that the Code of 1649 made one exception to the rule forbidding peasants to complain against landlords, and that was when the complaint concerned actions detrimental to the gosudar and his *gosudarstvo*. The range of such anti-state crimes was broad; included were offences which in the language of modern totalitarian jurisprudence would be called 'economic crimes', such as concealing peasants from census-takers or misinforming the Office of Pomestia about the true extent of one's landholdings. The Code placed great reliance on denunciation as a means of assuring that the state obtained the proper quantity of service and tiaglo. Several of its articles (e.g. Chapter II, Articles 6, 9, 18 and 19) made denunciation of anti-government 'plots' mandatory under penalty of death. The Code specified that families of 'traitors' (including their minor children) were liable to execution for failure to inform the authorities in time to prevent the crime from being committed.* In the seventeenth century crimes against the state (i.e. against the tsar) came to be known as 'word and deed' *(slovo i delo gosudarevo)*, that is, either expressed intention or actual commission of acts injurious to the gosudar. Anyone who pronounced these dreaded words against another person, caused him to be arrested and subjected to torture; as a rule, the accuser suffered the same fate, because the authorities suspected him of having concealed some information. 'Word and deed' often served to settle personal vendettas. Two aspects of this practice require emphasis, because they foreshadow a great deal of later Russian jurisprudence dealing with political crimes. One is that where the interests of the monarch were concerned, no distinction was drawn between the intention to commit a crime and the deed itself. Secondly, that at a time when the state did not concern itself with crimes committed by one subject against another, it laid down very harsh punishments for crimes directed against its own interests.

Denunciation would not have been half as effective a means of control were it not for the collective responsibility inherent in tiaglo. Since the taxes and labour services of anyone who fled his tiaglo community fell on its remaining members (until the next cadaster, at any rate), the government had some assurance that tiaglo payers would attentively

* This legal monstrosity was revived by Stalin in 1934 when he was about to launch his terror. Supplementary clauses to Article 58 of the Criminal Code added that year provided for a minimum sentence of six months of imprisonment for failure to denounce 'counter-revolutionary crimes'. In one respect Stalin went beyond the authors of the 1649 Code in that he established severe penalties (five years of prison) for members of families of citizens guilty of particularly heinous anti-state crimes, such as desertion abroad, even if they had had *no* prior knowledge of the culprit's intentions.

watch one another. Shopkeepers and artisans were particularly keen to note and denounce any attempts of their neighbours to conceal income.

So the state watched its subjects, and the subjects watched one another. The effect of this mutual surveillance on the collective mind of Russian society can be readily imagined. No one could allow someone else in his group or caste to improve his lot because it was as likely as not done at his expense. Self-interest required social levelling.* The Russian was required to denounce and he was eager to do so; indeed, in the early eighteenth century, the only legitimate way a serf had of gaining freedom was to turn in a landlord for concealing peasants from census-takers. Under such conditions, society could neither develop any sense of common cause nor undertake joint resistance against authority. A kind of police mentality impressed itself so deeply on the state apparatus and the population, that later on attempts of enlightened rulers like Catherine II to eradicate it fell far short of success.

No one was allowed to escape the system. The frontiers of the state were hermetically sealed. Each highway leading abroad was blocked at frontier points by guards who turned back travellers unable to produce the proper authorization, a document called *proezzhaia gramota* obtainable only by petition to the tsar. A merchant who somehow managed to get away abroad without such papers suffered the confiscation of his belongings; his relatives were subjected to torture to elicit information on the reasons for his trip, and then exiled to Siberia. The Code of 1649 provided in Chapter VI, Articles 3 and 4, that Russians who had gone abroad without authorization and then, upon their return, were denounced for having done so, had to be questioned as to their motives; if found guilty of treason they were to be executed, but if making money was their purpose, then they were to be beaten with the knout. The principal reason for such draconian measures was fear of losing servitors and income. Experience indicated that Russians familiar with foreign ways did not wish to return home. 'Russians must not serve together with men of the king [of Poland] because they will be deceived', was the opinion expressed by Ivan Golitsyn in the seventeenth century. 'After

---

* This is what Andrei Amalrik has to say about contemporary Russians (*Will the Soviet Union Survive Until 1984?* (London 1970), p. 33): 'Despite the apparent attractiveness of the idea of justice, if one examines it closely, one realizes that it represents the most destructive aspect of Russian psychology. In practice, "justice" involves the desire that "nobody should live better than I do" (but not a desire for the much-vaunted notion of equalizing wages, since the fact that many people live worse is willingly accepted) . . . . As I have observed myself, many peasants find someone else's success more painful than their own failure. In general, when the average Russian sees that he is living less well than his neighbour, he will concentrate not on trying to do better for himself but rather on trying to bring his neighbour down to his own level. My reasoning may seem naïve to some people, but I have been able to observe scores of examples in both village and town, and I see in this one of the typical traits of the Russian psyche.'

one summer spent together in the service, the following summer we won't have left even half of Russia's better men – not only boyars, of whom there will remain behind only those too old to serve and those who don't want to – but of the poor, not one man will remain.'[18] It was never forgotten that of the dozen or so young dvoriane whom Boris Godunov had sent to England, France and Germany to study, not a single one chose to come back.

Great difficulties also confronted all foreigners who wished to enter Russia. Frontier guards were under strict orders to turn away any foreigner lacking an entry permit; it was absolutely impossible to come to Muscovy on one's own initiative to practice a trade or vocation. Even those who had the necessary documents were narrowly limited in their choice of residence and length of stay. Natives were discouraged from establishing contact with visitors from abroad:

All conversations between [Muscovite] Russians and foreigners exposed the former to serious suspicion not only concerning their loyalty to native religion and customs, but also their politics. According to contemporary accounts, perhaps exaggerated, a foreigner could not stop on the street to look at something without being taken for a spy.[19]

Perhaps nothing conveys better the attitude of the Muscovite state towards its population than the fact that until January 1703 all domestic and foreign news in Russia was deemed a state secret. News was carried in reports called *kuranty* (from the Dutch *krant*, meaning newspaper), which the Office of Ambassadors prepared on the basis of foreign sources. They were for the exclusive use of the tsar and his top officials; all others were denied access to this information.

CHAPTER 5

THE PARTIAL DISMANTLING OF THE PATRIMONIAL STATE

The system we have described was so immune from pressures from below that, in theory at least, it should have perpetuated itself *ad infinitum*. The crown's monopoly on political authority, its ownership of nearly all the landed, commercial and industrial wealth, its tight grip on the social classes, and its ability to isolate the country from unwanted foreign influences all seemingly combined to assure perpetual stasis. One can see no way that the Muscovite population could have altered the system had it wanted to; and, as has been indicated, it had excellent reasons to dislike changes. The great patrimonial states of the Hellenistic world with which the Muscovite state had much in common collapsed not from internal causes but as a result of conquest. The same held true of the related regimes of the 'oriental despotic' type in Asia and Central America.

Yet in Russia the patrimonial system did experience significant change, though it was change induced, in the first place, from above, by the government itself. The reason why the Russian monarchy found it necessary to tamper with the closed and self-perpetuating system which had cost it so much trouble to establish has mainly to do with Russia's relations to western Europe. Of all the regimes of the patrimonial and oriental-despotic type, Russia was geographically closest to western Europe. Furthermore, as both a Christian and a Slav country, she was culturally the most sensitive to western influences. She was the first, therefore, to become aware of the inadequacies of her rigid, regulated system when confronted – especially on the field of battle – with the more flexible and 'scientifically' managed institutions of the west. Russia was the earliest of the non-western countries to undergo that crisis of self-confidence which other non-western peoples have experienced since; a crisis caused by the realization that inferior and odious as it may appear, western civilization had discovered the secrets of power and wealth which one had to acquire if one wished successfully to compete with it.

This awareness dawned upon Russia's leadership in the second half of the seventeenth century, two hundred years before a similar shock was to jolt Japan, another uncolonized non-western power. After overcoming initial perplexity, Russia launched a process of internal reform which, ebbing and flowing, has continued ever since. First to be reformed was the army. But it soon became evident that the mere copying of western military techniques was not enough, because the more fundamental sources of the west's strength lay in the social, economic and educational base; this too then had to be emulated. Increased contact with the west made the rulers of Russia realize that their might was more apparent than real; the system under which the crown owned or controlled everything set strict limits on what they could accomplish because it deprived them of support from a freely acting society. In response, the crown began cautiously to alter the system. Initially it hoped merely to graft individual western borrowings on the patrimonial system and thus enjoy the best of both worlds. 'We need Europe for a few decades, and then we must turn our back on it', Peter the Great once confided to his collaborators.[1] But once set in motion the process could not be stopped at will because as the social élite gained strength and independence from the government's reforming moves it began to pressure the monarchy on its own behalf, wresting from it rights which it had not intended to give them. The end result was the dismantling – partly vuluntarily, partly under duress – of three out of four mainstays of the patrimonial regime. During the ninety-nine years which elapsed between 18 February 1762, when dvoriane were formally exempt from obligatory state service, and 19 February 1861, when the serfs received their freedom, the hierarchy of social estates bound to the crown was dissolved. The 'ranks' (*chiny*) were set free and, transformed into estates (*sosloviia*), allowed to pursue their own interests. Concurrently, the crown gave up its proprietary claim to the country's economic resources. In the second half of the eighteenth century, it surrendered its monopoly on land by giving dvoriane full and unconditional title to their estates, and abolished nearly all the monopolies on trade and industry. Finally, the country was thrown open to the virtually unimpeded flow of foreign ideas.

These developments seemed to presage Russia's ultimate political westernization as well, that is, to lead to an arrangement under which state and society would coexist in some kind of an equilibrium. The patrimonial system from which the social, economic and cultural supports had been withdrawn appeared doomed. Or so it seemed to the majority of observers of imperial Russia, native and foreign alike. It is, however, a matter of historical record that this denouement did not occur. The reforms carried out by the imperial government fell short of their promise. While willing to concede its population considerable economic opportunities, civil rights and intellectual liberties, the monarchy insisted on retaining its monopoly on political authority. The patrimonial idea, even if truncated, survived behind the façade of the imperial state, and only the most perceptive observers who refused to be deceived by the mirage of 'historical trends' realized this fact – among them Speranskii, Chaadaev and Custine. Why the imperial government failed to take the final, decisive step and 'cap the edifice', as it was euphemistically called in the nineteenth century, is a complex problem that will be discussed in the proper place. Suffice it to say that it firmly refused to share political power with society; and even when finally compelled in 1905 by revolutionary events to grant a constitution it yielded more in form than in substance.

Incomplete reform injected a fatal contradiction into the relationship between state and society in Russia. For reasons of national power and prestige, the population was encouraged to educate and enrich itself, to develop a public spirit, to come – when asked – to the aid of 'its' government. At the same time it was expected to tolerate a paternalistic regime which acknowledged for itself no restraints or norms, and not only excluded the citizenry from participating in the formulation of laws but forbade it under severe penalties openly to contemplate any such participation.

Such was the main source of the tension which underlies the course of post-Petrine Russian history. An older system which for all its limitations had been at least consistent was abandoned in favour of something half-old, half-new. This arrangement steadily deprived the rulers of Russia of the power they had once enjoyed without giving them in return any of the benefits of liberal and democratic government.

The ultimate outcome was the erosion of royal power and, in as much as royal power was in Russia the only source of legitimate authority, general political disorganization. In order to divert the attention of the élite from politics, the monarchy amply gratified its material wants. Catherine the Great in effect divided the Russian empire into two halves, each of which she handed over for exploitation to one of the two constituent elements of the service class, dvoriane landowners and bureaucrats. The two groups were allowed undisturbed to exploit the country as long as they delivered to the crown its quota of taxes and recruits, and refrained from meddling in politics. Russia was now for all practical purposes farmed out to private interests. As a price for maintaining autocratic prerogative under conditions where it no longer made sense, the crown had to surrender most of its title to the country.

The resulting arrangement was curious in the extreme. The formal powers of Russia's sovereigns in the eighteenth and nineteenth centuries were as impressive as ever, and tsars determined to accomplish anything specific could not be deterred; they could legislate at will, create, reform and abolish institutions, declare war and peace, dispose of state revenues and state properties, raise or ruin individual subjects. But their grip on the country at large and their ability to intervene in its day-to-day affairs was tenuous and declining. The history of Russian politics of the imperial period is filled with incidents indicative of the inability of the sovereigns to have their will on fundamental policy issues. It is as if they were captains of a ship in full command of crew and passengers but without much say about the ship's operations or course. The pattern so often noted in the lives of Russian monarchs (Catherine ii, Alexander i and Alexander ii) – from liberalism to conservatism – was due not to the absence on their part of genuine desire for reform but to the realization which dawned on each as he or she accumulated experience that they simply lacked the capacity to lead their empire where they wanted and that the best they could hope for was to keep it from sliding into chaos. 'Autocracy' increasingly came to stand for a negative quantity, namely the exclusion of society from political decision-making; it ceased to mean the crown's control of the country. Paradoxically, by their insistence on the monopoly of political power Russian autocrats secured less effective authority than their constitutional counterparts in the west.

Such is the general scheme of the changes which occurred in the structure of the Russian state and in its relationship to society during the eighteenth and first half of the nineteenth centuries. We shall now take a closer look at the circumstances in which these developments took place.

Even more than the western monarchies of the early modern age, Moscow was organized for warfare. No European country had so long and exposed a frontier, such a mobile population expanding outward in search of land and promysly, and such vast territory to garrison. The principal resources of the empire were channelled into military purposes. When we say that in the second half of the seventeenth century, 67 per cent of all the tiaglo people lived on land of secular proprietors (p. 104), we are saying in effect that two-thirds of the labour of the country went directly for the support or 'feeding' of the military. This figure becomes even more impressive if one considers that the bulk of the moneys which the crown secured from taxes as well as from its properties and business activities was also devoted to these purposes.

Despite this immense outlay, the results were far from satisfactory. During the seventeenth century evidence accumulated that Russia's traditional manner of waging war ceased to be effective. At this time, the core of the Russian army still consisted of cavalry manned by boyars and dvoriane. This force was supported by commoners serving on foot.

While the ratio of horsemen to infantry was one to two, the cavalry constituted the senior arm. As in medieval western Europe, except for the personal force of the Great Prince's household, the Muscovite army was demobilized and sent home in the autumn and reassembled in the spring. The men reported for service with whatever weapons they could lay their hands on: firearms of all types, axes, pikes and bows. There were no regular formations, or chains of command, or battle tactics. The cavalry, usually massed in five regiments, followed by a mob of men on foot, rode into battle at a given signal, and then it was every man for himself. This essentially medieval mode of waging war, learned when the Russians had fought in the Mongol armies, was good enough when the enemy was the Tatar who fought in the same manner but was even less well equipped. The Russian soldier was just as tough and undemanding as his oriental opponent. According to Herberstein, a sixteenth-century traveller, on campaign Russians subsisted on a bagful of oats and a few pounds of salted meat which they carried with them. But confronting the armies of the great powers – Poland, the Ottoman Empire and Sweden – especially in offensive operations, Muscovite troops found themselves hopelessly outclassed. This was the lesson Ivan IV learned at heavy cost in 1558 when, fresh from his triumphs against the Tatars, he turned west and challenged Poland and Sweden to a war over Livonia. After a quarter of a century of tremendous exertions which left the country exhausted, he not only failed to capture Livonia but had to surrender several of his own cities. Russian troops fared no better against foreigners during the campaigns of the Time of Troubles (1598–1613).

The difficulties encountered by Russian troops on western fronts can be traced principally to the fact that they had failed to keep up with technological changes in warfare. In the late sixteenth and early seventeenth centuries western European states developed a style of 'scientific' warfare which made obsolete the traditional levies of landed gentry and their retainers. Gradually, warfare became professionalized and mercenaries came to shoulder the brunt of the fighting. A particularly important event was the invention of the flintlock and bayonet which made redundant the pikemen who in the past had been required to support soldiers armed with slow-firing muskets. In the west, the infantry now replaced the cavalry as the principal arm of the service. A profound change in tactics accompanied these technical innovations. In order to gain the greatest possible advantage from the new weapons, soldiers were drilled so that, like automata, they advanced unflinching against the enemy, alternately firing and loading their guns, until, having reached his lines, they charged with fixed bayonets. Chains of command were established, with heads of each unit responsible for the behaviour of their troops on and off the battlefield; unwieldy armies were broken down into brigades, regiments and battalions; artillery was separated into a distinct arm; special engineering and sapper units were formed to carry out siege operations. The introduction of military uniforms which occurred at this time symbolized the transition from medieval to modern warfare. Such full-time, professional armies had to be supported year round by the treasury. The cost was immense and in the long run contributed heavily to the ruin and collapse of absolute monarchies throughout Europe.

The Muscovite state had had in the streltsy a regular infantry of sorts, used to guard the tsars and garrison cities. But the streltsy knew nothing of formations or battle tactics either, and presented no match to modern armies, the more so as between campaigns, instead of training, they had to support themselves and their families by trade. After the Time of Troubles, impressed by the performance of foreign forces on its territory, the Russian government began to engage officers from abroad to form and command 'new' regiments of a western type. In 1632–3 a large Russian force, composed partly of these new units (some of them manned by western mercenaries), and partly of old-fashioned cavalry, was sent to capture Smolensk from the Poles. The campaign ended in the defeat and surrender of the Russian army. Subsequent campaigns against the Poles (1654–67) also brought no success, despite the fact that Poland was then also fighting a desperate war against Sweden. Between 1676 and 1681 Moscow undertook several inconclusive campaigns against the Turks and Crimeans, whose armies could hardly be described as modern. Despite these disappointments, the formation of western-type regiments continued apace and by the 1680s they outnumbered the cavalry. Still, victory proved elusive. In 1681 a boyar commission was appointed to ascertain the reasons for the poor performance of Russian troops. Its principal recommendation was to abolish mestnichestvo (1682), but this measure did little good as in 1687 and 1689 Russian armies suffered new reverses in campaigns against the Crimea. One source of trouble was that the service class, the mainstay of Russia's military force, scorned units fighting on foot and commanded by foreign officers, and insisted on serving in the traditional cavalry. The new regiments, therefore, were manned either with the poorest dvoriane who could not afford to buy themselves a horse, or with peasants whom the landlords and the government regarded as expendable, i.e. who presumably were as unfit for the sword as for the plough. Furthermore, the new regiments, just like the old, were disbanded every autumn to spare the government the expense of supporting them in idleness during winter months – a practice which made it impossible for foreign officers to train them into disciplined fighting units.

The question naturally arises why in the late seventeenth century Russia required a large and modern standing army, considering that it was already the largest country in the world and strategically one of the least vulnerable. (The existing forces, as noted, were adequate to protect Russia along its exposed eastern and southern frontiers.) In its broadest sense, the question is a philosophical one and can be posed with equal justice in regard to France of the Bourbons or Sweden of the Vasas. The seventeenth century happened to have been an age of intense militarism, and Russia, whose contacts with the west were increasing, could hardly have escaped being influenced by the spirit of the times. When we seek more specific answers, however, we find that the standard ones given by Russian historians, pre- and post-revolutionary alike, fail to convince. In particular, it is difficult to accept the proposition that Russia needed a powerful modern army in order to realize alleged 'national tasks': the recovery from the Poles of the lands which had once been part of the Kievan state, and access to warm-water ports. It is a matter of the historical record that the realization of both these 'tasks' in the course of the eighteenth century did nothing to assuage Russia's appetite for land. Having secured in the partitions of Poland what she regarded as its rightful patrimony, she went on in 1815 to absorb the Duchy of Warsaw which had never been in Russian possession and even to demand Saxony. As soon as she had gained the northern shore of the Black Sea with its warm sea ports, she began to claim the southern shore with Constantinople and the Straits. Having gained access to the Baltic, she seized Finland. Since it is always possible to justify new conquests on the grounds that they are required to protect the old – the classical justification for all imperialisms – explanations of this kind can be safely discounted: the logical sequence of such reasoning is mastery of the globe, for only at that point can any state be said to be fully protected from external threats to its possessions.

Setting aside the philosophical questions of the reasons for the appeal of warfare, two explanations can be suggested for Russia's obsession with military power and territorial expansion.

One explanation has to do with the manner in which the national state in Russia had come into being. Because in their drive for absolute authority the rulers of Moscow had to acquire not only autocratic powers but also what we have defined as monocracy (p. 58), ever since they had instinctively identified sovereignty with the acquisition of territory. Expansion in breadth, along the earth's surface, joined in their mind with expansion in depth, in the sense of political power over subjects, as an essential ingredient of sovereignty.

The second explanation concerns the inherent poverty of Russia and the perpetual hunger of her inhabitants for fresh resources, especially cultivable land. Every major conquest carried out by the Russian state was promptly followed by massive handouts of land to servitors and monasteries and the opening of the acquired territories to peasant colon- ization. In the case of Poland, partitioned in the eighteenth century, we dispose of statistical information to illustrate this connection. As is known, Catherine II liked to make use of land grants as a means of con- solidating her shaky internal position. During the first decade of her reign (1762–72) she distributed approximately 66,000 serf 'souls'. With the First Partition of Poland in 1772, she gained new territories from which to make handouts to favourites: the majority of the 202,000 'souls' whom she distributed between 1773 and 1793 came from areas taken in the First and Second Partitions. This done, Catherine ran out of re- sources; in 1793 she even had to renege on the promise of gifts made to generals and diplomats who had distinguished themselves in the recent Turkish war. Only after the Third Partition of Poland could these promises be made good. On a single day, 18 August 1795, Catherine handed out over 100,000 'souls', the majority once again in areas taken from Poland.[2] Of the approximately 800,000 male and female serfs of whom Catherine made gifts to dvoriane during her reign, well over half came from territories seized by force of arms from the Polish Common- wealth. We have here clear proof that concealed behind lofty slogans of 'national tasks' lay the very mundane reality of seizing resources to satisfy Russia's insatiable appetite for land, and in the process, shoring up the internal position of the monarchy. The situation has not changed today. For example, census figures show that in Latvia and Estonia, occupied by the USSR in 1940 in consequence of the Nazi– Soviet pact, there has occurred in the subsequent thirty years (1940–70) a very substantial influx of Russians. This migration combined with mass deportations to Russia proper of Latvians and Estonians, has more than tripled the number of Russian inhabitants in these two conquered republics (from 326,000 to 1,040,000) and nearly tripled their proportionate share of the population (from 10·8 per cent to 28·0 per cent).[3]

In the case of Peter the Great, the creator of modern Russia's military might, there were additional reasons for keen interest in military mat- ters. Although he is remembered primarily as a reformer, Peter thought of himself first and foremost as a soldier. His inexhaustible energy direc- ted itself from the earliest towards activity involving competition and physical danger. He began to walk when barely six months old and already as a teenager liked nothing better than to play with live soldiers. When grown to his full giant stature, he loved to share the life of ordi- nary soldiers on campaigns. When a son was born to him, Peter jubilant- ly announced to the nation that the Lord had blessed him with 'another recruit'. Peter firmly believed that military power was essential to every country's welfare. In letters to his very un-military son he emphasized the dominant role which war had played in history.[4] Little wonder that during the thirty-six years of Peter's reign, Russia knew only one solid year of peace.

It took Peter no time to discover that with the hodge-podge of old and new regiments which he had inherited from his predecessors he could realize none of his military ambitions. This became painfully clear in 1700 when 8,500 Swedes, commanded by Charles xii, routed 45,000 Russians besieging Narva and then (to use Charles's own words) gunned them down like 'wild geese'. Nine years later, at Poltava, Peter exacted his revenge. But his triumph was really less impressive than it is usually made to appear because the Swedes, led by their erratic king deep into enemy territory, found themselves exhausted, outnumbered and out-gunned when the decisive battle took place. Two years after Poltava Peter suffered the ignominy of having the Turks surround his army on the Prut; a predicament from which only the diplomatic skill of P.P. Shafirov, a converted Jew in his service, managed to extricate him.

The establishment of a large standing army which Peter initiated constitutes one of the critical events in the history of the Russian state. At Peter's death Russia had a powerful force of 210,000 regular and 110,000 supplementary troops (Cossacks, foreigners, etc.), as well as 24,000 sailors. Relative to the population of Russia at the time (12 or 13 million) a military establishment of this size exceeded almost three times the proportion regarded in eighteenth-century western Europe as the norm of what a country could support, namely one soldier for each one hundred inhabitants.[5] For a country as poor as Russia, the mainten-ance of such an armed force represented an immense burden. To enable it to carry the load, Peter had to re-vamp the country's fiscal, adminis-trative and social structures, and, to some extent, transform its economic and cultural life as well.

Peter's most pressing need was for money; his military expenditures regularly absorbed 80–85 per cent of Russian revenues, and in one year (1705) as much as 96 per cent. After experimenting with various fiscal methods, in 1724 he decided to sweep away the whole complicated sys-tem of payments in money, goods and labour evolved over the centuries and substitute for it a single capitation or 'soul' tax imposed on adult males. Tiaglo was nominally abolished, although in fact it continued to be applied sporadically for the remainder of the century. Before Peter's reform, the taxable unit in the village had been either a defined area of sown land or (after 1678) the household. The older methods of taxation permitted the tax-payer to practise evasion: to reduce the tax on land he curtailed the acreage, and to reduce the tax on households he crammed as many relatives under one roof as it would cover. The soul tax, being levied on every adult male subject to taxation, precluded such practices. This method had the added advantage of encouraging the peasant to increase his cultivated acreage since he was no longer penalized by higher taxes for doing so. Peter also increased the rolls of tax-payers by eliminating the various interstitial groups between the tax-paying and service-bearing estates which in the past had managed to escape all state obligations, such as slaves (kholopy), impoverished dvoriane who worked like ordinary peasants and yet were regarded as members of the service class, and clergymen without assigned parishes. All such groups were now integrated with the peasantry and reduced to the status of serfs. This reclassification alone increased the number of tax-payers by several hundred thousand. Characteristically, the amount of the soul tax was determined not by what the individual subjects could pay but by what the state needed to collect. The government estimated its military expenditures to be four million roubles, which sum it apportioned among the tax-paying groups. On this basis the soul tax was initially set at 74 kopeks a year for serfs of private owners, 114 kopeks for peasants on state and crown lands (who, unlike the former, owed no obligations to the landlord) and 120 kopeks for the posad people. The money was payable in three annual instalments and until its abolition in 1887 for most categories of peasants remained for the Russian monarchy a fundamental source of revenue.

The new taxes led to a threefold increase in state income. If after 1724 the government squeezed three times as much money out of peasants and traders as before, then obviously the financial burden of the tax-paying population tripled. The money cost of supporting the standing army which Peter had created was henceforth borne primarily by the tax-paying groups which, it must be kept in mind, contributed also indirectly to the military effort by supporting with their rents and labour the service class.

And they bore this cost not only in money and services. In 1699, Peter ordered the induction into the army of 32,000 commoners. This measure was not an innovation, since, as noted, the Muscovite government had claimed and exercised since the fifteenth century the right to call conscripts known as *datochnye liudi* (p. 99, above). But what previously had been a means of raising auxiliary manpower now became the principal method of complementing the armed forces. In 1705 Peter set a regular recruitment quota, requiring each twenty households, rural and urban, to furnish annually one soldier – a ratio of approximately three recruits for each thousand inhabitants. Henceforth, the bulk of Russia's armed forces consisted of recruits drawn from the tax-paying classes.

These measures represented an innovation of major historic significance. West European armies in the seventeenth century were manned almost exclusively by volunteers, i.e. mercenaries; and although here and there men were pressed into service in a manner which came close to forceful induction, no country before Russia practised systematic conscription. Spain introduced compulsory levies in 1637, and so did Sweden during the Thirty Years' War; but these were emergency measures, and the same held true of the conscription adopted by France during the War of the Spanish Succession. In western Europe, compulsory draft became the norm only after the French Revolution. Russia anticipated this modern development by nearly one century. The system of annual drafts of peasants and posad people introduced by Peter early in his reign, remained until the military reform of 1870 the normal way of providing manpower for Russia's armed forces. Russia therefore has every right to claim priority as the first country with compulsory military service. Although a recruit and his immediate family received automatic freedom from serfdom, the Russian peasant regarded induction as a virtual death sentence; required to shave his beard and to leave his family for the remainder of his life, the prospect he faced was either to be buried in some distant place or, at best, to return as an old, perhaps disabled man to a village where no one remembered him and where he had no claim to a share of the communal land. In Russian folklore there exists a whole category of 'recruit laments' (*rekrutskie plachi*) resembling funeral dirges. The farewell given a recruit upon induction into service by the family also resembled funeral rituals.

As far as Russia's social structure was concerned, the main consequence of the introduction of the soul tax and recruitment obligation was to consolidate what had traditionally been a fairly loose and diversified body of commoners, ranging from destitute dvoriane to ordinary slaves, into a single homogeneous class of tax-payers. The payment of the soul tax and (after dvoriane had been freed from state service) compulsory military service became hallmarks of the lower class. The contrast between it and the élite became sharper than ever.

Peter's successors made the landlords responsible for the collection of the soul tax from their serfs and formally liable for arrears. It further charged them with the duty of supervising the delivery of recruits from their villages (the selection of the recruits was entrusted to the community, although this power, too, gradually passed into the hands of landlords). With these measures, the state transformed landlords into its fiscal and recruiting agents, a fact which could not help but enhance their authority over the population, more than half of which was then living on private, secular estates. The most onerous period of serfdom begins with Peter's reforms. The government now continues to abandon the proprietary serfs to their landlords' arbitrary authority. By the end of the eighteenth century, the peasant no longer has any civil rights left and in so far as his *legal* status is concerned (but not social or economic condition), he can scarcely be distinguished from a slave.

The service estate also did not escape the reformer's heavy hand. Peter wanted to make absolutely certain that he extracted from this group the best performance possible, and with this aim in mind introduced several innovations concerning education and service promotion which, as long as he was alive to see that they were enforced, made their lives more onerous as well.

Pre-Petrine Russia had no schools and its service class was overwhelmingly illiterate. Apart from the higher echelons of the officialdom and the scribes (*d'iaki*) few servitors had more than a nodding acquaintance with the alphabet. Peter found this situation intolerable because his modernized army required men capable of assuming administrative and technical responsibilities of some sophistication (e.g. navigation and artillery plotting). Hence he had no choice but to create schools for his servitors and to make sure that they attended them. A series of decrees made it obligatory for dvoriane to present male pre-adolescents for a government inspection, following which they were sent either into the service or to school. Henceforth, hordes of young boys, torn out of their rural nests, were called for periodic inspections to towns to be looked over (sometimes by the Emperor himself) and registered by officials of the Heroldmeister's office which assumed the duties of the old Razriad. A decree of 1714 forbade priests to issue dvoriane marriage certificates until they could present proof of competence in arithmetics and the essentials of geometry. Compulsory education lasted five years. At fifteen, the youths entered active service, often in the same Guard regiment in which they had received their schooling. Peter's educational reform had the effect of pushing back the age of compulsory state service to the very threshold of childhood. Of his reforms, this was one of the most despised.

Another of Peter's reforms which deeply affected the life of the service class concerned the conditions of advancement. Traditionally in Russia, promotion in service rank depended less on merit than on ancestry. Although mestnichestvo had been abolished before Peter's accession, the aristocratic element remained well embedded in the service structure. Members of clans enrolled in the Moscow dvorianstvo enjoyed distinct advantages over the provincial dvoriane in appointments to the choicer offices, while commoners were barred from the service altogether. Peter would have found discrimination of this kind distasteful even if it redounded to his advantage. Given his view of the Muscovite upper class as ignorant, irrationally conservative and xenophobic, it was a foregone conclusion that sooner or later he would try to eliminate aristocratic privileges.

In 1722, after thorough study of western bureaucracies, Peter introduced one of the most important pieces of legislation in the history of imperial Russia, the so-called Table of Ranks (*Tabel' o rangakh*). The ukaz set aside the traditional Muscovite hierarchy of titles and ranks, replacing it with an entirely new one based on western models. The Table was a chart listing in parallel columns positions in the three branches of state service (armed services, civil service, and court), each arranged in fourteen categories, one being the highest and fourteen the lowest. The military and civil services were formally separated for the first time, being assigned their own nomenclature and ladder of promotion. The holder of a position listed on the Table was entitled to a rank or *chin* corresponding to it, much as in a modern army, for example, the commander of a company normally holds the rank of captain. It was Peter's intention that every dvorianin, regardless of social background, should begin service at the bottom, and work his way up as high – and only as high – as his talents and accomplishments would carry him. In the army he was to start as an ordinary soldier. The richer and physically stronger dvoriane were permitted to begin in one of the two Guard Regiments (Preobrazhenskii or Semenovskii) where, after a few years of schooling they were commissioned and either left to serve or else transferred to a regular field regiment; the others began as soldiers in regular regiments but promptly received their commissions. In the civil service, dvoriane began in the lowest position carrying chin. Common scribes, like soldiers and non-commissioned officers, had no ranking and therefore were not considered to belong to the dvorianstvo.

Peter was not content to establish a framework within which landowners were encouraged to better their performance. He also wished to give opportunities to commoners to join the service, and to this end he provided that soldiers, sailors and clerks who had distinguished themselves in their duties and qualified to hold positions listed on the Table of Ranks were to receive the appropriate chin. Such commoners at once joined the ranks of the dvorianstvo because in Petrine Russia all who had chin and they alone enjoyed the status of dvoriane. Once on the list, they competed with dvoriane by birth. According to the Table, commoners who attained the lowest officer rank in the military were automatically elevated to hereditary dvoriane, i.e. gained for their sons the right to enter state service at the fourteenth rank and all the other privileges of this estate. Commoners who made a career in the civil or court services had to reach the eighth rank before acquiring hereditary status; until then they were considered 'personal' (*lichnye*) dvoriane (the term came into existence later, under Catherine II) and as such could neither own serfs nor bequeath their status.* In this manner provisions were introduced for advancement by merit – an intention that ran contrary to other tendencies intensifying social cleavages, for which reason, as will be shown, it was only partially realized.

Before long the Table of Ranks turned into a veritable charter of the service class. Since at that time power and wealth in Russia were attainable almost exclusively by working for or with the state, acquisition of chin bestowed on the holder uniquely privileged status. He was assured of a government job for himself and, in most cases, for his offspring as well. He also enjoyed the most valuable of all economic privileges, the right to own land worked by serf labour. In the words of the Decembrist Nicholas Turgenev, Russians lacking chin were 'en dehors de la nation officielle ou légale' – outside the pale of the nation in the official or legal sense of the word.[6] Entry into the service and advancement in it became a national obsession for Russians, especially those from the lower middle class; clergymen, shopkeepers and scribes developed a consuming ambition for their sons to acquire the rank of a cornet in the army or commissar or registrar in the civil service, which carried the fourteenth chin, and in this way gain access to the trough. The kind of drive that in commercial countries went into accumulation of capital in imperial Russia tended to concentrate on the acquisition of chin. Chin now joined chai (tea) and shchi (cabbage soup) to form a triad around which revolved a great deal of Russian life.

In retrospect, Peter's attempt to change the character of the élite by an infusion of new blood seems to have been more successful in the lower echelons of the service class than at the top. Analysis of the composition of the highest four ranks, the so-called generalitet, reveals that in 1730 (five years after Peter's death) 93 per cent of its members were drawn from families which had held high office and often analogous positions in Muscovite Russia.[7] It was below these exalted heights, between the fourteenth and tenth chiny that the greatest changes took place. The Table of Ranks accomplished a considerable broadening of the social base of the service class. The class as a whole grew impressively. The increase can be accounted for by the promotion of commoners to officer rank in the greatly expanded military establishment, the granting of chin to holders of lower administrative posts in the provinces, and the enrolment in the ranks of dvorianstvo of landowning groups in such borderlands as the Ukraine, the Tatar regions on the Volga and the newly conquered Baltic provinces.

---

* In 1845 hereditary dvorianstvo was limited to the topmost five ranks, and in 1856 it was further restricted to the highest four. In the first half of the nineteenth century, personal, non-hereditary dvoriane constituted between a third and a half of all the dvorianstvo.

The reform measures so far described were intended to squeeze out of the country more money and services. In that sense they were mere improvements on Muscovite practices, and far less revolutionary than they appeared to contemporaries who, overawed by the energy of Peter and the foreign format of his reforms, failed to see their antecedents. Essentially, Peter rationalized the Muscovite system in order to make it more efficient.

Just how traditional Peter's methods were can be seen in the procedures he used to construct his new capital in St Petersburg. The decision to erect a city on the Neva estuary was first taken in 1702, but little progress was made until the victory at Poltava assured its security from the Swedes.[8] In 1709 Peter tackled the job in earnest. Because dvoriane and merchants were reluctant to settle in the new city noted for its raw climate and lack of amenities, Peter resorted to compulsion. In 1712 he ordered the transfer to St Petersburg of one thousand dvoriane and an equal group of merchants and artisans. The government assured these new settlers of the necessary labour and building materials for the construction of their residences, but the costs of building had to come out of their own pockets. The designs of the residences were strictly prescribed. Owners of more than 3,500 'souls' had to build houses of stone; less affluent dvoriane could use wood or mud. The dimensions and façades of all the private buildings had to conform to designs authorized by the city's chief architect. Only in furnishing the interiors were the proprietors free to use their imagination – a gesture with unintended symbolic meaning for the future of Russia's westernized upper class. Lists were drawn up containing the names of the families selected for transfer; they included representatives of the most eminent boyar clans. In all these measures the votchina background was clearly in evidence. As one historian puts it, such resettlements of dvoriane by government order 'had much in common with the resettlement of serf peasants from one estate to another at the landlord's command'.[9]

The construction of the new city under extremely adverse climatic and geological conditions required a steady supply of manual workers. For this purpose recourse was had to forced labour. In Muscovite Russia, forced labour for construction purposes had been usually employed in the immediate vicinity of the worker's village or posad. Since the area surrounding St Petersburg had few indigenous inhabitants, Peter had to import labour from other parts of the country. Requisition orders calling for 40,000 peasants to perform several months of labour in St Petersburg were issued every year. Like the new Russian army, the force was assembled on the basis of quotas set by the authorities of one worker for anywhere from each nine to sixteen households. The labour conscripts, carrying their tools and food, were driven in gangs over distances of hundreds of miles, usually under military escort and sometimes loaded down with chains to prevent desertions. Despite these precautions, so many escaped that according to recent estimates, Peter in no one year secured more than 20,000 men. Of this number many died from exposure and disease.

By such Asiatic means was constructed Russia's 'window on the west'.

The truly revolutionary element in Peter's reforms was concealed from contemporaries, and even Peter himself scarcely understood it. It lay in the idea of the state as an organization serving a higher ideal – the public good – and in its corollary, the idea of society as the state's partner.

Until the middle of the seventeenth century, Russians had no notion of either 'state' or 'society'. The 'state', in so far as they thought of it at all, meant to them the sovereign, the *gosudar'* or *dominus*, that is, his person, his private staff and his patrimony. As for 'society', it was not perceived as a whole but as fragmented into discrete 'ranks'. In the west, both these concepts had been well developed since the thirteenth century under the influence of feudal practices and Roman law and even the most authoritarian kings did not lose sight of them.* The idea of state as an entity distinct from the sovereign entered the Russian vocabulary in the seventeenth century, but it gained currency only at the beginning of the eighteenth, in the reign of Peter. 'Society' made its appearance later yet; at any rate, the Russian word for it, *obshchestvo*, seems to have originated in the reign of Catherine the Great.

As one might expect, Russians drew their idea of statehood mainly from western books. The transmittal, however, was, in the first instance indirect. The agents responsible for its transplantation to Russia were Orthodox clerics from the Ukraine, where ever since the Counter Reformation, the Orthodox church had been subjected to strong Catholic pressures. Resistance to it compelled the Ukrainian Orthodox establishment to familiarize itself with western theology and other branches of learning of which the Muscovite fraternity in its isolation remained blissfully ignorant. In 1632 the Ukrainian clergy founded in Kiev (then still under Polish rule) an academy for the training of Orthodox priests, the curriculum of which was modelled on the Jesuit schools in Poland and Italy which many of its faculty had attended. After Kiev had come under Russian authority (1667) these Ukrainians began to exert a powerful intellectual influence on Russia. Peter much preferred them to the Muscovite priesthood because they were more enlightened and more

* The famous pronouncement of Louis xiv, '*L'État, c'est moi*', which breathes a sentiment so contrary to the entire western tradition, is of doubtful provenance and probably apocryphal. Far more characteristic, as well as being authentic, are the words uttered by Louis on his deathbed: 'I am going but the state lives for ever'; Fritz Hartung and Roland Mousnier in *Relazioni del X Congresso Internazionale di Scienze Storiche* (Florence 1955), IV, p. 9.

favourably disposed to his reforms. The leading political theorist of Peter's reign, the man who introduced the concept of sovereignty to Russia, Feofan Prokopovich, came from this milieu. The works of Grotius, Pufendorf and Wolff which Peter ordered to be translated into Russian helped further to popularize concepts of western political thought.

As had been noted, Peter was interested in power, especially military power, not in westernization. In a sense, this had also been true of his predecessors in the seventeenth century. But unlike them, Peter, having been to western Europe and having formed close friendships with western Europeans, understood something about the nature of modern power. He realized, as they did not, that the practice of merciless skimming of the national wealth for the benefit of the treasury prevented the accumulation of more valuable forms of wealth lying underneath the surface – riches of an economic and cultural nature. Such resources had to be given a chance to mature. Borrowing terminology from another discipline, we may say that before Peter Russian rulers had treated their realm as would people at the hunting stage of civilization; with Peter, they turned into cultivators. The impulse towards instantaneous seizure of any desirable object in view now yielded gradually (and with occasional relapses) to the habit of development. Peter was only dimly aware of the implications of his steps in this direction, which he took less from philosophical preconceptions than from the instinct of a born statesman. His vigorous support of Russian manufacturers was motivated by the desire to free his military establishment from dependence on foreign suppliers; its actual long-term effect, however, was greatly to expand the foundations of Russian industry. His educational measures were intended, in the first place, to prepare gunnery experts and navigators. Peter himself had had a superficial education and valued only learning of a technical, applied kind. But in the long run his schools did for Russia much more than merely provide cadres of technicians; they created an educated élite which eventually became highly spiritualized and, indeed, turned violently against the whole service-oriented mentality which had made their existence possible in the first place.

It is under Peter that there emerges in Russia a sense of the state as something distinct from and superior to the monarch; narrow fiscal concerns now yield to a broader national vision. From the time of his accession, Peter talked of 'the common good', 'general welfare' and 'the benefit of the whole nation'.[10] He was the first Russian monarch to articulate the idea of *bien public*, and to express an interest in improving the lot of his subjects. Under Peter, public and private welfare appear for the first time in Russia as interconnected. A great deal of Peter's domestic activity had as its aim to make Russians conscious of a link between private and common good. Such, for example, was the purpose behind his practice of attaching explanations to imperial decrees from the most trivial (e.g. an ukaz prohibiting the grazing of cattle on the boulevards of St Petersburg) to the most weighty (such as the decree of 1722 changing the law of imperial succession). No monarch before Peter had thought such explanations necessary; he was the first to take the people into his confidence. In 1703 he launched Russia's first newspaper, *Vedomosti*. This publication not only made a major contribution to Russia's cultural life; it also marked a dramatic constitutional innovation, for with this act Peter abandoned the Muscovite tradition of treating national and international news as a state secret.

These and related measures posited a society functioning in partnership with the state. But this assumption was not thought out, and herein lies the central tragedy of modern Russian politics. It was not necessary for Peter and his successors to take their people into confidence, to treat them as partners rather than as mere subjects, to inculcate in them a sense of common destiny. Numerous regimes of the patrimonial or despotic type had managed to carry on for centuries without taking this drastic step. But once it had been decided that the interests of the country required the existence of a citizenry conscious of its collective identity and of its role in the country's development, then certain consequences inevitably followed. It was clearly contradictory to appeal to the public sentiments of the Russian people and at the same time to deny them any legal or political safeguards against the omnipotence of the state. A partnership in which one party held all the power and played by its own rules was obviously unworkable. And yet this is exactly how Russia has been governed from Peter the Great to this day. The refusal of those in authority to grasp the obvious consequences of inviting public participation generated in Russia a condition of permanent political tension which successive governments sought to attenuate sometimes by loosening their reins on the realm, sometimes by tightening them, but never by inviting society to share the coachman's seat.

With the idea of the state came the notion of political crime, and this, in turn, led to the establishment of the political police. The Code of 1649 which had first defined crimes against the tsar and his realm under the category of 'Word and Deed' offences had not as yet created special organs to ferret out political dissenters. At that time the tsarist government relied on denunciation by private citizens for information concerning seditious activities. The disposal of such cases was entrusted to individual prikazy; only the most serious ones came before the tsar and his Duma.

Peter continued to rely heavily on denunciation; for example, in 1711 he ordered that anyone (serfs included) denouncing dvoriane evading service should receive their villages as a reward. But he no longer could afford to treat political crimes as an occasional nuisance because his enemies were legion and scattered among all the strata of society. He created, therefore, a separate police bureau, the Preóbrazhenskii Prikaz, which he charged with over-all responsibility for dealing with political offences in the empire. This institution was introduced so surreptitiously that historians to this day have not been able to locate the decree authorizing its establishment or even to determine the approximate date when it might have been issued.[11] The first solid information concerning this organ dates from 1702 when a decree came out detailing its functions and authority. According to its provisions, the head of the Preobrazhenskii Prikaz had the right to investigate at his discretion any institution and any individual, regardless of rank, and to take whatever steps he thought necessary to uncover pertinent information and forestall seditious acts. In contrast to the other branches of administration created under Peter, its functions were defined very vaguely – a fact which served to enhance its powers. No one – not even the Senate which Peter had set up to supervise the country's administration – had the right to inquire into its affairs. In its chambers thousands were tortured and put to death, among them peasants who resisted the soul tax or recruitment orders, religious dissenters and drunks overheard to make disparaging remarks about the sovereign. The uses of the police, however, were not confined to political offences, broadly defined as these were. Whenever the government ran into any kind of difficulty, it tended to call upon its organs for help. Thus, the complex task of managing the construction of St Petersburg, after various unsuccessful attempts was in the end entrusted to that city's police chief.

The Preobrazhenskii Prikaz seems to have been the first institution in history created to deal specifically and exclusively with political crimes. The scope of its operations and its complete administrative independence mark it as the prototype of a basic organ of all modern police states.

It is one of the few dependable rules of history that, given enough time, private interests will always triumph over public ones simply because their advocates, as they stand both to lose and to gain more than do the guardians of public property, are infinitely more resourceful.

The dvoriane listed with the Office of the Heroldmeister in St Petersburg as serving under the Table of Ranks were even under Peter's semimeritocratic regime recipients of exclusive privileges, holding as they did the bulk of the country's arable land and of its working population. Their hold on this property, however, was tenuous, being conditional on the satisfactory performance of state service and also subject to many legal restrictions. Nor did the dvoriane enjoy any safeguards to protect them from the arbitrariness of the state and its officials. As one might expect, their foremost desires were to transform their conditional possession of land and serfs into outright ownership and to acquire guarantees of personal inviolability. They also wished for greater business opportunities than they had under a system of rigid state monopolies. Finally, to the extent that they became educated and curious about the outside world, they wanted the right of free travel and access to information. Most of these wishes were granted to them during the four decades which followed Peter's death (1725); the remainder, before the century was over. The climacteric was the reign of Catherine the Great; for although Catherine is mainly remembered for her love affairs it was she, rather than Peter, who revolutionized the Russian system and set it on its western course.

The dismantling of the patrimonial structure occurred with astonishing rapidity. Unfortunately, historians have paid much less attention to its decline than to its origins with the result that much of that history is covered by obscurity. We must confine our explanation to several hypotheses, the validity of which only further study can determine:

1. In the imperial period, the dvorianstvo grew very impressively in numbers; between the middle of the seventeenth and the end of the eighteenth centuries its male contingent increased nearly threefold, and from the end of the eighteenth to the middle of the nineteenth, once again more than fourfold; from approximately 39,000 in 1651, to 108,000 in 1782, to 464,000 in 1858.[12]

2. A number of Peter's measures bearing on the dvorianstvo had had the effect of consolidating its position:

a. By regularizing procedures for service promotion, the Table of Ranks helped to free the dvorianstvo from total dependence on the personal favour of the tsar and his advisers; it made the service establishment more autonomous, a development which the crown was unable subsequently to reverse;

b. Compulsory education required of young dvoriane brought them together and tended to heighten their sense of class solidarity; the Guard Regiments where the élite of dvoriane was schooled and given military training acquired extraordinary power;

c. The increase in the authority of the landlord resulting from the introduction of the soul tax and conscription transformed dvoriane into virtual satraps on their estates;

3. In 1722, after his conflict with Tsarevich Alexis, Peter abolished the regular law of succession, based on primogeniture, and empowered every monarch to pick his own successor. The Russian monarchy for the

remainder of the century became an elective office; from Peter's death until the accession of Paul I in 1796, Russia's rulers were chosen by high-ranking officials acting in collusion with officers of Guard Regiments. These groups favoured women, especially women with frivolous reputation, thought unlikely to take more than a perfunctory interest in affairs of state. In return for the throne, these empresses made generous presents of serfs, landed estates and various privileges to those who had helped them gain it.

4. The military reforms of Peter and his successors gave Russia an army second to none in eastern Europe. Poland, Sweden and Turkey no longer counted, the more so as each was in the throes of an internal political crisis; it was now their turn to fear Russia. During the eighteenth century, the nomads of the steppe were finally brought to heel as well. With increased power and external security came a growing desire for enjoyment of life and a corresponding de-emphasis on service.

5. The same reforms, by shifting the burden of military service onto conscripts, reduced the state's need for dvoriane whose main function henceforth was to officer the troops.

6. It has been said that under Peter Russia learned western techniques, under Elizabeth western manners, and under Catherine western morals. Westernization certainly made giant progress in the eighteenth century; what had begun as mere aping of the west by the court and its élite developed into close identification with the very spirit of western culture. With the advance of westernization it became embarrassing for the state and the dvorianstvo to maintain the old service structure. The dvorianstvo wished to emulate the western aristocracy, to enjoy its status and rights; and the Russian monarchy, eager to find itself in the fore-front of European enlightenment, was, up to a point, cooperative.

In the course of the eighteenth century a consensus developed between the crown and dvorianstvo that the old system had outlived itself. It is in this atmosphere that the social, economic and ideological props of the patrimonial regime were removed. We shall discuss economic liberalization in Chapter 8 and the unshackling of thought in Chapter 10, and here outline the social side of the process, namely the dismantling of the service structure.

Dvoriane serving in the military were the first to benefit from the general weakening of the monarchy which occurred after Peter's death. In 1730, provincial dvoriane frustrated a move by several old boyar families to impose constitutional limitations on the newly elected Empress Anne. In appreciation, Anne steadily eased the conditions of service which Peter had imposed on the dvorianstvo. In 1730 she repealed Peter's law requiring landowners to bequeath their estates to one heir (p. 176 below). The next year she founded a Noble Cadet Corps, reserved for dvoriane, where their children could begin to soldier among their peers, unsullied by contact with commoners. An important edict issued by Anne in 1736 raised from fifteen to twenty the age at which dvoriane were required to begin state service, and at the same time lowered its duration from life to twenty-five years; these provisions made it possible to retire at forty-five if not earlier, since some dvoriane were inscribed in the Guard Regiments at the age of two or three and began to accumulate retirement credit while still in their nurses' arms. In 1736 dvoriane families who had several men (sons or brothers) were permitted to keep one at home to manage the property. From 1725 onwards it became customary to grant dvoriane lengthy leaves of absence to visit their estates. Compulsory inspection of youths was done away with, although the government continued to insist on the education of dvoriane children and required them to present themselves for several examinations before joining active service at twenty.

These measures culminated in the Manifesto 'Concerning the Granting of Freedom and Liberty to the Entire Russian Dvorianstvo', issued in 1762 by Peter III, which 'for ever, for all future generations' exempted Russian dvoriane from state service in all its forms. The Manifesto further granted them the right to obtain passports for travel abroad, even if their purpose was to enroll in the service of foreign rulers – an unexpected restoration of the ancient boyar right of 'free departure' abolished by Ivan III. Under Catherine II, the Senate on at least three occasions confirmed this Manifesto, concurrently extending to the dvorianstvo other rights and privileges (e.g. the right, given in 1783, to maintain private printing presses). In 1785 Catherine issued a Charter of the Dvorianstvo which reconfirmed all the liberties acquired by this estate since Peter's death, and added some new ones. The land which the dvoriane held was now recognized as their legal property. They were exempt from corporal punishment. These rights made them – on paper, at any rate – the equals of the upper classes in the most advanced countries of the west.*

* The scheme given here according to which, yielding to the pressures of dvorianstvo, the Russian monarchy emancipated and transformed it into a privileged and leisured class, is the view held by most Russian historians before and since the Revolution. It has recently been challenged by two American scholars, Marc Raeff (*Origins of the Russian Intelligentsia: The Eighteenth Century Nobility* (New York 1966), especially pp. 10–12, and an article in the *American Historical Review*, LXXV, 5, (1970), pp. 1291–4) and Robert E. Jones (*The Emancipation of the Russian Nobility, 1762–1785* (Princeton, N.F. 1973)). These authors argue that it was not the dvoriane who emancipated themselves from the state, but, on the contrary, the state that freed itself from dependence on the dvoriane. The state had more servitors than it needed, it found the dvorianstvo useless in administering the provinces, and preferred to bureaucratize. The argument, while not without merit, appears on the whole unconvincing. If indeed the monarchy had too many servitors (which is by no means demonstrated) it could have solved its problem by demobilizing them temporarily and provisionally instead of 'for ever, for all future generations'. Furthermore, since salaries were rarely paid, no major

In the eyes of the law, these provisions applied equally to the land-owners serving in the military and the salaried personnel holding executive posts in the civil service because all persons holding positions listed on the Table of Ranks were technically dvoriane. In practice, however, in the eighteenth century a sharp distinction came to be drawn between the two categories with their vastly different social backgrounds. It became customary to reserve the term dvorianin for landowners, officers and hereditary dvoriane, and to call career civil servants *chinovniki* (singular *chinovnik*), i.e. holders of chin or rank. A well-to-do landowner, especially one of old lineage, appointed to a high administrative post, such as a governor or the head of a ministry in St Petersburg, was never called a chinovnik. On the other hand, an impoverished landlord's son forced to take a clerical job would lose in the eyes of society the status of a dvorianin. The distinction was accentuated by Catherine's creation of corporate organizations called Assemblies of Dvoriane which allowed only land-owners to vote. The growing gulf between the two categories of dvoriane ran contrary to Peter's expectations. Fearing that many dvoriane would seek to escape military service by enrolling in the bureaucracy, he had imposed quotas on the number of persons from each family who could choose such a career. In fact, dvoriane shunned office work, especially after they had been freed from obligatory state service and no longer required a loophole to escape it. Always short of competent bureaucrats, the government was forced to fill the ranks of the civil service with sons of clergymen and burghers, thus further lowering its social prestige. Sometimes, when the shortage of bureaucrats grew acute, as happened during Catherine's provincial administration reforms, the government resorted to forceful drafts of students attending religious seminaries.

Like the landowning dvoriane, mid-eighteenth-century chinovniks began to press the state for concessions. They too wished to be rid of the most disagreeable features of the state service system, especially that provision of the Table of Ranks which had made promotion in rank dependent on the availability of a corresponding post. They much preferred the old Muscovite system – restricted as it had been to the small high echelon of the civil service – whereby possession of a chin entitled the holder to a corresponding post in state service. The force of this Muscovite tradition was so strong that even in Peter's lifetime the basic premises of the Table of Ranks had been grossly violated; this must have

savings were effectuated by the wholesale dismissal. Nor is it apparent why bureaucratization required the emancipation of dvoriane, in so far as bureaucrats also belonged to this class. The trouble with this interpretation is that it ignores the entire process of society's 'manumission' of which the emancipation of dvoriane was only one chapter, and which cannot be explained satisfactorily by the desire to save money or by other, narrowly conceived considerations of *raison d'état*.

been true of the holders of the four uppermost ranks, the *generalitet*, who, as had been noted, in 1730 nearly to a man descended from titled Muscovite servitors. Under Peter's successors merit requirements were further lowered. For example, to encourage education, Elizabeth allowed graduates of institutions of higher learning to bypass the lowest ranks. Still, at any rate as far as the lower grades of the bureaucracy were concerned, the Petrine principle held, and the average official had to wait for a suitable vacancy before being promoted to the next higher rank.

This principle was abandoned in the early years of Catherine II, at almost the same time that the monarchy surrendered the principle of compulsory state service and much for the same reason, namely to win support. On 19 April 1764, Catherine issued instructions that all high civil servants who had held rank uninterruptedly for seven or more years were to be promoted to the next higher rank.* Three years later, the Senate asked the Empress what she wished done about those officials who had fallen short of the seven-year requirement by a few months and remained frozen in their rank while their more fortunate colleagues had moved up a notch. Catherine gave a casual reply destined to have the most weighty consequences; she ordered the general and automatic promotion of all civil servants who had served for a minimum of seven years in a given rank. This decision, dated 13 September 1767, set a precedent which was faithfully followed; henceforth it became the rule in Russia to promote civil servants on the basis of seniority without much regard to personal qualifications, attainments, or vacancies. Later on, Catherine's son, Paul, lowered the waiting period for most ranks to three years; and since it had become customary to bypass Ranks 13 and 11 anyway, a civil servant now had reasonable assurance that once he had reached the lowest chin and stayed in the service without getting into trouble with his superiors, he would in good time reach the coveted eighth rank and gain for his descendants hereditary dvorianstvo. (It was partly this threat of being flooded with ennobled bureaucrats that influenced Nicholas I and Alexander II to limit hereditary dvorianstvo to the uppermost five or four ranks; see above, p. 125.) Catherine's policies put the Table of Ranks on its head; instead of rank coming with office, office now came with rank.

The Manifesto of 1762, reinforced by the Charter of 1785, deprived the monarchy of control over the landed estate; the Edict of 1767 deprived it of control of the bureaucracy. The crown henceforth no longer had any choice but to convey up the automatic escalator of promotion

---

* This order, of utmost importance for the history of imperial Russia, is reproduced neither in the Full Collection of Laws nor in the appropriate volume of the Senate Archive (*Senatskii Arkhiv*, XIV, St Petersburg, 1910). No historian seems to have seen it, and it is known only from references.

officials who had logged a prescribed number of years in one rank. In this manner, the bureaucracy secured a stranglehold on the apparatus of state, and through it, on the inhabitants of state and crown lands for whose administration it was responsible. Already at the time keen observers noted the disastrous effects of such a system. Among them was a political *émigré* from one of the most aristocratic houses, Prince Peter Dolgorukov. Writing on the eve of the Great Reforms of the 1860s, he urged the abolition of chin as a prerequisite to any meaningful improvement of conditions in Russia:

The Emperor of All the Russias, the would-be Autocrat, finds himself utterly deprived of the right, claimed not only by all constitutional monarchs but even by presidents of republics, the right to choose his functionaries. In Russia, to hold a position, it is necessary to hold a corresponding rank. If the sovereign finds an honest individual, capable of performing a certain function but lacking in the rank required for the position he cannot appoint him. This institution is the most powerful guarantee given to nullity, to servility, to corruption. Hence, of all reforms it is the one most antipathetic to the all-powerful bureaucracy. Of all the abuses, chin is the most difficult to uproot because it has so many and such influential defenders. In Russia, merit is a great obstacle to a man's advancement ... In all civilized countries, a person who has devoted ten or fifteen years of his life to study, to travels, to agriculture, industry and commerce, a person who has gained specialized knowledge and is well acquainted with his country, such a person will come to occupy a public post where he is able to perform useful work. In Russia, it is quite different. A man who has left the service for several years cannot rejoin it except at a rank which he had held at the moment of his resignation. Someone who has never been in the service cannot enter it except at the lowest rank, regardless of his age and merit, while a scoundrel, a semi-moron, provided that he never leaves the service, will end up by attaining the highest ranks. From this derives the singular anomaly that in the midst of the Russian nation, so intelligent, endowed with such admirable qualities, where the spirit, so to speak, roams the villages, the administration is distinguished by an ineptitude, which, invariably increasing as one approaches the highest ranks, ends up in certain high administrative echelons by degenerating into veritable semi-idiotism.*[13]

The judgement, for all its impassioned harshness, cannot be faulted in

---

* This system of automatic promotion through seniority later penetrated the armed forces, and contributed to the lowering of the quality of the officer staff. Solzhenitsyn blames on it the Russian disasters in the First World War: 'The Russian army perished because of *seniority* – the supreme indisputable reckoning and the order of promoting by seniority. As long as you *did not make a slip*, as long as you did not offend your superiors, the very march of time would bring you at the appropriate time the desired next chin, and with the chin, the assignment. And everybody so accepted this wisdom . . . that colonel hurried to learn of another colonel and general of another general not where he had fought but from what year, month, and day dated his seniority, i.e. at what stage of promotion he was towards his next appointment': *August 1914*, Chapter 12.

its essential charge. It suggests, incidentally, an important cause for the estrangement of Russia's educated classes from the state. Attempts to correct the situation, were, of course, made because every monarch in the nineteenth century wished to regain control over his civil service, so lightheartedly forfeited by Catherine. The most celebrated of these was an order issued by Alexander I in 1809 on the advice of Count Speranskii, requiring officials to pass examinations before qualifying for promotion to Rank 8, as well as permitting, also by means of examinations, direct advancement from Rank 8 to Rank 5. But this and similar attempts always broke against the solid resistance of the bureaucratic establishment.

From the 1760s onwards a kind of dyarchy was introduced into Russia which until then had been governed in a strictly hierarchical fashion from a single centre. The monarch continued to enjoy unlimited authority in the sphere of foreign policy and the right to dispose of at his pleasure that part of the revenues which actually reached the Treasury. In governing the country, however, he was severely constrained by the power of his one-time servitors – dvoriane and chinovniki. In effect, the population of Russia was turned over to these two groups for exploitation. Their respective areas of competence were fairly well delineated. One historian divides post-Catherinian Russia in two parts, one of which he calls dvoriane-run (*dvorianskie*), the other bureaucratic (*chinovnye*), depending on the proportion of each group in the region's population. In the former category he includes twenty-eight provinces concentrated in the geographic centre of the country, the heartland of serfdom. As one moved outward from the centre, towards the borderlands, the bureaucrats took over.[14] Herzen who had been twice in provincial exile noted a similar phenomenon: 'The power of the governor', he observes in his *Memoirs*, 'generally grows in direct proportion to the distance from St Petersburg, but it grows at a geometric rate in the provinces where there is no dvorianstvo, such as Perm, Viatka, and Siberia.'[15]

Having conceded the direct exploitation of the country to some 100,000 landlords and 50,000 bureaucrats with their respective families, staffs, and hangers-on, the monarchy assumed towards the country at large an attitude more like that of an occupying power than of an absolute monarchy in the western sense. It no longer interceded on behalf of the population of commoners against the élite's abuses even in that limited sense in which it had done so in Muscovy. Indeed, in his legislation Peter referred to the landlords' serfs as their 'subjects' (*poddanye*), employing a term from the vocabulary of public law to describe what seemingly was a purely private relationship. At the same time, as will be noted (p. 181) dvoriane in dealing with the crown were in the habit of calling themselves 'slaves' (*raby*). 'If slaves were called subjects, then subjects, too, were called slaves', remarks a Russian historian, thus calling attention to the survival of strictly patrimonial relations in an age of seeming westernization.[16] The money which the crown extracted from the country through the intermediacy of its agents it spent not on the inhabitants but on the court and armed forces. 'It spent no more on the provinces than it had to spend in order to exploit them.'[17]

After 1762, the Russian monarchy became in large measure the captive of groups which it had originally brought into existence. The trappings of imperial omnipotence served merely to conceal its desperate weakness – as well as to camouflage the actual power wielded by dvoriane and chinovniki.

Under these circumstances, the situation seemed ripe for the élite to move in and seize the political prerogatives claimed by the crown. To understand why this did not happen we must investigate the condition and political attitudes of the principal social groupings.

II
SOCIETY

CHAPTER 6

THE PEASANTRY

The reason for beginning a survey of the social classes in old regime Russia with the peasantry does not call for elaborate explanation. As late as 1917, four-fifths of the empire's population consisted of people, who although not necessarily engaged in farming, were officially classified as peasants. Even today, when the census shows the majority of Russia's inhabitants to be urban, the country retains unmistakable traces of its peasant past: a consequence of the fact that most of the inhabitants of Soviet cities are one-time peasants or their immediate descendants. As will be shown later, throughout its history the urban population of Russia has preserved strong links with the countryside and carried with it rural habits into the city. The Revolution revealed how tenuous the urbanization of the country had been. Almost immediately after its outbreak, the urban population began to flee to the countryside; between 1917 and 1920, Moscow lost a third of its population and Petrograd a half. Paradoxically, although it had been carried out in the name of urban civilization and against the 'idiocy of rural life', the 1917 Revolution actually increased the influence of the village on Russian life. After the old, westernized élite had been overthrown and dispersed, the ruling class which had replaced it consisted largely of peasants in their various guises: farmers, shopkeepers and industrial workers. Lacking a genuine bourgeoisie to emulate, this new élite instinctively modelled itself on the village strong man, the *kulak*. To this day it has not been able to shake off its rural past.

In the middle of the sixteenth century, when they were being fixed to the soil, the peasants began to abandon the slash-burn method of cultivation in favour of the three-field system (*trekhpol'e*). Under this farming pattern the arable was divided into three parts, one of which was sown in the spring with summer crops, another in August with winter crops, and the last left fallow. The following year, the field which had been under winter crops was sown with spring crops, the fallow with winter crops, and the spring-crop field was set aside for fallow. The cycle was completed every three years. It was not a very efficient method of utilizing land, if only because it placed a third of the arable permanently out of commission. Already in the eighteenth century agrarian specialists criticized it and much pressure was exerted on the peasant to abandon it. But as Marc Bloch has shown in the instance of France and Michael Confino has confirmed in that of Russia, agricultural techniques cannot be isolated from the entire complex of peasant institutions. The muzhik fiercely resisted pressures to abandon the three-field routine and it remained the prevalent pattern of cultivation in Russia well into the twentieth century.[1]

Observers of the Russian village had often commented on the extreme contrast in the tempo of its life during the summer months and the remainder of the year. The brevity of the growing season in Russia calls for the maximum exertion during a few months which are followed by a long period of inactivity. During the middle of the nineteenth century in the central provinces of Russia 153 days in the year were set aside for holidays; most of them fell between November and February. On the other hand, from approximately April to September there was time for nothing else but work. Historians of the positivist age, who had to find a physical explanation for every cultural or psychic phenomenon, saw in this climatic factor an explanation of the Russian's notorious aversion for sustained, disciplined work:

There is one thing the Great Russian believes in: that one must cherish the clear summer working day, that nature allows him little suitable time for farming, and that the brief Great Russian summer can be shortened further by an unseasonal spell of foul weather. This compels the Great Russian peasant to hustle, to exert himself strenuously, so as to get much done quickly and quit the fields in good time, and then to have nothing to do through the autumn and winter. Thus, the Great Russian has accustomed himself to excessive short bursts of energy; he has learned to work fast, feverishly, and extensively, and to rest during the enforced autumn and winter idleness. No nation in Europe is capable of such intense exertion over short periods of time as the Great Russian; but probably also nowhere in Europe shall we find such a lack of habit for even, moderate, and well distributed, steady work as in this very same Great Russia.[2]

Spring comes to Russia suddenly. Overnight, the ice breaks on the rivers, and the waters, freed from their confinement, push the floes downstream, crushing everything in their path and spilling over the banks. White wastes turn into green fields. The earth comes to life. This is *ottepel'* or thaw, a natural phenomenon so striking in its suddenness that it has long served to describe awakenings of spirit, thought or political life. As soon as it has arrived, the peasant faces a period of highly concentrated physical work: before the introduction of machinery, eighteen hours a day were not uncommon. The rapidity with which field work had to be completed made for one of the most onerous features of serf-dom. The serf could not schedule the duties he owed his master so as to have time in which undisturbed to carry on his own work. He had to do both concurrently. Landlords sometimes required serfs to attend to domainial land before allowing them to till their own. When this happened, it was not unusual for peasants to have to work round the clock, tilling the landlord's strips daytime and their own at night. Work reached its highest pitch of intensity in August when the spring harvest had to be collected and the winter harvest sown. The agricultural season allowed so little margin for experimentation that one is not surprised at the conservatism of the Russian peasant where any change in working routine was concerned; one false step, a few days lost, and he faced the prospect of hunger the next year.

As soon as the soil, hard as rock in the winter, softened, the peasant household went into the fields to plough and plant the spring crop. In the northern and central regions, the principal spring crop was oats, and the principal winter crop rye, the latter of which went into the making of black bread, the staple of the Russian peasant. In the nineteenth century, the peasant consumed on the average three pounds of bread a day, and at harvest time as much as five pounds. Wheat was less cultivated there, partly because it is more sensitive to the climate, and partly because it requires more attention than rye. To the south and east, rye yielded to oats and wheat, the latter grown mostly for export to western Europe. The potato came late to Russia and did not become an important crop in the nineteenth century, with only $1\frac{1}{2}$ per cent of the cultivated acreage given to its cultivation (1875). The coincidence of a major cholera epidemic accompanying the introduction of the potato into Russia in the 1830s caused all kinds of taboos to be associated with it. In the garden plots attached to their houses, the peasants grew mainly cabbages and cucumbers which, next to bread, constituted the most important items in their diet. They were usually eaten salted. Vegetables were essential to the peasant diet because the Orthodox church prescribed that on Wednesdays and Fridays, as well as during three major fasts lasting several weeks each, its adherents were to abstain not only from meat but from all foods derived from animals, milk and its by-products included. The national drink was *kvas*, a beverage made of fermented bread. Tea became popular only in the nineteenth century. The diet was acrid and monotonous but healthy.

Peasants lived in log cabins called *izby* (singular, *izba*). (Plates 3–4, 6–8.) They furnished them sparingly with a table and benches and little more. They slept on earthen stoves which occupied as much as a quarter of the izba's space. As a rule, no chimneys were constructed, and the smoke

drifted into the huts. Each izba had its 'Red' or 'Beautiful' corner
(*krasnyi ugolok*), where hung at least one ikon, that of the patron saint,
most commonly St Nicholas. No guest spoke until he had made obeis-
ance to the icon and crossed himself.* Hygienic provisions were rudimentary. Each village had a bathhouse (*bania*), copied from the Finnish
sauna. (Plate 40.) Peasants visited it every Saturday afternoon to wash
and put on fresh linen. The rest of the week they went unwashed. The
everyday clothing was simple. Poorer peasants wore a combination of Slavic and Finnic dress, consisting of a long linen shirt, tied at the
waist, and linen trousers, with boots made of bark or felt, all of home
manufacture. Those who could afford to buy their clothing, tended towards oriental fashion. In the winter, the peasant wore a sheepskin coat
called *tulup*. The women tied on their heads a kerchief, probably a
legacy of the veil.

The Great Russian village was built on a linear plan: a wide, unpaved
road was flanked on both sides by cottages with their individual vegetable plots. Farm land surrounded the village. Individual farmsteads
located in the midst of fields were mainly a southern phenomenon.

We now come to serfdom, which, with the joint family and commune,
was one of the three basic peasant institutions under the old regime.

To begin with, some statistics. It would be a serious mistake to think
that before 1861 the majority of Russians were serfs. The census of
1858–9, the last taken before Emancipation, showed that the Empire
had a population of 60 million. Of this number, 12 million were free
men: dvoriane, clergy, burghers, independent farmers, Cossacks and so
forth. The remaining 48 million divided themselves almost equally between two categories of rural inhabitants: state peasants (*gosudarstvennye
krest'iane*), who, although bound to the land, were not serfs, and proprietary peasants (*pomeshchch'i krest'iane*), living on privately owned
land and personally bonded. The latter, who were serfs in the proper
sense of the word, constituted 37·7 per cent of the empire's population
(22,500,000 persons).[3] As Map 31 indicates, the highest concentration of
serfdom occurred in two regions; the central provinces, the cradle of the
Muscovite state, where serfdom had originated, and the western provinces, acquired in the partitions of Poland. In these two areas, more
than half of the population consisted of serfs. In a few provinces the proportion of serfs rose to nearly 70 per cent. The farther one moved away
from the central and western provinces, the less serfdom one encoun-

---

* The communist regime has made interesting use for its own purposes of such peasant
symbols. *Krasnyi*, which to the peasant meant both 'beautiful' and 'red' has become the
emblem of the regime and its favourite adjective. The coincidence between the words
'*bol'shak*' and Bolshevism – in both instances the source of authority – is self-evident.

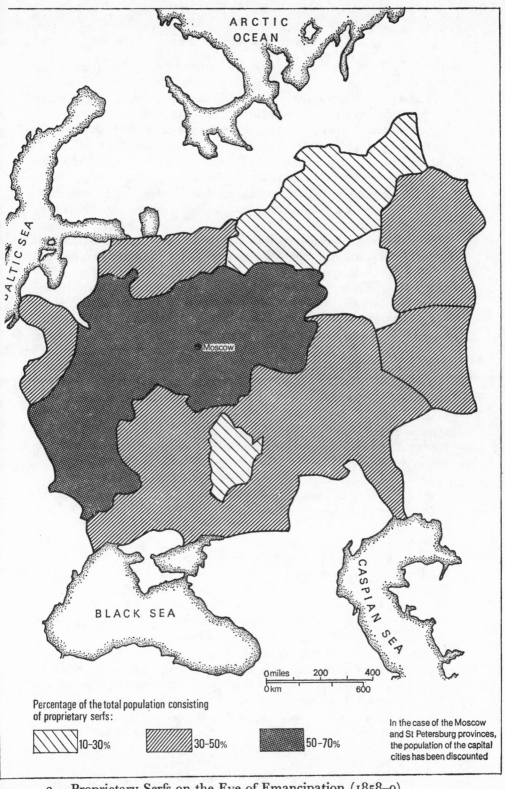

ARCTIC
OCEAN

BALTIC SEA

Moscow

BLACK SEA

CASPIAN SEA

0 miles   200   400
0 km   600

Percentage of the total population consisting
of proprietary serfs:

10–30%   30–50%   50–70%

In the case of the Moscow
and St Petersburg provinces,
the population of the capital
cities has been discounted

3.   Proprietary Serfs on the Eve of Emancipation (1858–9)

tered. In most of the borderlands, including Siberia, serfdom was unknown.

The state peasantry was made up of a variety of disparate groups. Its nucleus consisted of inhabitants of crown estates and the remnant of 'black peasants', the majority of whom the monarchy had distributed to its service personnel. Both these groups had been bound to the land in the second half of the sixteenth century. To them were added in the eighteenth century: peasants from secularized monastic and church holdings; sundry non-Russians, among them Tatars, Finnic peoples inhabiting central Russia, and the nomads of Siberia and central Asia; and individual farmers unattached to any of the regular estates, including *déclassé* dvoriane. Because they neither paid rent nor performed labour on behalf of landlords, state peasants were required to pay a higher soul tax than proprietary peasants. They were not allowed to leave their villages without authorization of officials. Otherwise they were quite free. They could inscribe themselves in the ranks of urban tradesmen by paying the required licence fee, and indeed from their ranks came a high proportion of Russia's merchants as well as manufacturers and industrial workers. Although they did not hold title to the land which they tilled, they disposed of it as if they did. Activity of peasant speculators moved the government in the middle of the eighteenth century to issue decrees severely limiting commerce in state land; it is doubtful, however, whether these had much effect. At this time, too, the authorities forced state peasants, who until then had held their land by households, to join communes. The bane of the state peasant's existence was the extorting official, against whom there was no recourse. It was to remedy this situation that Nicholas I instituted in the late 1830s a Ministry of State Domains charging it with the administration of state peasants. At this time, state peasants were given title to their land and allowed to form organs of self-government. From then on, they were, for all purposes, freemen.

Within the category of proprietary peasants, that is, serfs proper, a distinction must be made between peasants who fulfilled their obligations to the landlord exclusively or primarily by paying rent, and those who did so with labour services or corvée. The distribution of the two in large measure corresponds to the division between the forest zone in the north and the black earth belt in the south and south-east.

Until the beginning of the nineteenth century, when it shifted decisively to the black earth belt, the main area of agriculture in Russia lay in the central region of the taiga. It has been noted that the soil and the climate here are such that they normally allow the inhabitants to sustain life, but not to accumulate much surplus. It is for this reason that a large number of peasants in the forest zone, especially those living near Moscow, remained farmers in name only. They continued to be attached to the commune in which they were born and to pay the soul tax and their share of rent, but they no longer tilled the land. Such peasants roamed the country in search of income, working in factories or mines, hiring themselves out as labourers, or peddling. Many of the cab drivers and prostitutes in the cities, for example, were serfs who turned over part of their earnings to their landlords. Rent-paying serfs often formed co-operative associations called *arteli* (singular, *artel'*) which worked on contract for private clients and divided the profits among their members. There were numerous arteli of masons and carpenters. One of the most famous was an association of bank messengers whose members handled vast sums of money, with their organization's guarantee, apparently with utmost reliability. In the 1840s, in the north-eastern provinces of Russia between 25 and 32 per cent of all male peasants were regularly living away from their villages.[4] In some localities, the serfs leased their land to other serfs from neighbouring villages or to itinerant farmhands, and themselves went over to full-time manufacture. Thus there arose in the first half of the nineteenth century in northern Russia numerous villages where the entire serf population was engaged in the production of a great variety of commodities, headed by cotton fabrics, a branch of industry which serf manufacturers came virtually to monopolize.

Because agriculture in the north brought small returns, landlords here preferred to put their serfs on rent (*obrok*). Experience demonstrated that, left to their own devices, peasants knew best how to raise money; and rich peasants meant high rents. Masters of affluent serf merchants and serf manufacturers, of the kind we shall discuss in the chapter devoted to the middle class, imposed in the guise of rent a kind of private income tax which could run into thousands of rubles a year. On the eve of emancipation, 67.7 per cent of the proprietary serfs in seven central provinces were on obrok; here corvée tended to be confined to smaller estates with one hundred or fewer male serfs. The northern serf had more land at his disposal, because his soil being less productive the landlord was less interested in it. Unless very rich, the landlord here tended to turn over the estate to his serfs for a fixed rent and move into the city or enter state service. The average land allotment per male soul in the north was 11.6 acres, compared to 8.6 acres in the black earth belt.

In the south and south-east, proprietary peasants faced a different situation. Here the fertility of the soil encouraged landlords to settle down and take over the management of their estates. The process began in the second half of the eighteenth century, but it became pronounced only in the nineteenth. The more the northern landlords curtailed agriculture, the greater was the inducement to intensify it in the south, in so far as the northern provinces offered a growing market for food produce.

The inducement grew stronger yet with the opening of foreign markets. After Russia had decisively beaten the Ottoman Empire and established mastery over the northern shores of the Black Sea, Odessa and other warm-water ports were built from which grain could be shipped to western Europe. Once Britain repealed her Corn Laws (1846), the exports of wheat grown in the south of Russia rose sharply. The net result of these developments was a regional division of labour; in the 1850s, the black earth belt became Russia's granary, which produced 70 per cent of the country's cereals, while the northern provinces accounted for three-quarters of the country's manufactured goods.[5] Landlords in the south began now to rationalize their estates on the English and German model, introducing clover and turnip crops, and experimenting with scientific cattle-breeding. Such proprietors were less interested in rents than in human labour. In 1860, only 23 to 30 per cent of the serfs in the south were on rent: the rest, representing approximately two-thirds of the serf population, were on corvée (*barshchina*). Ideally, the land worked under corvée was divided in two halves, one of which the peasant tilled on behalf of the landlord, the other for himself. But the norm was not legally fixed. A great variety of alternatives was possible, including various combinations of rent and labour services. The most onerous form of corvée was *mesiachina* (p. 19 above).*

What was the condition of Russian serfs? This is one of those subjects about which it is better to know nothing than little. The idea of men owning men is so repugnant to modern man that he can hardly judge the matter dispassionately. The best guidance in such problems is that provided by John Clapham, a great economic historian, who stressed the importance of cultivating 'what might be called the statistical sense, the habit of asking in relation to any institution, policy, group or movement the questions: how large? how long? how often? how representative?'[6] The application of this standard to the social consequences of the Industrial Revolution has revealed that notwithstanding well-entrenched mythology, the Industrial Revolution from the beginning had improved the living standards of English workers. No such studies have as yet been carried out concerning living standards of Russian peasants. Enough is known, however, even now to cast doubts on the prevailing view of the serf and his condition.

To begin with, it must be stressed that a serf was not a slave and a pomestie was not a plantation. The mistake of confusing Russian serf-

* Because of the relative profitability of farming in the south it should come as no surprise that this area had a greater proportion of large farms than the north. In 1859, in four typical northern provinces (Vladimir, Tver, Iaroslavl and Kostroma) only 22 per cent of the serfs lived on properties of landlords who owned over a thousand serfs. In the black earth region (Voronezh, Kursk, Saratov and Kharkov) the corresponding figure was 37 per cent.

dom with slavery is at least two centuries old. While studying at the University of Leipzig in the 1770s, an impressionable young Russian gentleman, Alexander Radishchev, read Abbé Raynal's *Philosophical and Political History of the Settlements and Commerce of the Europeans in the Indies.* In the Eleventh Book of this work there is a harrowing description of slavery in the Caribbean which Radishchev connected with what he had seen in his native land. The allusions to serfdom in his *Journey from St Petersburg to Moscow* (1790) were among the first in which the analogy between serfdom and slavery was implicitly drawn by stressing those features (e.g. absence of marriage rights) which indeed were common to both. The abolitionist literature of the following decades, written by authors raised in the spirit of western culture, turned the analogy into a commonplace; and from there it entered the mainstream of Russian and western thought. But even when serfdom was in full bloom, the facile identification was rejected by keener observers. Having read Radishchev's book, Pushkin wrote a parody called *Journey from Moscow to St Petersburg* in which the following passage occurs:

Fonvizin, who [late in the eighteenth century] travelled in France, writes that in all conscience the condition of the Russian peasant seems to him more fortunate than that of the French farmer. I believe this to be true ...

Read the complaints of English factory workers; your hair will stand on end. How much repulsive oppression, incomprehensible sufferings! What cold barbarism on the one hand, and what appalling poverty on the other. You will think that we are speaking of the construction of the Egyptian pyramids, of Jews working under Egyptian lashes. Not at all: we are talking about the textiles of Mr Smith or the needles of Mr Jackson. And note that all this are not abuses, not crimes, but occurrences which take place within the strict limits of legality. It seems there is no creature in the world more unfortunate than the English worker ...

In Russia, there is nothing like it. Obligations are altogether not very onerous. The soul tax is paid by the mir; the corvée is set by law; the obrok is not ruinous (except in the neighbourhood of Moscow and St Petersburg, where the diversity of industry intensifies and stimulates the greed of owners). The landlord, having set the obrok, leaves it up to the peasant to get it whenever and by whatever means he chooses. The peasant engages in whatever enterprises he can think of and sometimes travels two thousand kilometres to earn money ... Violations are everywhere numerous; crimes are dreadful everywhere.

Take a look at the Russian peasant: is there a trace of slavish degradation in his behaviour and speech? Nothing need be said of his boldness and cleverness. His entrepreneurship is well known. His agility and dexterity are amazing. A traveller journeys from one end of Russia to the other, ignorant of a single word of Russian, and he is everywhere understood, everyone fulfils his requests and enters into agreements with him. You will never find among the Russian people that which the French call *un badaut* [an idler or loafer]: you will never see a Russian peasant show either crude amazement or ignorant contempt for what is foreign. In Russia there is not one man who does not have his *own* living quarters. A poor man who goes into the world leaves *his* izba. This does not exist in other countries. Everywhere in Europe to own a cow is a sign of luxury; in Russia not to have one is a sign of dreadful poverty.[7]

Even Pushkin's magisterial authority is no substitute for statistical evidence. But his judgement merits more than casual attention because he happened to have known the Russian village from firsthand experience and to have been endowed, in addition, with a very commonsensical outlook.

As Pushkin notes, unlike the slave of north or Central America, the Russian serf lived in his own house, not in slave quarters. He worked in the fields under the supervision of his father or elder brother, rarely under that of a hired steward. On many Russian estates, the land of the proprietor, cut into narrow strips, was intermingled with that of the peasants, creating a situation quite unlike that on a typical plantation. And most important of all, the product of the serf's labour was his own. Although, legally speaking, the serf had no right to hold property, in fact he did so throughout the existence of serfdom – a rare instance where the disregard for law prevalent in Russia benefited the poor.

The relationship of the landlord to the serf also differed from that of master to slave. The *pomeshchik* owed his authority over the serf in the first instance to his responsibilities as the state's fiscal and recruiting agent. In these capacities he could wield a great deal of arbitrary power, and in the reign of Catherine II his mastery over the serf indeed approximated to that of a slave owner. Still, he never had title to the serf; he owned only the land to which the serf was attached. In the Emancipation settlement, landlords received no compensation for their peasants. The law strictly forbade traffic in serfs. Some landlords did so anyway in defiance of the law, but basically the Russian serf had the assurance that if he so chose he could live out his days in his izba and in the midst of his family. The recruitment obligation introduced by Peter I was for the peasants such a calamity precisely because it violated this entrenched tradition, tearing away year after year thousands of young men from their families. The fact that immediately upon induction a recruit, his wife and children automatically received their liberty did not seem to make army service any more palatable. The peasants treated induction as a sentence of death.

As previously noted, nearly half of the serfs in the empire – roughly, a quarter in the south, and three-quarters in the north – were tenants on rent. These peasants were free to come and go, and to engage in any occupation they chose. Their lives were free of landlord interference. For them, serfdom meant essentially the payment of a tax, either fixed or adjusted to income, to dvoriane who happened to own the land to which they were ascribed. Whatever the morality of such a tax, it was not an institution related to slavery; rather, it was a 'feudal' relic.

Serfdom in any meaningful sense was confined to peasants who performed exclusively or mostly labour services, and especially to those who belonged to landlords with small or medium-sized estates inhabited by fewer than a thousand 'souls'. It may be roughly estimated that between seven and nine million of corvée-obligated peasants of both sexes were in the latter category. This group, representing in 1858–9, 12–15 per cent of the empire's population, were serfs in the classical sense of the word; bound to the land, subject to the direct authority of their landlords, forced to perform for him any services demanded.

It is, of course, quite impossible to attempt any generalizations about the condition of so large a group, the more so that we are dealing with some fifty thousand landlords (the approximate number of those who had peasants on corvée). Until more scholarly studies on the subject become available, all we can go by are impressions. These do not bear out the picture, derived largely from literary sources, of widespread misery and oppression. The obvious injustice of serfdom must not be allowed to colour one's perception of its realities. Several Englishmen who wrote accounts of their experiences in Russia found that the Russian peasant's condition compared favourably with what they knew at home, especially in Ireland, thereby confirming independently Pushkin's estimate. The following two excerpts come from such accounts. The first is by an English sea captain who in 1820 undertook a four-year journey on foot across Russia and Siberia which gave him unique opportunities to observe rural life at first-hand:

I have no hesitation ... in saying, that the condition of the peasantry here is far superior to that class in Ireland. In Russia, provisions are plentiful, good, and cheap; while in Ireland they are scanty, poor, and dear, the best part being exported from the latter country, whilst the local impediments in the other render them not worth that expense. Good comfortable log-houses are here found in every village, immense droves of cattle are scattered over an unlimited pasture, and whole forests of fuel may be obtained for a trifle. With ordinary industry and economy, the Russian peasant may become rich, especially those of the villages situated between the capitals.[8]

The second is by a British traveller who had gone to Russia for the express purpose of finding material which would cast on it a less favourable light than that found in the literature of the time:

On the whole ... so far at least as mere [!] food and lodging are concerned, the Russian peasant is not so badly off as the poor man amongst ourselves. He may be rude and uneducated – liable to be ill-treated by his superiors – intemperate in his habits, and filthy in his person; but he never knows the misery to which the Irish peasant is exposed. His food may be coarse; but he has abundance of it. His hut may be homely; but it is dry and warm. We are apt to fancy that if our peasantry be badly off, we can at least flatter ourselves with the assurance that they are much more comfortable than those of foreign countries. But this is a gross delusion. Not in Ireland only, but in parts of Great Britain usually considered to be exempt from the miseries of Ireland, we have witnessed wretchedness compared with which the condition of the Russian boor is luxury, whether he live amid the crowded population of large towns, or in the meanest hamlets of the interior. There are parts of Scotland, for instance, where the people are lodged in houses which the Russian peasant would not think fit for his cattle.[9]

The evaluation of these witnesses carries the more weight that they had no sympathy whatever with serfdom or any other of the disabilities under which the vast majority of Russian peasants were then living.

It is particularly important to be disabused concerning alleged landlord brutality toward serfs. Foreign travellers to Russia – unlike visitors to the slave plantations of the Americas – hardly ever mention corporal punishment.* The violence endemic to the twentieth century and the attendant 'liberation' of sexual fantasy encourage modern man to indulge his sadistic impulses by projecting them on to the past: but the fact that he longs to maltreat others has no bearing on what actually happened when that has been possible. Serfdom was an economic institution not a closed world created for the gratification of sexual appetites. Isolated instances of cruelty are no evidence to the contrary. It is simply not good enough to cite the notorious case of one Saltykova, a sadistic landlady immortalized by historians, who whiled away her idle hours by torturing to death dozens of her domestic servants. She tells us about as much about imperial Russia as does Jack the Ripper about Victorian London. Where statistics happen to be available they indicate moderation in the use of disciplinary prerogatives. Every landlord, for example, had the power to turn unruly peasants over to the authorities for exile to Siberia. Between 1822 and 1833, 1,283 serfs were punished in this fashion; an annual average of 107 out of over twenty million proprietary serfs is hardly a staggering figure.[10]

For the serfs, the most onerous feature of landlord authority seems to have been interference with their family life and working habits. Landlords were eager to have serfs marry young, both because they wanted them to breed, and wished to put to work young women, who were customarily exempt from corvée until after marriage. Many landlords

---

* Nor must it be forgotten that the Russian peasant did not share modern man's horror of this kind of punishment. When in the 1860s rural (*volost'*) courts were empowered to impose on peasants either monetary fines or physical punishment, it was found that most peasants, given the choice, preferred to suffer a beating.

compelled their serfs to marry as soon as they were of age, if not earlier, and sometimes even chose partners for them. Sexual licence was not uncommon; there are enough authenticated stories of landlords who staffed regular harems with serf girls. All of this the peasants deeply resented, and on occasion repaid with arson and murder. Landlord interference with the peasant's working routine was an even greater cause of discontent. The intention did not matter: a well-meaning landlord, eager, at his own expense, to improve the lot of his peasants was as disliked as a ruthless exploiter. 'It is enough for a landlord to order that the soil be ploughed one inch more deeply', Haxthausen reports, 'to hear the peasant mutter: "He is not a good master; he torments us." And then woe to him if he lives in the village!'[11] Indeed, a solicitous landlord, because he tended to meddle more with the working routine of his serfs, was often more despised than his callous neighbour whose only care was for higher rents.

The impression one gains is that the serf accepted his status with the same fatalism with which he bore the other burdens of peasant existence. He was grudgingly prepared to set aside a part of his working time and of his income as tribute to the landlord because that was what his ancestors had always done. He also bore patiently his landlord's eccentricities, provided they did not touch what mattered to him the most: his family and his work. His principal grievance had to do with land. He was deeply convinced that all the land – arable, meadow, forest – was rightfully his. From the earliest times of colonization, the peasant carried away the belief that virgin land belonged to no one and that cultivated land was the property of him who cleared and tilled it. This conviction was strengthened after 1762, when dvoriane were freed from compulsory state service. The serfs understood in some instinctive way the connection between the dvorianstvo's service obligations and their own servitude. Word spread in the villages that at the same time that he had issued the Manifesto of dvorianstvo's liberties in 1762, Peter III had issued another edict turning the land over to the peasants, but the dvoriane had suppressed it and thrown him into jail. From that year onwards the peasants lived in the expectation of a grand 'black repartition' of the country's entire private landholdings, and nothing would persuade them they were wrong. To make matters worse, the Russian serf had got into his head the totally mistaken notion that while he belonged to the landlord, the land – all of it – was his, whereas in fact neither happened to be true. This belief intensified tension in the countryside. Incidentally, it suggests that the peasant had no strong feelings against serfdom as such.

This de-emphasis of brutality and insistence on distinguishing serfdom from slavery is not intended to exonerate serfdom; it is merely meant to shift attention from its imaginary to its real evils. It was unquestionably a dreadful institution, a disease whose scars Russia bears to this day. A survivor of Nazi concentration camps said of life there that it was not as bad as commonly believed and yet infinitely worse, by which he must have meant that the physical horrors meant less than the cumulative effect of daily dehumanization. *Mutatis mutandis*, and without drawing invidious comparisons between concentration camps and the Russian village under serfdom, we can say the same principle applies to the latter as well. Something fatal attends man's mastery over man, even when benevolently exercised, something which slowly poisons master and victim, and in the end disintegrates the society in which they live. We shall deal with the effects of serfdom on the landlords in the next chapter, and here concentrate on the influence it had on the peasant, especially on his attitude towards authority.

There exists broad agreement among contemporary observers that the worst feature of Russian serfdom was not the abuse of authority but its inherent arbitrariness, that is, the serf's permanent subjection to the unbridled will of other men. Robert Bremner, who in the passage cited above compared favourably the living standards of Russian peasants with those in Ireland and Scotland (pp. 151–2), goes on to say:

> Let it not be supposed, however, that, because we admit the Russian peasant to be in many respects more comfortable than some of our own, we therefore consider his lot as, on the whole, more enviable than that of the peasant in a free country like ours. The distance between them is wide – immeasurable; but it can be accounted for in one single word – *the British peasant has rights; the Russian has none!* [12]

In this respect the lot of the state peasant was not much different from that of a serf, at any rate until 1837 when he was placed in the charge of a special ministry (p. 70). Russian peasants did enjoy a great variety of customary rights. Although generally respected, they had no legally binding force which meant they could be violated with impunity. Prohibited from lodging complaints against landlords and indeed forbidden to appear in court, the peasant was completely defenceless *vis-à-vis* anyone in authority. Landlords, as we happen to know, made exceedingly rare use of their right to exile serfs to Siberia; but the mere fact that they could do so must have served as a very effective deterrent. This was only one of many manifestations of arbitrariness to which the serf was subjected. In the 1840s and 1850s, for example, anticipating emancipation, and hoping to reduce the number of peasants working in the fields so as to have fewer of them to share the land with, landlords quietly transferred to their manors to work as domestics over half a million serfs.

1 'Take a look at the Russian peasant: is there a trace of slavish degradation in his behaviour and speech?' (Pushkin): Russian peasants from the Orel region, second half of the nineteenth century.

2 (below) A clearing in the *taiga*.

3 (opposite) The construction of a peasant hut or *izba*.
The hatchet is the only tool used.

4 (above) A village in central Russia around 1800.

5 (below) A village council, *c.* 1800.

6 (above) The exterior of an *izba*.

7 (below) An *izba* interior. In the rear, on the right, is the oven on which the family slept. The peasants are wearing *lapti*, the bast-shoes of home manufacture. Left rear, the Beautiful Corner with its icons.

8 A Russian village around 1870.

9/10 Russian peasant women in the reign of Catherine II (1782).

11 Holiday merrymaking in a village. On the right, a story-teller; on the left a band of revellers returning from a *kabak*.

12 Inside a village tavern or *kabak*: a bag-pipe player sounds off, the inn-keeper toasts his customers.

ПЕСНЯ

13 A popular print from the nineteenth century, titled 'Song'.

14 A serf Horn Orchestra; each horn sounded only one note.

15 A serf kowtowing to a dvorianin (1789).

16/17 Punishments: (above) a serf punished with rods *(batogi)* while the landlord and his family look on; (below) a serf girl punished with birches *(rozgi)*.

18 Market selling frozen meat, frequented mostly by the poorer urban people (*c.* 1800).

19 A shopkeeper using his abacus (1838).

20 (opposite) An itinerant ikon pedlar.

21 (above) Pedlars of live fish and caviar.

22/23 Peasant amusements: (top) *gorodki*, a game related to skittles; (bottom) holiday clowning.

24 The Great Embassy of Ivan IV in 1576 to the Holy Roman Emperor at Regensburg.
In front, the five Legates, dressed in up-to-date Persian outfits; behind them, men carrying
sables, presents for the Emperor.

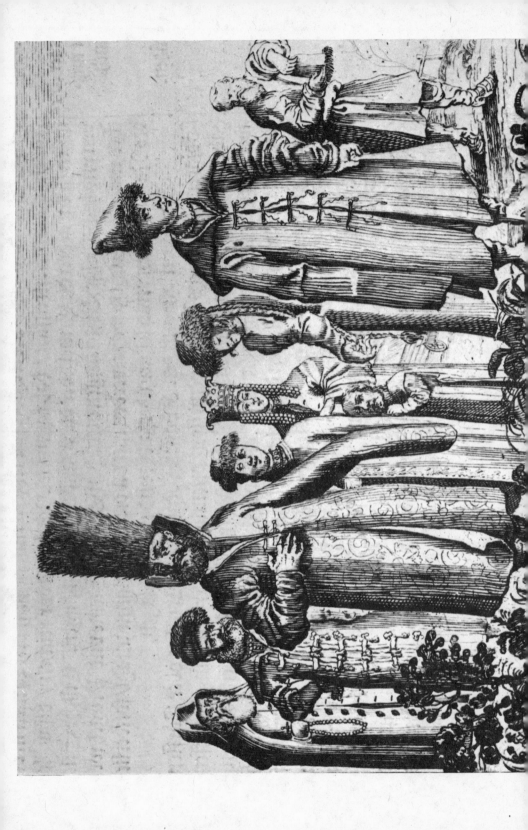

25 (top) Russian boyars in the middle of the seventeenth century; the dress indicates Polish influence.
26 (bottom) The residence of a dvorianin in Moscow (*c.* 1790).

Occa fluu

fluu

27 (opposite) Nizhnii Novgorod in the seventeenth century; the *posad* is inside the walls, towards the river, the *sloboda* outside them. In the upper part of the picture are the churches and fortifications of the *gorod*.

28 (below) A Russian city of the seventeenth century, composed of identical, closely clustered *izby*.

29 The banks of the Moscow River near the Kremlin in the 1790s (the white house on the left is the same as that seen in Plate 26). Although in the centre of tsarist Russia's most populous city, the scene is quite rural in character.

30 The city of Kazan in the middle of the nineteenth century.

31/32 A Russian merchant and
a merchant's wife, around 1800.

33 A group of stolid merchants sipping tea oriental fashion at the annual Nizhnii
Novgorod fair, 1905.

34 (top) A merchant family, first half of the nineteenth century. The lady is a progenitor of the wives of Soviet notables.

35 (bottom) Evening amusements at the Nizhnii Novgorod fair, where each summer East met West.

36 City amusements: swings *(kacheli)* erected at Easter time; to the left a *balaganshchik* or clown show. In the lower right, the revellers from Plate 11, somewhat reduced in number, seem to have made their way to the city.

37 City amusements: 'mountains of ice' often built in the flat lands around big cities for sledding.

38 City amusements: kicking the ball, a favourite pastime of cabbies waiting for fares (1798).

39 City amusements: more Easter fun.

40 (opposite) The Saturday bath, a democratic institution for all ages and classes.
41 (above) Russian religious services performed by the 1576 Embassy to Regensburg
(see Plate 24).

42 A Patriarch (Nikon).

43 A Parish Priest *(pop)*.

44/45 (above) 'Black' priests
(monks).
46 (opposite) An Old Believer.

47 An audience of Western ambassadors by the Tsar and Boyar Council in the Kremlin, mid-seventeenth century.

48/49 Bureaucratic types based on Gogol's *Dead Souls*: clerks.

50/51 Bureaucratic types based on Gogol's *Dead Souls*: (above) Director of the Chancery; (below) The Governor *(Nachal'nik)* himself.

52 The evolution of the seal of Novgorod the Great in the hands of Muscovite designers: the original fifteenth-century seal of the independent city-state (upper left) showing the steps of the *veche* tribune and the symbol of sovereignty, is gradually transformed until in the seventeenth century the steps have become the tsarist throne, and the symbol of sovereignty, the tsarist sceptre.

There was no recourse against such measures. Nor could anything be done to thwart well-meaning pomeshchiks who forced peasants to use unfamiliar farm machinery imported from abroad or to alter their routine of crop rotation. When the government of Nicholas I, for the best of reasons, compelled some state peasants to set aside a part of their land for potatoes, they rebelled. From the peasant's viewpoint the master's motives were immaterial; good and bad intention alike appeared as an external will acting upon him. Unable to distinguish between the two he often repaid his would-be benefactors in a most cruel fashion.

Totally lacking in legally recognized personal rights, the peasant regarded all authority as by its very nature alien and hostile. He complied when confronted with superior strength, especially if it was applied decisively. But in his mind he never acknowledged the right of someone outside his village community to tell him what to do.

Rural violence was actually much less prevalent in imperial Russia than it is generally thought. Compared to most twentieth-century societies, the Russian countryside of the imperial age was an oasis of law and order. It is, of course, an easy thing to compute statistics of rural 'disturbances' and on this basis to argue a steady rise in violence. The trouble, however, lies with definitions. In imperial Russia any formal complaint against his peasants lodged by a landlord was classified by the authorities as a 'disturbance' (*volnenie*) whether it actually occurred or not, and without regard to the nature of the offence: refusal to obey an order, idleness, drunkenness, theft, arson, manslaughter and premeditated murder were indiscriminately lumped together. A catalogue of such occurrences resembles a police blotter and has about as much value in the computation of criminal statistics. As a matter of fact, the majority of the so-called peasant 'disturbances' involved not acts of violence but of ordinary insubordination (*nepovinovenie*).[13] They performed the same function as do strikes in modern industrial societies and are equally unreliable as a gauge of social instability or political discontent.

Approximately once a century, Russian peasants went on a rampage, killing landlords and officials, burning estates and seizing properties. The first great jacquerie occurred in the 1670s under the leadership of Stepan (or Stenka) Razin, the second a century later (1773–5) under Emelian Pugachev. Both had their beginning on the periphery of the state, in land inhabited by Cossacks, and they spread like wildfire owing to the very weak administration in the provinces. There were no major peasant uprisings in nineteenth-century Russia, but two occurred in close succession in the twentieth, one in 1905, the second in 1917. A common quality of these major rebellions, as well as of the more localized ones, was the absence of political aims. Russian peasants never revolted against tsarist authority: indeed, both Razin and Pugachev claimed to have been the true tsars come to reclaim their throne from usurpers. Their hatred was directed against the agents of autocracy, those two classes which, under the dyarchic arrangement then in effect, exploited the country for their private benefit. From his intimate knowledge of the peasant, Leo Tolstoy foresaw that the muzhik would not support moves to subvert the autocratic system. 'The Russian revolution', he noted in his diary in 1865, 'will be directed not against the tsar and despotism, but against the ownership of land.'

Desperately violent as he could be on occasions, in daily life the serf tended rather to employ non-violent means to have his way. He elevated the art of lying to great heights. When he did not want to do something, he played stupid; when found out, he feigned contrition. 'The peasants show the landlord almost in all circumstances of life the darkest side of their nature', complained Iurii Samarin, a Slavophile expert on rural conditions. 'In the presence of his master, the intelligent peasant assumes the pose of a clown, the truthful one lies right to his face, untroubled by conscience, the honest one robs him, and all three call him "father".'[14] This behaviour towards his betters contrasted vividly with the peasant's honesty and decency when dealing with equals. Dissimulation was not so much part of peasant character as a weapon against those from whom he had no other defence.

The authority of other men, onerous as it was, was not the only force constraining the peasant and frustrating his will. There was also the tyranny of nature on which he was so dependent – that which the novelist Gleb Uspenskii called the 'the power of the earth'. The earth held the peasant in its grip, sometimes giving, sometimes withholding, for ever mysterious and capricious. He fled it as eagerly as he fled the landlord and the official, turning to peddling, handicrafts, casual labour in the cities or any other work that would free him from the drudgery of field work. There is no evidence that the Russian peasant loved the soil; this sentiment is to be found mainly in the imagination of gentry romantics who visited their estates in the summertime.

If one considers the vice in which the peasant was held by the arbitrary will of his master and the only slightly less arbitrary will of nature – forces which he understood little and over which he had no control – it is not surprising that his fondest wish was to be totally, irresponsibly free. His word for this ideal condition was *volia*, a word meaning 'having one's way'. To have volia meant to enjoy licence: to revel, to carouse, to set things on fire. It was a thoroughly destructive concept, an act of revenge on the forces that for ever frustrated him. The literary critic Vissarion Belinskii, a commoner by origin who knew the muzhik better than his genteel friends, put the matter bluntly when he disputed their dream of a democratic Russia:

Our people understand freedom as volia, and volia for it means to make mischief. The liberated Russian nation would not head for the parliament but it would run for the tavern to drink liquor, smash glasses, and hang the dvoriane who shave their beards and wear a frock-coat instead of a *zipun*.[15]

Indeed, the handiest means of escape was drink. The Russian Primary Chronicle, in its account of Russia's conversion to Christianity, explains the Kievan princes' rejection of Islam by its prohibition of alcohol. *Rusi est' vesele piti, ne mozhet bez nego byti* – 'Russians are merrier drinking – without it, they cannot live' – Prince Vladimir of Kiev is said to have told the Muslim delegates who had come to win him over. The story is, of course, apocryphal, but it canonizes, as it were, drinking as a national pastime. Until the sixteenth century Russians drank mead and fruit wines. Then they learned from the Tatars the art of distillation. By the middle of the seventeenth century drunkenness was so serious a problem that Patriarch Nikon and his party of church reformers sought to enforce total prohibition. Russians did not take vodka regularly, in small doses, but alternated between abstinence and wild abandon. Once a Russian peasant headed for the tavern – a government licensed shop called *kabak*, which dispensed no food – he liked to consume several glasses of vodka in rapid succession in order to sink as quickly as possible into an alcoholic stupor known as *zapoi*. A saying had it that a proper binge required three days: one to drink, a second to be drunk, and a third to sober up. Easter was the high point. At that time Russian villages, emerging from the long winter and about to begin the arduous cycle of field work, lay prostrate in a fog of alcoholic vapours. Attempts to combat drinking always ran into snags, because the government derived an important share of its income from the sale of spirits and therefore had a vested interest in their consumption. At the end of the nineteenth century, this source was the largest single item of revenue in the imperial budget.

The peasant of old regime Russia had what the older generation of anthropologists like Levy-Bruhl used to call a 'primitive mind', an outstanding quality of which is an inability to think abstractly. The peasant thought concretely and in personal terms. For example, he had great difficulty understanding 'distance', unless it was translated into so many units of *versta*, the Russian counterpart of a kilometre, the length of which he could visualize. Similarly with time, which he could perceive only in terms of specific activity. 'State', 'society', 'nation', 'economy', 'agriculture', all these concepts had to be filled with people they knew or activities they performed in order to be grasped.

This quality accounts for the charm of the muzhik when on his best behaviour. He approached other people free of national, religious or any other prejudice. Of his spontaneous kindness toward strangers there are innumerable testimonies. Peasants showered with gifts exiles *en route* to Siberia, not from any sympathy for their cause, but because they regarded them as *neshchastnye* – unfortunates. In the Second World War, Nazi soldiers who had come to conquer and kill met with similar acts of charity once they had been made prisoners. In this un-abstract, instinctive human decency lay the reason why radical agitators met with such resistance when they tried to incite peasants to 'class war'. Even during the revolutions of 1905 and 1917 rural violence directed itself against specific objectives: to wreak vengeance on a particular landlord, to seize a coveted plot of land, to cut down a forest. It did not aim against the 'system' as a whole, because the peasant had no inkling of its existence.

But this particular aspect of the peasant mind also had its detrimental side. Among the abstractions the peasant could not comprehend was law, which he tended to confound with custom or common sense. He did not understand due process. Russian customary law, enforced by village communities, recognized the accused person's confession as the most satisfactory proof of guilt. In the rural (*volost'*) courts established in the 1860s to deal with civil offences and run by the peasants themselves, in the majority of cases confession was the only evidence submitted.[16] Similarly, the peasant had great difficulty comprehending 'property', confusing it with usage or possession. To him, an absentee landlord had no rightful claim on the land or its product. The peasant would readily appropriate an object which he felt the legal owner had no need of (e.g. firewood from the landlord's forest), yet, at the same time reveal a very keen sense of ownership where land, livestock or agricultural implements of other peasants was concerned because these were required to make a living. The legal profession created by the Court Reform of 1864 was regarded by peasants as only another breed of corrupt officials: for did not lawyers take money to get people out of trouble with judges? Impatience with forms and procedures and inability to understand abstract principles, whether of law or government, made the peasant ill-suited for any political system except an authoritarian or anarchistic one.

The Russian peasant shared with other primitive men a weakly developed sense of personal identity. Private likes and dislikes, private ambition, private conscience, tended to be submerged in family and community – at any rate, until he obtained an opportunity to make money on a large scale at which point acquisitive instincts came to the surface in their crassest form. *Mir* – the village commune – meant also 'the world'. The community restrained the unsocial impulses of the muzhik: the collective was superior to its individual members. Khomiakov once said that 'a Russian, taken individually will not get into heaven, but there is no way of keeping out an entire village'.[17] But then the ties binding the inhabitants of a village and socializing them were intensely personal. The outside world was perceived through very clouded glasses as something distant, alien and largely irrelevant. It consisted of two parts: one, the vast, holy community of the Orthodox, and the other, the realm of foreigners, who were divided into Orientals (*Busurmane*) and Occidentals (*Nemtsy*). If foreign residents can be trusted many Russian peasants as recently as the nineteenth century did not know and would not believe that there were in the world other nations and other monarchs than their own.

The peasant was very conscious of the difference between equals and superiors. Everyone not in authority, he addressed as *brat* (brother); those in authority he called *otets* (father) or, more familiarly, *butiushka*. His manner toward equals was surprisingly ceremonious. Travellers to Russia were struck by the elaborate manner in which peasants greeted one another, bowing politely and tipping their hats. One of them says that in *politesse* they yielded nothing to Parisians promenading on the Boulevard des Italiens. To superiors, they either kowtowed (a habit acquired under the Mongols) or made a deep bow (Plate 15). Foreigners also commented on the peasant's gay disposition, readiness to mimic or break into song and his peaceful disposition: even drunk he rarely came to blows.

But when one turns from these descriptions to peasant proverbs one is shocked to find neither wisdom nor charity. They reveal crude cynicism and complete absence of social sense. The ethic of these proverbs is brutally simple: look out for yourself and don't bother about the others: 'Another's tears are water.' The socialist-revolutionaries who in the 1870s 'went to the people' to awaken in them a sense of indignation at injustice learned to their dismay that the peasant saw nothing wrong with exploitation as such; he merely wanted to be the exploiter instead of the object of exploitation. A leading agricultural expert, who had spent many years working among peasants, sadly concluded that at heart the Russian peasant was a kulak, that is, a rural speculator and usurer:

> The ideals of the *kulak* reign among the peasantry; every peasant is proud to be the pike who gobbles up the carp. Every peasant, if circumstances permit, will, in the most exemplary fashion, exploit every other. Whether his object is a peasant or a noble, he will squeeze the blood out of him to exploit his need.[18]

And this is what Maxim Gorky had to say on the subject:

> In my youth [during the 1880s–90s], I eagerly looked in the villages of Russia for [the good-natured, thoughtful Russian peasant, the tireless seeker after truth and justice which Russian literature of the nineteenth century had so convincingly and beautifully described to the world]. I looked for him and

failed to find him. I found in the villages a stern realist and a man of cunning who – when it suits him – knows very well how to appear a simpleton ... He knows that the 'peasant is no fool, but the world is dumb', and that 'the world is strong like water, and stupid like a pig.' He says 'Fear not devils, fear people', 'Beat your own people and others will fear you.' He holds a rather low opinion of truth: 'Truth won't feed you', 'What matter if it's a lie as long as you've got enough to eat', 'An honest man, like a fool, is also harmful'.[19]

Allowing for the fact that by the end of the nineteenth century, when Gorky was on his quest, the peasant was demoralized by economic difficulties, the fact remains that even before Emancipation had compounded his problems he displayed many of the characteristics with which Gorky credits him. Grigorovich's novels of peasant life brought out in the 1840s and Dal's collection of peasant proverbs, published in 1862, present an unattractive picture by any standard.

One possible resolution of the contradiction between these two images is to assume that the peasant had a very different attitude towards those with whom he had personal dealings and those with whom his relations were, so to say, 'functional'. The 'others' whose tears did not matter, who were stupid, who could be lied to and beaten, were outside his family, village or personal contact. But since they were precisely those who made up 'society' and 'state', the breach of the walls isolating the small peasant *mir* from the large *mir* – the world – an event which occurred in the nineteenth and twentieth centuries, left the peasant utterly bewildered and at a loss what to do. He was ill-prepared to enter into decent *im*personal relations, and, when compelled to do so, revealed promptly his worst, most rapacious characteristics.

In his religious life, the peasant displayed a great deal of external devotion. He crossed himself continually, attended regularly the long church services, observed the fasts. He did all this from a conviction that scrupulous observance of church rituals – fasts, sacraments, and the constant making of the cross – would save his soul. But he seems to have had very little if any understanding of the spiritual meaning of religion or of religion as a way of life. He did not know the Bible or even the Lord's Prayer. He had nothing but contempt for the village priest or *pop*. His attachment to Christianity was on the whole superficial, resting primarily on the need for formulas and rituals with which to gain access to the nether world. It is difficult to quarrel with Belinskii's judgement as made in his famous Open Letter to Gogol:

According to you the Russian people is the most religious in the world. That is a lie! The basis of religiousness is pietism, reverence, fear of God, whereas the Russian man utters the name of the Lord while scratching himself somewhere. He says of the icon: If it isn't good for praying it's good for covering the pots.

Take a closer look and you will see that it is by nature a profoundly atheistic people. It still retains a good deal of superstition, but not a trace of religiousness. Superstition passes with the advances of civilisation, but religiousness often keeps company with them too; we have a living example of this in France, where even today there are many sincere Catholics among enlightened and educated men, and where many people who have rejected Christianity still cling stubbornly to some sort of god. The Russian people is different; mystic exaltation is not in its nature; it has too much common sense, a too lucid and positive mind, and therein, perhaps, lies the vastness of its historic destinies in the future. Religiousness has not even taken root among the clergy in it, since a few isolated and exceptional personalities distinguished for such cold ascetic contemplation prove nothing. But the majority of our clergy has always been distinguished for their fat bellies, scholastic pedantry, and savage ignorance. It is a shame to accuse it of religious intolerance and fanaticism; instead it could be praised for exemplary indifference in matters of faith. Religiosity among us appeared only in the schismatic sects who formed such a contrast in spirit to the mass of the people and who were numerically so insignificant in comparison with it.[20]

How superficial a hold Orthodoxy exercised over the masses is evidenced by the relative ease with which the communist regime succeeded in uprooting Christianity in the heartland of Russia and replacing it with an ersatz cult of its own. The job proved much more difficult to accomplish among Catholics, Muslims and Orthodox Dissenters.

The true religion of the Russian peasantry was fatalism. The peasant rarely credited any event, especially a misfortune, to his own volition. It was 'God's will', even where responsibility could clearly be laid at his own doorstep, e.g. when carelessness caused a fire or the death of an animal. Russian proverbs are full of fatalistic sentiments. When, towards the end of the nineteenth century, the muzhik began to be acquainted with the Bible, he first learned the passages stressing humility and passive acceptance of one's fate.

Finally, as concerns politics. The Russian peasant was undoubtedly a 'monarchist' in the sense that he could conceive of no source of worldly authority other than that emanating from the tsar. He regarded the tsar as God's vicar on earth, a bolshak of all Russia, created by the Lord to give him orders and to take care of him. He gave the tsar credit for all that was good and blamed whatever went wrong either on God's will or on the landlords and officials. He believed the tsar knew him personally and that if he were to knock on the door of the Winter Palace he would be warmly received and his complaints not only heard but understood in their smallest detail. It is because of this patriarchal outlook that the muzhik felt a familiarity towards his sovereign which would have been completely out of place in western Europe. De Segur on his travels in Russia with Catherine the Great observed with surprise the unaffected manner which simple country people adopted when speaking to their empress.

A powerful factor in the peasant's monarchist sentiments was the firm belief that the tsar wished them to have all the land, that his desire was frustrated by the landlords, but that some day he would overcome this resistance. Serf emancipation of 1861 transformed this belief into firm conviction. The socialist-revolutionary propagandists of the 1870s were driven to desperation by the peasants' unshakeable faith that the 'tsar will give' (*tsar' dast*).[21]

Hence the chaos which enveloped Russia after the sudden abdication of Nicholas II; hence, too, Lenin's haste to have the tsar and his family murdered once communist authority seemed endangered and Nicholas could have served as a rallying-point for the opposition; hence the constant efforts of the communist regime to fill the vacuum which the demise of the imperial dynasty had created in the minds of the masses by mammoth state-sponsored cults of party leaders.

The imperial government attached great importance to the monarchist sentiments of the peasantry, and many of its policies, such as hesitation to industrialize or to build railroads and indifference to mass education, were inspired by the wish to keep the muzhik exactly as he was, simple and loyal. Belief in the monarchist loyalties of the peasant was one of the cornerstones of imperial policy in the nineteenth century. Correct up to a point, the government misconstrued the peasant's attitude. The peasant's loyalty was a personal loyalty to the idealized image of a distant ruler whom he saw as his terrestrial father and protector. It was not loyalty to the institution of the monarchy as such, and certainly not to its agents, whether dvoriane or chinovniki. The peasant had no reason whatever to feel attachment to the state, which took from him with both hands and gave nothing in return. To the peasant, authority was at best a fact of life which one had to bear like disease, old age, or death, but which could never be 'good' and whose clutches one had every right to escape whenever given a chance. Loyalty to the tsar entailed no acceptance of civic responsibility of any kind, and indeed concealed a profound revulsion against political institutions and processes. The personalization of all human relations, so characteristic of the Russian peasant, produced a superficial monarchism which appeared conservative but was in fact thoroughly anarchist.

Beginning with the latter part of the eighteenth century it was becoming apparent to an increasing number of Russians that serfdom was not compatible with Russia's claim to being either a civilized country or a great power. Both Alexander I and Nicholas I had serious reservations about this institution, and so did their leading counsellors. Public opinion, nationalist-conservative and liberal-radical alike, turned hostile to serfdom. Indeed, serfdom had no genuine arguments in its favour: the best case that could be made for it held that after centuries of bondage the muzhik was as yet unprepared for the responsibilities of freedom and therefore that it would be best if it were given to him later rather than sooner. If, these growing abolitionist sentiments notwithstanding, serfdom was not done away with until 1861 the principal reason must be sought in the monarchy's fear of antagonizing the 100,000 serf-owning dvoriane on whom it relied to staff the chief offices, command the armed forces and maintain order in the countryside. Within the narrow limits open to it, however, the government did what it would to reduce the number of serfs and to improve their condition. Alexander forswore to hand out any more state or crown peasants to private persons. He also introduced procedures by which Russian landlords could carry out private emancipations, and authorized the liberation (without land) of the serfs belonging to the German barons in Livonia. The cumulative effect of these measures was gradually to reduce the proportion of serfs in the empire's population from 45–50 per cent at the close of the eighteenth century, to 37·7 per cent in 1858. Serfdom was clearly on the wane.

The decision to proceed with emancipation, come what may, was taken very soon after the accession of Alexander II. It was carried out in the teeth of strong resistance of the landowning class and in disregard of formidable administrative obstacles. Scholars had once believed that the step was taken largely on economic grounds, namely as a result of a crisis in the serf economy. This belief, however, does not appear well grounded. There is no evidence that economic considerations were uppermost in the government's mind when it took the decision to proceed with emancipation. But even had they been, it is questionable whether improvements in rural productivity required the liberation of serfs and the replacement of bonded with hired labour. The decades immediately preceding emancipation were a period of the most efficient utilization of serf labour because landlords, freed from compulsory state service, devoted more attention to rationalizing their rural economies to serve the expanding Russian and foreign markets. In his pioneering historical studies, Peter Struve has shown that serfdom attained the very peak of economic efficiency on the eve of its abolition.[22]

It is much more plausible that the decisive factors behind the government's decision were political. Until Russia's humiliating defeat in the Crimean war it had been widely believed, even by persons unfriendly to the absolute monarchy, that at the very least it assured the empire of internal stability and external power. Internal stability remained as yet unchallenged, although the probability of another Pugachev uprising occurring if serfdom survived did not escape the new emperor. But the myth of autocratic Russia's military might was irreparably shattered once the empire proved itself unable to defend its territory from the armies of the 'corrupt' liberal states. In the crisis of self-confidence which followed the defeat, all institutions came under critical scrutiny, serfdom most of all: 'At the head of current domestic problems which we must tackle stands – as a portent for the future and as an obstacle which precludes at the present time a substantial improvement of anything whatever – the question of serfdom'. Samarin wrote during the Crimean War, 'From whatever end our internal reconstruction should begin we will inevitably confront this issue'.[23] Human bondage now appeared as a ballast around Russia's neck, a weight which dragged it down into an abyss: on this there was wide agreement, which only those unable to see beyond their immediate personal interests did not share.

Russian serfdom as it developed historically consisted of two disparate elements: the authority of the landlord over the serf, and the serf's attachment to the land. The Emancipation Edict, issued after prolonged deliberations of 19 February 1861, immediately abrogated the landlord's authority. The one-time serf now became a legal person allowed to own property, to sue in court and to participate in elections to local self-government boards. Traces of his previous inferior status, however, remained. In many crimes of a civil nature he came under the jurisdiction of special rural courts operating according to customary law which could impose corporal punishment. He continued to pay the soul tax from which the other estates were exempt; and he was required to petition his commune every time he wished to absent himself for a longer period of time.*

The government approached the second ingredient of serfdom, attachment to the land, very gingerly. In this respect the peasant became fully free only half a century later. The reasons for keeping the peasant bound to the land were partly political, partly fiscal. The authorities knew how ready the Russian peasant was to abandon the soil and roam the country in search of easier and more remunerative work. It feared that an uncontrolled mass movement of the peasantry would provoke social unrest and make it impossible to collect taxes. In the final settlement, therefore, the government attached the peasant to the community which, in addition to its traditional powers (e.g. the right to repartition land strips) acquired some of the authority previously enjoyed by the landlord. The commune was retained where it had already existed and introduced where it had been unknown.

The authorities resolved early that upon his emancipation the ex-serf would receive an adequate land allotment to support himself and his

---

* This disability survives in the USSR, where kolkhoz members are not issued regular internal passports and cannot move away without authorization.

family. After hard bargaining with representatives of landed interests, minimum and maximum norms were set for the various regions of the country: landlords whose peasants tilled on their own behalf land in excess of the maximum norms could request to have it reduced; where the allotment fell below the minimum norm, they had to increase it. In the end, Russia's landlords retained approximately two-thirds of the land, including most of the pasture and woodland; the rest was distributed among the one-time proprietary peasants. Because in the eyes of the law both parts were property of the landlord, the peasants had to pay for their share. The government advanced to the landlords on the peasants' behalf 80 per cent of the price of the land, as determined by assessors, which the peasants had to repay over a period of forty-nine years in the form of 'Redemption Payments'. The remaining 20 per cent of the purchase price the peasant paid the landlord directly: in money if he had it, in services if he did not. To assure that the 'Redemption Payments' were accurately delivered the government entrusted the property title to the peasant allotment to the commune rather than to the individual household.*

The Act of 19 February 1861 placed the peasant in an ambivalent situation. He was freed from the detested authority of the landlord; thus the single worst feature of serfdom was done away with. But at the same time, he remained in many respects separated from the rest of the population and continued to be attached to the land.

At the time of its promulgation, the Emancipation settlement appeared a success. Only a small group of radical critics found fault with it on the grounds that all the soil should have been turned over to the peasants and that they should not have been required to pay for their allotments. The Emperor of Russia achieved with one stroke of his pen the abolition of bondage which took the President of the United States four years of civil war. In retrospect, the achievement appears less impressive. In fact, after 1861 the economic situation of the Russian peasant deteriorated, and in 1900 he was, by and large, worse off than he had been in 1800. For the rural population, especially in the black earth belt, the second half of the nineteenth century turned out to be a period of progressive decline and demoralization. The crisis had several causes, some traceable to human error, some to factors beyond human control.

To begin with, the imposition of Redemption Payments on one-time serfs on top of their regular taxes placed on them unrealistic burdens. The peasants had extreme difficulty meeting their new fiscal obligations, especially in the areas where corvée had been the traditional method of paying rent and there were few opportunities for making money. To

---

* The Emancipation Edict left it up to the ex-serf to decide whether or not he wished to buy his share of land. Purchase became obligatory only in 1883.

lease or buy more land, they borrowed money, first at exorbitant rates from village usurers, and later, at more advantageous ones, from the Peasant Bank. This indebtedness, on top of their current obligations, caused them to fall into arrears. In 1881 the government reduced by a quarter the moneys due under the Emancipation settlement, but this measure did not suffice. In 1907 bowing to the inevitable, it abolished the Redemption Payments altogether and cancelled arrears. But the harm had been done. The radical critics of the settlement who had argued the land should have been given the peasants free of charge appear in retrospect to have been right not only on moral but also on practical grounds.

The retention of the commune also seems to have been a mistake although it is more difficult to see how that one could have been avoided, because the peasants cleaved to it. The commune inhibited the emergence in Russia of a vigorous farming class, in so far as the hard-working and enterprising commune members had to bear fiscal responsibility for the indolent, inept and alcoholic ones. The whole arrangement fostered routine at the expense of innovation. Peasants had little interest in investing in the land which they stood to lose in the next round of repartition; they had every reason to squeeze out of it all they could, mindless of the future. The Emancipation Edict contained provisions which permitted a peasant household to consolidate its strips and separate itself from the commune; but these arrangements were hedged with so many formalities that few took advantage of them. In any event, in 1893 the government revoked them. By retaining and strengthening the commune the government undoubtedly achieved a certain measure of social stability and fiscal control, but it did so at the expense of economic progress.

The unwillingness of the authorities to entrust the peasant with full civil rights also represented an error of judgement. Understandably, it seemed more prudent to introduce the peasant to the obligations of full citizenship piecemeal. But the actual effect of the post-emancipation system which subjected peasants to so many separate laws and institutions was to perpetuate their peculiar status in society, and to postpone yet further the development in them of that civic sense which they so sadly lacked. The flaw was aggravated further by the creation in 1889 of rural officials called Land Commandants (*zemskie nachal'niki*). Chosen by the bureaucracy from among conservative landlords of the district, they were assigned a wide range of arbitrary powers over the peasantry, not unlike those the landlords had once enjoyed over their serfs.

Finally, the land settlement contained iniquities which over the long run produced very pernicious economic consequences. The Emancipation settlement left in the hands of landlords the bulk of the meadow land and forest which under serfdom the peasants had freely shared with them. Whereas a well-balanced rural economy in Russia required that every two acres of arable be matched by one acre of meadow, in Russia around 1900 the ratio was 3:1 and in places 4:1. Lumber and firewood were a constant bone of contention between peasants and landlords.

Common to all the human flaws in the Emancipation settlement was an excess of caution. The settlement was, if anything, too carefully thought out and therefore too rigid; it allowed too little scope for self-correction. A more liberal, more flexible arrangement might have caused more trouble at first but in the long run it would have been better able to absorb the kind of pressures outside human control which in the end undermined it altogether; little revolutions might have prevented the big one.

Of these natural pressures the most devastating was the sudden spurt in population; a phenomenon which affected not only the one-time serfs, but all who made their living off the land. In 1858, Russia had 68 million inhabitants; in 1897, 125 million. Its compounded annual rate of population growth in the second half of the nineteenth century was 1·8 per cent; the corresponding figure in south-western Europe was 0·4–0·5 per cent and in north-western Europe, 0·7–1·1 per cent. The overwhelming majority of the new people, of course, was born in the rural districts of European Russia, where between 1858 and 1897 the population increased by some 50 per cent without a corresponding increase in resources, as yields remained pitifully low. At the turn of the century, the average net income from a desiatina (2·7 acres) of land (arable and meadow) in Russia was 3·77 rubles, or not quite $2.00 in the then US currency. In the province of Moscow in the closing decade of the nineteenth century, where the average net per desiatina was about 5.29 rubles and the average peasant holding 7.5 desiatinas (about 20 acres), the net income was just below 40 rubles a year, or £4 ($20.00). If one counts the peasant's labour as wages, and adds to it his outside earnings, the most generous esstimate of a farming family's net income in the Moscow region in the 1890s would come to 130–190 rubles (£13–20 in British currency of the time) which fell far short of its needs.[24] The imperial government which alone had the capital to invest in the amelioration of Russian agriculture preferred to place it in railways and heavy industry, although it drew the bulk of its revenues from the countryside.

The combined pressure of excessive fiscal burdens, social and economic disabilities and an uncontrollable population growth created a situation which made it increasingly difficult for the Russian peasant to support himself from agriculture. In 1900, it was estimated, he covered only between a quarter and a half of his needs from farming; the remainder he had to make up in some other way. The solution readiest at hand was to hire himself out to landlords or rich peasants as a labourer, or else to lease land and till it either on a sharecrop basis or in return for various services; in the latter event, he reverted to the status of a semiserf. In 1905, peasants residing in European Russia held outright (mostly communally) 160 million desiatinas, and leased another 20–25 million, leaving only 40–45 million of cultivable land in private hands. (The state and crown owned, in addition, 153 million desiatinas, but nearly all of this land was either forest or soil unsuitable for cultivation; the arable was largely on lease to peasants.) Still, they did not have enough. The Russian peasant knew no other way of augmenting his food supply than by putting more land under the plough, and there simply was not enough unclaimed land to accommodate a population growing at so fast a rate. The peasants' belief in an imminent national 'black repartition' aggravated their plight, because they often refused to buy land offered them for purchase on advantageous terms. Some of them preferred to till the land until it was utterly exhausted than to pay for that which would be theirs before long for nothing.

The northern peasant suffered from an additional handicap. He had traditionally earned a large portion of his supplementary income from household industries. This source of income began to dry up with the development of modern mechanical industries. The crude cloth, shoes, utensils or hardware produced in cottages during the long winter months could not compete either in quality or price with machine-made products. Thus at the time when the peasant stood in greatest need of supplementary income he was deprived of it by industrial competition.

Finally, the rural crisis was exacerbated by a spontaneous social development, the dissolution of the joint family. As soon as the personal authority of the landlord and official over them had been lifted peasants split up their common properties and broke up into individual households. This was decidedly a regressive step from the point of view of rural productivity. The peasants apparently knew this to be the case, yet they not only did not want to live under the same roof with their parents and kin but preferred not to work jointly with them. The authority of the bolshak waned and with it weakened an important stabilizing force in the village.

As can be readily seen, there was no easy solution to the Russian agrarian crisis as it unfolded towards the end of the nineteenth century. The problem was not, as is often thought, mere shortage of land; nor was the solution to take land away from landlords and state and turn it over to the peasants. The entire rural economy was enmeshed in interrelated difficulties. The economic crisis enhanced the peasant's anarchist proclivities. The muzhik, whom foreigners at the end of the eighteenth century described as naturally gay and good natured, travellers around 1900 depict as sullen and hostile.

This ugly mood, exacerbating the peasants' instinctive hostility to the outside world, created at the beginning of the twentieth century a situation ripe for violence. It needed only some outward sign of weakening of state authority for the village to explode. This signal was given in the winter of 1904–5 by the liberal intelligentsia which through the Union of Liberation launched an open campaign of meetings and assemblies to demand a constitution. The government whose forces were tied down on the Far Eastern front against the Japanese had to temporize, and by so doing created the impression it was not averse to some kind of constitutional arrangement. In the confusion which ensued, the bureaucracy alternated concessions with brutal shows of strength. In January 1905, after troops had fired on the peaceful procession of workers marching to the Winter Palace, the cities were thrown into turmoil. The village, held in the grip of winter, had to await the coming of the thaw. As soon as the snow had melted and the ice on the rivers had broken, the peasantry went on the rampage, looting and burning estates and appropriating what they had so long coveted, namely the landlord's land. Once the situation was brought under control (1906–7) the government undertook a belated agrarian reform. Redemption Payments were abolished. Disappointed in the commune's failure to act as a stabilizing force, the government issued an edict on 9 November 1906 which allowed peasants to consolidate their holdings and leave the commune without its permission to set up individual farmsteads; the commune's authority over peasant movement through passport control was abolished. The government now appropriated large sums to finance the resettlement eastward of peasants from the overpopulated black earth provinces. Money was also set aside to help them purchase land from landlords. The consequences of these measures were indeed gratifying. In 1916, self-employed peasants (i.e. those who did not use hired labour) owned in European Russia outright about two-thirds of the cultivated land in private possession; with the leased land included, they had at their disposal nearly 90 per cent of such land. They also owned nine-tenths of the livestock.[25]

The events of 1905 gave the peasants a sense of power such as they had never possessed before. When in February 1917 Nicholas II suddenly abdicated, there was no force left to restrain them. In the spring of 1917 the muzhiks once again went on the rampage, this time to complete what the first revolution had left undone. The object now was no longer arable land; this time they concentrated on cutting down state and private forests, harvesting crops sown by others, appropriating produce stored for sale, and, of course, once again looting and burning country manors. Peasant violence in 1917 was directed primarily against the large, productive estates. It was on the crest of this rural revolution (of which the dissolution of the peasant army was an aspect) that Lenin and his party rode to power.

In the end, the Russian monarchy was destroyed by the peasant whom it had viewed as its staunchest supporter. Conditions aborted the development of a conservative rural estate in Russia. Latent peasant anarchism first delayed reform, then influenced it in an overly cautious direction, and finally, becoming overt, generated chaos which brought the inadequately reformed state down. At no point in history was the peasant in Russia that anchor of stability which he had been in Germany or France.

CHAPTER 7

DVORIANSTVO

[In Europe] people believe in the aristocracy,
some to scorn it, others to have something to
hate, others yet to profit from it or to satisfy
their vanity, and so on. In Russia none of this
exists. Here one simply does not believe in it.
Pushkin[1]

In the west, society's instrument in restraining the state (where such restraint was, in fact, exercised) was either the nobility or the bourgeoisie, that is groups controlling, respectively, land and money. In some western countries the two acted in concert, in others separately and at cross purposes; sometimes one led and the other followed. The next chapter, devoted to the middle class, will suggest why it had virtually no influence on the course of Russian politics. But even without detailed analysis it should be apparent that in an agrarian country with little money in circulation and no commercial credit such as Russia was until the 1860s, the middle class could not have been very influential by the very nature of things. If the Russian monarchy were to be limited, the job had to be done by the landed estate, the dvoriane, who by the end of the eighteenth century owned outright the bulk of the country's productive wealth, and on whom the crown depended to administer and defend its realm. It was by all odds the strongest and richest social group, best protected by laws, as well as the best educated and politically the most conscious.

And yet, whatever its potential, the dvorianstvo's actual political accomplishments were pitiful indeed. Its occasional acts of defiance were half-hearted, mismanaged, or both. In any event, they never involved more than a thin layer of the very rich, cosmopolitan élite, whom the provincial rank and file mistrusted and refused to follow. Most of the time, the Russian equivalent of the nobility did as it was told. The personal liberties which it won from Peter III and Catherine II it used to solidify its economic and social privileges, not to acquire political rights. Instead of accumulating the properties with which it was showered in the eighteenth century, it tended to carve up and dissipate them. In the end, whatever contribution the dvoriane made to political life they made not as a social and economic group standing up for its particular interests, but as a supra-class body fighting for what it conceived to be the general good: that is, not as a dvorianstvo but as an intelligentsia.

The historian N. Khlebnikov, writing a century ago, was among the first to inquire into the reasons for the political impotence of the Russian upper class as compared with the western. In his analysis he proceeded on the premiss that the latter's power rested on two foundations: control of local government and great landed wealth. Where it proved especially effective, for instance in England, the nobility combined the two powers, aristocrats dominating the countryside in the double capacity of administrators and proprietors. Khlebnikov noted that the dvorianstvo in Russia enjoyed too little of either power to be able to stand up to the monarchy.[2] This scheme provides a convenient starting point for an investigation of the dvorianstvo's politics.

The basic fact which one must take into account in dealing with the historical evolution of the dvorianstvo is the absence in Russia of a tradition of land ownership. As has been noted earlier, the relationship of property in land to the growth of statehood had been in Russia the reverse of that encountered in the history of western Europe. In the west, conditional land tenure preceded the emergence of royal absolutism; with the growth of the national monarchy and centralized statehood conditional possession in land was transformed into outright property. In Russia, alodial property existed only as long as there was no monarchy. As soon as it came into being, the monarchy proceeded to eliminate alodial property, replacing it with tenure conditional on service. During the three centuries separating the reign of Ivan III from that of Catherine II the Russian equivalent of the nobility held its land on royal sufferance. The Russian state grew and took shape without having to contend with entrenched landed interests – an absolutely fundamental factor in its historic evolution.

But even without clear title to its landed estates and serfs the dvorianstvo might have been able to secure a solid economic base; after all, the line separating possession from ownership is never as sharp in reality as it appears in legal manuals. To have done so, however, called for certain conditions which were missing. Everything conspired to make the dvorianstvo dependent on the monarchy, and to divert its attention from the struggle for its long-term interests to the satisfaction of its immediate needs.

From what has been said of the early Russian state it should be clear why the monarchy never allowed its service class to sink roots in the countryside. It desired its dvoriane to be mobile, ever ready to change jobs and residences. Sovereignty in Russia had been built on the ruins of private property, by a ruthless destruction of appanages and other votchiny. Once the rulers of Moscow had subjugated rival princes, they made certain that neither they nor their descendants, nor the boyars and the newly created dvorianstvo obtained a grip on regions such as had existed during appanage system. We have noted to what trouble Moscow went to prevent its provincial administrators from ensconcing themselves in their localities by prohibiting servitors from holding office in any area where they had estates and by rotating them at annual or biannual intervals. The Prussian *Indigenatsrecht*, which required administrators to reside and therefore, in effect, to own landed property in the province where they officiated would have been unthinkable in Russia. Hereditary office-holding was unknown as well. Western royalty, too, would have preferred its nobility not to become entrenched in the provinces, but in most countries it was unable to prevent this from happening and so it concentrated on weakening the nobility's political influence at the centre and replacing it gradually with a bureaucracy. In Russia, the issue was viewed with much greater gravity. A dvorianstvo enjoying local roots would have challenged the very principle of monocracy, a basic ingredient of tsarist authority as historically evolved, and as such could never have been tolerated. The mass deportations carried out by Ivan III, Basil III and Ivan IV did the job so thoroughly that afterwards even the mightiest of Russian grandees, possessors of millions of acres and hundreds of thousands of serfs, could not lay proprietary claim to any one part of Russia.

The Muscovite government made sure that the landholdings of its servitors were well dispersed. The Razriad and the Prikaz of Pomestia, which controlled the land reserve, issued estates to servitors without regard to their place of birth or the location of their other holdings. A petitioner, requesting additional land for himself or his son, had to take it wherever it was assigned, sometimes hundreds or more miles away from the family estate. As new frontier areas were opened to Russian colonization, dvoriane were encouraged and occasionally ordered to pick up their household and move with their serfs to new locations. The turnover of properties in Muscovite Russia was remarkably high. In the Moscow region during the sixteenth century, over three-quarters of all the pomestia are known to have changed hands in one twenty-five year period; in Kolomna during that same century, half the estates acquired new landlords in the course of sixteen years. In the seventeenth century, after a lapse of some fifty to sixty years, only a third of all the pomestia in the central regions of Muscovy still remained in the possession of the same owners.[3]

The wide scattering of properties and their rapid turnover continued throughout the imperial period. The recipients of the munificent gifts bestowed by Catherine II and Paul I did not obtain their holdings concentrated in one place: what they got were bits of property here and there, exactly as had been the case in the sixteenth and seventeenth centuries. As a result, even the largest fortunes in Russia consisted not of latifundia but of numerous scattered holdings. The Morozovs who thanks to their family links with the royal house became the richest landlords of mid-seventeenth-century Russia had their 9,000 peasant households dispersed in 19 different provinces. The extensive properties which the Vorontsovs managed to accumulate in the course of the eighteenth century from imperial grants – 5,711 peasant households with 27,000 male serfs living on 700,000 acres – were located in 16 provinces. The same held true of P. Sheremetev's fortune, the largest in the reign of Catherine II: his 186,000 serfs and 2.7 million acres lay scattered in 17 provinces.[4] In other words, imperial, like Muscovite, Russia had nothing resembling ducal properties – properties sufficiently large and concentrated to give their owners, as a by-product of ownership, a decisive voice in local politics. A Russian magnate resembled a modern 'diversified' investor who owns stock in many companies but not enough in any one of them to have a controlling voice. This was even truer of owners of medium and small estates. The poorest landlords had strips of arable in one or more villages which they shared with several proprietors. It is difficult for a person educated on western history to realize how extreme was the *morcellement* of estates in Russia. It was not uncommon for a complex of villages (*selo*), inhabited by 400 or 500 peasants, to be co-owned by 30 or 40 landlords. In the late eighteenth century *the majority* of Russian villages are said to have belonged to two or more landlords; single ownership was rather the exception.[5] Haxthausen was shown a village of 260 peasants belonging to 83 proprietors. Such a situation, incidentally, precluded enclosures or other measures designed to rationalize the rural economy.

Dvoriane continued to turn over land at a rapid rate throughout the imperial age, even after it had been declared their property and they no longer depended on the whimsy of government agencies. The practice of centuries had become habit. Romanovich-Slavatinskii, the leading historian of the dvorianstvo, estimates that in imperial Russia estates rarely remained in the same family longer than three or four generations. Foreigners were for ever astonished at the casual manner in which Russians disposed of their landed inheritance, and Haxthausen states flatly that nowhere in Europe did landed properties change hands as frequently as in Russia.

One needs only to compare this situation with that prevailing in

England, Spain, Austria or Prussia to understand the implications. The extreme dispersal and constant turnover of holdings deprived the dvorianstvo of a solid territorial base, and greatly reduced the political power latent in its vast collective resources.

Nor did the situation look much better in terms of absolute wealth. The Morozovs, Vorontsovs and Sheremetevs were rare exceptions. In Russia, there was always a very wide gap between the few rich families and the rest. Suffice it to say that in 1858–9, 1,400 of the wealthiest landowners in the empire, constituting 1·4 per cent of all the serf-owners, held 3 million serfs, whereas 79,000 of the poorer ones, or 78 per cent of the serf-owners, held only 2 million. The vast majority of Russian dvoriane at any time in history lived at the bare subsistence level or on a standard that made them indistinguishable from peasants.

There are no precise figures on medieval incomes from land in Russia, but enough is known to suggest how meagre they were. It has been previously noted (p. 80) that over three-quarters of the landlords in fifteenth-century Novgorod could not afford to equip themselves for war. Alexander Eck estimates that in the second half of the sixteenth century, a horse in Russia cost one to three rubles, a cavalryman's weapons one ruble, and his clothing two; this at a time when an average landed estate yielded a cash income of from five to eight rubles.[6] In other words, the outlay for miliary equipment which a servitor was required to make could absorb more or less his entire income. There was no surplus. Little wonder that Herberstein observed Muscovite 'nobles' pick up the lemon peelings and melon rinds which he and his colleagues in the embassy had cast aside. Many Muscovite dvoriane either had no serfs or not enough to turn over to them the cultivation of their pomestia. Such men had to till the land themselves. They formed a class of *odnodvortsy* ('single-householders") whom Peter later subjected to the soul tax and thereby merged with ordinary serfs.

The situation did not improve in the imperial period, despite the country's expansion into fertile areas. The great majority of imperial dvoriane remained destitute. Their incomes were so small they could not educate their children or afford any of the amenities associated with aristocratic life to which they now began to aspire. An Englishman who visited Russia around 1799, describes the typical provincial pomeshchik with evident revulsion:

You will then find him throughout the day, with his neck bare, his beard lengthened, his body wrapped in sheep's hide, eating raw turnips, and drinking kvass, sleeping one half of the day, and growling at his wife and family the other. The same feelings, the same wants, wishes, and gratifications ... characterize the nobleman and the peasant ...[7]

Indeed, a full quarter of the dvoriane in Riazan, a province in the Central Agricultural Region, some 1,700 families, were reported in 1858 to 'constitute a single family with their peasants, partake of food at the same table and live together in one *izba*'.[8]

Part of the problem lay in the fact that, as indicated, dvoriane multiplied more rapidly than any other social group in imperial Russia; they were demographically the most dynamic social estate of all. Between 1782 and 1858, the dvorianstvo grew 4·3 times, whereas the country's total population increased only twofold and the peasantry even somewhat less than that.[9] This growth put heavy pressures on the land resources and contributed to the over-all impoverishment of the élite.

In the final reckoning, however, the blame for the poverty of dvoriane must be placed on the primitiveness of the Russian economy and the lack of alternative opportunities which compelled the élite to rely much too heavily on income from land and serf labour. The Russian land-owning class never developed entail or primogeniture, two institutions essential to the well being of any nobility, because there was hardly anything that young men deprived of their share of the landed estate could draw income from. The son of a dvorianin, stripped of his inheritance, had nowhere to turn; he was worse off than would be a peasant expelled from the commune. Peter the Great, hoping both to strengthen his service class and to induce it to branch out into the many fields of endeavour which his reforms had opened up, issued in 1714 an edict requiring landlords to bequeath their immovable properties to a single heir (not necessarily the eldest). But this law ran so much against traditions and economic realities that it was consistently evaded and in 1730 had to be repealed. Russian landlords always insisted on carving up their estates into more or less equal parcels for distribution among their sons. The constant subdivision contributed as much to the decline of the Russian élite as did all the government policies. Veselovskii has shown in the example of five Muscovite boyar families – the kind that elsewhere might have founded influential aristocratic houses – how, owing mainly to the practice of property subdivision by testament, each in its turn fell apart and disappeared. Far from gaining influence, some of their offspring in the third and fourth generation actually sunk to the level of slaves.[10]

The political consequences of these facts become apparent when one considers the English nobility, a class in every respect the antithesis of the Russian dvorianstvo. In England, the nobility has showed a consistent concern for keeping landed property consolidated in family hands. As a recent study has demonstrated, this concern was in evidence as early as the fourteenth century.[11] The introduction in the seventeenth century of 'strict settlement' – a legal device by virtue of which the title-holder to a landed estate was treated as only its life tenant – greatly solidified the English nobility's hold on the land. Under 'strict settlement' a proprietor could alienate an estate only for as long as he was alive. By the eighteenth century, an estimated half of England was subject to this arrangement, which had the effect both of keeping this much of the country's territory in perpetuity in the hands of the same noble families and out of those of the *nouveaux riches*. Ample opportunities to earn a living outside agriculture, of course, made such practices feasible. Over the centuries, the richer English nobility steadily expanded its holdings at the expense of the smaller proprietors, causing land ownership to become heavily concentrated. It is estimated that in 1790 between 14,000 and 25,000 families owned 70 to 85 per cent of the cultivated land in England and Wales.[12] Even the least affluent in this select group drew from their properties incomes large enough to lead the life of gentlemen.

Elsewhere in western Europe the economic position of the nobility was perhaps less brilliant but still throughout the west the application of entail and primogeniture assured at least the wealthier landed families of a strong economic base. The meshing of this landed wealth with administrative functions enabled the western nobility to resist royal absolutism in its most extreme forms.

As the following statistics will show, in Russia the situation was diametrically the opposite; land was not accumulated but relentlessly cut up into ever smaller lots, with the result that the overwhelming majority of dvoriane lacked economic independence and could not afford to live in the style of landed gentry.

In 1858-9, there were in the Russian empire approximately one million dvoriane of both sexes. Of this number, slightly more than a third belonged to the category of non-hereditary (*lichnoe*) dvorianstvo legally barred from owning serfs (see above, p. 124). The number of hereditary dvoriane of both sexes is estimated at 610,000.[13] More than half of this number – 323,000 – were Polish *szlachcice* who had come under Russian rule following the Partitions. These can be ignored for our purposes, since they directed their political aspirations towards the restoration of Polish independence rather than reform in the internal government of Russia. There were also Turco–Tatar, Georgian, German and other non-Russian nobles who must be set aside. After these exclusions, there remain approximately 274,000 hereditary dvoriane, male and female, residing in the 37 provinces constituting Russia proper.* The ratio of

---

* These are the gubernii of Archangel, Astrakhan, Vladimir, Vologda, Voronezh, Viatka, the Region of the Don Cossacks, Ekaterinoslavl, Kazan, Kaluga, Kostroma, Kursk, Moscow, Nizhnii Novgorod, Novgorod, Olonetsk, Orenburg, Orel, Penza, Perm, Poltava, Pskov, Riazan, Samara, St Petersburg, Saratov, Simbirsk, Smolensk, Taurida, Tambov, Tver, Tula, Ufa, Kharkov, Kherson, Chernigov and Iaroslavl.

men to women in this group may be set, following data obtained in the 1897 census, at 48 to 52, which yields a figure of 131,000 men.

According to the 1858–9 census, in these 37 provinces lived approximately 90,000 serf-owners of both sexes. Unfortunately, there is no way of knowing the ratio of males to females among the serf-owners. But if we assume the ratio to have been two to one in favour of the males, we arrive at the figure of 60,000 hereditary male dvoriane owning estates; if the ratio is assumed to have been 1:1, the number of male serf-owners drops to 45,000. In the former case, one out of two male dvoriane (60,000 out of 131,000) had a landed estate worked with serf labour; in the latter, only one out of three (45,000 out of 131,000).

Setting aside the two-thirds of hereditary dvoriane of both sexes who had no serfs (184,000 out of 274,000) let us inquire into the condition of those who did. In imperial Russia, the possession of 100 'souls' was regarded as the minimum which a dvorianin needed to qualify as a gentleman. This criterion, employed already in the eighteenth century, received official sanction from Nicholas 1 in an edict of 1831 which decreed that only dvoriane with 100 or more 'souls' had the right to a direct vote in the Assemblies of the Dvoriane. Following this standard, landlords with fewer than 100 male serfs can be defined as in varying degrees impoverished. Those with more can be subdivided into the moderately wealthy 'gentry' (100–1,000 'souls') and the grand seigneurs (over 1,000). With these criteria in mind, let us look at the distribution of serf-ownership in Russia proper during the imperial period:

TABLE I *Serf-owning Landlords, Male and Female, in European Russia*[14]

Category in terms of male serfs ('souls') owned	1777 Percentage	1858–9 Number	1858–9 Percentage
Grand Seigneurs (over 1,000 souls)		1,032	1·1
'Gentry'	16		
501–1,000 souls		1,754	2·0
101–500 souls		15,717	18·0
Impoverished dvoriane			
21–100 souls	25	30,593	35·1
Fewer than 20	59	38,173	43·8

These statistical tables indicate that on the eve of Emancipation nearly four-fifths of Russian dvoriane (male and female) fortunate enough to own serfs (18,503 out of 90,000) did not own enough to live off the land in a manner regarded by the authorities as commensurate with their social status. Or, to put it in another way: in 1858–9 only 18,503 Russian dvoriane in the 37 provinces of Great Russia secured enough income from their estates to enjoy financial independence. The number of dvoriane able to rely on corvée and agrarian rents was always exceedingly small. The 1831 decree of Nicholas I restricting the right of direct vote in Assemblies of the Dvoriane to owners of 100 or more 'souls' had the effect of reducing the roll of such voters in the empire as a whole to 21,916, a figure close to the 18,503 given in Table I for the 37 provinces of Russia proper.[15] What makes these figures even more telling is that the 38,173 dvoriane listed as in possession of fewer than 20 'souls' had on average only 7 male serfs each. The situation in the reign of Catherine II, the 'Golden Age' of dvorianstvo, was, if anything, more dismal yet, as the figures for 1777 indicate. All of which should serve as a warning not to think of the Russian 'nobility' as a profligate class wallowing in luxury in the midst of poverty and backwardness. The Rostovs, Bezukhovs and Bolkonskys of *War and Peace* are in no sense typical: they were members of an exclusive club of some 1,400 grand seigneurs in an Empire in which a million persons claimed 'noble' status of some kind.

Thus, although the dvorianstvo was indeed a landed estate in the sense that prior to Emancipation it owned nearly all of the privately held, cultivated land in the empire and drew much of its income from it, it was not a landowning aristocracy in the western meaning of the word. Ninety-eight per cent of them either had no serfs or not enough of them to be able to rely on their labour and rents for a decent living. These people – unless they had relatives or patrons willing to support them – had to depend on the largesse of the crown. Even after it had gained its liberties in 1762 and 1785, therefore, the dvorianstvo could not dispense with the monarchy's favours; it alone had the jobs, the pomestia and the serfs needed for its survival. The members of this large group were no more a landed aristocracy than a modern salaried employee who invests a part of his savings in some industrial shares is a capitalist entrepreneur. But even that 2 per cent of the dvorianstvo which had enough land to live off its proceeds did not resemble a true landed aristocracy. The scattering and rapid turnover of properties, noted above, precluded the formation of strong local attachments, so essential to the aristocratic spirit. For them, land was a way of making a living, not a way of life.

If poor, landless dvoriane depended on the crown for jobs, those affluent enough to own estates were dependent on it for the preservation of serfdom.

It is one of the anomalies of Russian social history that for all its critical importance to the country's evolution, serfdom was always allowed to remain in a kind of legal limbo. No edict enserfing peasants had ever been issued, nor did the crown ever formally certify the landlord's title to their serfs. The institution grew up in practice from an accumulation.

of numerous edicts and customs, and it was maintained by common consent but without explicit official sanction. It was always understood – though again, never spelled out – that the landlords did not actually own their serfs; rather, they were managing them, as it were, on behalf of the crown. The latter assumption acquired particular validity after Peter the Great and his successors had made landlords agents of the state charged with the collection of the soul tax and the gathering of conscripts. For all their reliance on serfs, the landlords' title to them and their labour was vague, and it remained so even after 1785, the year they received title to the land. The favour of the crown, therefore, was essential to all those who benefited from serf labour. What the crown had once entrusted, it could at any time revoke. Fear of being deprived of serfs by state decree greatly mitigated the dvorianstvo's interest in politics, especially after its liberation from compulsory state service. The *status quo* assured them of free labour; any change was bound to upset the situation to their detriment. It was a condition understood as part of the dyarchic arrangement under which Russia operated that if they wished to go on exploiting serf labour, the dvoriane had to stay out of politics.

Serf-owners further relied on the crown to keep their serfs under control. The Pugachev uprising of 1773–5 had thoroughly frightened them. Landlords were convinced – rightly, as subsequent events were to show – that at the slightest sign of weakening of state authority the muzhik would take the law in his own hands and once again murder and pilfer as he had done in Pugachev's day. Their most effective weapon to keep serfs obedient was the right to call in troops, and to turn over recalcitrant peasants to the authorities for induction into the army or exile to Siberia. From this point of view, too, the influential serf-owning part of dvorianstvo had an interest in the maintenance of a strong autocratic regime.

Another factor which exerted a strongly negative effect on the political situation of the dvorianstvo was the absence in Russia of corporate institutions and corporate spirit.

Enough had been said of the Muscovite monarchy and its conception of the service class to make it superfluous to have to explain why it never issued collective charters. But in their insistence on the patrimonial power of the monarchy, the tsars went further, using every means at their disposal to humiliate anyone who by virtue of ancestry, office or wealth may have been inclined to become self-important. They habitually referred to their servitors as slaves (*kholopy*). Muscovite protocol required every boyar and dvorianin, even the scion of a 'pedigreed' clan, to address his sovereign with the formula: 'I, so-and-so [the diminutive form of the first name, e.g. "Ivashka"], your *kholop*.' This practice was stopped only by Peter; but even after him and throughout the eighteenth century, it was quite customary for great and small lords in addressing the crown to continue referring to themselves as slaves by another name, *raby*.

Corporal punishment was applied indiscriminately to dvoriane and commoners: a boyar or a general was lashed with the knout exactly as the meanest serf. Peter in particular liked to show his displeasure by beating his associates. The upper class was exempt from corporal punishment only in 1785 by terms of the Dvorianstvo Charter.

The status of a dvorianin was always insecure. Even in the eighteenth century, when the fortunes of the dvorianstvo stood at their zenith, a servitor could be demoted into the ranks of commoners at a moment's notice and without the right of appeal. Under Peter, a dvorianin who failed to educate himself or who concealed serfs from the census-takers was cast out of the ranks of his estate. A dvorianin enrolled in the civil service who after a five-year trial period proved unsuited for clerical work was sent to the army as a common soldier. In the nineteenth century, as the number of dvoriane swelled from the influx of commoners and foreigners, the government conducted occasional 'purges'. In the 1840s, for example, Nicholas I ordered 64,000 members of the Polish *szlachta*, previously admitted into the ranks of Russian dvorianstvo, to be reduced to the ranks of commoners. Under this ruler deprivation of noble status was a common punishment for political and other offences.

The institution of mestnichestvo, on the face of it, reflected a spirit of corporatism, but over the long run it contributed heavily to the undermining of the corporate position of the upper class *vis-à-vis* the monarchy. Mestnichestvo accounts did compel the crown to take account of boyar wishes in making appointments. Yet the net effect of the elaborate inter-clan and intra-family 'placement' ladders was to promote rivalries within boyardom. The endless petitions and suits lodged by boyars against one another made it impossible for them to combine forces against the crown. Mestnichestvo was only in appearance an instrument of boyar control over the state. Its actual result was to eliminate the possibility of any internal cohesion within the Muscovite upper class.

The monarchy never allowed the boyars and dvoriane to form a closed corporation. It insisted on keeping the ranks of its service class open to newcomers from the lower classes and from abroad.

We have noted the effect of the elevation of ordinary dvoriane to the privileges of the boyar class which occurred in the latter phase of the Muscovite state. The Table of Ranks merely perpetuated this tradition, emphasizing more than ever the element of merit over ancestry. The influx of commoners into the ranks of dvorianstvo by way of service promotion greatly displeased those who enjoyed their title by right of inheritance. In the middle of the eighteenth century, dvorianstvo pub-licists, led by the historian Prince Michael Shcherbatov, sought to dis-suade the monarchy from promoting commoners into its ranks, but to no avail. Sympathetic as Catherine was to its interests, she refused to transform the dvorianstvo into a closed estate and the inflow continued.

In addition to commoners, an important source of dilution of the ranks of dvorianstvo were foreign nobles. The Russian monarchy gener-ally welcomed foreigners willing to enter its service. In the sixteenth and seventeenth centuries, a large number of Tatars were converted and inscribed into the ranks of Russian dvorianstvo. In the following cen-tury, Ukrainian Cossack 'elders', Baltic barons, Polish szlachta and Caucasian princes were accorded the same privilege. All along, Germans, Scotsmen, Frenchmen and other west Europeans who came to Russia with permission or by invitation of the government were inscribed in dvorianstvo rolls. As a result, the proportion of ethnic Russians in the ranks of dvorianstvo remained relatively small. An historian who has analyzed the background of 915 service clans, largely on the basis of the rolls of the Razriad at the end of the seventeenth century found the following ethnic distribution: 18·3 per cent were descendants of the Riurikides, that is, of Norman blood; 24·3 per cent had Polish or Lithuanian ancestry; 25·0 per cent, other west European; 17·0 per cent, Tatar and other Oriental peoples; 10·5 per cent unknown; and only 4·6 per cent, Great Russian.[16] Even if one counts the descendants of the Riurikides and all the 'unknowns' as Great Russian, it would still follow from these computations that in the final decades of the Muscovite period more than two-thirds of all the servitors of the tsars were of foreign extraction. In the eighteenth century, owing to territorial expansion and the introduction of regular procedures for ennoblement, the proportion of foreigners in the service class increased further. While it is true that in imperial Russia fashion dictated that one trace one's ancestry to foreign shores, so that the available figures are undoubtedly inflated in favour of non-Russians, the proportion of non-Russians in the service was high by any reckoning. Modern compilations indicate that of the 2,867 civil servants holding the top ranks during the imperial period (1700–1917), 1,079 or 37·6 per cent were of foreign nationality, mostly western and pre-eminently German; in the middle of the nineteenth century, Lutherans alone held 15 per cent of the highest posts in the central administration.[17] No other nobility was so open to the inflow of aliens or so lacking in deep native roots.

Last but not least among the factors working against the transforma-tion of the dvorianstvo into a corporate body was the insignificance of noble titles. Just as all the sons of a boyar or a dvorianin inherited equal shares of his landed estate, so they inherited, if he was a prince, their father's title. The result was a proliferation of princely families in Russia; and since most of the princes were poor, the title carried little prestige and no power. Englishmen travelling in imperial Russia found among the many oddities of that exotic country not the least surprising that a prince, whom they greeted with due deference, was not automatically a 'noble', and indeed sometimes was a pauper. The only title that mattered was that obtained in the service – that is, rank or chin – and that was dependent not on heredity but on government favour. Thus an important element of patrimonial systems, the ranking of the élite by state function rather than by social origin not only survived Muscovy but was strengthened under the imperial regime.

Under these conditions, well-meaning attempts to transplant into Russia western aristocratic institutions were bound to fail. Catherine II made a tentative attempt in this direction. In 1785, in her Dvorianstvo Charter, she provided for Assemblies of Dvoriane, the first corporate organizations (together with the concurrently formed urban corporations) ever granted in Russia to a social group. Her purpose was to give her newly emancipated dvoriane something to keep them busy and incidentally to have them assist the local administration in its duties. But the rules governing the Assemblies were hedged with so many limitations and the members were anyway so strongly disinclined to participate in public responsibilities that they never came to be more than harmless social gatherings. Their administrative functions were fully absorbed by the bureaucracy, whose provincial representatives made sure the Assemblies never overstepped their narrowly prescribed limits. Speranskii, at one time the principal adviser of Alexander I, who had visions of transforming Russian dvoriane into something resembling the English peerage, was driven to desperation by their complete indifference to the opportunities which the Assemblies provided. 'The nobles run away from elections to the Assemblies,' he complained in 1818, 'and soon it will be necessary to convoke them using gendarmes in order to compel the nobles to take advantage of their rights.'[18]

The facts adduced help to explain an apparent paradox that a social class which by 1800 had managed to get hold of the bulk of the country's productive wealth (not only land but, as will be pointed out in the following chapter, also much of its industry) and to acquire, in addition, personal rights and estate privileges extended to no other group, nevertheless did not translate its advantages into terms of political power. Wealthy as the dvorianstvo may have been collectively, individually more than nine-tenths of its members were indigent. These people remained economically heavily dependent on the crown. Nor could the affluent minority consolidate its influence because its properties – thinly scattered, for ever subdivided, and prevented from fusing with local administrative authority – gave them no solid regional footing. Fear of losing serfs acted as a further deterrent to political involvement. The absence until 1785 of corporate institutions and the spirit that grows out of them prevented the dvorianstvo from closing its ranks. Thus the gains made in the eighteenth century – freedom from state service, a charter of rights, and full title to landed property – had no political results. They improved the condition of the upper class without bringing it nearer to the sources of power.

In Russian history there were only three significant attempts, each a century apart, on the part of the service élite to stand up to the monarchy and restrain its unlimited power. The first occurred during the Time of Troubles when a group of boyars entered into a compact with the Polish crown. They offered the Russian throne to the son of the King of Poland, on condition that he consent to specified terms under which he would exercise royal authority. The Poles agreed but the compact was annulled when they were expelled from Russia shortly afterwards. The Romanov dynasty which took over in 1613 was not required to subscribe to any terms. Next, in 1730, during an interregnum, a group of upper class civil servants sitting in the Supreme Privy Council, prominent among whom were members of the ancient princely clans of Golitsyn and Dolgorukii, requested and obtained from Empress Anne her signature to a set of 'Conditions'. These severely limited her power to dispose of state revenue, promote servitors and conduct foreign policy. Prodded by the provincial dvorianstvo, however, Anne renounced these terms after assuming office and reverted to unlimited autocratic authority. Finally, in December 1825, a group of officers from the most distinguished families tried to stage a *coup d'état*. Their purpose was to abolish the autocracy and re-place it either with a constitutional monarchy or a republic. The mutiny was quelled in no time at all.

All three of these attempts had certain features in common. In each case, the effort was led by the topmost élite, descendants of the 'pedi-greed' clans or wealthy *nouveaux riches* who identified with the western aristocracy. They acted on their own without being able to draw on any support from the masses of provincial dvoriane. The latter profoundly mistrusted all constitutional attempts which they saw not as moves in-tended for the common good but as cleverly camouflaged designs to introduce an oligarchic form of government. Given its dependence on the state for jobs and landed estates, the rank and file greatly feared the state falling into the hands of the great landed families who (so they believed) would use the power to enrich themselves at their expense. In 1730, at a critical juncture in Russia's constitutional development, the spokesmen for the victorious party of provincial dvoriane who opposed any 'conditions' being imposed on the crown stated their fears as follows: 'Who will guarantee us that in time, instead of one sovereign, we shall not have as many tyrants as there are members sitting in the Council, and that their oppressive policies will not worsen our bondage?'[19] The political philosophy of the mass of dvorianstvo was not all that different from the peasantry's; both preferred unlimited autocracy to a constitutional arrangement, seeing behind the latter manipulations of private interests acting for their own benefit. And without such rank-and-file support, the political ambitions of the uppermost élite had no chance of success.

The second factor common to the three constitutional attempts was that each was an 'all or nothing' effort, centred on a *coup d'état*. The patient, steady accumulation of small bits of political power was missing. The fate of constitutional change in Russia always hinged on dramatic gambles. This is not, however, how society has usually succeeded in wresting power from the state.

The government never really felt it had much to fear from the dvorianstvo's political ambitions. It was perhaps disappointed in this estate's failure to come to its assistance in administering the realm, and willy-nilly kept on increasing the bureaucracy to replace the landed service class as the mainstay of the regime. Nicholas I mistrusted the upper class because of its participation in the Decembrist revolt. But he too did not fear it. The view from the top was accurately expressed in 1801 by Count Paul Stroganov, a member of Alexander I's inner cabinet known as the Unofficial Committee. He had been in France during the Revolution and observed the reactions of the Western aristocracy when its privileges were threatened. At one of the sessions of the Committee, when worries were expressed that dvoriane might object to a certain government proposal, he spoke as follows:

Our nobility consists of numerous people who had become gentlemen solely by way of service, people who had had no education, whose only concern it is to see nothing superior to the Emperor's power. Neither law nor justice, nothing is capable of awakening in them the idea of the least resistance. This is a most ignorant estate, the most corrupt, and, as far as its *esprit* is concerned, the stupidest. Such is the approximate picture of the majority of our rural dvoriane. Those with a somewhat better education are, first of all few in number, and, in their majority, also permeated with a spirit which makes them utterly incapable of standing up to any government measures ... A large part of the dvorianstvo which is on active service has its spirit moved by other considerations: unfortunately, it is inclined to find in the execution of state commands wholly their private advantage, and this very often lies in cheating but never in resisting. Such is an approximate picture of our nobility; one part lives in the village, sunk in the profoundest ignorance, while the other, that which serves, is permeated with a spirit in no wise dangerous. The grand seigneurs need not be feared. What remains then, and where are the elements of dangerous discontent? ...

What was not done in the previous reign [of Paul 1] against justice, against the rights of these people, against their personal security? If ever there was a time to fear anything it was then. But did they ever breathe a word? Quite the contrary – all the repressive measures were carried out with amazing scrupulousness, and it was precisely the gentleman [*gentilhomme*] who executed the measures designed against his fellow noble, measures which happen to have run against the interests and honour of this estate. And one wants that a body totally devoid of public spirit do things which call for *esprit de corps*, clever and a little persistent conduct, and courage ![20]

Twenty-four years after these scornful remarks had been uttered came the Decembrist uprising, in which spirit and courage certainly were not lacking. But nevertheless, Stroganov's opinion is correct as pertains to the dvorianstvo as a whole. For the remainder of the Imperial regime it never again gave it much trouble.*

In dealing with the politics of a class as diversified as the Russian dvorianstvo, it is necessary to draw a distinction between its three constituent elements, the rich, the middling and the poor.

The poor can be ignored for this purpose. For although they constituted more than nine-tenths of all the dvoriane, they had no evident political aspirations. Their concerns were of an immediate material nature. Like the peasants, whose way of life many of them shared, they looked to the crown for help and reacted to any effort to liberalize the system of government as a move undertaken in the interest of the magnates. As Stroganov aptly put it, this type, especially when ennobled by way of service, was concerned only to 'see nothing superior to the Emperor's power'. These people, so brilliantly depicted in the novels of Gogol and Saltykov-Shchedrin, made for a profoundly conservative force.

The very rich – members of some one thousand families with a thousand or more souls each (they owned, on the average, four thousand adult serfs of both sexes) – presented a different picture. They tended to live in oriental splendour, surrounded by hordes of friends, retainers and domestics. Very few of them had any clear idea of their incomes and expenditures. They usually squandered all the rents, and got into debt which their heirs had to sort out the best they could. At a pinch, they

---

* It is, of course, true that the bulk of the opposition to the imperial regime in the nineteenth and twentieth centuries came from people born dvoriane. But the liberals and radical dissenters were struggling not for the interests of their class, which is what concerns us here. They were struggling for national and social ideals of society as a whole – a struggle which sometimes compelled them to move against the interests of their own class. Surely, Bakunin, Herzen, Kropotkin, Lenin, Struve, Shipov, though of dvoriane background, cannot be said to have been in any sense exponents of dvorianstvo causes.

could always sell one of the many scattered properties of which such great fortunes were normally composed, and go on living in their accustomed style. The Rostovs of *War and Peace* give a faithful portrait of such a family.

It was customary for Russian grandees to keep an open house to which even the slightest acquaintances were freely admitted to share in lavish offerings of food and drink – the surplus from estates for which there was no worth-while market. Much money was spent on foreign luxuries, such as tropical fruits and wines; it was said that imperial Russia consumed each year more champagne than was produced in all the vineyards of France. The hospitality of the great Russian houses could probably not be duplicated anywhere else in Europe. It was possible only where no one kept a close watch on the account books.

An essential feature of life of the very rich were hordes of domestics who catered to their every whim. One general had 800 servants, 12 of whom were assigned exclusively to care for his illegitimate children. A profligate count employed 400 domestics, including 17 lackeys, each of whom had assigned a single duty; one to bring his master water, another to light his pipe, and so on. Another seigneur a special hunting orchestra of serfs, each of whom produced only one sound (Plate 14). Rich households had also their contingents of clowns, 'Arabs' (Negroes), 'Holy People', story-tellers of all sorts, to help while away long winter evenings. Most of the domestics did little work, but prestige required one to have as many of them as possible. Even the poorer dvoriane liked to have a couple of servants in attendance.

A household of this kind, when it ventured on a trip, resembled a tribal migration. In 1830 Pushkin met the son of a grand seigneur who described to him how his father used to travel in the reign of Catherine the Great. This is what Pushkin wrote down:

When my father was about to undertake a journey somewhere, he moved with his entire household. In front, on a tall Spanish horse, rode the Pole Kulikovskii ... It was his function in the house to ride out on market days on a camel and show the peasants the *lanterne magique*. On the road he gave the signal to stop and go. Behind him followed my father's gig, and behind it, a carriage for use in case of rain; under the seat was the place of my father's favourite clown, Ivan Stepanich. These were followed by carriages loaded with us children, our governesses, teachers, nursemaids, and so on. Then came a grated cart with the fools, Negroes, dwarfs – in all, thirteen persons. Then again an identical cart with the sick borzois. Next came a gigantic box with horn instruments, a buffet carried by sixteen horses, and finally wagons with Kalmyk tents, and all sorts of furniture, because my father always stopped overnight under the open sky. You can judge yourself how many people were involved, musicians, cooks, dog-watchers, and other helpers.[21]

Some of the very affluent settled permanently abroad where they astonished Europeans with their profligacy. One Russian aristocrat lived for a while in a small German town where he liked to amuse himself by sending his servants early in the morning to the market to buy out all the produce in order then to watch out of his window local housewives frantically run round in circles in search of food. The gambling casinos and spas of western Europe well knew these free-spending Russian potentates. It is said that Monte Carlo never recovered from the Russian Revolution.

People of this kind had very little interest in politics, so absorbed were they in the pursuit of pleasure. In 1813–15 many younger members of these rich families, having spent time in western Europe with the army of occupation, came under the spell of liberalism and nationalism. It is these people who founded the Russian counterparts of the German *Tugenbunde* and in 1825, inspired by uprisings of liberal officers in Spain, Portugal and Naples, made a move to abolish absolutism in Russia. But the Decembrist revolt had no antecedents and no issue, it was a solitary event, an echo of distant happenings. It shattered the spirit of the great families who had no inkling of its approach and could not understand what madness had seized their youth. In general, the very rich liked to enjoy life, without much thought for their own tomorrow, let alone for the general good.

It is the middle group, the gentry, in possession of 100 to 1,000 'souls' which was potentially the most active political body in the country. In 1858, they owned in the 37 provinces of Russia on the average 470 serfs of both sexes – a number sufficient to enable them to live independently and to provide themselves and their children with an up-to-date education. They were likely to know French well, and yet also to be at home in Russian. The richer among them travelled to Europe, sometimes for a year or longer on a 'grand tour' or to attend university. Many joined the military service for a few years not so much to make a career or to gain money, but to see something of their country and make friends. They had libraries and kept up with news from abroad. Although they preferred to live in the city, they spent the summers on their estates, and this custom reinforced their links with the village and the people inhabiting it. This group provided a unique bridge between the culture of rural Russia and that of the modern west, and from its ranks came most of the political and intellectual leaders of imperial Russia. A charming picture of such a provincial gentry family, rather of the less affluent sort, can be found in Serge Aksakov's autobiographic *Family Chronicle*.

Yet as a whole, this group also was uninterested in political activity. In addition to all the reasons mentioned above, partly to blame for this apoliticism was the memory of state service. After they had been freed from it, dvoriane remained very suspicious of all civic responsibility. They were inclined to view the crown's attempts to involve them in local government as a device surreptitiously to reharness them in its service. They shied away, therefore, even from the limited opportunities granted them to involve themselves in provincial life, the more so that the bureaucracy always breathed down their necks; it was only too common in Russia for an elected representative of the district dvorianstvo to find himself drawn into the orbit of the civil service and end up being accountable to St Petersburg instead of his constituency. It was a most unfortunate legacy of the Muscovite tradition of life-long state service that even those dvoriane who had the means and the opportunity to participate in public life on the local level preferred to abstain, so deep was their aversion to all work on behalf of the state. Like peasants who could not distinguish between benevolent interference with their lives by well-meaning landlords and thoughtless exploitation, so most dvoriane did not separate compulsory state service from voluntary public service. In both cases, the decisive consideration was an instinctively negative reaction to someone else's will and the wish – without regard to the substance of the issue – to have one's *volia* or licence.

The other inhibiting factor was that mentioned by Dolgorukov (p. 136), namely the rigidity of the ranking system in the Russian civil service. An educated dvorianin could not enter the civil service at a rank appropriate to his qualifications; he had to start at the bottom and work his way up in competition with professional bureaucrats whose sole concern was with personal advancement. The better educated and more public-minded dvoriane found this intolerable and avoided the civil service. Thus an important opportunity to attract to the government the most enlightened element was lost.

The middle dvoriane tended to be most interested in culture: literature, drama, art, music, history, political and social theory. It is they who created a public for Russian novels and poetry, who subscribed to the periodical press, who filled the theatres, who enrolled at the universities. Russian culture is to a very large extent the product of this class, of some 18,500 families from whose ranks came both the talent and the audience which gave Russia, at long last, something that the rest of the world could recognize and adopt as part of its own heritage. But what culture gained politics lost; the genius which went into literature and art shied away from humdrum affairs of government. Once some members of this group interested themselves in public affairs with any degree of commitment – this occurred in the 1830s – they did so at a visionary level which had little to do with political reality. We shall encounter them later as the founders of the Russian intelligentsia.

Whatever hope there might have been that the dvorianstvo would develop into a politically active class vanished in 1861. The emancipation of serfs was a calamity for the landlords. It is not that the provisions of the emancipation settlement were ungenerous: the dvoriane received good money for the land they had to give up to the peasants; indeed, suspicion has been voiced that the assessments for this land had been set artificially high to include at least some compensation for the loss of the serfs. The trouble was that the landlords were now on their own. Under serfdom they did not have to keep accurate account books because, at a pinch, they could always squeeze out a bit more out of the serf. Under the new conditions this was no longer possible. To survive, one had to be able to calculate the costs of rents and services, and exercise some control over expenditures. Nothing in its background had prepared the dvorianstvo for such responsibilities. Most of them did not know how to count roubles and kopeks, and indeed scorned doing so. It is as if, after long tradition of free living, they were suddenly put on a strict allowance.

This was the ultimate vengeance of serfdom. Having lived for so long off rents and corvée, whose quantity they were free to set, they were totally unsuited for a self-reliant existence. Despite the fact that after 1861 land values and rents rose sharply, dvoriane got deeper into debt and had to mortgage their land or sell it to peasants and merchants. By 1905, dvoriane had lost a third of the land they had kept as part of the Emancipation settlement; after the agrarian disorders of 1905 they began to dispose of it even more rapidly. About half of the land left in private possession at this time was mortgaged. In the northern provinces, by the end of the nineteenth century dvoriane landholding virtually vanished. Unable to manage, dvoriane sold most of the arable land, retaining mainly forests and pastures which they could lease at good prices without much trouble to themselves. In the south, dvoriane landholding did survive but here too it was on the defensive, retreating under the combined pressure of the land-hungry peasantry and capitalist farming working for export. Efforts of the monarchy to shore up the eroding economic position of dvorianstvo by means of easy credit failed to reverse the process. As pointed out above (p. 169), by 1916 self-employed peasants owned two-thirds of all the cultivated land in Russia not in state possession (and the state had little arable land), as well as nine-tenths of the livestock. As a class, the dvorianstvo lost its economic foundation in the final decades of the imperial regime, and politically it no longer represented any force whatever.

CHAPTER 8

THE MISSING BOURGEOISIE

That the Russian middle class was small and inconsequential is one of the commonplaces of historical literature. Russia's inability to produce a large and vigorous bourgeoisie is usually seen as a major cause of its deviation from the political patterns of western Europe, and of the failure of liberal ideas significantly to influence its political institutions and practices. The stress on this element is understandable if one considers the historic function performed by the western bourgeoisie. In its methods the western bourgeoisie was not always consistent. In France, for example, it initially allied itself with the monarchy to help reduce the power of the landed aristocracy, then reversed itself, and headed the struggle against the monarchy which ended with the latter's destruction. In England, it sided with the aristocracy against the crown and together with it, whittled down its prerogatives. In the Netherlands, having expelled a foreign power ruling the country, it took over. In Spain, Italy and the Holy Roman Empire, where it failed to remake national governments to its liking, at least it managed to extract from the monarchy and the feudal aristocracies corporate rights which it used here and there to establish capitalist enclaves in the form of sovereign city-states. But whatever the strategy employed, the spirit and the aim of the western middle class was everywhere the same. It stood for its business interests, and since these required the rule of law and the safeguarding of personal rights, it fought for a public order consonant with what later came to be articulated as liberal ideals. This being the case, it is reasonable to assume a more than casual connection between the notorious under-development in Russia of legality and personal freedom and the impotence or apathy of its middle class.

What accounts for the insignificance of the Russian middle class? The first answer which suggests itself has to do with the country's economy. The bourgeoisie is by definition the moneyed class, and, as is well known, Russia never had much money in circulation. It was situated too far from the principal routes of international trade to earn bullion from commerce; nor did it have its own precious metals because it began mining them only in the eighteenth century. The shortage of money was sufficient cause to have prevented the emergence in Russia of a moneyed class comparable to the western bourgeoisie of the classical age of capitalism. But this point conceded, the problem is by no means settled. For Russia at all times was a country whose inhabitants had a remarkable penchant for trade and manufacture; where indeed the natural poverty of the soil compelled them to become businessmen. One must not be misled by statistics indicating that under the old regime nearly the entire population of Russia consisted of either dvoriane or peasants. The social categories of old Russia were legal in nature, and designed to distinguish those who paid taxes from those who rendered full-time service, and both from the clergy which did neither; they were not meant to define economic occupations. In fact, Russia always had a much larger proportion of its inhabitants engaged in trade and manufacture than the official census figures indicate. It is probably true to say that when its state was in the process of formation (sixteenth to eighteenth centuries), proportionately more of Russia's inhabitants pursued non-agricultural activities part-time or full-time than was the case in any other European country. Western travellers to Muscovy were invariably struck by the business enterprise of its citizenry. Johann de Rodes, a Swedish commercial agent, noted in 1653 that in Russia 'everyone, from the highest to the lowest, practises [trade] ... No doubt, in this respect this nation's zeal almost excels that of all the others ...'[1] Twenty years later a German visitor, Johann Kilburger, made similar observations: no one was better suited to trade than Russians, because of their passion for it, their favourable geographic location, and their very modest personal wants. He believed that some day Russians could become a great commercial nation.[2] Foreigners were especially impressed that in contrast to the west, where trade was regarded as an occupation below the dignity of the nobility, in Russia no one disdained it: 'All the boyars without exception, even the ambassadors of the Great Prince to foreign sovereigns everywhere occupy themselves with commerce,' wrote another seventeenth-century traveller, 'they sell, buy, and barter without hypocrisy and concealment.'[3]

This intense trade activity was not quite equalled by Russia's industrial development. But even that was never quite as negligible as is generally supposed. In the eighteenth century, Ural foundries, working mainly for the English market, smelted the largest quantity of iron in Europe. The cotton spinning industry, the first in Russia to be mechanized, produced in the 1850s more yarn than that of Germany. All through the eighteenth and nineteenth centuries Russia had a bustling cottage industry, whose enterprising leaders differed little from self-made entrepreneurs of the Americas. The surge in all branches of heavy industry which got under way in 1890 attained a pace which Russia has not been able to match since. Thanks to it, on the eve of the First World War Russia's industrial production attained fifth place in the world.

None of which is intended to imply that Russia under the old regime was at any time a predominantly commercial or manufacturing country. Without question, until the middle of the twentieth century, agriculture constituted the foundation of Russia's national economy and the main source of her wealth. The *per capita* income from non-agrarian occupations remained low even after the aggregate industrial figures had grown impressively. But on the face of it, it would certainly seem that a country which in 1913 ranked, in value of industrial output, only behind the United States, Germany, Great Britain and France did possess an adequate economic basis for some kind of a middle class – not a flourishing one, perhaps, but one which should have been able to make its weight felt. Commercial and industrial fortunes were in fact made in Russia from the seventeenth century to the early twentieth. The intriguing question is why these fortunes tended to dissipate rather than grow, why rich merchants and manufacturers failed to found bourgeois dynasties, and, above all, why Russian money did not acquire political ambitions. The solution to these questions is best sought in the political environment in which Russian business had to operate.

As noted before, the small and unreliable returns from agriculture had compelled Russians from the time of their earliest settlement in the forest to supplement income obtained from the land with other revenues. Called promysly they were of a most diverse character: fishing, hunting, trapping, apiculture, salt distilling, leather tanning and weaving. The mingling of agricultural and non-agricultural occupations which economic conditions forced upon the population accounted, among other things, for a weak division of labour and the absence of highly skilled (that is, full-time) traders and artisans. For a long time it also inhibited the rise of a commercial and industrial culture; for where trade and manufacture were regarded as natural sources of supplementary income for all, neither could become a separate vocation. Foreign accounts of Muscovy do not mention merchants as a distinct estate, lumping them with the mass of 'little men' or muzhiki. Already in the appanage period, princes, boyars, monasteries and peasants were quick to seize every opportunity to earn additional income from such promysly as came their way. In the testaments of the Great Princes, promysly are treated as an intrinsic part of the princely patrimony, and carefully apportioned among the heirs along with towns, villages and personal valuables.

As the might and the ambitions of the Muscovite dynasty grew, it began to concentrate in its hands the major branches of trade and nearly all manufacturing. This process paralleled the crown's centralization of political power and its appropriation of landed wealth. Proceeding from the premiss underlying patrimonialism, namely that the tsar owned his realm, the rulers of Moscow sought to appropriate all the promysly along with all the authority and all the land. The manner in which political power and landed property became the exclusive domain of the tsars in the fifteenth and sixteenth centuries is reasonably well known. The same cannot be said of the acquisition of control over trade and manufacture, a subject largely unnoticed and uninvestigated by historians. Here a process of expropriation not unlike that carried out earlier in respect of landed property seems to have taken place in the sixteenth and even more so in the seventeenth century. By a succession of decrees bearing on specific promysly, the crown imposed royal monopolies, eliminating thereby the threat to itself of private competition. In the end, just as he had earlier become the country's largest landowner and *de jure* title-holder of all the landed estates, the tsar became also the exclusive proprietor of industries and mines, and both *de jure* and *de facto* monopolist in regard to all but the most trivial commercial activities. In his business affairs, he was assisted by cadres of specialists drawn from the ranks of the service class, topmost merchants, and foreigners. The trading and artisan class, in the proper sense of the term, that is, the membership of the posad communities, was in large measure excluded from these activities.

This fact is absolutely essential for the understanding of the fate of the middle class in Russia. Like everything else, trade and industry in Muscovy had to be carried out within the context of the patrimonial state, whose rulers regarded monopoly on productive wealth a natural complement to autocracy. In his letter to Queen Elizabeth, cited above (p. 77), Ivan IV taunted her that English merchants – presumably in contrast to his own – 'seek their own merchant profit', as proof that she was not a genuine sovereign. Given this view of the function of the trading class, the Muscovite state could hardly have been expected to show concern for its well-being. The richest among them it harnessed in its service; the remainder it treated as a breed of peasants whom it taxed to the limit; and rich and poor alike it expected to fend for themselves.

In his commercial capacity, the tsar handled a large variety of commodities. These he obtained from three sources: 1. surplus produced by his private domains; 2. tribute from administration and subjects; 3. purchases made for resale. As a rule, any commodity in which the crown acquired a major interest was declared a royal monopoly and withdrawn from public commerce.

The most important of the regalia in the category of surplus from royal domains were cereals, trade in which was a crown monopoly until 1762.

Vodka, which is distilled from grain (rather than potatoes, as is often mistakenly believed), was likewise a crown monopoly until the eighteenth century when the monopoly was turned over to dvoriane. It was dispensed exclusively in licensed shops.

Among commodities derived from tribute, the place of honour belonged to precious furs. These the tsar obtained from the regular tribute (*iasak*) levied on the inhabitants of Siberia; a tax collected from Siberian merchants requiring them to turn over to the Treasury the best pelt out of ten in their stock; and contributions of voevody who had to sell to the Treasury at fixed prices all the furs given them by the populace as part of their 'feeding'. These mountains of skins were sold either to western merchants resident in Russia or dispatched to the Middle East and China. Whenever they went abroad, Russian ambassadors took with them trunks filled with furs which having given out the presents (Plate 24), they sold to cover their expenses. Private dealers were allowed to trade only in the less valuable skins, unfit for export.

Many of the goods used in tsarist commerce were imported from abroad. The tsar asserted the right of first refusal on all foreign merchandise landed in the country. Before being offered to private traders, all such merchandise had to be submitted for inspection to tsarist agents who bought whatever they liked on his behalf at non-negotiable prices. A foreigner who refused the price offered could not sell the merchandise in question to anyone else in Russia. Goods obtained in this manner were either used by the tsarist household or resold for domestic consumption. This practice enabled the crown to corner the wholesale trade in luxuries. The crown also claimed a monopoly on the export of certain commodities in great demand abroad, such as caviar, flax, tar, potash and leather.

Last but not least, the crown made extensive use of regalia, claiming the sole right to commerce in any commodity it chose. The government rarely failed to impose royal monopolies whenever private initiative demonstrated the existence of a market for some previously untraded item. Thus, for example, in 1650 the government learned that the inhabitants of Astrakhan were doing brisk business with Persia in madder, a plant used in the manufacture of dyes. It immediately declared madder a state monopoly, ordering it to be henceforth sold exclusively to the Treasury at fixed prices; the Treasury, in turn, resold it to the Persians at negotiable prices. A similar injunction was imposed twelve years later on several commodities which tsarist agents discovered private businessmen had been selling at a handsome profit to westerners: Russian leather, flax, meerschaum and beef fat.[4] In practice, any product which entered into commerce became the subject of a state monopoly. It is difficult to conceive of a practice more fatal to the entrepreneurial spirit.

If the crown tightly controlled trade, it may be said to have held Russia's manufacturing industry in exclusive ownership. Apart from iron, salt and coarse cloth, all produced by very primitive domestic methods, Muscovite Russia had no indigenous industries. Its first industrial establishments were founded in the seventeenth centuries by foreigners who had come to Russia with tsarist permission and worked under state licence. Thus, the foundries at Tula and Kashira, from which developed the Russian iron industry, were the creation of Dutch and German mining experts, Andries Winius (Vinius) and Peter Marselis, who in 1632 undertook to furnish the government with weapons. Marselis also laid the foundations of Russia's copper industry. Paper and glass manufactures were founded by Swedes. The Dutch erected in Moscow the first woollen mill. These and other enterprises to which Russia's industry owed its rise were sponsored by the crown, financed by a combination of tsarist and foreign capital and directed by foreign experts. They worked exclusively for the monarchy to which they sold, at cost, whatever share of the production it required. Their profit came from the sale on the open market of the surplus. Although the Muscovite government insisted on foreign licensees training Russians in their arts, the management as well as skilled labour employed in these early establishments came almost exclusively from abroad. Native capital and managerial personnel were as conspicuous by their absence as they would have been in any western colonial dependency.

The monarchy lacked an administration to supervise its commercial activities and such promysly as salt manufacture and fisheries which were dispersed throughout the empire. It therefore made frequent use of the practice of farming out those branches of business on which it claimed a monopoly to individuals on the understanding that from the proceeds they would turn over to the Treasury a fixed annual sum. The surest way of becoming rich in Muscovite Russia was to obtain a concession of this sort. The Stroganovs, peasants who became the richest merchant family of Muscovy, owed their start to a licence to manufacture salt in conquered Novgorod. From this beginning, they gradually branched out into other profitable enterprises, but always operating either under state licence or in partnership with the state.

To supervise the business activities in which it participated directly, the crown relied on experts drawn from the ranks of native and foreign merchants. The highest echelon of such state-employed businessmen were the Moscow gosti, an élite which in the middle of the seventeenth century numbered some thirty persons. Gost' was an ancient word, derived from the same root as gosudar' (p. 77). Originally it designated all foreign merchants but, like the term 'boyar', from the end of the sixteenth century it became an honorific title bestowed by the tsar. To qualify for it, a merchant had to have large capital, because the tsar often exacted from gosti deposits which were used to make good any arrears. In terms of relative wealth, the Moscow gosti came close to the urban patricians of the west, and in the historical literature they are sometimes compared to them, but the analogy is difficult to sustain. Gosti were not free entrepreneurs; they were royal factors, appointed by the tsar and working for him. In fact, few ever requested the honour; more often than not, they were dragooned. As soon as it came to the attention of the government that a provincial merchant had accumulated a fortune, he was ordered to move to Moscow and appointed a gost. The status was more of an onerous burden than a distinction because of the risks involved in having part of one's capital tied up as collateral. Furthermore, gosti competed with one another not for goods and customers, but for royal favours, and the income they made was compensation for the services rendered the tsar. Just below gosti, in terms of social status and economic power, were members of commercial bodies called 'hundreds', namely the *gostinnaia* and *sukonnaia sotni*.

Gosti and persons enrolled in these two 'hundreds' performed the most diverse functions; they collected customs and liquor duties, appraised the goods which the tsar had an interest in buying, sold them on his account, supervised some manufactures and minted money. They constituted a kind of pool of businessmen whose members the monarchy in characteristic fashion never allowed to specialize because it did not wish to become overly dependent on them. They made their profits on handling government goods as well as on their private undertakings. In legal theory, gosti belonged with the tiaglo-bearing population; but thanks to privileges, confirmed in personal charters, they were peers of the noblest servitors. The most valuable of these privileges were exemptions from tariffs and taxes, and immunities from the detested voevoda courts; foreign gosti were tried by the Office of Ambassadors, while native ones went before a boyar designated by the tsar. They had the right to purchase votchiny, and, on certain conditions, to travel abroad. The members of the *gostinnaia* and *sukonnaia sotni* were somewhat less generously rewarded.

With all his wealth and privileges, however, the gost was a very different creature from the western bourgeois. He fawned on authority, in the preservation of whose absolute power he had an abiding interest. He bore heavy responsibilities to the state. He was an enemy of free trade. His association with royal authority and support of its monopolies made him an object of hatred of the mass of ordinary traders. The richest businessmen in Muscovy never became spokesman of the trading community at large.

Apart from gosti and the two 'hundreds' the only merchants favoured by the crown were westerners. In 1553 an English ship in search of a northern passage to China touched Russian soil not far from what later became the port city of Archangel. Its crew was escorted to Moscow where Ivan IV greeted them warmly, and offered them privileges if they would open a regular trade route between the two countries. Two years later, the Muscovy Company was formed in London for this purpose, the first of the great chartered companies of merchant adventurers. It obtained from Ivan IV the exclusive right to the northern route which its members had discovered, exemptions from tariffs and taxes, and the right to maintain in several cities its own warehouses. Although forbidden to carry on retail business, the Company did so anyway, employing for the purpose Russian front men. Later on, somewhat less generous privileges were granted to the Dutch, Swedes, Germans and other westerners. The Muscovite élite strenuously opposed the crown's policies favouring foreigners, but it could do little about them because the crown derived great profit from trade in western merchandise.

The Muscovite state made its presence felt in trade and manufacture in such an overpowering manner that even without additional evidence it should be apparent how difficult were the conditions under which the ordinary Muscovite merchant had to operate. He was barred by the crown more or less permanently from trading in the most lucrative commodities. As soon as he discovered on his own some new line of business, the crown was certain to take it away from him by declaring it a state monopoly. Gosti, members of the merchant *sotni*, and foreigners, all of them trading tax free, offered unfair competition. Manufacturing and mining, for which he had neither capital nor the know-how, were controlled by the crown and its foreign managers. The trading and artisan class therefore had left to itself nothing but scraps from the table of the tsar and his servitors; and even this little, as we shall see, it was not allowed to enjoy in peace.

To a western reader, the words 'trade and industry' used in a premodern context automatically evoke the image of the city; protective walls within which the commercial and manufacturing classes go about their affairs free and secure from arbitrary authority. In dealing with Russia, it is well at once to divest onself of such associations. There, the centre of trade and manufacture lay not in the city but in the countryside; the commercial and industrial classes did not constitute the bulk of the urban population; and residence in the city guaranteed neither security nor freedom, even in the limited sense in which these terms were applicable to Russia.

Max Weber noted that in its fully matured form the city was five things: 1. a fortress with a military garrison, 2. a market-place, 3. the seat of an autonomous court, 4. a corporation with legal status, and 5. a centre of self-government.[5] Populated centres satisfying the first two elements of this definition can be found from the beginning of recorded history in every area of the world; wherever there is organized human life of some kind, there are market places, and wherever there is political authority there are also fortified places near by. But it is only in western Europe and areas colonized by its immigrants that one meets with cities which, in addition, render their inhabitants special legal and administrative services. The city as a body of men enjoying rights not shared by the rural population is a phenomenon peculiar to the civilization of western Europe. As so much else, it came into being in the Middle Ages as a by-product of feudalism. The city originally constituted itself into a community by virtue of a grant from the feudal lord authorizing a place to be set aside for trade and crafts. Then, as the result of its members undertaking joint business ventures, the burghers acquired corporate status. As their wealth and power grew, the burghers challenged their feudal lords, transforming their corporate status into self-rule by winning special urban laws and courts, separate systems of taxation, and organs of city-government. Essentially, the urban population of continental western Europe gained its rights and transformed itself into a bourgeoisie in the course of conflict with the feudal nobility and at this nobility's expense.

The city of the western European kind did emerge between the twelfth and fifteenth centuries in north-western Russia, most notably in Novgorod and Pskov which were in close contact with the German city-states and imitated their institutions. They could also be found on the territory of the Polish-Lithuanian Commonwealth, whose urban inhabitants enjoyed autonomy based on the law of the Hanseatic town of Magdeburg. But these were short-lived exceptions. Moscow could not tolerate privileged sanctuaries from which a genuine urban civilization might have developed because they violated the kingdom's patrimonial constitution. Moscow deprived Novgorod and Pskov of their liberties as soon as it had conquered them, and it promptly curtailed the guarantees of the burghers of Poland-Lithuania when this area fell under Russian control. Long before the devastations of the Second World War such once proud metropolitan centres as Novgorod, Pskov and Smolensk degenerated into seedy large villages; and the city of Moscow owes whatever grandeur it can lay claim to not to its commercial but to its autocratic and aristocratic heritages.

Although quite unlike its western counterpart, the Russian city was still an institution of considerable complexity in whose history administrative, taxatory and economic elements overlapped in bewildering fashion.

As far as the monarchy was concerned, a city (*gorod*) was any locality, regardless of size or economic function, which had in residence a voevoda (see above, p. 96). From its point of view, the city was a military-administrative outpost *par excellence*. Muscovite Russia, and even more so imperial Russia had many centres larger, more populous, and even economically more productive than those officially designated as cities which nevertheless did not qualify as such because they lacked a voevoda or his equivalent, and therefore could not perform the functions which the state required of its cities.

In their internal structure, Muscovite cities did not differ from populated places in the countryside. All were the property of the crown, privately held cities having been liquidated concurrently with alodial land tenure. There was in the cities no private property in land; it was all held conditionally, for which reason there could be no commerce in urban real estate. In all cities large tracts were set aside for the benefit of the servitors who garrisoned them; these were held on the same terms as rural pomestia. Side by side with them, lay properties of the crown and lots inhabited by 'black' people. The tax-paying population was organized, exactly as its rural counterpart, into communities which were held collectively responsible for the fulfilment of state obligations.

Muscovite cities were few and far between, and their populations were small. If one adopts a very formal criterion and counts as cities only places with a resident voevoda, the figure is 63 cities under Ivan III, 68 under Ivan IV and 138 in 1610. If one broadens the definition to include every fortified place maintained at government expense, then the figure in the mid-seventeenth century is 226 cities containing an estimated 107,400 households or 537,000 inhabitants. Moscow at that time had between 100,000 and 200,000 inhabitants, Novgorod and Pskov 30,000 each, and of the remainder none exceeded 10,000; many so-called cities, especially on the frontier, were small fortified places manned by a few hundred soldiers. The typical Russian city in the middle of the seventeenth century had 430 households with an average of 5 inhabitants each.[6] It was a rambling agglomeration of low wooden residential buildings, churches, monasteries and bazaars, set in the midst of vegetable patches and meadows. The streets were wide and unpaved, the river banks unregulated. (Plates 26–30.) They always seemed more impressive from a distance than on closer inspection because due to their low population density they were disproportionately large. Olearius wrote that on the outside a Russian city looked like Jerusalem, but on the inside like Bethlehem.

Artisans and shopkeepers constituted only a minority of Muscovy's minuscule urban population. In Muscovy the terms 'urban' and 'artisan-trading' were far from coterminous. Because cities served primarily

administrative and military purposes, their inhabitants were mostly service personnel with their families, dependents and serfs, as well as clergy.
It is estimated that in the middle of the seventeenth century tiaglo
people comprised only 31·7 per cent of the inhabitants of Russian cities,
while 60·1 per cent were service personnel, and 8·2 per cent proprietary
serfs. In the central provinces, the tiaglo people were in a majority; but
in the frontier towns to the west, east and south, their proportion of the
total urban population was anywhere from 8·5 to 23·5 per cent.[7]

The traders and artisans were formed into communities like those in
which the majority of farmers were then living. These were called the
'*posad* community' (*posadskaia obshchina*) to distinguish it from the agricultural community called *sel'skaia* or *krest'ianskaia obshchina*. In the earlier
period, the posad was often a separate city quarter, adjoining the fortress, called *kreml'* or *gorod* (see Plate 27). But by handing out in the mercantile quarters properties to persons exempt from taxation and therefore
not part of the posad community the government confused the picture.
In the late Muscovite and early imperial periods the posad was more a
legal than a territorial entity. It had no intrinsic connection with the
city. Nearly one out of every three cities in Muscovy was without a
posad; conversely, there were posad settlements in the countryside,
especially near monasteries. At the close of the sixteenth century, only
sixteen cities had five hundred or more posad households.

In the eyes of the law, the posad constituted a legal entity because its
members, like those of a rural community, bore collective responsibility
for the fulfilment of their tiaglo obligations. However, it was in no sense
a privileged corporation, as was the urban commune in the west. The
posad bore extremely heavy tiaglo obligations, and if anything, the lot
of its members was inferior to that of rural serfs. These obligations
included ordinary and extraordinary taxes, work on fortifications, and
(for the more affluent) assisting the authorities in the collection of taxes
and tariffs. An historian of the eighteenth-century posad lists its various
possible obligations on three pages and warns that the catalogue is not
complete.[8] The status of a person belonging to a posad was hereditary
and he and his descendants were forbidden to leave it. As noted, the land
on which urban residences stood belonged to the tsar and therefore
could not be sold. Except that they plied trade and crafts as their vocation and agriculture as an avocation, whereas the black peasants did the
opposite, the two groups were barely distinguishable.

Since 1649 members of posad communities enjoyed (along with gosti
and members of the two 'hundreds') the exclusive right to produce
articles for sale and maintain shops, but the right had little value because all the estates took advantage of it without bearing their share of
the tiaglo. Some groups – e.g. the Streltsy and Cossacks – were legally

entitled to do so. But the posad also faced competition from serfs of the service people and the clergy. Peasants living on 'white' properties of lay and clerical landlords set up in most cities and in many rural localities regular markets known as *slobody* (a corruption of *svoboda*, meaning freedom) where they traded without bearing their share of tiaglo. In some localities the posad was a mere nucleus surrounded by slobody and occasionally a prosperous sloboda turned into a large market town. How significant such competition was may be gathered from the situation in Tula where at the end of the sixteenth century the posad people owned only a fifth of the stalls, while the remainder belonged to soldiers and peasants.[9] Competition from this quarter caused great bitterness and bred constant conflicts in the Muscovite city. From time to time the government took steps to placate the posad population, but without success. The posad never succeeded in shaking off the deadly rivalry of tiaglo-exempt groups.

Given these circumstances, no one stood much to gain from membership in the posad, and all the prohibitions notwithstanding, posad people in droves fled their communities. The best chance of making good their escape lay in finding a landlord or a monastery willing to take them under its wings and thus enable them to trade without bearing tiaglo. How desperate the situation of the posad community must have been may be gathered from the not uncommon practice of their members bonding themselves as slaves. Apparently the status of a slave (which carried with it exemption from all state obligations) was preferable to that of a shopkeeper or artisan – a telling commentary on the conditions of the Russian middle class. The government had to take drastic measures to stop the exodus of such people, imposing heavy penalties for unauthorized separation from the posad. To help the posad communities fulfil their responsibilities, it pressed into their depleted ranks vagabonds, impoverished dvoriane and anyone else whom it caught living outside the service-tiaglo structure. But the effect was minimal and the exodus continued. The modest growth in the number of cities during the seventeenth century was due to the expansion of Russia and the construction of military-administrative outposts along the eastern and southern frontiers.

The Muscovite city reflected accurately the threefold division of Muscovite society at large – servitors, bearers of tiaglo and clergy; it was a microcosm not a world unto itself. The servitors, peasants and clergy, who made up over two-thirds of the urban population of Muscovite Russia had their roots outside the city, while the trading-artisan class was enserfed. The diverse social gorups comprising the city population not only enjoyed no administrative and judicial autonomy but even lacked any legal status binding them to one another. The Muscovite city never belonged to itself; it was always the property of someone else – at first often of private owners, and later of the state – and its entire population was dependent on him on whose land it stood.

A century ago, a historian of the Muscovite city made a remark which subsequent researches have in no way invalidated: 'Essentially, the history of the [Russian] city is nothing else but the history of regimentation, of transformations of the commercial and industrial population of cities carried out by sovereign authority. The course of these transformations was determined by the sovereign authority's view of *state* interests.'[10] These interests centred on internal and external security and the flow of taxes. Lacking independent status, the Muscovite city could not have had a history different from that of the rest of society. Attempts by modern Russian historians to magnify its historic role are wide off the mark. It is not enough to demonstrate (as they are able to do) that Muscovy had more urban-type concentrations than the official counts of cities indicate, and many busy market-places scattered throughout the country. Historically speaking, the significance of the city lies not in numbers of inhabitants or in the intensity of economic activity – both of which were absurdly low in Muscovy in any event – but in the acquisition by its residents of judiciary, fiscal, and administrative autonomy. And of this there was no trace.

Muscovite merchants had to adapt themselves to the difficult conditions under which they lived; accordingly, their business activities tended to be small in volume, oriented towards quick profit, and conducted largely on a barter basis.

The central region of Russia – the Volga-Oka mesopotamia where the state of Muscovy was born – seems to have become first involved in long-distance trade at the beginning of the fourteenth century, when the country was under Mongol rule. The Golden Horde insisted on its tribute being paid in silver. Since Russians did not then mine precious metals, they had to look for them abroad. Around 1300 merchants from Russia established at Sarai, the capital of the Horde, a commercial colony from where they traded under Mongol protection with the Crimea and northern Iran. Thus, unlike Novgorod and Pskov, whose commercial ties were with Germany, Moscow's trade tended to be Asiatic in orientation. The most striking testimony of the debt which Russian commerce owes to the Mongols and their Turko-Tatar allies is the large number of words in the Russian vocabulary having to do with finance, merchandise, storage and transport derived from the languages of these nationalities. The Mongol origin of the Russian words for money, customs and treasury has already been noted (p. 75). The Russian word for merchandise – *tovar* – comes from the Turko-Tatar term for cattle or

possessions in general; from this same root derives *tovarishch* which originally denoted a business partner and *tovarishchestvo*, meaning a business
company. *Pai*, the Russian word for share or security, is likewise of
Tatar origin. *Chemodan* (suitcase), *sunduk* (trunk or chest) and *torba* (bag)
are of Mongol-Tatar derivation, as are the terms for many articles of
clothing, such as *karman* (pocket), *shtany* (trousers) and *shapka* (cap), and
for the means of communication and transport (e.g. *iamshchik* or postil-
lion, *telega* and *tarantass* both denoting kinds of carts in which goods were
carried). *Kniga* (book) derives from the Chinese *küen* (scroll) by way of
the Turko-Tatar *Kuinig*.[11] Such etymologies acquire special significance
when one considers that there is virtually no trace of Mongol or Turko-
Tatar influence in the vocabulary of Russian agriculture.

Russian trade remained oriented towards the east even after the
Golden Horde had dissolved and Moscow entered into regular commer-
cial relations with western Europe. The conquest in the 1550s of Kazan
and Astrakhan, both of them important entrepots of oriental and Middle
Eastern goods, increased Russian involvement with eastern markets.
Until the eighteenth century, Russia's foreign trade was directed primarily towards the Middle East, especially Iran; of the three bazaars in
Moscow in the second half of the seventeenth century, one dealt exclusively with Persian merchandise. Through Armenian, Tatar, Bukharan,
Chinese and Indian intermediaries, commercial contacts were maintained also with other parts of Asia. The Russians sold abroad raw
materials and semi-finished products (e.g. furs and leather) and imported
weapons and luxury articles.

The long tradition of Levantine trade made a deep and lasting impression on the Russian merchant class, which was not erased by subsequent
relations with the west. The point is that in Asia the Russians traded
more or less directly and on equal terms, whereas in the west, where
they faced a highly sophisticated market, they had to rely on foreign
intermediaries. Russian merchants almost never ventured on business to
western Europe – it was westerners who came to Russia to buy and sell.
Because of its eastern contacts, the merchant class became the main
carrier of Levantine influences in Russia, much as the service class (after
Peter the Great) transmitted western influences, the clergy Greek-
Byzantine, and the peasantry remained loyal to native Slavic culture.

The oriental background of the Muscovite merchant class was most
in evidence in his appearance and domestic habits.* Clothed in sump-
tuous caftans cut from imported brocades, with their tall, fur-fringed
hats and high boots with pointed toes, the gosti resembled wealthy
Persians. (Plate 24). Merchant wives painted their faces in exotic

---

* Because the boyars were also actively engaged in trade, these remarks in some measure
apply to them as well.

white and red tints. As a rule, Muscovite ladies of quality were confined to a separate quarter, called *terem* (from the Greek *teremnon*). Even as late as the middle of the nineteenth century, merchant women never worked in their husbands' shops. During the eighteenth century, the boyars and dvoriane succumbed to westernization, and by the beginning of the nineteenth they shed all traces of oriental legacy, except perhaps for a love for ostentation. The merchant class proved more conservative in this respect, and retained until the turn of the present century a characteristic eastern appearance: a beard (now usually trimmed), a long, blue coat adapted from the kaftan and usually buttoned on the left side, tall hat, baggy trousers and boots (Plates 31–4).

The oriental influence was also very much in evidence in the Russian manner of keeping shop. Following Mongol practices, the Muscovite government collected an *ad valorem* tax (*tamga*) on all goods in commerce. The collection of this tax required shops to be concentrated. The government allowed trade to be carried out only in designated market-places where officials or private persons to whom the collection of the tax had been farmed out could supervise it. Local merchants set up their rows (*riady*) of stalls, arranged by specialities, while out of town and foreign merchants had to display their wares at the *gostinnyi dvor*, a typical oriental combination of shelter for men and animals and bazaar, of which every town had at least one. The value of the goods which each shop carried was minimal. Many of the shopkeepers – and in the principal towns and posady most of them – were also the producers of the goods offered for sale. Unlike western shopkeepers, the Muscovites did not reside at their place of business. Consisting of row upon row of tiny stalls arranged by speciality, Muscovite trade centres were a type of *suq* such as one can see to this day in any Middle Eastern city. The *gostinnyi dvor* serving travelling merchants was a variant of the *karavansarai* or *khan*; like them it was located in the midst of the market-place and provided shelter but no food or bedding. As late as the middle of the nineteenth century a traveller in the provinces of Russia had to carry his own provisions and bedding because except for a few hotels in Moscow and St Petersburg, run by westerners for westerners, Russian inns provided neither.

The business mentality of the Russian merchant retained a strong Levantine stamp. We find here little of the capitalist ethic with its stress on honesty, industry and thrift. The buyer and seller are seen as rivals pitted in a contest of wits; every transaction is a separate event in which each party tries to take all. The dishonesty of the Russian merchant was notorious. It is repeatedly stressed not only by foreign travellers, whom one might suspect of prejudice, but also by native writers, including Ivan Pososhkov, Russia's first economic theorist and an ardent patriot.

Caveat emptor – 'let the buyer beware' – was rendered in Muscovite Russia as 'the pike plies the seas to keep the carp awake'; the saying was apparently so much in circulation that even foreigners were able to quote it. Mackenzie Wallace writing at the end of the nineteenth century aptly described Russian businessmen, small and large alike, as basically horse-traders. How highly they esteemed cunning may be gathered from a story told by a seventeenth-century traveller to Moscow of a Dutchman who so impressed the local merchants by his ingenuity in defrauding customers that they petitioned him to teach them his art. There is no indication that these eager students of business practices had a comparable interest in the creative sides of Dutch commerce.

Except for twenty or thirty gosti, and their companions in the two *sotni*, Muscovite merchants lived in a state of perpetual anxiety, being defenceless against the service class which administered, judged and taxed them, and in the process pitilessly bullied them. Giles Fletcher was struck by the intimidated traders he had met in Russia:

If they have anything, they conceal it all they can sometimes conveying it into monasteries, sometimes hiding it under the ground, and in woods, as men are wont to do where they are in fear of foreign invasion ... I have seen them sometimes when they have laid open their commodities for a liking [for approval] (as their principal furs and such like) to look still behind them and towards every door; as men in some fear that looked to be set upon and surprised by some enemy. Whereof asking the cause, I found it to be this, that they have doubted lest some nobleman or *syn boiarskii* of the Emperor's had been in company and so laid a train upon them to pray upon their commodities per force.[12]

Under such conditions capitalism could hardly take root. And indeed, Russian commerce tended towards natural forms of exchange. In terms of money and credit, it remained until the middle of the nineteenth century at a level which western Europe had left behind in the late Middle Ages. Trade in Muscovite Russia and in considerable measure in Russia of the imperial period was mainly carried out by barter; money was employed mostly for small-scale cash-and-carry transactions. The principal form of capital was merchandise. It was not unusual for Muscovites to buy from foreigners on credit some commodity and later to offer it to them for repurchase at a discount. This practice perplexed foreigners but it makes sense if one allows for the acute shortage of money. The Russians used goods as collateral for loans from monasteries or rich individuals, which they employed in quick speculations. Once the profit had been pocketed, the merchandise was of no further use and, if necessary, could be disposed of at a loss. As late as the nineteenth century, Jewish merchants were reputed to sell grain in Odessa at a lower price than they had paid the producers and still come out ahead.

The primitive, pre-capitalist character of Russian commerce is demonstrated by the importance of fairs. Common in medieval Europe, fairs disappeared from there following the introduction of bills of exchange, letters of credit, joint stock companies, stock exchanges and all the other marvels of modern commerce. In Russia they remained in widespread use until the end of the nineteenth century. The largest of these, the summer fair at Nizhnii Novgorod, attracted annually a quarter of a million traders. The goods offered for sale included oriental merchandise, headed by tea, for which international prices were set here, textiles, metals and products of Russian household industry (Plates 33, 35). Nizhnii Novgorod's was the largest fair in the world; but beside it there were in the middle of the nineteenth century several thousand fairs of medium and small size scattered throughout Russia. Their decline set in only in the 1880s with the spread of railways.

Given the extreme scarcity of money in circulation, it is not surprising that until modern times Russia had virtually no commercial credit or banking. Nothing so dispels the deceptive panoramas of a flourishing Russian capitalism painted by communist historians, partly out of misplaced patriotism, partly to justify the triumph of 'socialism' in a backward country, than the fact that the first successful commercial banks in Russia were founded only in the 1860s; until then, the country got along with two banks owned and operated by the state. Capitalism without credit is a contradiction in terms; and business ignorant of credit is no more capitalist than urban inhabitants without self-government are bourgeois.

The Russian merchant had no knowledge of that whole elaborate structure of commerce on which western European wealth was built. He was usually illiterate, even when doing business in the millions; and even if he knew how to read and write, he usually had no idea how to keep account books, preferring to rely on memory. Ignorance of bookkeeping was a major cause of business failures in Russia and a great deterrent to growth of firms. Many a successful enterprise collapsed after the death of its founder because his heirs could not carry on for want of account books. Risk capital, the sinews of capitalist development, was absent; what there was of it came either from the state treasury or from foreign investors. As late as the early twentieth century, the Russian middle class regarded the investor as the lowest species of businessman, far below the manufacturer and merchant in prestige.[13]

The Russian government first began to interest itself in the well-being of its business class in the middle of the seventeenth century, and from then on it never ceased to encourage private enterprise and promote an indigenous bourgeoisie. Given the power of the Russian state, these policies might in time have produced something resembling a middle class were it not that they were vitiated by other measures favouring the dvorianstvo. The crown in effect gave the landowning class all the economic privileges, including monopoly on serf labour, while concurrently throwing trade and manufacture open to the other estates. The result was to undercut the more narrowly circumscribed middle class.

In 1648, the posad people of several towns rebelled. After order had been restored, the government made an effort to satisfy their worst grievances. The Code of 1649 formally granted members of the posad communities something they had long demanded, namely the exclusive right to engage in trade and manufacture. It also deprived slobody of their tax immunities and eliminated 'white' (i.e. tiaglo-exempt) places from the cities. However, these measures proved unenforceable, as seen from the steady stream of edicts required to reconfirm them. Russian peasants were forced by economic conditions to keep on selling at markets and fairs their agricultural surplus and the products of household industry, and they did so with the connivance of landlords. Measures against foreigners were easier to enforce. In the same year (1649), under the pretext that the English nation, by executing its legitimate king, had forfeited the claim to favoured treatment, Moscow revoked the century-old privileges of the Muscovy Company. The New Trading Statute (*Novotorgovyi Ustav*), issued in 1667, considerably restricted the liberties of all foreign merchants, forbidding them once again under the penalty of confiscation to engage in retail trade. By such measures, this time strictly enforced, foreign commercial competition was gradually eliminated.

The government's attitude towards the business class changed even more noticeably in the latter's favour with the accession of Peter I. On his voyages to the west, Peter was greatly impressed by the prosperity which he saw all around him. Quickly grasping the basic principles of mercantilism on which national wealth was then believed to rest, he decided to make the Russian economy self-sufficient. He went out of his way to protect indigenous business, introducing the first comprehensive protective tariff (1724). By requiring all merchants and manufacturers to hold licences, he tried to restrict these occupations to members of the urban estates. His attempt to fashion a bourgeoisie failed, but the effort, once initiated, was never abandoned. The government henceforth no longer treated traders and artisans as sheep to be fleeced and began to act as their patron.

To stimulate private enterprise Peter abolished in 1711 royal commercial monopolies in all commodities but grain, vodka, salt and tobacco. For a while Russia enjoyed something close to internal free trade. But the merchants, taught by experience, were in no hurry to take advantage of the opportunities, probably fearing that Peter's measures were temporary, and that once monopolies were reinstituted they would suffer losses. Indeed, soon after Peter's death the monarchy reclaimed its commercial monopolies and things went back to normal.

Peter had more success in his industrial undertakings because here vital military considerations were involved. The standing army which he had created required uniforms and weapons in quantities far exceeding Russia's manufacturing capacity. They could not be imported from abroad for lack of money; and even had money been available, Peter could hardly have agreed to become a hostage of foreign suppliers in a matter affecting national security. He had no choice, therefore, but to construct his own defence industries. Calculations by modern historians indicate that during his reign the number of manufacturers and mining enterprises quadrupled. Nearly all the new industries worked for the military. As a rule, the government founded industries at its own expense and either operated them itself through the College of Manufactures and the College of Mining, or farmed them out to individual entrepreneurs chosen from the ranks of dvorianstvo and the merchant class. In the latter event, the state retained the property rights exactly as it did in the case of pomestia. Private entrepreneurs enjoyed only the right of possession, accorded to them and their heirs as long as they ran the enterprises to the government's satisfaction – otherwise they reverted to the crown.*
Under Peter, as in the seventeenth century, the manufacturers and mines worked exclusively for the state. Only that part of their output which the state did not need could be sold on the open market. The government bought the product of privately operated industrial and mining enterprises at fixed prices, usually at cost. Profits had to be made on the sale of the surplus. The quality and quantity of the product were specified; failure to meet the specifications entailed penalties, and, in case of recurrence, confiscation and fines. In return for this service, industrial and mining entrepreneurs were exempt from service obligations and taxes. In this manner some private fortunes were indeed made, e.g. that of the Demidov family, which supplied the state, at low cost, with armaments from their Tula foundries.

The energy with which Peter tackled industrial development and the success he had in raising productivity must not obscure the fact that he was acting in a very traditional Muscovite manner. He treated his entrepreneurs as he would ordinary dvoriane, that is without the slightest

---

* For which reason it is grossly misleading to assert (as is done, for example, by E.I. Zaozerskaia in *Voprosy Istorii*, No. 12, 1947, p. 68, and many other historians) that a large proportion of the manufactures founded under Peter I 'belonged' to merchants or dvoriane. Even those founded wholly or partly with private capital, were not private property in the true sense of the word, since the government could at any time take them away from the 'proprietors'. Soviet historians have understandable difficulty in grasping the difference between ownership and possession.

regard for their personal interests or wishes. The history of the Moscow Woollen Manufacture (*Moskovskii Sukonnyi Dvor*) during his reign may serve as a case in point. This enterprise, founded by Dutchmen in 1684, was a major supplier of cloth to the army. Displeased with the high costs of its operations and the low quality of the product, Peter decided on the advice of his Scottish friend, Ia.V.Bruce, to transfer its management into private hands. To this end he created a 'Commercial Company', the first chartered business enterprise in Russia. Knowing how unventuresome Russian traders were, he appointed the members of the Company by picking names from lists of the Empire's leading merchants. This done, he sent soldiers to fetch the victims and bring them to Moscow on 'temporary exile' (*vremennaia vysylka*) 'whether they wished to or not'. They were given by the treasury some capital without interest, and told that they had to deliver to the state, at cost, whatever woollen cloth it required; the remainder they could sell for their own profit free of sales tax. As long as they operated the enterprise satisfactorily, the manufacture was their 'hereditary property' (!); should they fail, the state would claim it back and punish them to boot.[14] The first business company in Russia thus came into being as a result of the government literally dragooning the entrepreneurs. The model for such procedure was clearly Muscovite state service, not western capitalism. Little wonder that under Peter instances of requests by private persons for the privilege of operating manufactures and mines were rare; the risks were great and the profits uncertain. It is only under the more favourable conditions established by his immediate successors, Anne and Elizabeth, that merchants and manufacturers began to display greater initiative. During these two reigns (1730–61), the practice of instituting crown monopolies on objects of trade and manufacture, and then farming them out to private persons reached its peak.

To provide labour for the manufactures and mines, Peter at first relied on the impressment of subjects not attached to any of the regular estates, such as convicts, vagabonds, prisoners of war, soldier wives and prostitutes. When this source proved inadequate, he transferred whole villages of state peasants from central Russia to the Urals. In the end he had no choice but to break with precedent which limited possession of serfs to the state, its service class and clergy, and in 1721 issued an edict granting merchants the right to purchase villages for the purpose of acquiring serfs for industrial and mining enterprises. The 'possessional serfs', as bonded industrial labour came to be known, were attached by an ukaz of 1736 with their families and descendants 'in perpetuity' to the factories and mines in which they were employed. These people – an industrial counterpart of rural serfs – formed the nucleus of Russia's working class.

The industrial development launched by Peter, though new in spirit was entirely traditional in execution. The state owned the means of production, set the prices and absorbed nearly all the output; the management was on good behaviour; the working force was enserfed. Assured of bonded labour and a market, the state-appointed or state-licensed entrepreneurs had no incentive to rationalize production. In short, though there was industry under Peter, there was no industrial capitalism.

The greatest break in the economic policies of Russia prior to the industrial drive of the 1880s–90s, occurred in 1762 during the brief reign of Peter III and the first few months which followed Catherine's accession. Inspired by Physiocratic ideas, the new administration dismantled the old, elaborate structure of state-run commerce and manufacture, with its network of concessions and licences, and threw both open to free public participation. The first step in this direction had been taken a decade earlier, in 1753, with the abolition of all internal tolls and tariffs in Russia. On 23 March 1762, Peter III did away with many of the royal monopolies and opened to general commerce all but a few commodities; cereals, traditionally one of the regalia, were among the items in which free trade was allowed. Catherine, who in an expansive mood once claimed commerce as 'her child', confirmed this edict upon her accession. By virtue of these laws, merchants retained the exclusive right to trade and manufacture granted them by the 1649 Code; dvoriane and peasants were permitted to sell only that which they themselves produced in the villages. But since the bulk of merchandise traded in Russia had always consisted of agricultural produce and items of household industry, the distinction had little practical significance. It meant, in effect, the introduction of freedom of trade in Russia. Even more consequential in the long-run were two edicts issued that same year concerning manufacture. On 29 March 1762, Peter III revoked the decree of his grandfather, Peter the Great, which authorized merchants to purchase serfs for use as labourers; henceforth, they could hire labour only for wages. The ownership of serfs from now on was restricted to dvoriane.* On 23 October 1762, Catherine gave permission to all the estates to found manufactures anywhere except in Moscow and St Petersburg; a Manifesto of 17 March 1775 gave Russians the right to establish every kind of manufacturing facility.

The cumulative effect of this legislation, designed to stimulate the economy, was to deliver the *coup de grâce* to Russia's ailing middle class. With one hand, the government deprived merchants of access to serfs, the principal source of labour then available in Russia and certainly the

---

* Paul I in 1798 temporarily returned to merchants the right to own serfs, but his son, Alexander I, abolished it permanently.

cheapest; with the other, it opened up to others the opportunity to do openly and legally what until then they had been doing surreptitiously, namely to compete with the merchants as traders and manufacturers. The legislation ensured that its major beneficiary would be dvoriane and peasants. Trade and manufacture were reunited with agriculture, and the centre of economic activity shifted to the village. The crown's withdrawal from direct participation in economic activity (it retained control only of the major defence industries) not only did nothing to help the middle class, but confronted it with the competition of the rural classes, more ubiquitous and formidable even than royal monopolies.

The consequences made themselves felt soon enough. Peasants throughout Russia began now to trade on an unprecedented scale, cornering much of the market in foodstuffs (cereals, garden produce and cattle) and implements for the home and farm. Already at Catherine's Legislative Commission (1767–8), the merchants loudly complained of peasant competition. By the beginning of the nineteenth century the bulk of the trade in Russia was controlled by peasants who could trade openly without paying the onerous annual certificate fee imposed by the government on merchants belonging to the urban guilds, and without bearing the various responsibilities which the merchants had to shoulder on behalf of the state.

In industry, too, the new laws produced dramatic results. Dvoriane now proceeded to take away from the merchants some of the most profitable branches of manufacture and mining in which the latter had established a strong presence between 1730 and 1762. Alcohol distilling had become a dvoriane monopoly in the eighteenth century: a privilege which allowed them to make profitable use of surplus grain. After 1762, many of the Ural mines and metallurgical industries fell under the control of wealthy landed families like the Stroganovs (merchants by origin, enobled early in the eighteenth century) and Vorontsovs, who had at their disposal unlimited servile labour. These gentlemen-industrialists of the eighteenth century edged out merchants from a number of industries. Already in 1773 a fifth of the factories belonged to dvoriane, the turnover of which was equal to nearly one-third of the turnover of all the Russian manufactures.[15] In the decades that followed, dvoriane extended their hold on manufacture. Statistics compiled in 1813–14 indicate that, in addition to all the distilleries, they owned 64 per cent of the mines, 78 per cent of the woollen mills, 60 per cent of the paper mills, 66 per cent of the glass and crystal manufactures, and 80 per cent of the potash works.[16] The merchants now had to watch helplessly as some of the most profitable branches of industry were taken over by classes based in the countryside and rooted in agriculture. The posad population remained stagnant in the course of the eighteenth century, barely exceeding 3 per cent or 4 per cent of the total; of this number nearly half were concentrated in Moscow and adjoining areas to the north and north-east.

No less serious competition came from peasants. A remarkable by-product of Catherine's economic legislation was the emergence of large-scale serf industry. Although not unique to Russia – a similar phenomenon has been observed in eighteenth-century Silesia – in no other country has it attained comparative economic importance. It is among the obrok-paying peasants of the central provinces, especially from the Moscow region, that the capitalist spirit first made its appearance in Russia. When between 1767 and 1777, in order further to stimulate rural enterprise, Catherine passed laws allowing the establishment of textile manufactures without registration, both state and proprietary peasants began to expand their household looms into large mills employing hundreds of hands. A high proportion of such entrepreneurs were Old Believers, a religious minority which compensated for the disabilities inflicted on it (such as double soul tax) by developing a strong economic drive and a sense of social discipline. Especially active were state peasants and serfs of very rich landlords, rural groups which traditionally enjoyed the greatest freedom. On the estates of Count Sheremetev, Russia's wealthiest landed proprietor, several villages developed into major industrial centres, the entire adult population of which engaged in manufacture.

Peasant entrepreneurs from the beginning concentrated on the mass consumer market which state and dvoriane manufacturers largely ignored. Cotton textiles were their most important product, but they also played a leading role in the manufacture of pottery, linen cloth, hardware, leather goods and furniture. Whole villages specialized in the production of a single item, for example, ikons. Peasant entrepreneurs living on private properties remained serfs even after having amassed vast fortunes. Such bonded magnates paid rents running into thousands of rubles a year. If the landlord consented to give them their freedom – which, for obvious reasons, he was loath to do – they were required to pay enormous sums. The serfs of Sheremetev paid for their redemption 17,000–20,000 rubles; on occasion the price could rise as high as 160,000 rubles.* Some had serfs of their own, and lived in truly seigneurial style.

The peasant entrepreneur in Russia worked under the most adverse conditions imaginable. He had one advantage, and that was proximity to the soil; his labour costs were low and in bad times his working force could always fall back on farming. But his personal situation was very

* The early nineteenth-century silver ruble can be roughly estimated as equivalent to 75 cents in US currency of the time.

precarious. As a serf, he lacked elementary civil rights. His master could at any time appropriate his wealth and send him back to the fields. He had neither access to interest-free loans nor an assured buyer as did the dvorianin-industrialist or the merchant working for the state. It is only thanks to a strong inner drive that so many serfs triumphed over their handicaps. The story of N.N.Shipov may be unusual, for few could have encountered and overcome as many adversities as this remarkable peasant, but it is typical of the spirit of this breed of self-made men. Shipov was the son of a very successful serf merchant who at the beginning of the nineteenth century made a fortune dealing in cattle and furs. After he died, his assistants stole much of the property and connived with officials to imprison his heir. In 1832 Shipov *fils* fled from his landlord and for the next five years wandered from place to place doing business under assumed names. Someone betrayed him to the authorities, and after spending four years in prison, he was returned to his legitimate master. He then obtained a passport valid for six months, on which he travelled to Bessarabia where he purchased a glue factory. On the passport's expiration, the authorities refused to renew it, and Shipov had to give up his business and once again return home. At that time he learned of a law that a serf who escaped from the captivity of the north Caucasian mountaineers, against whom the government was waging war, was to be granted freedom. Driven to desperation, Shipov made his way to the Caucasus, attached himself to the army, let himself be captured and then, having made good his escape, received his freedom and with it at last the right to carry on business free of private and official chicanery.[17]

It was thanks to men of Shipov's iron determination that rural industries made rapid progress. The deterioration in the legal status of the peasantry under Catherine should not obscure the fact that at the same time their economic conditions improved. Russian peasants were probably never as prosperous as during her reign when the liberalization of economic policies gave them virtually unlimited access to trading and manufacture.

Until 1839, when an enterprising German, Ludwig Knoop, settled in Russia, Russia's rural textile industry relied on manual labour; it was a form of cottage industry and suitably primitive in its technology. Knoop, who represented in Russia a major English textile firm, knew how to get around English prohibitions on the export of spinning machines. He won the confidence of some rich peasant manufacturers (most of them recently emancipated serfs) whom he persuaded to invest in machinery. His clients were so successful that he was soon swamped with orders. Knoop arranged credit for his peasant-clients, engaged the managers and foremen, laid out the plants, procured the raw material, and as an active shareholder often supervised actual operations. In all, he founded 122 spinning mills and died in 1894, the richest industrialist in Russia.

It is significant that these undertakings which laid the foundations of Russia's first mechanized industry were controlled not by merchants but by peasants. Prohibited from acquiring serfs, merchants had to confine themselves to supplying the raw materials to peasant-entrepreneurs and selling the finished product of their factories. The industrial processes themselves were not in their hands. Mechanical spinning of cotton yarn, the industry which in England had launched an economic and social revolution, in Russia accommodated itself perfectly well to serfdom and indeed matured within its womb. The result of technological innovation was a peculiar blend of modern technology imported from the west and servile labour inherited from Muscovy, a mixture which contradicted the nineteenth-century belief that industrialism and bondage were incompatible.

Viewed against the background of these economic facts, the attempts of eighteenth-century monarchs to build up in Russia western-type cities inhabited by a western-type bourgeoisie appear to have been singularly misguided.

It would be tedious to recount in detail the urban legislation of that age, not only because the provisions were most elaborate, but because they bore little relationship to reality and rarely produced any results. Suffice it to say that all the rulers, notably Catherine II, tried to overcome the traditional formlessness of Russian cities by consolidating all their actual inhabitants into a cohesive and legally recognized class enjoying self-government. The City Charter of 1785, issued by Catherine concurrently with her Dvorianstvo Charter, was a particularly ambitious step in this direction, because it granted the Russian urban population for the first time in history the right to form corporations and elect its own officials. But none of this meant much. The urban inhabitants continued as before to owe primary allegiance to their respective social estates; a dvorianin who happened to live in the city and to hold property there, though technically an urban inhabitant under Catherine's definition, in fact felt nothing in common with his fellow-burghers, and the same could be said of the urban peasants and clergy. In effect, the city population remained split and the merchants and artisans continued to live in isolation from the rest of society. The seemingly generous powers of self-rule granted the cities in the Charter of 1785 were immediately nullified by other provisions assuring the bureaucracy a tight reign on urban corporations.

Despite their promises, eighteenth-century governments treated cities much as their Muscovite predecessors had done, that is, as out-posts of royal authority in the countryside. Catherine prided herself that in a single decade (1775–85) she had doubled the number of cities in the empire. Investigation of her new cities reveals, however, that the increase was accomplished by the simple procedure of reclassifying villages as urban centres. Shaken by the ease with which Pugachev and his rebels had taken over vast stretches of Russia, Catherine decided in 1775 to tighten her control over the countryside. The provinces (*gubernii*) now were cut down to more manageable size, and subdivided further into districts (*uezdy*), each with its capital. How this reform was carried out can be gathered from the activities of Count R.L.Vorontsov who in 1778 was placed in charge of the reorganization of the Vladimir region. On the completion of his assignment, Vorontsov reported to the Empress that he had 'designated' (*naznachil*) thirteen cities to serve as capitals of as many districts: of this number, seven had had the status of cities already; the remaining six he picked from among villages favoured by a convenient location and good access to transport.*[18] Haxthausen aptly observes that Catherine 'designated' cities as she promoted officers. She also demoted them, for subsequently several dozen cities were punished by being deprived of their urban status.

It may be noted that at the time when she transformed villages into cities, Catherine allowed many large commercial and manufacturing centres to retain their rural status. This was done as a favour to dvoriane and had the effect of exempting their trading and manufacturing serfs from all taxes save the soul tax. An outstanding example was Ivanovo, a property of the Sheremetevs, which at the height of its economic development in the 1840s employed thousands of industrial workers, and yet still remained technically a 'village'. The administrative relabelling of the population clearly had not the slightest effect on the quality of life in the cities or on the mentality of its inhabitants, which (except for Moscow and St Petersburg) remained indistinguishable from the rural. The tripling of urban inhabitants, allegedly accomplished between 1769 and 1796, was a figment of the bureaucratic imagination.

There is no indication that in the eighteenth century Russian cities gained in economic importance. Leading authorities on urban history believe that the extremely low level of urban activity, characteristic of Muscovite Russia did not change in the eighteenth century, largely owing to the steady shift of trade and industry from town to village.[19] Nor did the population structure of the cities change. In Moscow in 1805, there were still three times as many peasant serfs as merchants.

* Sometimes the status of a village was elevated by a change of name. Thus in the Full Collection of Laws (PSZ, No. 14,359) there is an edict of 1775 changing the name of the village Black Muck (Chernaia Griaz) to Imperial City (Tsaritsyn).

Despite the monarchy's earnest efforts to stabilize it, the merchant class was in constant flux. Well-to-do merchants – *kuptsy* of the first and second guilds – liked to marry their children to dvoriane because in this way they assured them of superior social status, access to government jobs and the right to buy serfs. Once ennobled, they and their capital were lost to the middle class, although they did not necessarily cease to offer competition to their less fortunate brethren, for if they wished they could continue to trade by buying temporary licences. Merchants unable to raise the annual certificate fee required of guild members, sunk to the level of *meshchane*, lower-class urban inhabitants subject (until 1775) to the soul tax. Peasant-entrepreneurs, on acquiring the minimum capital necessary, immediately joined the ranks of the merchant class by enrolling in the third guild, and once in there were able to float upwards; their grandchildren often entered the ranks of dvoriane. The middle estate thus became a kind of half-way house for those moving up and down the social ladder. At the end of the nineteenth century, the majority of Moscow's twenty or so leading business families were of rural origin; 'one half had risen from the peasantry within the last three generations, while the other half looked back to an ancestry of small artisans and merchants who had come to Moscow in the late eighteenth or early nineteenth century.[20] The gosti of Muscovite Russia disappeared as tracelessly as did most of the ancient boyar families.

In the historical and belletristic literature one occasionally encounters a Russian merchant who meets the bourgeois ideal. But these are rare exceptions. The nineteenth-century Russian merchant is much more frequently depicted as a conceited boor interested only in money, devoid of any sense of personal calling or public responsibility, both ignorant and scornful of learning. In the sixteenth and seventeenth centuries he had to conceal his wealth; but as the monarchy introduced legislation protecting private property, he became vulgarly ostentatious in his private habits, overeating and overdrinking, and overfurnishing his home. He cultivated chinovniki, whose favours were important for him. As a rule, he kept one son at home to help out with the business and sent the others into the service. The thought that a son may know more than his father offended the patriarchal spirit of the Russian merchant class, for which reason children were not allowed to educate themselves. The author of an important study of the Moscow merchant class, and himself a descendant of one of its more prominent families, says that in all Russian literature written by the 'intelligentsia' he knows only of one place where a private entrepreneur is treated in a favourable light.[21]

This prevalent view of the merchant was undeniably unfair. Towards the end of the nineteenth century some of the leading merchant and industrial families attained a high level of cultivation. But even that cultivated minority evinced little interest in public affairs, shying away from all politics and the limelight which politics brought with it. Its non-commercial energies were directed primarily towards cultural patronage, in which towards the end of the nineteenth century businessmen displaced the impoverished landed class. The wife of a self-made railway magnate discreetly subsidized Tchaikovsky; another railway builder, Savva Mamontov, founded the first opera company in Russia, and helped support Mussorgskii and Rimskii-Korsakov. Chekhov's Moscow Art Theatre was financed with merchant money. The best collection of the Russian school of painting was assembled by the Moscow merchant Tretiakov. It was the descendants of two serf entrepreneurs, Morozov and Shchukin, who put together Russia's outstanding collection of French Impressionist and post-Impressionist art.

These were the visible upper echelons. The rank and file continued to live in a world of its own, isolated and self-contained – a world which the critic Dobroliubov called the 'Kingdom of Darkness'. Its outstanding characteristics were an intense nationalism coupled with fear of western influences, and deep loyalty to autocracy whose protective tariff policy enabled this class to withstand foreign competition.

When in the 1880s, the Ministry of Finance began to promote large-scale industrial development, native entrepreneurship once again showed little inclination to commit itself. The situation resembled that familiar from the seventeenth century: state initiative, foreign money and management. The second phase of Russia's industrialism, involving the development of steel, coal, petrol, chemical and electrical industries, found Russia's middle class unprepared and unwilling. Russia had missed the chance to create a bourgeoisie at a time when that had been possible, that is on the basis of manufacture and private capitalism; it was too late to do so in an age of mechanized industry dominated by joint-stock corporations and banks. Without experience in the simpler forms of capitalist finance and production, the Russian middle class lacked the capacity to participate in economic activity involving its more sophisticated forms.

It is enough to survey the leading branches of heavy industry created in Russia in the late nineteenth century to see the decisive role which foreigners played in their development. The modern coal and steel industries located in the Donets–Krivoi Rog region of the Ukraine were founded by the English and financed by a combination of English, French and Belgian capital. The Caucasian oilfields were developed by English and Swedish interests. Germans and Belgians launched Russia's electrical and chemical industries. Indeed, the textile mills of central Russia, founded by serf entrepreneurs, were the only truly modern industry of native origin.* The great surge of Russian industrial production in the 1890s, which attained a pace unmatched either before or since, was not so much the outgrowth of Russia's own, internal economic development, as the result of the transplantation of western money, technology and above all, management.† Russian capitalists – rich landowners and merchants alike – were too ignorant of the techniques of modern investment to be able to initiate the kind of financial operations which were required; and in any event, they preferred to place their money in the securities of the imperial government, in the safety of which they had unbounded faith, than to take a chance on industrial ventures. Only after foreigners had borne the brunt of the risk did native capital flow into heavy industry. Hence, on the eve of the Revolution a third of Russia's industrial investment and a half of the bank capital of her major banks were of foreign provenance.[22]

The political outlook of these self-made people was influenced by a simple economic fact, namely high tariffs. Fledgling Russian industries would not have been able to survive English or German competition without the aid of tariff measures, which became increasingly stringent as the nineteenth century drew to a close.

Hence, the timidity and conservatism of the Russian moneyed class in economic activities was duplicated by its political behaviour. Its own sympathies were certainly monarchist and nationalist, but it preferred not to expose itself. It stood aside when the great conflict between the intelligentsia and government got under way in the middle of the nineteenth century. In 1905, a group of leading businessmen attempted to form their own political party, but it never got off the ground and most of them ended up in the ranks of the conservative Octobrists. The First Duma (1906) had among its deputies two industrialists and twenty-four merchants – 5·8 per cent of the total membership; surely a pitiful share

* The railway boom, in which Russian capital did participate in a major way, when not directed by high government officials or generals, was promoted largely by Jews or naturalized Germans.

† It is noteworthy that in the historical evolution of Russian industry, native resources have always proved inadequate to the task of making the transition to more advanced methods of production. Having learned in the seventeenth century the basic techniques of manufacture and mining with disciplined human labour, Russians used them for two centuries. The next phase, heavy industry operated by steam and electric power, was introduced again by westerners in the 1880–90s. It has served as the basis of the Soviet economy which until recently kept on developing the foundations of mechanized industry of the first generation but has shown no ability to make the leap into automated methods of production distinguishing the post-Second World War economy of the west. Here again, in the 1960s–70s, the Russian government has been forced to rely on foreign capital and foreign technology, paying for both, as it had done throughout its history, with raw materials. This accounts for the ironic situation that half a century after the Revolution one of whose goals was to liberate Russia from 'colonial' economic dependence, the Soviet government once again invites foreign capital and grants concessions to foreign enterprises.

for the 'bourgeoisie' in an institution supposed to have embodied 'bourgeois' rule in Russia. This political impotence was due, first and foremost, to a conviction, acquired from centuries of experience that in Russia the path to wealth lay not in fighting the authorities but in collaborating with them, with the corollary conviction that when contenders for political power were locked in combat it was wisest to sit tight.

It is not surprising, therefore, that industrialists and merchants remained inactive in 1917, when their fate hung in the balance. They supported neither the tsarist regime, nor the Provisional Government, nor the anti-communist White Movement. Those who had the money, quietly folded their tents and fled abroad; those who did not, sat on the sidelines, watching the radical intelligentsia fight it out with the nationalist officers and awaiting the better times that never came.

CHAPTER 9

THE CHURCH AS SERVANT OF THE STATE

> Between ourselves, there are two things that I
> have always observed to be in singular accord:
> supercelestial thoughts and subterranean
> conduct.
>
> Montaigne

Externally, the most striking quality of Orthodox Christianity is the
beauty of its art and ritual. Even after centuries of destruction, the
churches and monasteries which have survived in Russia stand out as
the most attractive product of human hands in an otherwise bleak and
monotonous landscape. This holds true of the majestic cathedrals in
Novgorod, Vladimir and the Moscow Kremlin, but no less of the more
modest stone churches built at the expense of princes, boyars and merchants, and the wooden chapels erected by the peasants themselves. Of
their original decorations little remains, but the best medieval ikons
preserved in museums (some, no doubt, of Greek origin) are rendered in
a manner which suggests a highly refined taste. Russian liturgical music,
unfortunately, was heavily penetrated in the eighteenth century by
Italian influences. Still, even in its corrupt form it rarely fails to produce
a strong impression, especially during Easter when Orthodox services
reach the height of splendour. If these combined visual and aural effects
dazzle modern man, it takes little effort to imagine the overwhelming
effect they must have had on peasants. It is not without significance for
the role which the Orthodox church assigns sensory impressions that
according to the Russian Primary Chronicle the decisive consideration
in Russia's conversion to Christianity was the effect produced on Kievan
emissaries by Constantinople's Hagia Sophia.

The basic doctrinal element in Orthodoxy is the creed of resignation.
Orthodoxy considers earthly existence .an abomination, and prefers
retirement to involvement. It has always been keenly receptive to cur-
rents emanating from the orient which preached withdrawal from life,
including eremitic and hesychast doctrines striving for total dissocia-
tion from earthly reality. In the eighteenth and nineteenth centuries

when religious leaders in the west, passion and enthusiasm safely behind them, were worrying how to accommodate faith to science or the needs of society, Russians were experiencing personal conversions leading in the very opposite direction, towards renunciation, mysticism, hypnosis and ecstasy. Among Russian peasants in that age of rationalism there spread sectarian movements of an extreme irrational type such as western Europe had not seen since the Reformation.

An aspect of this resignation is humility and dread of *hubris*. Orthodox theologians claim that their church has remained truer to the teachings of Christ and the practices of early Christianity than either the Catholic or the Protestant ones on the grounds that the latter, having become contaminated by contact with classical civilization, have assigned far too great a role to analytic reason, a concession which has inexorably led them to the sin of presumption. Orthodoxy preaches patient acceptance of one's fate and silent suffering. The earliest canonized saints of the Russian church, the medieval princes Boris and Gleb, attained saint-hood because they had let themselves be slaughtered without offering resistance.

If one were dealing with the religion of Eastern Christianity one would naturally dwell on its aesthetics and ethics. But our concern is with the political performance of the Russian church and especially with its involvement in the relationship of state to society, not with what the best religious minds preached and practised, but with what the church as an institution did. And once the inquiry shifts to this ground one quickly discovers that notwithstanding its extreme other-worldliness, the Orthodox church of Russia was to an uncommon degree implicated in all the sordid business of survival. In actual practice, it turned out to be much less spiritual than faiths like Judaism and Protestantism which regard involvement in worldly affairs as essential to the fulfilment of religious obligations. Observing its fate one is reminded of Montaigne's saying placed at the head of this chapter, linking supercelestial thought with subterranean behaviour. It can hardly be otherwise since anyone who renounces involvement in life is without principles to guide him whenever life compels him to become involved. Lacking rules of practical conduct, the Russian church did not know how to adapt itself to its circumstances and still uphold, even if in an imperfect, compromised form what it regarded as its fundamental spiritual values. The result was that it placed itself more docilely than any other church at the disposal of the state, helping it to exploit and repress. In the end, it lost its institutional identity and allowed itself to be turned into an ordinary branch of the state bureaucracy. All of which made it unusually vulnerable to shifts in political alignments and trends in public opinion. Unlike the other churches, it failed to carve out for itself an autonomous sphere of activity. It had nothing to call its own, and identified itself to such an extent with the monarchy that when the latter fell, it went right down with it. The relative ease with which the communists succeeded in eliminating the church from public life in Russia contrasts tellingly with the resistance they encountered in Catholic Eastern Europe where, having attempted the same and failed, in the end they had to accept the church as an independent institution.

Except for the Hungarians, the Russians were the last east Europeans to be converted to Christianity. Formal conversion occurred in 987 (rather than 988–9, as the chronicles report) when Prince Vladimir and his court, followed by the rest of the warrior class received baptism from the Greek clergy. The Slavic population at large was converted slowly and often under duress; for many centuries afterwards it continued to adhere to pagan practices. The choice of Orthodoxy for Kievan Russia was a perfectly natural one if one takes into account the wealth of Byzantium in the tenth century and the superiority of its culture relative to Rome's, as well as the importance to Kiev of commercial relations with it.

The fact that Russia received its Christianity from Byzantium rather than from the west had the most profound consequences for the entire course of Russia's historic development. Next to the geographic considerations discussed in the opening chapter of this book, it was perhaps the single most critical factor influencing that country's destiny. By accepting the eastern brand of Christianity, Russia separated itself from the mainstream of Christian civilization which, as it happened, flowed westward. After Russia had been converted, Byzantium declined and Rome ascended. The Byzantine Empire soon came under siege by the Turks who kept on cutting off one by one parts of its realm until they finally seized its capital. In the sixteenth century, Muscovy was the world's only large kingdom still espousing eastern Christianity. The more it came under the assault of Catholicism and Islam, the more withdrawn and intolerant it grew. Thus, the acceptance of Christianity, instead of drawing it closer to the Christian community, had the effect of isolating Russia from its neighbours.

The Orthodox Church, being composed of independent national units, is by its very nature decentralized. It has no papacy to give it cohesion; its units tend to be 'autocephalous' or 'self-headed'. Major doctrinal and administrative issues are settled by councils (synods) which on important occasions assume the format of international church congresses. This practice too is more faithful to the spirit of early Christianity, but it does tend to weaken Orthodoxy's ability to stand up to secular authority. Its structural decentralization is reinforced by the right of national branches of the Orthodox church to make use of local languages in liturgies and theological writings. Intended to bring the church closer to the people, the practice has the effect of separating the members of the Orthodox community still further. Orthodoxy has nothing corresponding to Latin to give its members a sense of oneness transcending national boundaries. The Russian clergy, for example, were ignorant of Greek, and had to import monks from the Balkans whenever they needed to consult Byzantine books.

The whole trend of Orthodox Christianity may be said to be centrifugal, away from the ecumenical towards the regional. And this trend, in turn, has tended to blur the distinction between church, state and nation. The Orthodox church never had the power and the cohesion needed to defend its interests from secular encroachments. Divided into many national branches, each separated from the rest by frontiers and barriers of language, each under its own hierarchy, it had little choice but to adapt itself to whatever temporal power it happened to live under. A perceptive French observer noted already in 1889, long before the Revolution had demonstrated the fact, the utter dependence of the Russian church on the shifting winds of politics:

In Eastern Orthodoxy, the ecclesiastical constitution tends to model itself on the political, while the boundaries of the churches tend to reproduce the boundaries of states. These are two correlative facts, inherent in the national form of the Orthodox churches. Confined within the frontiers of the state, deprived of a common head and religious centre abroad, independent of one another, these churches are more susceptible to the influence of temporal power, more vulnerable to the backlash of revolutions of lay society. With their everywhere identical hierarchy of identical priests and bishops, the Orthodox churches adapt themselves, depending on the time and place, to the most diverse regimes: the mode of their internal administration always ends up by harmonizing with the mode of the political organization.[1]

The close, almost symbiotic identification of church and state characteristic of eastern Christianity has deep roots in historic and doctrinal factors.

To begin with the historic. The eastern church was fortunate to enjoy from its inception the patronage of the Roman Emperors who, after conversion, transplanted their capital to Constantinople. In Byzantium, the emperor was head of the church, and the church 'was within the state and ... part of the state organization'. In the words of Emperor Justinian there existed a relationship of 'harmony' between secular and ecclesiastical authorities which in practice meant that the Emperors participated in some of the most important church functions, including formulation of canon law, summoning of general church councils, and the appointment of bishops. In return, the state used the power at its disposal to uphold the decisions of the synods and to maintain on their territory religious orthodoxy.[2] For Byzantine theorists it was axiomatic that the church could not subsist without protection of the state. The matter was stated succinctly by the Patriarch of Constantinople in a letter he sent to Prince Basil I of Moscow around 1393. Objecting to Basil's reputed assertion that Muscovy had a church but no emperor, the Patriarch reminded him that it was the duty of emperors to convoke synods, support church rules, and fight heresies. Hence 'it is not possible for Christians to have a church and not to have an emperor. Imperial authority and church exist in close union and communication with one another, and the one cannot be separated from the other.'[3]

In the west, the conditions making for such close collaboration were absent. After the imperial capital had been transferred to Constantinople, Rome found itself in a political vacuum which its bishops promptly filled. The western church for a long time had no monarchy to contend with, and developed strong secular interests of its own. When, therefore, independent secular authority made its appearance in the west, the situation tended towards confrontation. The western church was not in the least shy in asserting its superiority; already Pope Gregory the Great (590–604) boldly proclaimed the supremacy of church over state. Precisely because it had developed under politically more auspicious circumstances, the eastern Church made on its behalf more modest claims. Then, as Byzantium went under, it became yet more dependent on secular authority for physical protection and financial assistance, whereas the papacy grew richer and more powerful and had less reason than ever to acknowledge secular authority as its equal.

The doctrinal factor which pushes the Orthodox church into the arms of the state has to do with its inherent conservatism. This church considers itself to be the custodian of truths eternally revealed; its mission is to make certain that these are not tampered with or diluted. Purity of doctrine and ritual are for it matters of the gravest importance. Reform movements within orthodoxy have generally aimed at the removal of what were perceived as innovations rather than at a return to scriptural Christianity or an adaptation to modern conditions. The ultimate authority in its eyes is not the Gospels but church tradition. (The Holy Scriptures in Russia were first translated and published as late as the 1860s–70s.) Because of the importance which attached to the outward manifestations of religion, its magical elements, the Orthodox church has always staunchly resisted changes in ritual, iconography or any other practice. Byzantium still experienced conflicts over doctrine; but by the tenth century when Russia underwent conversion, these had been largely resolved, so that she received the faith in a finished and supposedly perfect form – a fact which made its ecclesiastical establishment more conservative than even the mother church.

Its inherent conservatism causes Orthodoxy to want strong secular authority at its side. The land must be pure and 'holy', unpolluted by false faiths. No deviation from tradition can be tolerated. As the Byzantine Patriarch Photius put it, 'Even the smallest neglect of tradition leads to complete contempt of dogma'; in other words, every slip is the beginning of apostasy. This and much else connected with the strict interpretation of the revealed truth impelled Orthodox religion towards theocracy, which, given the historic circumstances under which it had evolved, in practice signified heavy reliance on secular authority.

The Golden Age of the Orthodox Church in Russia coincided with Mongol domination. The Mongols exempted all the clergy living under their rule from the burdens which they imposed on the rest of the subjugated population. The Great Iasa, a charter issued by Genghis Khan, granted the Orthodox church protection and exemption from tribute and taxes in return for the pledge to pray for the khan and his family. The privilege was an immense boon to the church at a time when the rest of Russia suffered from heavy exactions and violence, and its wealth grew by leaps and bounds. The main beneficiaries of Mongol favour were the monasteries. In the fourteenth century, Russian monks undertook vigorous colonization, and before it was over built as many new abbeys as had been established since the country's conversion four hundred years ealier. Around 1550, there were in Russia some two hundred monasteries, some of immense size, among them the St Sergius Monastery of the Trinity, the Beloozero Monastery of St Cyril, and the Solovetskii Monastery. Much of the monastic land came from the princes of Moscow in gratitude for the numerous services which the church performed on its behalf, especially by backing its claim to monocratic and autocratic power. Additional land came from boyars who customarily made provisions for monasteries in their wills. That which the clergy got it kept because, unlike secular landholders, it enjoyed institutional continuity, and, of course, did not practice subdivision.

As their holdings grew, the monks no longer were able to till their land and had to resort to tenant labour. Monasteries were among the first landlords to petition the crown for charters fixing peasants to the soil. The larger abbeys grew into vast business enterprises quite indistinguishable from boyar votchiny. At its height, the St Sergius Monastery of the Trinity had 100,000 peasant 'souls' cultivating its estates scattered in fifteen provinces. In the middle of the seventeenth century, the properties attached to the office of the patriarch alone had some 35,000 serfs. Foreign travellers of the sixteenth century are in agreement that the Russian clergy owned a third of the land, and this estimate, even if somewhat suspect because of its unanimity, is generally accepted by modern historians. It must be emphasized, however, that because of the decentralized structure of Orthodox Christianity, this wealth did not belong to the 'church' as a whole. Like boyar land, ecclesiastical properties were subdivided into many votchiny, large, medium and small, and widely dispersed. The actual owners were the patriarch, bishops, churches, abbeys and parishes. (Although it is true that the patriarchal office collected taxes from all these holdings.) In many instances, properties nominally belonging to a monastery were held by individual monks, who went about their business as would any other landlord or merchant. The great disparity in wealth between the few rich and the rest, which has been noted in the case of secular landholders and the merchant class, held also true of church wealth in Russia. At one end of the spectrum stood the great abbeys (*lavry*) whose combined holdings equalled those of the most affluent boyars; at the other, parish churches whose priests supported themselves by tilling their plots just as did the peasants to whom they ministered. Clerical holdings had to be reconfirmed by every new khan or (later) Great Prince, exactly as was the case with lay properties. Its wealth placed the Russian church in an ambivalent situation *vis-à-vis* secular authority, because while the priests and monks in their clerical capacity were subject to archbishops, in their capacity as landlords they were subject to the jurisdiction of the local prince. In sum, clerical land in Russia was every bit as decentralized and dependent on secular authority as was lay landholding, and therefore politically just as impotent.

Care of its properties absorbed most of the time of the monastic or 'black' clergy. It was even more worldly than the monastic clergy of late medieval western Europe. In a typical Russian abbey of the fourteenth and fifteenth centuries the monks lived not within their walls but in the towns and villages belonging to them, where they supervised the agricultural and commercial activities and the promysly of their chapters. The majority of Russian monks were not even ordained as priests.

The worldly corruption of the Russian clergy was furthered by its ignorance. The church language in Russia was old Slavonic, a bookish language created in the ninth century by the missionaries Cyril and Methodius on the basis of the Slavic spoken in their native Macedonia. While not identical with Russian, it was close enough to it to be mastered with a minimum of education. Neither Greek nor Latin was taught at the Russian monasteries, and little literary work was carried out except for some rudimentary chronicle-writing and hagiography. The Russian clergy was unbelievably ignorant. Unless we assume that all foreign visitors to Muscovy conspired to tell lies, the picture which emerges from their accounts of religious life there is appalling:

Foreigners state that ordinary laymen knew neither the story of the Gospels, nor the symbol of the faith, nor the principal prayers, including 'Our Father' and 'Virgin, Mother of God', naively justifying their ignorance on the grounds that all this was 'very subtle science fit only for the tsar and the patriarch, and altogether lords and clergy who did not have to work'. But the same foreigners give also the most devastating evidence against those who did have the leisure and even a special leisure to acquire this knowledge. Olearius ... writes that in his time hardly one [Russian] monk in ten knew 'Our Father'. At the end of the seventeenth century Wahrmund mentions a monk begging for alms in the name of a fourth member of the Holy Trinity, who turned out to be St Nicholas. After this, it is not surprising to read in Fletcher ... that the Bishop of Vologda was unable to tell him from which book of the Holy Scriptures he had just finished reading aloud at Fletcher's request and how many evangelists there were; nor to learn from Olearius and Wickhart (seventeenth century) that the patriarchs of their time were extremely ignorant in matters of faith and could not engage in theological arguments with foreigners.[4]

In the fourteenth and fifteenth centuries, the Russian church immersed itself so deeply in secular affairs that it ceased to uphold Christianity in any but the most primitive magic-ritualistic sense. And even in this respect it found it difficult to resist shortcuts. Thus, for instance, to compress their interminable services, Muscovite churches and monasteries adopted the practice of *mnogopenie* which had several priests or monks chanting successive parts of the liturgy at the same time, with resultant bedlam.

This worldliness in time produced the inevitable reaction which, for all its superficial resemblance to the western Reformation, was an event *sui generis* with an entirely different outcome.

Russian frontiers were never as hermetically sealed as the government wished, and in the late Middle Ages foreign reform movements succeeded in penetrating Muscovy. One of these, the *Strigol'nik* heresy, spread in the middle of the fourteenth century in Novgorod, the Russian city in closest contact with the west. Though little authentic information is available about this movement because its adherents were eventually extirpated and their writings destroyed, it appears to have been a typical proto-Reformation heresy similar to the Catharist (Albigensian). Preaching on street corners, its adherents castigated the ordained clergy and monks for their corruption and worldliness, denied the validity of most of the sacraments, and demanded a return to the 'apostolic' church. In the 1470s a related heresy of the so-called 'Judaizers' emerged in Novgorod. Its adherents also attacked the church for its materialism, especially its ownership of great landed wealth, and called for a simpler, more spiritual religion. The Judaizing heresy became very dangerous to the established church because it gained converts among priests close to the tsar and even members of his immediate family.

But the gravest challenge to the established church came from within its own ranks, from elements whose doctrinal and ritualistic orthodoxy was beyond suspicion. The roots of this particular reform movement lay in Greece. In the latter part of the fifteenth century among the monks living at Mt Athos, the centre of Orthodox monasticism, there spread talk of an imminent end of the world. Some monks left their abbeys to settle in hermitages. Here, living in utmost simplicity, they prayed, studied and meditated. This so-called 'hesychast' movement was imported to Russia by the monk, Nil Sorskii, who had been to Mt Athos. Around 1480, Nil moved out of his monastery and dug himself a pit in the marshy forest wilderness north of the upper Volga, where he henceforth lived in solitude praying and studying the scriptures and patristic writings. Other monks followed his example, settling in the vicinity of Nil's hermitage or pushing on further north. These 'Transvolga Elders', did not at first seem to threaten the interests of the established church because the kind of life they advocated was too rigorous to attract many followers. But in time Nil became involved in a debate concerning the principle of monastic landholding, and when that happened, the church was thrown into a crisis.

By the end of the fifteenth century, its claim to monocratic authority well established, the Muscovite monarchy required much less urgently the worldly favours of the church. In fact, it was beginning to cast a greedy eye on the church's properties to whose growth it itself had made major contributions, as these yielded neither taxes nor services and could be put to better use by being carved up for distribution as pomestia. Ivan III indicated his attitude clearly enough when in conquered Novgorod he confiscated most of the ecclesiastical holdings on his own behalf. The friendly reception accorded the Judaizing movement at his court may have had something to do with this heresy's outspoken opposition to monastic wealth. His son, Basil III, began to supervise closely monastic revenues and occasionally even helped himself to them. He probably also issued some kind of an order prohibiting monasteries from acquiring additional land without royal approval because a decree to this same effect issued early in the reign of Ivan IV (1535) made reference to a previous law. Many boyars also sympathized with the vision of a spiritual church, partly to deflect the crown's attention from their own holdings, partly to help it acquire more land for distribution to servitors. There are suspicions that it was either the tsar or boyars close to his court who prevailed on Nil Sorskii to leave his anchorage and denounce the monasteries for owning land. This occurred in 1503 when Nil suddenly made his appearance at a synod to urge that the church renounce its wealth and resort to alms. His appeal threw the assembly into panic. The synod unanimously rejected the proposal, passing a resolution which reconfirmed the inalienability and sacredness of ecclesiastical holdings. But the issue would not die quite so easily. Nil's speech was only the opening shot in a war between two clerical parties later labelled 'anti-property' (*nestiazhateli*) and 'pro-property' (*liubostiazhateli*) which went on until the middle of the sixteenth century.

The quarrel was not, in the first instance, over politics; at issue were differing conceptions of the church. Nil and the other Transvolga Elders envisaged an ideal church, unencumbered by worldly responsibilities, serving as a spiritual and moral beacon in a dark and evil world. One of the leading figures in Nil's party was Maxim the Greek, a native of Corfu who had studied in Italy and there fallen under the influence of Savonarola. Having come to Russia to help translate Greek books, he was appalled by the debased quality of the clergy. Why were there in Russia no Samuels to stand up to Saul and no Nathans to tell the truth to erring David, he asked; and the answer, given by Kurbskii or who-ever it was that wrote the epistles to Ivan IV credited to him was: be-cause the Russian clergy were so concerned with their worldly posses-sions that they 'lay motionless, fawning in every way on authority and obliging it so as to preserve their holdings and acquire still more'.[5] There was implied in this argument a clear political message, namely that only a poor church could look the tsar straight in the eye and serve as the nation's moral conscience. The conservative, 'pro-property' party, on the contrary, wanted a church which collaborated intimately with the monarchy and shared with it responsibility for keeping the realm truly Christian. To be able to do that, it needed income, because in fact only financial independence freed the clergy for excessive concern with worldly affairs. Each party could draw on historic precedent, the former with reference to early Christian practices, the latter by appeals to the Byzantine tradition. The monarchy's stand in this dispute was ambiva-lent. It did want to get hold of the church's properties, and with that in mind it encouraged at first the 'anti-property' group. But it preferred their opponents' political philosophy which viewed the church as the collaborator of the state. Allusions to Nathan and Samuel certainly could not appeal to patrimonial rulers who desired no independent institutions in their realm, least of all a church which took it upon itself to act as the nation's conscience. In the end, by skilful manoeuvring, the monarchy got the best of both worlds: it first supported the 'pro-property' faction; then, having with its help liquidated the proponents of an independent, spiritual church, reversed itself and, adopting the recommendations of the defeated 'anti-property' faction, proceeded to sequester church lands.

The leader and chief ideologist of the conservatives was Joseph, abbot of the Volokolamsk monastery. His was a very unusual monastic establishment, quite different from any then in existence in Russia. Voloko-lamsk operated on communal principles, which permitted the monks no private property: all the possessions of the abbey were institutionally owned. Its brethren were required to reside in the monastery, where they were subject to strict disciplinary codes drawn up by its abbot. Volokolamsk had property and yet it was not corrupt. Joseph's innova-tions showed that it was possible to combine ownership of land with the ascetic habits demanded by the church, that wealth did not necessarily lead to the abdication of moral responsibilities, as the Transvolga Elders were charging. It was for this reason that the clergy, shaken by Nil's speech, turned to Joseph to lead the counterattack. In upholding the principle of monastic landholding, Joseph had a powerful argument in his favour. Orthodox canon law requires the parish priests to marry but the bishops to remain celibate – a rule which forces the church to draw its bishops from the ranks of the monastic clergy. Referring to this rule, Joseph argued that it was unreasonable to expect Orthodox monks to spend all their time supporting themselves; for if they did so, they would have no time left to acquire the knowledge and the experience that they would need when called upon to administer a diocese. Further harm resulting from this practice would be the likelihood that the better sort of people, namely boyars, on whom the church heavily depended to manage its abbeys and bishoprics, would stay away from monasteries should they be required to perform menial labour. The argument was practical, almost bureaucratic, in nature. Joseph did not stop here but went on to question the motives of the Transvolga Elders. He was a rabid foe of the Judaizers, preaching that they be rooted out by sword and fire, without even being granted the opportunity to recant. Nil and his followers, while in no wise sympathetic to heresy, preferred excom-munication to the death penalty. Exploiting the more tolerant attitude of the 'anti-property' group, Joseph assailed their orthodoxy. In his principal work, a collection of essays gathered by his pupils in book form and inappropriately titled *The Enlightener* (*Prosvetitel'*), he piled citation upon citation from the scriptures and patristic writings to prove his points, intermingling arguments with diatribes against the Judaizers and anyone who had for them the least tolerance. In his opinion, the Russian church as it then stood was the purest and most perfect in the world: 'In piety, the Russian land now surpasses all the others.'[6] The implication of this view was that any reform would debase the country's religious standing and diminish its inhabitants' assurance of eternal salvation.

Joseph reinforced his arguments with ruthless intrigues at the court designed to turn the tsar against the reformers and their supporters among the courtiers and boyars. An advocate of the 'church militant', during his early career he had occasionally run foul of the crown; but now that church properties were in danger, he became an extravagant apologist of royal absolutism. In arguing the divinity of tsars – an idea he was the first to introduce into Russia – Joseph relied on the authority of Agapetus, a sixth-century Byzantine writer. From him he borrowed the central thesis of his political theory: 'Although an Emperor in his physical being is like other men, yet in his authority [or office] he is like God.'[7] To curry favour with the crown, in 1505 or 1506 he took a step for which there was no precedent in Russian history: he withdrew his abbey from the patronage of its local appanage prince (and incidentally, its generous benefactor) a younger brother of Ivan III, and placed it under the personal protection of the tsar. Thus, skilfully combining censure of heresy with eulogies of absolutism, and all the time reminding the crown of the church's utility to it, Joseph managed to turn the tables on the Transvolga Elders. The small band of hermits which strove for a spiritual church was no match for the conniving abbot. After Joseph's death (1515), the most important ecclesiastical position went to members of his party, and many Russian monasteries were reorganized on the model of Volokolamsk. A decisive event in the conflict occurred in 1525 when Metropolitan Danil, one of his disciples, in contravention of canon law, authorized Basil III to divorce his childless wife and remarry, offering to assume the sin, if such it was, on his own conscience. Henceforth, the grateful tsar completely backed the Josephites, to the extent of allowing them to imprison their opponents, among them Maxim the Greek. The Josephite party attained the apogee of its influence under Metropolitan Macarius. It was this ecclesiastic who planted in the mind of Ivan IV the idea of crowning himself tsar.

Fear for its properties, of course, was not the only motive behind the Russian church's drive to build up a powerful and unlimited monarchy. There were also other considerations; the need for state assistance in extirpating heresy, protecting Orthodox Christians living under Muslim and Catholic rule, and reconquering those parts of the Polish–Lithuanian Commonwealth which had once formed part of 'Holy Rus' '. The threat of secularization was only the most pressing factor, the one which made collaboration with secular powers especially urgent. Traditionally partial to strong imperial authority, in the first half of the sixteenth century, under threat of expropriation, the Russian Orthodox Church placed its entire authority behind the Muscovite monarchy, filling its mind with ambitions which on its own it was incapable of conceiving. The entire ideology of royal absolutism in Russia was worked out by clergymen who felt that the interests of religion and church were best served by a monarchy with no limits to its power. This ideology consisted of the following principal ingredients:

1. The idea of the Third Rome: the Romes of Peter and Constantine

had fallen as punishment for heresy; Moscow has become the Third Rome; as such it would stand for all eternity because there shall be no Fourth. This idea, formulated some time in the first half of the sixteenth century by the monk Philotheus of Pskov, became an integral part of official Muscovite political theory. Related to it was the belief that Muscovy was the purest, most pious Christian kingdom in the world;

2. The imperial idea: the rulers of Moscow were heirs of an imperial line which extended all the way back to the Emperor Augustus: theirs was the most ancient and therefore the most prestigious dynasty in the world. A genealogy to fit this scheme was worked out by clerics working under the supervision of Metropolitan Macarius and given official sanction in the tsarist Book of Degrees (*Stepennaia Kniga*);

3. The rulers of Russia were universal Christian sovereigns: they were emperors of all the Orthodox people in the world, i.e. they had the right to rule and protect them and, by implication, to bring them under Russian suzerainty. One of the occasions at which this was asserted was at the church synod held in 1561 (above, p. 73). In some writings, claims were made on behalf of the Russian tsar as the ruler of all the Christians, not only of those professing the Orthodox faith;

4. Divine authority of kings: all authority was from God, and the Russian tsar, in the exercise of his office, was like God. His authority extended over the church in all but doctrinal matters; he was the church's temporal ruler and the clergy had to obey him. Introduced into Russia by Joseph of Volokolamsk, the theory was subsequently confirmed by several church synods, including that convened in 1666.

By throwing its weight so fully behind royal absolutism, the Russian church achieved its immediate objectives: it uprooted dangerous heresies and saved (for the time being, at any rate) its properties. But it bought these victories at a terrible price. The refusal to adopt the reforms advocated by the anti-property clergy had a doubly negative effect: it progressively ossified the church within and forced it into increased dependence on the state. In effect, in the first half of the sixteenth century the Russian church placed itself voluntarily under the tutelage of secular authority. It was an exceedingly short-sighted policy that the leaders of the Russian church adopted at this critical juncture in its history. The results were not slow in making themselves felt as the church administration rapidly slipped under control of state organs. In the course of the sixteenth century it became customary for tsars to make on their own appointments of bishops and metropolitans, to decide who would attend church synods, and to interfere with church justice. In 1521 Basil III removed a metropolitan who had displeased him; the first time this had ever happened in Russia. He also appropriated moneys belonging to the church. By the end of the sixteenth century there was precious little left of the Byzantine ideal of 'harmony'. Just how subservient the church had become during this time can be seen from its support of government measures aimed at limiting its right to make further land acquisitions. A synod convoked in 1551 approved tsarist orders forbidding monasteries to make new acquisitions without royal approval (p. 229 above), and another synod in 1584 reconfirmed them. These were the first steps towards ultimate expropriation of clerical land. In the end, the Russian church forfeited its autonomy without by this surrender salvaging its wealth.

The Schism which in the 1660s split in two the Russian church was a religious crisis which only tangentially touched on the question of church-state relationship. Even so, it exerted a lasting effect on the political position of the Russian church. The reforms of Patriarch Nikon which led to the Schism alienated from the established church its most dedicated groups, draining it of most of its zeal which henceforth flowed into movements of religious dissent. The end result was the church's total dependence on the state. After the Schism, the Russian church required the full vigour of state support to prevent mass defections from its ranks; it could no longer survive on its own. Even one of its staunchest supporters conceded that if it were not for state prohibitions against the abandonment of Orthodoxy (a criminal offence in nineteenth-century Russia), half of the peasants would go over to the Schismatics, and half of educated society would be converted to Catholicism.[8]

The Schism resulted from reforms introduced into Russian religious practices to bring them closer in line with the Greek. Comparisons of Russian religious practices with their Greek models, begun in the sixteenth century but pursued with special vigour in the first half of the seventeenth, revealed beyond doubt that over time major deviations had occurred in Russian observances. Less apparent was the answer to the question whether such discrepancies were good or bad. Purists, headed by Nikon, maintained that all departures from Greek prototypes were corruptions and as such had to be eliminated. Under his guidance books were corrected and changes introduced into rituals. The conservatives and nationalists, a party which included the majority of the Russian clergy, argued that the Russian church as then constituted was purer and holier than the Greek, which had fallen from grace for agreeing at the Council of Florence in 1439 to merge with Rome. Since that act of apostasy, the centre of Orthodoxy had shifted to Moscow which had repudiated the Union. As Joseph of Volokolamsk had said a century earlier, Russia was the most pious land in the world; any tampering with its practices would bring on its head the wrath of heaven. The issue was a grave one. The problem dividing the two parties had profound personal significance at a time when people universally believed in the immortality of the soul, and associated spiritual salvation with the punctilious observance of religious rites. Korb, a German who visited Russia in 1699, was undoubtedly correct when at the head of a list of things Russians 'principally guarded against' he put 'lest the religion of their forefathers should be changed'.[9]

Nikon enjoyed the complete confidence of Tsar Alexis, an extremely pious man, whose natural inclination to do the proper thing was further encouraged by Greek prelates flattering him with visions of a revived Byzantine Empire under his rule. With his support, Nikon forced through many ritualistic changes, altering the manner of making the cross, pronouncing the Credo and painting ikons. He abolished *mnogopenie*, the custom of concurrent singing of different parts of the liturgy. But he went further yet, attempting to create in Russia a true Christian community by regulating the daily life of ordinary people in some detail. He and his supporters enforced strict rules of conduct which forbade card playing, drinking, cursing and sexual licence, and required every Russian to spend some four or five hours a day in church. So intimate was Nikon's relationship with Tsar Alexis that when the latter left for campaigns he turned over to him the management of state affairs. Through his friendship with the tsar, Nikon succeeded in restoring temporarily the balance between church and state.

Nikon, however, happened to have been a very difficult man, headstrong, tactless, and on occasion ruthlessly brutal. Having alienated with his reforms the mass of the clergy, he next aroused the anger of court dignitaries, resentful of his arrogation of sovereign prerogatives and generally overbearing manner. He was intrigued against by courtiers bent on estranging the tsar from him. Alexis gradually became persuaded that the patriarch had indeed overstepped the bounds of his authority, as his enemies charged, and visibly cooled to him. Hoping to force the tsar's hand, Nikon abandoned his post and retired to a monastery. But he miscalculated, for the tsar did not come to beg forgiveness as he had anticipated; instead, he waited and did nothing, allowing the patriarchal office to remain, in effect, vacant.

Finally, in 1666 Alexis convoked a major church synod to which he invited prominent ecclesiastics from Greece to settle his dispute with Nikon and pass judgement on his reforms. Defending himself from the charges brought against him, Nikon advanced a novel (to the Orthodox) theory of church supremacy over state:

Has thou not learned ... that the highest authority of the priesthood is not received from kings or emperors (lit. Tsars), but contrariwise, it is by the priesthood that rulers are anointed to the empire? Therefore it is abundantly plain that priesthood is a very much greater thing than royalty ...

In spiritual things which belong to the glory of God, the bishop is higher than the Tsar: for so only can he hold or maintain the spiritual jurisdiction. But in those things which belong in the province of this world the Tsar is higher. And so they will be in no opposition the one against the other. However, the bishop has a certain interest ... in the secular jurisdiction, for its better direction, and in suitable matters; but the Tsar has none whatever in ecclesiastical and spiritual administration ... For this cause, manifestly, the Tsar must be less than the bishop, and must owe him obedience.[10]

Nikon failed to persuade the synod, which reasserted the traditional idea of 'harmony': the tsar had the right to rule all his subjects, the clergy included, and the church establishment, from the patriarch down, had to obey him in all matters save those touching on doctrine. At the same time, the synod sustained Nikon's reforms which had brought Russian religious observances more in line with the Greek.

The synod's religious resolutions were not accepted by a sizeable part of the laity. (The clergy promptly fell in line.) Almost immediately defections from the official church began of parishes which refused to make the required revisions and adhered to the old ways. In the 1670s rumours spread that the end of the world was approaching, and entire communities of believers fled into the forests, shut themselves in coffins or set themselves on fire. At least 20,000 persons are believed to have burned themselves to death during this outburst of religious mania. Some fanatical Old Believers even talked of burning down all Russia.

It is only with the Schism that intense religious life in Russia begins on a mass scale. Dissent, which had great appeal to the peasantry because of its anarchist undertones, compelled every believer to choose between the official church and the schismatic, and by this very choice to make a religious commitment. Those who decided on a break then faced many further decisions concerning not only ritual but also conduct, and thus step by step they were drawn into religion of a more personal and spiritual kind. Foreigners found dissenters to be the only Orthodox people in Russia familiar with the Holy Scriptures and able to discuss religious questions. Adherence to dissent cost dearly both in money and exposure to government harassment which sometimes turned into outright persecution.

Russian dissenters are customarily divided in two basic groups: the Old Believers, known to themselves as 'Old Ritualists' (*Staroobriadtsy*) and to the official church as 'Splitters' (*Raskol'niki*), and the Sectarians. The former, who are stronger in the taiga, repudiate the Nikonian reforms and adhere to the old rituals, but in every other way remain faithful to Orthodoxy; the latter depart more or less consciously from the doctrines and practices of the Orthodox church, developing new forms of religion, some of which come closer to early Protestantism then to Orthodoxy. They have traditionally been the strongest in the Ukraine.

The Old Believers associated Nikon's reforms with the advent of the Anti-Christ. By cabalistic computations they concluded that the coming of the Anti-Christ would occur in 1699–1700, and the end of the world three years later. When Peter returned from his foreign journey in 1698, and instead of going to church began to cut off beards and execute rebellious streltsy, many of whom were adherents of Old Belief, the prophesy seemed about to be fulfilled. At this time incidents of self-immolation and other expressions of *mania religiosa* multiplied. When the end of the world did not occur, the Old Believers faced a quandary: how were they to conduct themselves like proper Christians in a world ruled by Anti-Christ? The most urgent question had to do with priests and sacraments. The Old Believers recognized only priests ordained before Nikon's reforms. These had been a minority to begin with, and they were dying out. Confronting this problem, the movement split in two factions, the Priestly (*Popovtsy*) and the Non-Priestly (*Bezpopovtsy*). Adherents of the former, after having run out of suitable ministers, consented to accept priests ordained by the official church and eventually made their peace with it. The more radical Non-Priestly solved the problem in a different way. Some concluded that once Anti-Christ had taken charge, no more intermediaries between man and God were required; now it was every Christian for himself. Others performed only those sacraments which were open to laymen. For the latter, the thorniest problem concerned the marriage rite, indubitably a sacrament requiring the services of an ordained priest. They got round the difficulty either by denying the sacramental character of marriage and performing it without priests, or else by practising celibacy. Extremists argued that in a world dominated by Anti-Christ it was a Christian's positive duty to sin, because by so doing one diminished the total amount of evil abroad. They indulged in sexual licence which often assumed the form of pre-Christian rites still surviving in the village. The Non-Priestly Old Believers, as many other religious dissenters, tended to vacillate between asceticism and dionysiac indulgence. Certain among them thought Napoleon to be the Messiah come to deliver Russia from the Anti-Christ, and worshipped him, for which reason it was not uncommon to find in Russian peasant huts the portrait of the French Emperor pinned to the wall alongside ikons. In the course of time, the Non-Priestly expanded at the expense of the Priestly, who gradually faded into the established church. Their domain was the remote northern forest: the territory of what had been the Novgorod republic, Karelia, the shores of the White Sea and Siberia. Organized in disciplined, self-governing communities they proved excellent colonists. After Peter I had imposed on them a

237

double soul tax, many Old Believers turned to commerce and industry at which they proved extremely adept. They enjoyed the reputation of being the most honest businessmen in Russia.

The Sectarians sought not so much to defend the old ways as to formulate new answers to religious questions. Sectarianism was a logical outgrowth of Old Belief, especially of its more radical Non-Priestly wing. Most sects issued from this source, although it appears that some antedated the Schism and represented a revival of heresies dormant since the Middle Ages and believed extirpated, such as that of the Judaizers. The basic quality common to the sects was the turning away from church tradition, books and rituals in quest of a 'Spiritual Christianity' based on an inner faith. Once the tie with the official church had been broken it was inevitable that many spontaneous religious trends would emerge. The process has by no means run its course as the contemporary Russian press reports time and again the discovery of some new sect. Most sects have had an ephemeral existence, revolving around a single inspired leader and falling apart upon his imprisonment or death. Some, however, established themselves more solidly. Among the better known are the following:

The *Khlysty* or Flagellants, a word which seems to be a corruption of *'Khristy'* or 'Christs', for the members of this sect did not practise flagellation. The sect originated in the central black earth region, apparently in the late seventeenth century. Its central idea held that Christ reincarnated himself by entering living individuals who thereby became 'Christs'; upon their death the spirit passed on to others. Many groups were formed under the inspiration of peasants seized by the spirits who would wander from village to village gathering followers. Meetings were held to the accompaniment of singing and dancing which often degenerated into mass hysterics. The Khlysty occasionally engaged in sexual orgies. They opposed marriage and engaged in free intercourse which they called 'Christ's love'. Persecuted for their activities they operated in great secrecy.

The minuscule sect of *Skoptsy* (from the word *skopets* meaning eunuch) were a late eighteenth-century offshoot from the Khlysty. They maintained that woman with her beauty was the main obstacle to salvation and to resist her temptations they castrated themselves.

The *Dukhobortsy* or 'Fighters for the Spirit' emerged in the second half of the eighteenth century, also probably from the Khlysty. Their theology was vague. They taught that human souls had been created before corporal bodies. Some, having sinned before the creation of the world, were punished by being cast into the material world without recollection of what had gone on before. All rituals and all institutions are the products of original sin. The Dukhobors also believed in Christ 'entering' the souls of living people. Aided by Leo Tolstoy, they migrated early in the twentieth century to Canada where they have distinguished themselves by spectacular acts of civil disobedience.

The *Molokane* (Milk-drinkers) were a moderate sect, identified by the practice of drinking milk and its products on fast days.

The *Stundists* emerged in the nineteenth century and spread after the Emancipation. They formed circles to study the bible. Baptism, which is probably the most dynamic sectarian movement in contemporary Russia, is its outgrowth. In the second half of the nineteenth century Stundism and Baptism made some converts among the educated in Moscow and St Petersburg.

All of these and many of the minor related sects have in common opposition to the state and the established church. The political views of their members can best be defined as Christian Anarchist. As such, and because they would not obey the official church, they suffered harsh persecution in the first century following the Schism. Under the tolerant reign of Catherine II the state left them alone, but under Nicholas I the harassment resumed, military expeditions being sent out to destroy sectarian strongholds, especially those of the more radical sects. Nevertheless, dissent kept on gaining adherents. Statistics of Russian dissenters are notoriously unreliable because the imperial government falsified census figures bearing on them by a factor of anywhere from five to thirty, so as to minimize defections from the official church. The 1897 census listed only 2 million Old Believers and Sectarians, but there are reasons to believe that their actual number then was closer to 20 million. Scholarly estimates place the number of dissenters at 9–10 million in the 1860s, between 12 to 15 million in the 1880s, and around 25 million in 1917, of whom 19 million were Old Believers and 6 million Sectarians.[11] These figures indicate that the dissenting churches more than held their own in terms of over-all population growth.

The Schism was a disaster for the Russian Orthodox church, robbing it of its most dedicated adherents and placing it more than ever at the state's mercy. 'After Nikon, Russia no longer had a church: it had a religion of state. From there to state religion it required but one step. The state religion was instituted by that power which in 1917 succeeded the imperial.'[12]

Although in large measure integrated into the state apparatus and subservient to the crown, until Peter the Great the Russian Church still preserved its institutional identity and some semblance of autonomy. The Byzantine principle of 'harmony', restated by the great synod of 1666, retained its theoretical validity. The church was an entity different from the state, with its patriarch, its administrative, judiciary and fiscal offices, and its properties whose inhabitants it taxed and judged. It was Peter who did away with this semi-autonomous status; he abolished the patriarchate, transformed its offices into branches of the secular administration, lifted its judiciary immunities, and, perhaps most importantly, confiscated its incomes. After Peter's reign, the Russian church became just another branch of the civil administration. The *coup de grâce* was dealt a victim so drained of all vitality that it hardly twitched; there were no protests, only silent submission. No church in Christendom allowed itself to be secularized as graciously as the Russian.

Peter heartily disliked the Orthodox church, especially its Great Russian branch; he much preferred the Ukrainian and especially the Protestant clergy. It troubled him that by virtue of privileges granted them in the Dark Ages tens of thousands of clergymen escaped taxes and service obligations, and at the same time devoured a good portion of the country's wealth in the form of labour services and rents. To him they were a lot of parasites. His animus towards the church was exacerbated by its support of his son Alexis with whom he was on bad terms. He was thus predisposed to cut the Orthodox church down to size in any event. What made it urgent to do so were fiscal considerations, so decisive in all of his reforms. On his accession the church remained rich, notwithstanding repeated injunctions against its making additional acquisitions of land. The custom of making provision for the church in one's will remained strongly ingrained among the service class; indeed, the tsars themselves continued making generous gifts to their favourite monasteries after they had decreed such practices illegal for ordinary landlords. Because of the rapid expansion of Russia, the percentage of the nation's wealth owned by the clergy diminished, but in absolute numbers it remained formidable: at Peter's accession they controlled an estimated 750,000 peasants out of a total of 12–13 million.

Peter began as early as 1696 to tamper with the right of the parish and monastic clergy freely to dispose of the incomes from church properties. Four years later, following the death of Patriarch Adrian, he decided to take advantage of the vacancy to abolish the whole separate church administration. Instead of appointing Adrian's successor, he selected a *locum tenens*, a learned but spineless Ukrainian divine. The actual authority over the church's properties and other worldly responsibilities he entrusted to a Monastery Prikaz, which he charged with administering, judging and taxing the inhabitants of ecclesiastical votchiny. Ecclesiastical properties were not actually secularized but they were incorporated to such an extent into the general administrative structure of the state that when it came, half a century later, secularization appeared a mere formality. After 1701 the principle was established – though like every other government policy it was irregularly enforced –

that the monasteries were to forward to the Treasury all their revenues in return for fixed salaries.

Peter's church policies culminated in a general charter called Ecclesiastical Regulation (*Dukhovnyi Reglament*), prepared under Peter's personal supervision and issued in 1721. It provided in the minutest detail for the operations of the parish and monastic clergy, laying down what they could and could not do, and even what they were required to do. The Regulation was a veritable bureaucratic constitution of the Russian church. Among its most important provisions was the formal abolition of the office of the Patriarch, vacant since 1700, and its replacement with a bureaucratic institution called initially Ecclesiastical College and later the Most Holy All-Ruling Synod. The Holy Synod was nothing more nor less than a ministry of religious affairs; its head, called Chief Procurator, need not have been a cleric and indeed in the course of the eighteenth century he was usually a military man. Until 1917, the Synod assumed full responsibility for administering the Russian church. With its establishment, the Russian church lost its distinct institutional existence and merged formally with the state apparatus.

The extent to which the church became politicized under Peter can be seen from some of the obligations which the Regulation imposed on the clergy. Ordained priests were required to take an oath in which they pledged to 'defend unsparingly all the powers, rights and prerogatives belonging to the High Autocracy of His Majesty' and his successors. Members of the Spiritual College (Holy Synod) swore an oath in which the following words appear: 'I swear by Almighty God that I resolve, and am in duty bound, to be a faithful, good, and obedient slave [*rab*] and subject to my natural and true Tsar and Sovereign...'[13]

Beyond this generalized promise, parish priests had to pledge they would denounce to the authorities any information prejudicial to the interests of the sovereign and his state which came their way even at confession:

If during confession someone discloses to the priest an unfulfilled but still intended criminal act, especially [one] of treason or rebellion against the Sovereign or the State, or an evil design against the honour or health of the Sovereign and the family of his Majesty ... the confessor must not only not give him absolution and remission of his openly confessed sins ... but must promptly report him at the prescribed places pursuant to the personal decree of His Imperial Majesty ... in virtue of which, for words reflecting on the high honour of His Imperial Majesty and prejudicial to the State, such villains are commanded to be apprehended with all dispatch and brought to the designated places [i.e. the tsar's Privy Chancellery and the Preobrazhenskii Prikaz].[14]

Subsequent to the Regulation, Russian priests regularly collaborated with the police. For example, towards the end of Peter's reign, when the government struggled to compile a national census preparatory to the imposition of the soul tax, the rural clergy were commanded to help in uncovering any evasions under the threat of 'merciless whipping' and exile to Siberia. In the nineteenth century, denunciation of political dissidents was considered a regular part of a priest's obligations.

The striking feature of the Ecclesiastical Regulation is not only that it should have been issued but that it met with no resistance. Peter simply sent high prelates copies of the document with instructions to sign; they duly complied, even though it must have been evident they were sealing the fate of their church. There are no record no cases of active opposition to the Regulation such as had been common during the Schism when ritual had been at stake. All of which suggests that in the Russian church it was the magic element in religion that mattered the most; and since Peter could not care less about liturgy, sacraments or any of its other rituals, the church was content to go along with whatever else he wanted.

Knowing this, one is not surprised to learn that the actual expropriation of church holdings also evoked no resistance. This was carried out in 1762 by Peter III who ordered all land belonging to churches and monasteries to be incorporated into state properties. Catherine II confirmed this ukaz two years later. At that time (1767) approximately one million peasants living on ecclesiastical lands were taken over by the state, and all the parish and black clergy placed on government salary. Of the several million rubles' annual income which the crown henceforth drew from secularized church properties it returned to the clergy only some 400,000, and kept the rest. Landless abbeys which brought the state no income were ordered to be shut down, with the consequence that the total number of monasteries in Russia decreased by more than half: of the 954 active in 1764, 569 were closed. Nor were all of those remaining allotted government funds; out of the 385 monasteries which survived secularization, only 161 were put on the government payroll, the remaining 224 had to fend for themselves. These measures too aroused no opposition. The secularization of ecclesiastical land – perhaps the most powerful single factor in the European Reformation – was in Russia carried out as calmly as if it were a mere book-keeping operation.

Once the state had assumed responsibility for supporting the clergy, it had to make certain that its payrolls were not padded by pseudo-clerics or priests who, although properly ordained, performed no duties for want of a parish. The government now began to draft regular personnel lists (*shtaty*) for clerical appointments such as it had for its civil service. Peter I issued instructions that 'superfluous' priests – that is, those without a parish of their own – either be conscripted in the army or included in the tax-paying estate. The principle was not strictly enforced, however, in the eighteenth century, for want of the required personnel. It was only in the 1860s that regular lists of the clergy were drawn up, and the state made certain that the number of paid clergymen corresponded to the number of active parishes. Catherine II took another step towards the full integration of the clergy into the state bureaucracy in the 1790s when she ordered the boundaries of bishoprics to be aligned with those of the provincial administration, to make it easier for the governors to control the church. As a result of all these measures, the Russian clergy was transformed in the eighteenth century into something very close to chinovniki.

The Orthodox church might have been able to improve its fortunes had it been able to command the loyalty of the population. This, however, it lacked. Peasants with a more than perfunctory concern for religion gravitated towards the Old Believers and Sectarians. The educated classes either had no interest in the church or felt themselves drawn to foreign religions, especially those of a secular (ideological) kind, in which history served as a surrogate for God. The Orthodox church never found a common language with the educated because its conservative outlook made it pronouncedly anti-intellectual. Following the medieval Russian precept, 'all evil comes from opinions', it showed little interest even in its own theology to which it resorted mainly when compelled to defend itself from heretics or foreigners. It met all attempts to revitalize it with instinctive suspicion which turned into hostility, sometimes accompanied by denunciation to the authorities and excommunication, whenever it felt that independent judgement was being brought to bear on its dogmas or practices. One by one, it pushed away from itself the country's finest religious minds: the Slavophiles, Vladimir Soloviev, Leo Tolstoy and the laymen gathered in the early 1900s around the Religious Philosophical Society. It also showed little interest in educating its flock. The Russian Orthodox church first began to involve itself in elementary schooling on any scale only in the 1860s, and then on orders of the state which was becoming alarmed over the influence of intellectuals on the masses.

It would be absurd to deny that in the imperial era many Russians, educated and illiterate alike, sought and found solace in the church, or that even among a clergy so subservient to the state there were individuals of the highest moral and intellectual calibre. Even in its deformed shape, the Russian church offered an escape from life's troubles. But viewed as a whole the church was not a popular institution during the imperial period, and what popularity it had it steadily lost. The clergy now became very much isolated from society, especially from the well-to-do and educated. In Kotoshikhin's time, in the mid-seventeenth century, it had been common for dvoriane and boyars to maintain at their own expense domestic chapels and support one or more priests. But already one century later, in the reign of Catherine II, an English traveller noted with surprise that during his five months' stay in St Petersburg he had not seen a single noble attended by a priest.[15] Other foreign travellers of the imperial era furnish similar negative evidence. There were several reasons for this growing isolation of the clergy from the country's élite. One was Peter's law forbidding the construction of family churches and the maintenance of family priests. Another was the widening gulf between the westernized, secular kind of education given the upper class and that offered by even the best seminaries. Social differences also played their part. The strict prohibitions imposed by the Muscovite government against nobles joining the clerical estate – prohibitions reinforced by Peter's legislation – prevented in Russia that blood kinship between nobility and upper ranks of the clergy usual in western Europe. In their vast majority, Russian clerics were commoners, often of the lower sort, culturally and socially close to the urban petty bourgeoisie. The westernized dvorianstvo simply did not feel at ease in the company of such people. The characters inhabiting the novels of Leskov, the chronicler of clerical life in Russia, seem to live in a world of their own, even more shut off from the world at large than the merchants inhabiting their 'dark kingdom'. They remained to the end of the imperial regime a closed caste, attending their own schools, marrying priests' daughters, and sending their offspring into the priesthood. Even in the early twentieth century, when it was possible to do so, Russian laymen rarely took holy orders. Impoverished, isolated and identified with the autocracy, the clergy commanded neither love nor respect; it was at best tolerated.

What could the church in Russia have been realistically expected to do? Given its conservative philosophy and traditional reliance on state authority, it could certainly not have acted as a liberalizing force. Still, it could have accomplished two important things. First, it might have upheld the principle of duality of temporal and spiritual authority as laid down in Matthew 22:16–22, and elaborated in the theory of the Byzantine church. Had it done so, it would have gained for itself sovereignty over the country's spiritual realm and by this very fact imposed a certain limit on the state's authority. By failing to do so, it enabled the state to claim power over men's minds as well as over their bodies, thereby contributing heavily to the monstrous development of secular power in Russia, then and even more so later.

Secondly, it could have stood up and fought for the most elementary Christian values. It should have protested against the institution of serfdom, so contrary to Christian ethics. It should have condemned the massacres of an Ivan IV or, later, of a Stalin. But it did neither (isolated cases apart), behaving as if righting wrongs were none of its concern. No branch of Christianity has shown such callous indifference to social and political injustice. One can fully sympathize with the words of Alexander Solzhenitsyn that Russian history would have been 'incomparably more humane and harmonious in the last few centuries if the church had not surrendered its independence and had continued to make its voice heard among the people, as it does, for example, in Poland'.[16]

The ultimate result of the policies of the Russian Orthodox Church was not only to discredit it in the eyes of those who cared for social and political justice, but to create a spiritual vacuum. This vacuum was filled with secular ideologies which sought to realize on this earth the paradise that Christianity had promised to provide in the next.

III

INTELLIGENTSIA VERSUS THE STATE

CHAPTER 10

THE INTELLIGENTSIA

> The title of poet and writer has long since eclipsed the tinsel of epaulettes and gaudy uniforms.
>
> *Vissarion Belinskii, 'Letter to Gogol' (1847)*
>
> A great writer is, so to speak, a second government of his country.
>
> *Alexander Solzhenitsyn,* First Circle (*1955–64*)

The sum total of the preceding analysis of relations between state and society in pre-1900 Russia is that none of the economic or social groups of the old regime was either able or willing to stand up to the crown and challenge its monopoly of political power. They were not able to do so because, by enforcing the patrimonial principle, i.e. by effectively asserting its claim to all the territory of the realm as property and all its inhabitants as servants, the crown prevented the formation of pockets of independent wealth or power. And they were not willing because, in so far as under this system the crown was the ultimate source of all material benefits, each group was strongly inclined to fawn on it. Dvoriane looked to the autocracy to keep their serfs in place, to conquer new lands for distribution to them as pomestia, and to preserve their various exclusive rights; the merchants depended on the crown to grant them licences and monopolies, and through high tariffs to protect their inefficient industries; the clergy had only the crown to safeguard their landed properties and, after these were gone, to pay them subsidies and keep their flock from defecting. Under the adverse economic conditions prevailing in Russia, groups aspiring to rise above the subsistence level had but one option open to them, and that was to collaborate with the state – in other words, to give up political ambition. Throughout Russian history,

private wealth came into being and was viewed as the consequence of government favour, as government reward for good political behaviour. It was by exercising humility not by struggling that dvoriane and merchants amassed large fortunes: they reached the summits of wealth at the price of complete political self-effacement.[1]

The underprivileged, the mass of muzhiki, also preferred absolutism to any other form of government except anarchy. That which they desired the most, namely free access to all the land not already under peasant control, they expected to obtain from the same tsar who had given personal liberty to their masters in 1762 and to them ninety-nine years later. For the impoverished dvoriane, the mass of petty traders and the overwhelming majority of peasants, constitution and parliament were a swindle which the rich and influential tried to foist on the country to enable them to seize hold of the apparatus of political power for their personal benefit. Thus, everything made for conservative rigidity.

Apart from economic and social interest groups there existed still one other source of potential resistance to absolutism, namely regional interest. The phenomenon was not unknown to Russia and it even enjoyed a certain degree of constitutional recognition. The governments of Muscovite and imperial Russia were usually in no hurry to dismantle the existing administrative apparatus of territories they had conquered; as a rule, they preferred to leave things fairly intact, at least for some time, content to transfer to Moscow or St Petersburg only the seat of power. At various periods Russia had self-governing regions over which the bureaucracy exercised only nominal control. In the reign of Alexander I ,when territorial decentralization was at its height, large segments of the empire were subject to charters which granted their inhabitants considerably more political self-expression than was enjoyed by any part of Russia proper. Under this ruler, Finland and Poland had constitutions and national diets empowered to legislate on internal matters; Courland and Livonia were administered in accord with charters, originally issued by the Swedes and confirmed by Peter I, which made them virtually self-governing provinces; the nomads of Siberia and central Asia lived under a very liberal arrangement, almost free of external interference; and the Jews were given internal autonomy in the Pale of Settlement through their religious communal organizations called *kahaly*. But if one inquires more closely into the circumstances under which these exceptions to the prevailing centralism had been made, one generally discovers that the decisive factor was not the recognition of the 'right' of non-Russians to self-government but administrative prudence and shortage of personnel. The historic trend of Russian imperial evolution has been the very opposite of the British or American, tending relentlessly towards centralism and bureaucratization. As the civil service expanded, the autonomy of minority groups and their territories was curtailed under one pretext or another, until by the early 1900s there was almost nothing of it left. The Polish constitution was abrogated in 1831, and the Finnish in effect suspended in 1899; the charters of Courland and Livonia were thoroughly subverted; and the nomads of Asia as well as the Jews were fully subordinated to Russian governors. On the eve of the 1917 Revolution only the central Asian protectorates of Khiva and Bukhara still retained their autonomous status, and they were liquidated and incorporated as soon as the new communist government came to power in the area.

Such being the case, political opposition, if it was to emerge at all, had to come from quarters other than those customarily labelled 'interest groups'. No social or economic group in Russia had an interest in liberalization; to the élites it spelled the loss of privilege, to the rural masses shattered hopes of a nationwide 'black repartition'. Throughout Russian history, 'interest groups' have fought other 'interest groups', never the state. The drive for change had to be inspired by motives other than self-interest, as the word is conventionally used – motives more enlightened, farsighted and generous, such as sense of patriotism, social justice and personal self-respect. Indeed, just because the pursuit of material rewards was so closely identified with the constitution of the old regime and subservience to the state, any aspiring opposition was bound to renounce self-serving; it had to be, or at any rate appear to be, utterly disinterested. Thus it happened that in Russia the struggle for political liberty was waged from the beginning exactly in the manner that Burke felt it ought never to be waged: in the name of abstract ideals.

Although the word *intelligentsia* is commonly believed to be of Russian origin, its etymological roots in fact lie in western Europe. It is a clumsy, Latinized adaptation of the French *intelligence* and German *Intelligenz* which in the first half of the nineteenth century came to be used in the west to designate the educated, enlightened, 'progressive' elements in society. In the discussions of the Austrian and German revolutionary parliaments in February 1849, for example, conservative deputies made reference to 'the intelligence' (*die Intelligenz*) as that social group – essentially urban and professional – which by virtue of its superior public spirit deserved heavier parliamentary representation.[2] The word entered the Russian vocabulary in the 1860s, and by the 1870s became a household term around which revolved a great deal of political discussion.

Intelligentsia, unfortunately, does not lend itself to precise and universally acceptable definition. Like so many terms in Russian history (e.g. boyar, dvorianin, muzhik, tiaglo), it has at least two meanings, one broad, the other narrow. In the broad sense, which is the older of the two, it refers to that portion of the educated class which enjoys public prominence – not far from what the French call *les notables*. In Turgenev's

'Strange story', written in 1869, there occurs an early example of such usage when the hero on a visit to a provincial town is invited to a reception at which, he is told, there will be present the town's doctor and teacher and 'the entire intelligentsia'. This broad definition gradually went out of use but it was revived after 1917 by the communist regime. Averse to the concept of an intelligentsia as a distinct social category, as it cannot be fitted into the Marxian class scheme, and yet unable to purge it from Russian speech, it employs 'intelligentsia' as an occupational category to describe what in the west would be called the white collar class. By this definition, the Chief of the KGB and Solzhenitsyn are both members of the 'Soviet intelligentsia'.

The narrow usage has a more complicated story. Very much as has been the case with the designation 'liberal' in English, 'intelligentsia' in time lost its descriptive and objective quality, and acquired a normative, subjective one. In the 1870s, young people holding radical philosophical, political and social opinions began to insist that they and they alone had the right to the title intelligentsia. The point was not immediately conceded by those whom such an exclusive definition would put outside the pale of progressive company. But by the 1890s it was no longer enough for a Russian to have an education and play a part in public life in order to qualify; one had to stand in staunch opposition to the entire political and economic system of the old regime, and be willing actively to participate in the struggle for its overthrow. In other words, to be an intelligent meant as much as to be a revolutionary.

The result of the concurrent expression of two quite different ideas through the medium of the same word was confusion. In 1909 a group of liberal intellectuals, several of them ex-radicals, published a volume of essays called *Vekhi* (*Signposts*) in which they took to task the Russian intelligentsia for what they considered lack of political sense, irreligiosity, low morals, superficial education and all other manner of sin. There was no doubt among the readers who was meant. Yet the authors of the symposium were certainly themselves members of the intelligentsia in the eyes of the government and its supporters.

Confronted with this situation, the historian must make up his own mind. It would certainly be wrong to adopt the exclusive definition of the intelligentsia insisted upon by its radical wing. The struggle against the autocracy was joined by many people acting on liberal or even conservative principles who would have nothing in common with the whole revolutionary ideology. To exclude them, would do violence to the historical record. The inclusive definition embracing the entire white-collar group is even less useful because it tells nothing of political and social attitudes which were the very thing separating those conscious of belonging to the intelligentsia from the rest of the nation. The definition which we shall adopt falls somewhere between the two described above. It employs as its touchstone the sense of commitment to public welfare: a member of the intelligentsia or an *intelligent* is someone not wholly preoccupied with his personal well-being but at least as much and preferably much more concerned with that of society at large, and willing, to the best of his ability, to work on society's behalf. Under the terms of this definition, one's level of education and class status are of secondary importance. Although a well-educated and affluent person naturally is in a better position to understand what is wrong with his country and to act accordingly, it does not follow that he cares to do so. At the same time, a simple, semi-literate working man who makes an effort to grasp how his society functions and to work on its behalf does qualify as an *intelligent*; it is in this sense that in late nineteenth-century Russia one spoke of a 'working-class intelligentsia' and even of a 'peasant intelligentsia'.[3]

An intelligentsia thus defined emerges wherever there exists a significant discrepancy between those who control political and economic power, and those who represent (or believe themselves to represent) public opinion. It is strongest and most vocal in countries where an authoritarian government confronts an educated élite receptive to new ideas; here, capacity to act and desire to act engage in bitter conflict, and the intelligentsia solidifies into a state within a state. In traditional despotisms, where there is no significant educated public, and in properly functioning democracies, where ideas can be readily translated into policies, the intelligentsia is not likely to emerge.*

In imperial Russia the emergence sooner or later of an intelligentsia was a foregone conclusion; and given the unyielding patrimonial outlook of the monarchy where political power was concerned, it was equally certain that the struggle between the intelligentsia and the regime would become a war to the bitter end.

There must have always been disaffected people in Russia, but the earliest political dissident about whom there is documentary evidence is one Prince I.A.Khvorostinin. This aristocrat of the early seventeenth century was denounced to the authorities for failure to practise Orthodoxy, keeping Latin books in his library, calling the tsar a 'despot', and complaining that among the 'stupid' populace of Moscow he found no one to converse with. He requested permission to leave for Lithuania, but this was denied to him and he ended up being exiled to a monastery

---

* Unless, of course, some part of the educated minority decides that it knows best what is good for the people. It can then disregard the popular vote on grounds that (1) it gives the people no 'real' choice, or (2) that the electoral process is manipulated, or, when all else fails, (3) that the masses have been brainwashed and vote against their own better interest.

in the far north.[4] Khvorostinin was a typical dissident of the pre-intelligentsia era, an isolated individual doomed to die without having exerted the slightest influence on the course of events. Such early intellectuals constituted no force or movement. Under the service regime of the seventeenth and early eighteenth centuries discontent was *prima facie* evidence of mutiny and had to be confined to private forms of expression.

Before Russia could have a public opinion it was necessary for the government to acknowledge public activity independent of its volition as legitimate and proper. This occurred only with the loosening of the conditions of state service after the death of Peter I. In the 1730s, and even more so in the 1740s and 1750s, it became progressively easier for dvoriane to pursue their private interests while nominally on active service. It was now quite easy to obtain prolonged leaves of absence and even to retire in early middle age. Thus, without any formal legislation, a leisure class began to form. But even for dvoriane in the armed forces time became available for other than military obligations. For instance, the training schedule at the Noble Cadet Corps, founded in 1731 (p. 132) was so undemanding that its young gentlemen had a great deal of free time left to amuse themselves with dramatic productions and poetry. The founders of the Russian theatre, A.P.Sumarokov and M.M. Kheraskov, began their literary careers while cadets and produced some of their most important writings at this ostensibly military institution. In the middle of the eighteenth century, literature emerged as a form of free activity, the earliest of its kind ever to be tolerated by a Russian government. The level of the writing was not high, and most of what was published imitated western models. But the significance of this literature was political, not aesthetic: 'What is important is that literature wrested itself free of the state, that the articulation of the artistic word ceased to be an official act. The carriers of literature began to distinguish themselves, their consciousness and the aims of their activity from the consciousness, activity and aims of state authority.'[5] A fissure thus appeared in the once solid patrimonial structure; literature became the first endeavour permitted to members of the tsarist service class that had nothing to do with promoting the sovereign's own interests. It never lost this unique status. From then on and to this day, literature has been a private realm, subject to different sovereigns and different laws.

The fate of this tendency depended on a further relaxation of service requirements. The Manifesto of 1762 by freeing dvoriane from compulsory service opened wide the flood-gates of intellectual activity. It both made possible the pursuit of literature as a profession, and created for the professional writer an audience. Proportionately, few of the retired dvoriane read books, and most of those who did were satisfied with French novels which it was customary to buy by the pound. But at least the habit of reading for pleasure began to form. The flowering of Russian literature in the nineteenth century could not have occurred but for the law of 1762 and the security which the upper stratum of dvoriane enjoyed under Catherine's benevolent reign. The more thoughtful in this group now began to acquire a taste for political ideas. There was special interest in western writings concerned with the role and rights of the noble estate with which the dvoriane of this reign tended to identify themselves. Montesquieu's *Spirit of Laws*, translated into Russian within a few years of its appearance, became for a whole generation of Russians a manual of statesmanship because of the stress it placed on the necessity of close cooperation between the crown and the nobility.

Catherine II actively encouraged this interest in political ideas. She was appalled by the prevailing ignorance and apathy among the upper class in Russia, and set out to create a body of public-minded citizens, as if to disprove Montesquieu's contention that Russia had only lords and slaves but nothing resembling a *tiers état*. She accomplished much more in this direction than she is usually given credit for. It is true that her *Instruction*, with its precepts cribbed from Montesquieu and Beccaria had no practical issue, and that the commission which she convened in 1767 to give Russia a new code of laws in place of the *Ulozhenie* of 1649 produced no code. Yet the experience was far from wasted. Printed in large numbers and widely disseminated, the *Instruction* familiarized the Russian élite with commonplace western political and social ideas. It may be said to have marked the beginning in Russia of discussion of government as an institution subject to moral norms. The abortive Legislative Commission provided the first opportunity in Russian history for representatives of the several estates frankly, publicly, and without fear of retribution to speak out about what troubled their constituencies. This was no longer a 'consultation of the government with its own agents', as the Muscovite Assemblies had been, but a national forum of a kind that would not convene again until the First Duma 140 years later. It was a school of politics as well, some of whose alumni played a major role in the development of public opinion in the latter part of Catherine's reign. The intellectual stimulus which the *Instruction* and the Legislative Commission gave Russian public life was of greater consequence for the future course of Russian history than any code could ever have been.

Catherine continued to encourage the ferment which she had generated after dissolving the Commission. The following year (1769), she launched Russia's first periodical, *Vsiakaia Vsiachina* (*A Bit of Everything*), a satirical journal to which she made pseudonymous contributions. She had emulators, and soon the small reading public was flooded with satirical publications. Most of the material in these journals was light-hearted nonsense meant to amuse, but on occasion satire assumed more earnest forms, turning into an instrument of social criticism. In Catherine's reign there appeared also various informative publications, including specialized periodicals for landowners and children. In the first decade after her accession, the number of book titles published in Russia increased fivefold. Towards the end of her reign, Catherine grew somewhat ambivalent towards the forces she had unleashed, and in the 1790s, frightened by the French Revolution, she tried to repress independent thinking. But this late reversal must not be allowed to obscure her lasting contribution. To Catherine belongs the credit for launching what Russians describe with the untranslatable *obshchestvennoe dvizhenie* (literally, 'social movement'), a broad current combining expressions of opinion with public activity, through which Russian society at long last asserted its right to an independent existence. The omnipotent Russian state brought into being even its own counterforce.

From its inception, public opinion in Russia flowed in two distinct channels from which in time branched out many forks. Both were critical of Russia as it then was, but for different reasons entirely. One can be described as conservative-nationalist, the other as liberal-radical.

The founder of the conservative-nationalist movement in Russia – and, incidentally, Russia's first clearly identifiable intelligent – was Nikolai Nikolaevich Novikov. In his youth, he had served in the Guard regiment which put Catherine on the throne, a stroke of good fortune which assured him of the Empress's protection and favour. He participated in the Legislative Commission working with the 'middle estate', a fact which acquires special significance in view of his pronouncedly 'bourgeois' outlook. In 1769, responding to Catherine's journalistic challenge, he issued the first of three satirical journals, *Truten'* (*The Drone*), which he then followed with some serious didactic publications.

In the very first issue of *The Drone*, Novikov posed a question destined to be the central preoccupation of the whole intelligentsia movement in Russia. Confessing that he had no desire to serve in the army, civil service or at the court, he asked 'What can I do for society?', adding, by way of explanation, that 'to live on this earth without being of use is only to burden it'.[6] His solution was to turn to publicistic and philanthropic work. Novikov's outlook falls wholly within the cultural tradition of the western European bourgeoisie, which is the more surprising since he had never been to the west and, according to his own admission, knew no foreign languages. In all his writings the principal target of attack was 'vice' which he identified with 'aristocratic' qualities of idleness, ostentatiousness, indifference to the sufferings of the poor, immorality, careerism, flattery, ignorance and contempt for knowledge.

'Virtue' was that which middle-class ideologists from Alberti to Benjamin Franklin had thought it it to be: industriousness, modesty, truthfulness, compassion, incorruptibility, studiousness. In his satirical publications, Novikov lashed out at life at the court and the estates of the rich in the name of these values. Catherine at first ignored his criticism, but his insistent harping on the dark sides of Russian life began eventually to annoy her, and she engaged him on the pages of her journal in literary polemics. That which Novikov lashed as 'vice' she preferred to treat as human 'weakness'. She called him intolerant and bilious. In one of their exchanges, Catherine charged Novikov with suffering from a 'fever', employing language which foreshadows some of the more bitter anti-intelligentsia polemics of the next century:

An individual begins to experience boredom and sadness, sometimes from idleness, sometimes from reading books. He begins to complain about everything around him, and in the end about the very universe. Having reached this phase, the disease comes to a head and overcomes reason. The afflicted person dreams of building castles in the air [complains] that everyone does everything wrongly, and that the government itself, try hard as it may, gives no satisfaction at all. In their minds, such people feel that they alone possess the ability to give advice and to arrange everything for the best.[7]

Novikov responded in more cautious language but without yielding an inch. On one occasion he even had the temerity to criticize the Empress's command of the Russian language.

This unprecedented exchange between sovereign and subject, unthinkable even one generation earlier, showed how rapidly the small fissure in the patrimonial structure had widened. In the reign of Elizabeth the emergence of *belles lettres* as an independent vocation represented a major constitutional change; in that of Catherine, the realm of independent thought came to extend to political controversy. Significantly, Novikov's disagreement with the Empress had for him no untoward consequences. Catherine continued to support him in a variety of ways, including subsidies. In the 1770s and 1780s, assisted by the Empress and wealthy friends, he initiated a programme of educational and philanthropic works of such grand scope that here one can do no more than list its peaks. His book publishing enterprises, designed to place informative rather than merely diverting literature in the hands of noble and burgher families, turned out over nine hundred titles. Through a Translators' Seminary, he made available to Russians many foreign works of a religious and literary nature. Part of the proceeds of his journalism and publishing went to support a school which he founded for orphans and indigent children, and a free hospital. During a famine, he organized relief. These would have been counted as good deeds anywhere in the world; but in Russia they were also a political innovation of revolutionary dimensions. Novikov broke with the tradition which held that the state and it alone had the right to act on behalf of 'the land'. From him and his associates, society first learned it could take care of its own needs.

Novikov is nevertheless classified as a political conservative because of his determination to work 'within the system', as one would put it today. A freemason and follower of Saint-Martin, he thought all evil stemmed from man's corruption, not from the institutions under which he lived. He mercilessly exposed 'vice' and promoted with such enthusiasm useful knowledge because of the conviction that only by improving man could one improve mankind. He never questioned the autocratic form of government or even serfdom. This stress on man rather than the environment became a hallmark of Russian conservatism.

Alexander Radishchev, the pioneer Russian liberal-radical, was a figure of far lesser import although thanks to the tireless and well-financed efforts of Soviet propaganda institutes he is the better known of the two. His fame rests on one book, *The Journey from St Petersburg to Moscow* (p. 149) in which, using the then popular device of a fictional travel account, he exposed the seamier sides of Russian provincial life. The writing is execrable and on literary merits alone the book would hardly deserve mention. The ideology is so confused that critics are still in fundamental disagreement about what the author intended: to advocate violent change or merely to warn that unless reforms were made in good time violence would inevitably break out. Unlike Novikov, whose intellectual roots were in freemasonry and Anglo–German sentimentalism (he abhorred Voltaire), Radishchev drank deeply at the source of French Enlightenment, showing a marked preference for its more extreme materialist wing (Helvetius and d'Holbach). In one of his last writings, completed before his death by suicide, he dealt with the question of the immortality of the soul; and although he came out on the affirmative side of the argument, the negative side clearly was written with greater conviction. In a last message before his suicide he wrote – anticipating Dostoevsky's Shatov – that only he who took his life was his own master.

A man holding such ideas was not likely to accept the old regime at face value or agree to work within its framework. His proposals, as has been said, were extremely vague, and yet because of his philosophic position and indubitable opposition to serfdom he has been acknowledged by liberals and radicals as their forerunner. Pushkin's instinct told him that Radishchev was an impudent fool, and it is probably no accident that the figure of Evgenii in the 'Bronze Horseman' bears such resemblance to Radishchev.[8]

Both Novikov and Radishchev were arrested during the panic which seized St Petersburg after the outbreak of the French Revolution and sentenced to lifelong exile. They were pardoned and released on the death of Catherine by her contrary son, Paul I.

The Decembrist movement, to which allusion has been made earlier (p. 188), was for sheer drama and the number and eminence of persons involved not equalled until the socialist-revolutionary turmoil of the 1870s. Yet it is difficult to make a case that it was a Russian movement properly speaking because its inspiration, ideals, and even forms of organization came directly from western Europe. They were all derived from the experience of post-Napoleonic France and Germany where many Russian dvoriane spent two or three years during the campaigns of 1812–13 and the occupation which ensued. It was testimony to the cosmopolitanism of young Russian aristocrats that they felt so completely at home in the political ferment of the Restoration era they thought it possible to transplant to their native land the political programmes of a Benjamin Constant, Destutt de Tracy, or the American constitution. Once the conspiracy failed, these ideas evaporated, and the next generation of intellectuals turned to an entirely different source.

That source was German Idealism. Not that Russian intellectuals understood the intricate and often exceedingly abstruse doctrines of the Idealist school: for few of them had the requisite philosophic training and some (e.g. the critic Belinskii) lacked knowledge of German and had to rely on secondhand accounts. But as is always the case with intellectual history – in contrast to history or philosophy – the important fact is not the exact meaning but the public reception of a man's ideas. Russian intellectuals of the 1820s–40s turned with such enthusiasm to the theories of Schelling and Hegel because they rightly sensed that they would find in them ideas capable of justifying what they felt and yearned for; and indeed they extracted from them only what they needed.

In Russia, as elsewhere, the principal consequence of Idealism was greatly to enhance the creative role of the human mind. Kant's critique of empirical theories had this inadvertent result that it transformed the mind from a mere recipient of sensory impressions into an active participant in the process of cognition. The manner in which intelligence, through its inbuilt categories, perceived reality was in itself an essential attribute of that reality. With this argument, the Idealist school which sprung up to overshadow Empiricism, gave a weapon to all those interested in promoting the human mind as the supreme creative force – that is, in the first place, the intellectuals. It was now possible to argue that ideas were every bit as 'real' as physical facts, if not more so. 'Thought' broadly defined to include feelings, sensations, and, above all, creative artistic impulses was raised to a status of equality with 'Nature'.

Everything fitted together; nothing was accidental: intelligence merely had to grasp how phenomena related to ideas. 'I owe to Schelling the habit I now have of generalizing the least events and the most insignificant phenomena which I encounter', wrote V.F.Odoevskii, a leading Schellingian of the 1820s.[9] In the late 1830s when Russian intellectuals became drunk on Hegel, the addiction acquired extreme forms. Alexander Herzen, having returned from exile, found his Moscow friends in a kind of collective delirium:

> Nobody at this time would have disowned such a sentence as this: 'The concrescence of abstract ideas in the sphere of the plastic represents that phase of the self-questing spirit in which it, defining itself for itself, is potentialized from natural immanence into the harmonious sphere of formal consciousness in beauty' ... Everything that *in fact* is most immediate, all the simplest feelings were erected into abstract categories and returned from thence as pale, algebraic ghosts, without a drop of living blood ... A man who went for a walk ... went not just for a walk, but in order to give himself over to the pantheistic feelings of his identification with the cosmos. If, on the way, he met a tipsy soldier or a peasant woman who tried to strike up a conversation, the philosopher did not simply talk with them, he determined the substantiality of the popular element, both in its immediate and its accidental manifestations. The very tear which might rise to his eye was strictly referred to its proper category: to *Gemüth* or the 'tragic element in the heart'.[10]

Secondly, and only slightly less importantly, Idealism injected into philosophy a dynamic element. It conceived reality, both in its spiritual and physical aspects, as undergoing constant evolution, as 'becoming' rather than 'being'. The entire cosmos was evolving, the process leading towards a vaguely defined goal of a perfectly free and rational existence. This 'historicist' element, present in all Idealist doctrines, has become ever since an indispensable ingredient of all 'ideologies'. It gave and continues to give the intelligentsia the assurance that the reality with which they happen to be surrounded and in varying degrees repudiate is by the very nature of things transitory, a stepping stone to something superior. Furthermore, it allows them to argue that whatever discrepancy there might exist between their ideas and reality is due to the fact that reality, as it were, has not yet caught up with their ideas. Failure is always temporary for ideologues, as success is always seen by them to be illusory for the powers that be.

The net effect of Idealism was to inspire Russian intellectuals with a self-confidence which they had never possessed before. Mind was linked with nature, both participating in a relentless unfolding of historical processes; compared to this vision, what were mere governments, economies, armies and bureaucracies? Prince Odoevskii thus describes the exaltation he and his friends experienced on being first exposed to these heady concepts:

What solemn, luminous, and joyful feeling permeated life once it had been shown that it was possible to explain the phenomena of nature by the very same laws to which the human spirit is subject in its evolution, seemingly to close forever the gap separating the two realms, and fashion them into a single receptacle containing the eternal idea and eternal reason. With what youthful and noble pride did we at that time envisage the share which had been allotted man in this universal existence! By virtue of the quality and right of thought, man transposed visible nature within himself and analyzed it in the innermost recesses of his own consciousness: in short, he became nature's focal point, judge and interpreter. He absorbed nature and in him it revived for rational and inspired existence ... The more radiantly the eternal spirit, the eternal idea reflected themselves in man, the more fully did he understand their presence in all the other realms of life. The culmination of the whole [Idealist] outlook were moral obligations, and one of the indispensable obligations was to emancipate within oneself the divine share of the world idea from everything accidental, impure, and false in order to acquire the right to the blessings of a genuine, rational existence.[11]

Of course, not all Russian intellectuals succumbed to such ecstasy. Idealism had also more sober followers, as, for example, among academic historians who took from Hegel little more than a general scheme of development of human societies. But in some degree, in the reign of Nicholas I (1825–55) Idealism was an all-pervading philosophy of the Russian intelligentsia, and its influence persisted well into the second half of the nineteenth century, after its principal tenets had been repudiated and replaced by materialism.

The first, 'Idealist', generation of the Russian intelligentsia was recruited almost exclusively from the ranks of dvoriane, especially the comfortably situated 'gentry'. But the social preponderance of dvoriane was a historic accident caused by the fact that in the first half of the nineteenth century they alone had the leisure and wherewithal for intellectual interests, especially of such an esoteric kind as demanded by Idealism. Even then, however, intellectuals from other estates were welcomed into the group whenever they chanced to appear, among them Belinskii, the son of a commoner, and V.P.Botkin, the son of a merchant. After the accession of Alexander II, as the country's estate structure began to dissolve, there was a steady inflow of non-dvoriane youths into the ranks of the intelligentsia. In the 1860s much was made of the sudden emergence as an intellectual force of *raznochintsy*, i.e. persons not attached to any of the standard legal categories, such as sons of priests who did not follow their fathers' footsteps (e.g. Nicholas Strakhov and Nicholas Chernyshevskii), children of lower rank, non-hereditary civil servants and officers, and so forth. The slow but steady spread of educational opportunities increased the number of potential dissidents. In secondary schools until the reign of Alexander III, the proportion of commoners in secondary schools rose uninterruptedly at the expense of dvoriane, as Table 2 shows; and since between eight and nine out of every ten secondary school graduates went on to the university or another institution of higher learning, it is clear that with each passing year the composition of all the student bodies became more plebeian.

TABLE 2 *Social Composition of Students in Russian Secondary Schools, 1833–85 (in percentages).*[12]

Year	Dvoriane and chinovniki	Clergy	Tax-paying groups
1833	78·9	2·1	19·0
1843	78·7	1·7	19·6
1853	79·7	2·3	18·0
1863	72·3	2·8	24·9
1874	57·7	5·5	35·7
1885	49·1	5·0	43·8

The free professions, virtually unknown in pre-Reform Russia, flourished in the second half of the nineteenth century. It is estimated that between 1860 and 1900 the number of professionally trained persons in Russia grew from 20,000 to 85,000.[13]

The educated class, from which the intelligentsia recruited its membership, thus steadily expanded and in expanding changed its character: what had been a small band of rich youths with troubled consciences and patriotic aspirations, became a large pool of people of all estates for whom intellectual work was a way of making a living. In the 1880s, Russia, already had a large intellectual proletariat. Nevertheless, to the end of the old regime, descendants of the old service class set the tone: the vast majority of the leaders of Russian opinion always came from well to do dvoriane or chinovniki of the upper ranks. It is they who formulated the ideology of a resentful mass of the intelligentsia.

The intelligentsia had to have institutions which would bring the like-minded together, allow them to exchange ideas and to form friendships based on shared convictions. In nineteenth-century Russia there were five such institutions.

The oldest of these was the salon. The open house maintained by rich landlords, especially in their spacious Moscow residences, provided an ideal setting of informal contact for people interested in public affairs. Although most of the aristocracy attending salons were preoccupied with gossip, match-making and cards, some salons were known to attract the more earnest and even to have a certain ideological colouring.

The controversy which later divided intellectuals into 'Westerners' and 'Slavophiles', for example, first broke out in salon conversations and only later found its way into print.

The second was the university. Russia's premier university, that of Moscow, had been founded in 1755, and although its Press proved useful to Novikov in his publishing ventures, it can hardly be said to have had much of an intellectual impact on the country. Its largely foreign faculty lectured in German and Latin to an uncomprehending audience composed of priests' sons and other plebeians; dvoriane saw no point in sending their sons there, the more so since years spent at the university did not count towards the accumulation of service seniority. This situation continued until the 1830s, when S. S. Uvarov took over the Ministry of Education. A conservative nationalist but also an eminent classical scholar, Uvarov believed that scientific and scholarly knowledge was the best antidote to subversive ideas then floating in the country. Under his ministry, higher learning began to flourish spectacularly in Russia. In the 1830s it became very fashionable for sons of aristocratic families to enrol at the University of Moscow. The government, anxious not to contribute to the creation of a large and unemployable intelligentsia, deliberately kept the number of students low: under Nicholas I it remained constant, barely exceeding three thousand throughout the empire. The government also placed great obstacles to the admission of commoners. With the death of Nicholas I, access to institutions of higher learning was eased. Many professional and technical schools were opened with the result that in 1893–4 Russia had 52 institutions of higher learning attended by 25,000 students. Several thousand more were enrolled at foreign universities. In an age when parental authority was strictly upheld by law and custom, the university provided a natural breeding ground for oppositional activity. It was here that young people from all parts of the empire first found themselves in a relatively free and informal society of their peers, where youth was in absolute and dominant majority. Here they heard articulated their privately nourished resentments and visions. Those who arrived without any strong public commitments were soon drawn into a vortex of common action which could only be resisted at the risk of ostracism: for the university was then, as it is today, one of the most effective means of enforcing intellectual conformity. In the early 1860s, unrest began to engulf Russian universities, and from then on the 'student movement' became a constant feature of Russian life. Protests, strikes, harassment and even violence against unpopular teachers and administrators were countered with mass arrests, expulsions and the closing down of universities. In the last half century of its existence, the old regime was in a state of permanent war with the student population.

The 'circle' (*kruzhok*) was throughout the nineteenth century a very popular vehicle for intellectual activity. It began in the age of salons, when separate circles were formed to study Schelling, Hegel and the French socialists, and continued into the era of university dominance when the salon ceased to play a significant role in the country's intellectual life. The circle was an informal gathering of persons sharing common intellectual interests who met periodically for study and discussion. At periods of severe repression, they acquired of necessity a clandestine and subversive character.

The fourth major institution of the Russian intelligentsia and on a par with the university in importance was the periodical, or as it was popularly known, the 'fat journal' (*tolstyi zhurnal*). This kind of publication came into vogue with the easing of censorship after 1855. Typically, it consisted of two parts, one belletristic, the other devoted to public concerns in the broadest sense of that word (politics, to the extent allowed by censorship, economics, sociology, science, technology and so on). Each journal espoused a philosophical-political line and appealed to a particular clientele. The polemics between them, waged in coded or 'aesopian' language to get by the censors, became for Russians a surrogate for open political debate. In the 1850s and early 1860s, the leading radical organ was *The Contemporary* (*Sovremennik*), and, after its closing in 1866, *Annals of the Fatherland* (*Otechestvennye Zapiski*) which, in turn, was followed by *Russian Wealth* (*Russkoe bogatstvo*). The *Messenger of Europe* (*Vestnik Evropy*) was the steady beacon of pro-western, liberal opinion, a role which after 1907 it shared with *Russian Thought* (*Russkaia Mysl'*). The conservative-nationalist point of view had its mouthpiece in the *Russian Messenger* (*Russkii Vestnik*), a periodical which owed much of its popularity to the fact that the great novelists of the age, among them Tolstoy, Dostoevsky and Turgenev, published many of their works there. Backing up these leading organs of opinion were scores of lesser known periodical publications.* The 'fat journal' performed a unique service in the development in Russia of public opinion. It broadcast throughout the vast empire information and ideas which otherwise would have remained confined to the two capital cities, and by so doing created multiple networks linking widely scattered individuals inhabiting provincial cities and rural estates. It is on this basis that political parties emerged in Russia so quickly at the beginning of the twentieth century. Within a year after he came to power Lenin shut down all the 'fat journals' without exception, no doubt because his

---

* In the reign of Nicholas I the number of political, social and literary journals hovered between 10 and 20. After 1855, their number grew rapidly: 1855, c.15; 1860, c.50; 1875, c.70; 1880, c.110; and 1885, c.140. *Entsiklopedicheskii slovar'* . . . *Ob'a Brogkauz i Efron* (St Petersburg 1899), xviia, pp. 416–417.

keen political sense told him what danger they presented to absolute authority.*

Finally, there were the *zemstva*. These organs of local self-government came into being in 1864, partly to replace the authority of one-time serf-owners, partly to carry out functions which the provincial bureaucracy was incapable of executing, such as elementary education, sanitation, maintenance of roads and bridges, agrarian improvement. Zemstva had limited powers of levying taxes and were authorized to use the money they raised to hire technical and professional personnel. Known as the 'third element', this personnel consisted of teachers, physicians, engineers, agronomists and statisticians. It numbered in 1900 some 47,000 persons. The political orientation of this group may be described as liberal-radical or liberal-democratic, that is, socialist but anti-revolutionary and anti-élitist. This 'third element' subsequently furnished the backbone of the liberal Constitutional Democratic Party, formed in 1905, and had much to do with its general leftward leanings. The landlords elected to zemstvo posts tended to be considerably more to the right, and in the main conservative-liberal; they disliked the bureaucracy and opposed all manifestations of arbitrariness, but they were cautious about introducing into Russia a constitutional regime, and especially a parliament based on a democratic franchise. In the 1880s and 1890s it was the fashion for liberals and non-revolutionary radicals to seek employment with zemstva. Committed revolutionaries, on the other hand, viewed all such work with suspicion.

These five institutions had this in common that they furnished society with means to resist the ubiquitous bureaucracy, for which reason they became the prime target of repression. In the final years of the nineteenth century, when the monarchy launched a determined political counter-offensive against society, the universities, journals and zemstva were singled out for harsh treatment.

The first controversy within the Russian intelligentsia broke out in the late 1830s and concerned the historic mission of Russia. Schellingian and Hegelian philosophy had raised in an acute form the question what was every major country's contribution to the advance of civilization. The German thinkers tended to dismiss the Slavic contribution and to relegate the Slavs to the category of 'unhistoric' races. The Slavs reacted by extolling themselves as the wave of the future. The first to develop a 'Slavophile' theory were the Poles and the Czechs, both under direct German pressure. In Russia the question was raised in an acute form

---

* In the Khrushchev era, the Soviet monthly *Novyi Mir* (*New World*) sought, with fair measure of success, to revive the 'fat journal's' political role as a critic of the *status quo*. With the dismissal of its editor, Alexander Tvardovskii, in 1970, this attempt came to an end.

somewhat later, after 1836, in response to a sensational article published that year by a leading figure of Moscow society, Peter Chaadaev. Chaadaev, who was deeply influenced by Catholic thought of the Restoration era and came close to conversion, argued that of all the major nations Russia alone had contributed nothing to civilization. Indeed, it was a country without a history: 'We live entirely in the present in its narrowest confines, without a past or future, amid a dead calm.'[14] Russia was a kind of historic swampland, a backwater where things stirred now and then but never flowed anywhere. This was so because Christianity had been drawn from a polluted source, Byzantium, which caused it to be isolated from the mainstream of spiritual life issuing from Rome. Officially pronounced insane for espousing these ideas, Chaadaev partly recanted, but towards the end of his life his pessimism about Russia reasserted itself. In 1854, during the Crimean War, he wrote these words:

Talking about Russia one always imagines that one is talking about a country like the others; in reality, this is not so at all. Russia is a whole separate world, submissive to the will, caprice, fantasy of a single man, whether his name be Peter or Ivan, no matter – in all instances the common element is the embodiment of arbitrariness. Contrary to all the laws of the human community, Russia moves only in direction of her own enslavement and the enslavement of all the neighbouring peoples. For this reason it would be in the interest not only of other peoples but also in that of her own that she be compelled to take a new path.[15]

Chaadaev's 1836 essay set off a controversy that raged for two decades splitting the Russian intelligentsia in two.

One camp, the Slavophile, produced what became the most seminal current in Russian intellectual history. It created the first ideology of Russian nationalism (as distinct from xenophobia) and it did so by borrowing ideas from western Europe to extol Russia at western Europe's expense. Its leading theorists came from the ranks of that middle level of the dvorianstvo which retained close links with the land. Their ideas were first elaborated in discussions held in Moscow salons during the late 1830s and the 1840s. In the 1850s, when their influence was at its peak, the Slavophiles formed a party grouped around the periodical *The Muscovite (Moskvitianin)*. Although they disavowed any interest in politics, they were constantly harassed by the authorities who treated with suspicion any ideology, even one favouring absolutism.

According to Slavophile theory, all the essential differences between Russia and the west were ultimately traceable to religion. The western churches had from their inception fallen under the influence of classical cultures and from them become poisoned with rationalism and *hubris*. Orthodoxy had remained constant to true Christian ideals. It was a truly communal church, which drew its strength from the collective faith and wisdom of the flock. This communal spirit (*sobornost'*) formed the quintessential feature of Russian national character and provided the basis of all Russian institutions. In the west, by contrast, the foundations of organized life were individualistic and legalistic. Thanks to Orthodoxy, Russians have managed to retain 'integral' personalities in which logic and faith fused to produce a superior kind of knowledge which Alexis Khomiakov, Slavophilism's outstanding theorist, called 'living knowledge' (*zhivoe znanie*).

Having succumbed to rationalism, western civilization has isolated the individual from the community: as each westerner follows the dictates of his understanding he comes to inhabit a world of his own making. To use a word which Hegel had made current, he is 'alienated'. In Russia, by contrast, every individual (except those who had become westernized) submerges in the community and feels at one with it. Russian intellectuals who have received a western education ought to find their way back to the community, to the peasantry. Spontaneous social organization, as exemplified by the rural commune and the artel was, in the Slavophiles' opinion, the natural form in which the Russians' social instincts expressed themselves. Legality and private property were alien to the Russian spirit.

These premises led to a peculiar anarcho-conservative political philosophy. According to the Slavophiles, it was in the Russian tradition to draw a sharp line of demarcation between the state or authority (*vlast'*) and the 'land' (*zemlia*). The land entrusted the management of high politics to the state, without imposing on it any legal limitations. The most that it ever asked for was to be heard when major decisions had to be taken. In return, the state did not interfere with society's right to lead its life as it saw fit. This mutual respect between state and society, unencumbered by any formalities, was the true Russian constitution. This tradition was violated by Peter the Great, and ever since his reign Russia had been following a path entirely alien to her nature. By creating in St Petersburg a bureaucratic machine, Peter had broken the communication between the crown and the people. Even worse was his interference with the nation's customs, manners and religion. The entire St Petersburg period in Russian history was a horrendous mistake. The country had to return to its heritage. There ought to be no constitution or parliament, but neither should there be a meddlesome, arbitrary bureaucracy. The 'land' should be give back to the people, who had a right to full freedom in all matters except politics. Serfdom should be abolished.

The Slavophile view of their country's past bore no resemblance whatever to the historic record, and did not long withstand scholarly critique. But then the facts about the development of Russian state and society outlined on the preceding pages were not known in the middle of the nineteenth century when Slavophile theory was formulated; in the main, they are the product of scholarly research carried out during the past hundred years. The Slavophile outlook probably owed more to the contemporary 'Young England' movement than to anything in Russia's own tradition. The Slavophiles greatly admired Britain (as they disliked France and Germany), and they wished Russia to have the same kind of unwritten constitution under which the relations between crown and nation were regulated by custom rather than written law, where the crown (ideally) allied itself with the laboring classes, where the bureaucracy was small and weak, and where it was taken for granted that the state did not interfere with society's right to go about its business. Of course, they knew next to nothing of the long historic antecedents of the Victorian compromise, or of the role played in it by the things they so hated, namely law, property and an institutionalized adversary relationship between rulers and ruled.

Their grotesquely idealized picture of the past permitted the Slavophiles to maintain that she was the country of the future, destined to solve the problems plaguing mankind. Her contribution would lie in the spread of voluntary associations, built in the spirit of love and brotherhood, and of a political system based on trust between authority and nation. By so doing, Russians would once and for all eliminate the world's political and class conflicts.

Because they like symmetry, historians have created a foil for the Slavophiles, a party they call 'Westerners', but it is difficult to perceive among the opponents of Slavophile theories any unity except that of a negative kind. They rejected the whole vision of Russia and of the west of the Slavophiles as compounded of ignorance and utopianism. Where the Slavophiles saw depth of religious feeling, they saw superstition verging on atheism (see Belinskii's letter to Gogol, cited above, p. 160). The historians among the anti-Slavophiles had no difficulty in demolishing one by one their most cherished beliefs; they could show that the modern repartitional commune was not of ancient and spontaneous, 'folkish' origin, but an institution created by the state to ensure collection of taxes (p. 17 above); that every one of Peter's 'revolutionary' innovations had had its antecedents in Muscovite Russia; that the alleged understanding between state and society had never existed, the Russian state always crushing society under its massive weight. They did not deny that Russia was different from the west, but they explained this difference by her backwardness rather than uniqueness. They saw virtually nothing in Russia worthy of preservation; the little there was, had been created by the state, and especially Peter the Great.

Apart from their rejection of Slavophile idealizations, the Westerners had no ideology in common. Some among them were liberal, others radical, even extremely so. But their radicalism was subject to change. Belinskii, for example, towards the very end of his life had a sudden illumination that what Russia needed was not socialism but a bourgeoisie, while Herzen, having spent his life as an eloquent advocate of drastic change, in one of his last writings ('Letter to an Old Comrade') rejected revolution. It might be better, therefore, to call the Westernizing movement the 'critical movement' because a highly critical attitude towards Russia, past and present, was its outstanding quality. Apart from history, its principal outlet was literary criticism. Belinskii, the most consistent Westerner of his generation, fashioned out of the book review and the literary essay a powerful instrument of social analysis. He used his considerable influence to expose all idealizations of Russian reality, and to promote what he considered the realistic school of literature. It was owing to him that the Russian writer first became conscious of fulfilling a social role.

The reign of Alexander II witnessed a sharp break in Russian public opinion. The Idealist generation had still been concerned primarily with the question: what are the Russians? The new post-1855 generation of 'Positivists' or 'Realists' raised the more pragmatic problem, first articulated by Novikov: what are we intellectuals to do? In responding, the intelligentsia became polarized into conservative and radical wings, with a small body of liberal opinion uneasily wedged in between. Unlike the preceding era, when ideological opponents continued to meet socially and observe ordinary civilities, in the reign of Alexander conflicts of ideas became personalized and not infrequently led to bitter enmities.

The occasion which brought about this change was the Great Reforms inaugurated by the new monarch, most of which have been mentioned in these pages already. There was the emancipation of the serfs, followed by the introduction of zemstva and organs of urban self-government, a reform of the court system (which will be touched upon in the following chapter) and the introduction of compulsory military service. This was the most ambitious effort undertaken in the history of Russia to bring society into active participation in national life short of allowing it to share in the political process.

The reforms generated a tremendous sense of excitement in society, especially among the young who suddenly saw opportunities opening up for public service such as had never existed before. They could now enter the professions (law, medicine or journalism); they could work in zemstva and city governments; they could seek careers in the military service, whose officer ranks were opened to commoners; and, above all, they could establish contact with the emancipated peasant and help him to raise himself to the status of a citizen. The late fifties and early sixties were a period of rare unanimity, as left, centre and right joined forces to help the government carry out its grand reform programme.

The first breach in the united front occurred in 1861 with the publication of the terms of the Emancipation settlement. The left, led by Chernyshevskii and his *Contemporary*, disappointed that the peasant received only half the land he had been cultivating and had to pay even for that, declared the whole Emancipation a cruel hoax. Student unrest of the early 1860s coupled with the Polish revolt of 1863 and a simultaneous outbreak of mysterious arson in St Petersburg persuaded many conservatives and liberals that a conspiracy was afoot. The *Russian Messenger*, until then an organ of moderate opinion, now swung sharply to the right and began to attack the left from a patriotic position. There was a further split within radical ranks themselves. The *Contemporary* launched vicious personal attacks on the intelligentsia of the older generation, accusing it of lack of serious commitment and inertia. Herzen replied in the pages of his London-based *Bell*, charging the younger generation with chronic biliousness. Chicherin then attacked Herzen for his revolutionary predilections, while Chernyshevskii called Herzen 'the skeleton of a mammoth'. By 1865, Russian opinion was thoroughly splintered. Still, the basic debate as it unfolded was a dialogue between radicals and conservatives who could agree on nothing except their common loathing of the sensible, pragmatic men of the middle. The 1860s and 1870s were the Golden Age of Russian thought, when all the major themes which have occupied the intelligentsia ever since were stated and examined.

The new radicalism developed on the basis of a 'scientific' or 'positivistic' philosophy which began to penetrate Russia from the west in the closing years of Nicholas' reign but fully conquered the radical left only under his successor. The spectacular achievements of chemistry and biology in the 1840s, notably the discovery of the laws of conservation of energy and the cellular structure of living organisms, led to the emergence in western Europe of an anti-Idealist movement committed to a crass form of philosophic materialism. The writings of Büchner and Moleschott, which young Russians read with a sense of revelation, told of a cosmos composed exclusively of matter in which all activity could be reduced to basic chemical or physical processes, a cosmos in which there was no room for God, soul, ideals or any other metaphysical substance. Feuerbach explained how the idea of God itself was a projection of human wishes; and his followers applied this psychological explanation to money, state and other institutions. Buckle, in the introduction to his *History of Civilization in England*, a best seller in Russia, promised that the science of statistics would make it possible to determine in advance with mathematical precision all manifestations of social behaviour. These ideas, seemingly backed by the prestige of natural science, suggested that the key to the understanding of man and society had at long last been found. Nowhere was their impact stronger than in Russia where the absence of a tradition of humanism and lay theology made intellectuals exceedingly vulnerable to deterministic explanations.

Left-wing youths now contemptuously rejected Idealist philosophy which had sent their elders into such raptures – at any rate, they rejected it consciously, because unconsciously they retained a great deal of personal idealism and a belief in historic progress which, strictly speaking, could not be justified on empirical grounds. In *Fathers and Sons*, Turgenev depicted this clash of generations in a manner which the protagonists at once recognized as accurate. The young 'nihilists' viewed the world in which they found themselves as a living relic of another, earlier phase of human development, now drawing to a close. Mankind stood on the eve of the stage of 'positivism', when all natural and human phenomena would be properly understood and therefore made to subject to scientific management. The immediate task was to smash what was left of the old order, of which Idealism, as a metaphysical doctrine, was part. Dmitry Pisarev, one of the idols of radical youth of the early 1860s, urged his followers recklessly to hit about them right and left, assailing institutions and conventions, on the premiss that whatever fell in the process was not worth saving. Such 'nihilism' was motivated not by a total absence of values, as conservative critics were to charge, but by the belief that the present already belonged to the past, and destruction, therefore, was creative.

Psychologically, the outstanding quality of the new generation of radicals was a tendency to oversimplify by reducing all experience to some single principle. They had no patience at all with complexities, refinements, qualifications. To deny the simple truth or to try to complicate it by introducing caveats was taken by them as an excuse for inaction: it was a symptom of 'Oblomovitis', as extreme sloth came to be known after the hero of Goncharov's novel. Each radical of this era had a formula, the adoption of which was certain radically to alter the entire human condition. Chernyshevskii's vision of a terrestrial paradise was a kind of oleograph of the prophetic writings he must have read in his seminary days; all was simple provided people would only see the truth, and the truth was that only matter existed and nought else.* Perfectly

* The Russian right was not far behind the left in its reductionism. 'Actually, it is all so simple' Dostoevsky wrote at the conclusion of the 'Dream of a Ridiculous Man', 'in one day, *in one hour*, everything could be arranged! The main thing is to love others as oneself — this is the main thing, and this is all, and nothing more is needed. As soon as you know this, everything will be arranged.'

reasonable objections to the philosophy of materialism Chernyshevskii and his allies shrugged off as undeserving of any attention. Needless to say, neo-Kantian criticism of mechanistic science, on which materialism was based, never reached Russian radicals, although they were closely attuned to developments in German thought. Chernyshevskii, on his death in 1889, still faithfully clung to Feuerbach and the other idols of his youth fifty years before, blissfully unaware what confusion was being spread in the field of natural science by recent discoveries. He even rejected Darwin. This selective treatment of science was very characteristic of the radical left, which shielded itself behind the prestige of science, but completely lacked the attitude of free and self-critical inquiry fundamental to genuine scientific thinking.

The radicals of the 1860s wished to create a new man. He was to be totally practical, free of religious and philosophical preconceptions, a 'rational egoist', and yet, at the same time, an absolutely dedicated servant of society and fighter for a juster life. The obvious contradiction between empiricism, which insisted that all knowledge derives from observation, and ethical idealism which has no equivalent in the material world was never faced by the radical intellectuals. The religious philosopher, Vladimir Soloviev, once stated their predicament in a pseudo-syllogism: 'Man is descended from the ape, and *therefore* he must sacrifice himself for the common good.' Emotionally some of the radical publicists came nearer Christian idealism than the hard-headed pragmatism they claimed to admire. The hero of Chernyshevskii's *What is to be Done?*, Rakhmetov, is a figure straight from Orthodox hagiology: his asceticism goes so far that he builds himself a bed studded with nails. The other figures in this novel (which exerted deep influence on the young Lenin) resemble early Christians in that like them they break with their corrupted, worldly families to join brotherhoods of those who had renounced the seductions of money and pleasure. The men and women in this book experience affection but not love and certainly no sex. But it is a vacuous religiousness, all zeal and no charity. Soloviev, annoyed by claims of an alleged identity of ideals of Christianity and socialism once reminded his readers that whereas Christianity told man to give away his own wealth, socialism exhorted him to expropriate the wealth of others.

The radicals were fully conscious how impotent was their small band confronting the full might of the autocratic state. However, they were not out to challenge the system politically. They were anarchists who had no interest in the state as such, regarding it as merely one of the many by-products of certain ways of thinking and of human relations based on them. Their assault against the *status quo* was directed in the first place against opinions, and their weapons were ideas, where they felt they enjoyed clear superiority over the establishment. In so far as (according to Comte) the progress of humanity expressed itself in the gradual widening of man's intellectual horizons – from the religious-magical through the philosophical-metaphysical to the positivist-empirical – the spread of the highest, positivist-material way of thinking was of itself a most powerful agent of change. Nothing could stand up to it because it sapped the very foundations of the system. The force of ideas would bring down states, churches, economies, and social institutions. Paradoxically, the triumph of materialism would be brought about by the action of ideas.

Hence, the crucial role of the intelligentsia. Defined by left publicists in the narrow sense to mean only that segment of society espousing the positivist-materialist outlook, the intelligentsia was the thin end of the historic wedge: behind, followed the masses. It was a fundamental tenet of faith of all the radical movements of the time that the intelligentsia was the prime mover of human progress. The Social Democrats, who became popular only in the 1890s, first abandoned this belief and shifted the emphasis to impersonal economic forces. But it is significant that the one offshoot of Russian Social Democracy which in the end attained success, Bolshevism, found it necessary to abandon reliance on impersonal economic forces, whose tendency rather pointed away from revolution, and revert to the traditional stress on the intelligentsia. Lenin's basic theory held that socialism could only be brought about by a cadre of professional revolutionaries which meant nothing else than the intelligentsia, since few workers or peasants could dedicate themselves to full-time revolutionary activity.

Between 1860 and 1880, the radical or, as it was then known, 'socialist-revolutionary' movement underwent constant evolution as a result of a frustrating inability to realize any of its goals. The changes concerned tactics only. The goal itself remained constant – the abolition of the state and all institutions tied to it – and so did the faith in positivist-materialist principles. But every few years, as fresh classes entered the university, new battle tactics were devised. In the early 1860s, it was believed that the mere act of breaking with the dying world was enough; the rest would take care of itself. Pisarev urged his followers to drop all other occupations and interests and concentrate on the study of natural science. Chernyshevskii exhorted them to cut ties with their families and unite in working communes. But these methods did not seem to lead anywhere, and around 1870 radical youths became increasingly interested in the newly emancipated peasant. The leading theoretical lights of this period, Michael Bakunin and Peter Lavrov, called on young people to abandon universities and go to the village. Bakunin wished them to carry the message of immediate rebellion. He believed that the muzhik was a born anarchist, and only a spark was needed to set the countryside on fire. That spark was to be carried by the intelligentsia in the form of revolutionary 'agitation'. Lavrov adopted a more gradual approach. Before he would turn into a revolutionary, the Russian peasant needed exposure to 'propaganda' which would enlighten him about the injustices of the Emancipation Edict, about the causes of his economic predicament, and about the collusion between the propertied classes, the state and the church. Inspired by these ideas, in the spring of 1874 several thousand youths quit school and went 'to the people'. Here disappointment awaited them. The muzhik, known to them largely from literary descriptions and polemical tracts, would have nothing to do with idealistic students come to save him. Suspecting ulterior motives – the only kind experience had acquainted him with – he either ignored them or turned them over to the rural constabulary. But even more disappointing than the peasant's hostility, which could be explained away by his ignorance, were his ethics. The radical youths scorned property because they largely came from propertied backgrounds: they associated concern for wealth with their parents, whom they rejected. Hence they idealized the rural commune and the artel. The muzhik, living from hand to mouth, looked at the matter quite differently. He desperately wanted to acquire property, and was not very choosy how to go about getting it. His idea of a new social order was an arrangement under which he took the part of the exploiting landlord. The intellectuals could indulge in talk of selfless brotherhood because, being supported by their families or the government (by means of stipends) they were not required to compete with one another. The muzhik, however, was always competing for scarce resources, and he treated conflict, including the use of force or duplicity, as right and proper.*

In response to these disappointments, the radical movement broke up into warring factions. One group, called *narodniki* from their unbounded faith in the *narod* or people, decided that it was improper for intellectuals to foist their ideas upon the masses. The toiling man was always right. Intellectuals should settle in the village and learn from the peasant instead of trying to teach him. Another group, convinced that this method would end in renunciation of revolution, began to veer towards terrorism (below, p. 297). A third developed an interest in western Social Democracy and, having concluded that no social revolution in Russia was possible until capitalism had done its work, braced themselves for a long and patient wait.

* It may not be out of place here to remark that the Revolution of November 1917, by sweeping away the old, westernized élite, brought to power a new élite rooted in the village and permeated with this kind of psychology. Why the radical intelligentsia, having learned much of the peasant's psychology, nevertheless still expected him to emerge as a selfless socialist, is one of the unexplained mysteries of Russian history.

The number of radical activists in Russia was always very small. Statistics on political repression carried out by a police disinclined to give suspects the benefit of the doubt, indicate that they constituted an infinitesimal part of the country's population (below, p. 307). What made them dangerous was the behaviour of the public at large in the mounting conflict between the radical left and the authorities. The imperial government invariably over-reacted to radical challenges, carrying out mass arrests where restraint would have been in order, and exiling where arrest and brief detention would have been sufficient punishment. By various bureaucratic-police devices, which will be detailed in the following chapter, the government increasingly restricted the civil liberties of all the Russians, alienating law-abiding citizens who otherwise would have had no truck with the opposition. The radicals, having quickly learned how beneficial to their interests government over-reaction was, developed elaborate techniques of 'provocation', that is of baiting the police into brutality as a means of gaining public sympathy for themselves and their cause. The net effect was for public opinion to shift steadily towards the left. The average liberal found himself in a great quandary as to how he should react to the mounting civil conflict. While he disapproved of violence, he saw that the authorities also did not stay within the bounds of law; his choice was not between 'law and order' and violence, but between two kinds of violence, one perpetrated by the (seemingly) all-powerful state, the other by misguided but (seemingly) idealistic and self-sacrificing youths, struggling for what they conceived to be the public good. Faced with such a choice, he tended to opt for radicalism. This kind of dilemma is clearly reflected in the writings of Turgenev, in this respect a typical Westerner and liberal. But even an arch-conservative like Dostoevsky could not entirely escape it. He for whom radicalism was explainable best by recourse to demonology admitted once to a friend that he would have been incapable of turning over to the police hypothetical terrorists overheard talking about a bomb planted by them in the Winter Palace.[16]

The unwilling, half-hearted, often tormented recruits from the centre constituted a critical asset for the radicals. The technique of purposefully driving the government to the extreme right and to violent excesses, first developed by Russian radicals in the late nineteenth century, has ever since served as the most effective weapon in the radical arsenal. It paralyses the liberal centre and prods it into joining ranks with the left against the increasingly extreme right, thereby assuring, over the long haul, liberalism's self-destruction.

The conservative movement in Russia under Alexanders II and III arose in response to radicalism, and in struggling against it acquired many of its qualities. It was a 'radical right' movement, characterized by contempt for liberalism and a tendency to assume all-or-nothing positions.[17]

It began as a critique of the 'nihilist' whose sudden appearance threw Russian society into disarray. Who was this type who negated everything that others cherished, deliberately flaunting all convention, and what was his parentage? This was the central problem of the conservative position. The battle was in large measure over Russia's future national type, in which the radicals' 'new man' was confronted with a no less idealized model of a 'man with roots'.

The most common diagnosis of the malaise responsible for 'nihilism' – the term being defined as a rejection of all values – was the separation of theory and theorists from raw life. The conservatives mistrusted all abstractions and inclined towards philosophical nominalism; if forced to generalize, they gave preference to the vocabulary of biology over that of mechanics. The intellect which they extolled was Khomiakov's 'living knowledge'. Detached from experience, the intellect fell into all kinds of aberrations, including the belief that it could completely alter nature and man. This charge against radicals was not unlike that which Catherine II had levelled a century earlier against Novikov, although Novikov himself, of course, entertained no such delusions. In Russia, according to conservative theorists, the divorce of thought from life assumed tragic dimensions because of the method of education adopted since Peter I. The education was western, whereas native culture, still preserved intact among ordinary people, was Slav and Orthodox. By virtue of its education, Russia's upper class, of which the 'nihilist' was an offshoot, was isolated from the native soil and condemned to spiritual sterility, of which the habit of negation was a natural expression. 'Outside the national soil', wrote Ivan Aksakov, 'there is no firm ground; outside the national, there is nothing real, vital; and every good idea, every institution not rooted in the national historical soil or grown organically from it, turns sterile and becomes an old rag.'[18] And Michael Katkov, the editor of *Russian Messenger*, thus diagnosed the 'nihilist' hero of *Fathers and Sons*:

Man taken separately does not exist. He is everywhere part of some living connection, or some social organization ... Man extracted from the environment is a fiction or an abstraction. His moral and intellectual organization, or, more broadly, his ideas are only then operative in him when he has discovered them first as the organizational forces of the environment in which he happens to live and think.[19]

The radicals, too, stressed the collective nature of man; but to them, the collective was freely formed by individuals who had broken with that environment in which accident of birth had happened to cast them, whereas to the conservatives in had to be the actual historically formed environment and nothing else. Dostoevsky went so far as to draw a direct line connecting western education with the desire to kill. He called a harmless professor of medieval history and a prominent Westerner, T. Granovskii, and the critic Belinskii 'fathers' of Nechaev, the anarchist who had organized the assassination of an innocent student youth, the story of which provided him with the plot for *The Possessed*.[20] In *The Brothers Karamazov*, the Western rationalist Ivan bears ultimate responsibility for parricide.

The immediate duty of the intelligentsia was to recover its lost roots. It must 'go to the people', not in the literal sense in which Bakunin and Lavrov advocated it, but in a spiritual one, urged by the Slavophiles. It must submerge itself in the nation and seek to dissolve in it. The intelligentsia was a poison in Russia's body for which 'folkdom' was the only efficacious antidote.

The political philosophy of the conservatives underwent considerable change as the warfare between the radicals and the authorities intensified. Basically, like the Slavophiles, the conservatives desired a government without parliamentary democracy or bureaucratic centralism; a government modelled on a mythical ancient Muscovite order. It was men, not institutions that mattered. The conservatives completely rejected the view of Bazarov, the archetypal 'nihilist' of *Fathers and Sons*, that 'in a well-constructed society it will be quite irrelevant whether man is stupid or wise, evil or good.' There could be no 'well-constructed society', unless the material was sound; and in any event, there were limits to the perfectibility of any society because man was inherently corrupt and evil. Dostoevsky, whose pessimism went further than that of most Russian conservatives, regarded humans as natural killers, whose instincts were restrained principally by fear of divine retribution after death. Should man lose belief in the immortality of his soul there would be nothing left to keep his murderous inclinations from asserting themselves. Hence, there was need for strong authority.

As the conflict between the left and the regime intensified, most of the conservatives unqualifiedly backed the regime, which in itself tended to exclude them from the ranks of the intelligentsia. They also grew steadily more xenophobic and anti-Semitic. In Pobedonostsev, the power behind the throne of Alexander III, conservatism found its Grand Inquisitor.

'If you please, the Venus of Milo is more indubitable than Russian law or the principles of 1789.'[21] This phrase of Turgenev's may appear strange at first sight. But its meaning becomes quite clear when set in the context of a crucial controversy which developed in Russia between the radical intelligentsia on the one hand and writers and artists on the other.

Literature was the first human activity to break away from patrimonial subservience in Russia; and in time it was joined by other spiritual activities, the visual arts, scholarship, science. One may say that by the middle of the nineteenth century, 'culture' and the pursuit of material interest were the only two spheres which the regime allotted to its subjects reasonably free of interference; but since the pursuit of material interest, as pointed out at the beginning of this chapter, tended in Russia to go in hand with complete political subservience, culture alone provided a possible base of opposition. It was natural, therefore, that it should become progressively politicized. One can state categorically that not one great Russian writer, artist, scholar or scientist of the old regime placed his work in the service of politics; the few who did, were without exception untalented third-raters. There is a fundamental incompatibility between politics, which requires discipline, and creativity, which demands freedom, for the two to make at best uneasy allies and most often, to confront one another as deadly enemies. What did happen, however, was that creative persons in Russia found themselves under immense pressure from the intelligentsia left of centre to place themselves and their work at the disposal of society. Poets were under pressure to write novels, and novelists to write social *exposés*. Painters were asked to use their art to bring vividly to the attention of all, especially illiterates, the suffering of the masses. Scholars and scientists were urged to occupy themselves with problems of immediate social relevance. This utilitarian approach was not unknown in contemporary western Europe, but in Russia its exponents were much more strident because of culture's, and especially literature's, unique function. As the high priest of utilitarian aesthetics, Chernyshevskii, put it:

In countries, where intellectual and social life has attained a high level of development there exists, if one may say so, a division of labour among the various branches of intellectual activity, of which we know only one – literature. For this reason, no matter how we rate our literature compared to foreign literatures, still in our intellectual movement it plays a much greater role than do French, German or English literatures in the intellectual movement of their countries, and there rests on it heavier responsibility than on any of the others. As things stand, [Russian] literature absorbs virtually the entire intellectual life of the people, and for that reason it bears the duty of occupying itself also with such interests which in other countries, so to say, have come under the special management of other kinds of intellectual activity ... In Russia literature has retained a certain encyclopedic importance which has been already lost by the literatures of more enlightened peoples. That which Dickens says in England, is also said, apart from him and the other novelists, by philosophers, jurists, publicists, economists etc., etc. With us, apart from novelists, no one talks about subjects which comprise the subject of their stories. For that reason, even if Dickens need not feel it incumbent upon him, as a novelist, to bear direct responsibility for serving as spokesman for the strivings of his age, in so far as these can find expression in fields other than *belles lettres*, in Russia the novelist cannot have recourse to such justification. And if notwithstanding this both Dickens and Thackeray do consider it the direct responsibility of *belles lettres* to touch on all questions which occupy society, then our novelists and poets ought to feel this responsibility a thousand times more strongly.[22]

The key word in this passage, repeated four times, is 'responsibility'. The utilitarian school of criticism, which enjoyed in Russia virtual monopoly from 1860 to 1890, insisted that all writers, but those of Russia particularly, had a sacred duty to 'act as spokesmen for the strivings of their age', in other words, to put their pen at the disposal of the peoples' social and political aspirations. An extreme theory of utilitarian aesthetics was put forward by the young Dmitry Pisarev. Applying the principle of conservation of energy, he insisted that a backward society could not afford the luxury of a literature that did not serve the purposes of social betterment. Intelligence to him was a form of capital which had to be conserved. 'We are stupid because we are poor, and we are poor because we are stupid', he wrote in an essay called 'Realists', concluding that it was an unpardonable waste of national resources to write (and read) literature whose primary aim was to please.

In the polemic which developed between utilitarians and the exponents of 'art for art's sake', the central figure of contention was Pushkin. Until the 1860s his place in Russian culture had been unchallenged. He was revered not only as Russia's greatest poet and the founder of her literature, but as a new national type. 'Pushkin is the Russian man as he is in the course of becoming,' Gogol wrote, 'such as he may appear, perhaps, in two hundred years hence.'[23] But Pushkin was known to have detested all who wished to make art serve some ulterior purpose. For him, 'the aim of poetry was poetry', and 'poetry stood above morality'.[24] It is because of these sentiments that the radical critics chose him as their target, seeing in him the central bastion of that Idealism which they were determined to bring down. To Chernyshevskii, the idea of art serving itself was callous to the point of treason. For him 'the useless had no right to exist.'[25] He attacked Pushkin on numerous occasions not only as an irresponsible and useless human being but as a second-rate poet, a mere imitator of Byron. Pisarev, the *enfant terrible* of his generation, called Pushkin a 'lofty cretin'.[26] Relentless campaigns of this sort not only sent Pushkin's reputation into temporary eclipse, but had a profoundly discouraging influence on all but the very greatest literary and artistic talents.

The great ones fought back. They refused to serve as propagandists, convinced that their social role, such as it was, was best fulfilled by holding up a clear mirror to life. To a friend who complained that Chekhov in his stories showed no moral preferences, the writer replied:

Your criticize me for objectivity, calling it indifference to good and evil, lack of ideals, and so on. You desire me, in depicting horse thieves to say: horse-stealing is an evil. But this has been known for a long time without me. Let juries judge horse thieves. My job it is only to show what kind of people they are. I write: you deal with horse thieves then know that these are not poor people but well-fed ones, that they are members of a cult and that for them stealing horses is not theft but a passion. Of course, it would be nice to combine art with preaching, but for me it is extremely difficult to do so and indeed for technical reasons virtually impossible.[27]

And Tolstoy put the matter succinctly in a letter to a fellow-writer:

The aims of the artist are incommensurable (as mathematicians might say) with social goals. The goal of the artist lies not in solving a question in an indisputable manner, but in making people love life in its infinite, eternally inexhaustible manifestations.[28]

The quarrel had far greater import than might appear from its literary context. It was not over aesthetics but over the freedom of the creative artist – and, ultimately, that of every human being – to be himself. The radical intelligentsia, in struggling against a regime which had traditionally upheld the principle of compulsory state service, began to develop a service mentality of its own. The belief that literature and art, and to a somewhat lesser extent scholarship and science, had a primary responsibility to society became axiomatic in Russian left-wing circles. Social Democrats of both Bolshevik and Menshevik persuasion held on to it through thick and thin; and hence it was not surprising that when they came to power and got hold of the apparatus of repression which allowed them to put their theories into practice, the Communists soon deprived Russian culture of that freedom of expression which it had managed to win for itself under the imperial regime. Thus the intelligentsia turned on itself, and in the name of justice for society throttled society's voice.

CHAPTER 11

TOWARDS THE POLICE STATE

Although Russia lacks a tradition of vigorous self-government, it does not necessarily follow that it has one of bureaucratic centralism. Before the coming to power of the communist regime, Russia's officialdom was relatively small and not very effective. The obstacles to bureaucratization were formidable: the size of the country, the thin distribution of the population, difficulties of communication, and, perhaps most of all, lack of money. Russian governments were always short of cash, and that which they had they preferred to spend on the military. Under Peter the Great, the administration of Russia – already then the largest state in the world – absorbed 135,000–140,000 rubles annually, or an equivalent of between 3 and 4 per cent of the national budget.[1] How paltry this sum was may be judged from the following example. Impressed by the order prevailing in Livonia, which he had recently conquered from the Swedes, Peter ordered in 1718 an inquiry into administrative practices there. The investigation revealed that the Swedish government had allotted as much money for governing this one province, measuring perhaps 50,000 square kilometres, as the Russian government was spending on the administration of the whole empire, measuring over 15 million.[2] Rather than attempt the impossible and copy Swedish methods, Peter dismantled the administration of Livonia.

The Russian bureaucratic establishment loomed small not only in the country's budget; it was also insignificant in relation to the number of inhabitants. In the middle of the nineteenth century, Russia had between 11 and 13 civil servants for 10,000 people. This ratio was three to four times below that prevailing at the same time in western Europe.[3] Muscovite and imperial Russias, whose bureaucracies enjoyed very wide latitude and behaved in a notoriously arbitrary fashion, were certainly administratively understaffed. The obstacles standing in the way of full-scale bureaucratization were removed only in October 1917, when the Bolsheviks seized power. By that time the means of transport and communication had been modernized to the point where neither distance nor climate prevented the centre from exercising close control over the far-flung provinces. Nor was money any longer a problem; the expropriation in the name of socialism of the country's productive wealth assured the new government of all the resources it needed for administrative purposes, while at the same time providing it with a legitimate excuse for the building up of an immense bureaucratic apparatus on which to spend them.

The administrative order of pre-1917 Russia rested on a peculiar system of farming out which resembled neither bureaucratic centralism nor self-government. Its prototype was the Muscovite institution of 'feeding' (*kormlenie*), which gave the civil service virtually free rein to exploit the country, demanding only that it turn over to the state its fixed share. What happened to the surplus squeezed out of the population did not much concern the crown. Catherine II explained the system with charming candour to the French Ambassador as it applied to her court establishment:

The King of France never knows precisely the amount of his expenditure; nothing is regulated or fixed beforehand. My plan, on the contrary, is as follows: I fix an annual sum, which is always the same, for the expenses of my table, furniture, theatres and fêtes, my stables, and in short, my whole household. I order the various tables in my palace to be served with a particular quantity of wine, and a particular number of dishes. It is the same in all other branches of this administration. So long as I am supplied exactly, in quantity and quality with what I have ordered, and no one complains of neglect on the subject, I am satisfied; I think it of little consequence whether out of the fixed sum I am cheated through cunning or economy ...[4]

Essentially, the same system prevailed throughout the Russian government, at any rate until the second half of the nineteenth century.

The notorious venality of Russian officials, especially those working in the provinces, and most of all in provinces far removed from the capital cities, was due not to some peculiar characteristic of the Russian national character or even to the low calibre of the people who chose a bureaucratic career. It was inherent in a government which, lacking funds to pay for the administration, not only had for centuries paid its civil servants no salary, but had insisted that they 'feed themselves from official business' (*kormiatsia ot del*). In Muscovite Russia, the right of civil servants to line their pockets was to some extent regulated by the strict limits imposed on the length of time anyone could hold a provincial administrative post. To make certain that voevody appointed to lucrative Siberian posts did not exceed what were regarded as reasonable levels of extortion, the government set up on the main road leading from Siberia to Moscow pickets which searched returning voevody and their families and confiscated the surplus. To avoid them, enterprising governors returned by back roads, stealing home like thieves in the night.

Peter the Great made a valiant effort to put an end to this whole system under which officials, while nominally serving the crown, were actually petty satraps mainly concerned with their private well-being. In 1714 he forbade the granting of pomestia to officials employed in the bureaux of the central administration and outlawed the whole practice of 'feedings' for the provincial functionaries. Henceforth, all state employees were to receive a salary. The reform did not succeed for want of money. Even under Peter's strict regime only officials of the central bureaux in St Petersburg and Moscow received their salaries, and irregularly at that; provincial bureaucrats continued to live off the land exactly as before. In 1723, a quarter of the funds budgeted for the civil service was sequestered to help reduce the general deficit. The Austrian traveller, J.G.Korb, reports that in Peter's time Russian functionaries had to bribe their own colleagues to obtain the salaries due to them. Under Peter's immediate successors the situation deteriorated further as the state treasury fell into disarray. In 1727, for example, salary payments for most categories of chancery scribes (*podd'iachie*) were officially abolished, and the functionaries affected told to fend for themselves. Matters improved somewhat under Catherine II who took a keen interest in provincial administration, authorizing an appreciable increase in moneys allotted for it; in 1767, nearly a quarter of the budget was set aside for that purpose. Steps were also taken to assure that officials received their salaries on time. But the basic problem remained. During Catherine's reign and after it, civil service salaries were so low that most officials could not depend on them to meet their basic living expenses, and had to look around for additional income. In the reign of Alexander I, lower clerks received from one to four rubles' salary a month, a sum equivalent to between ten pence and two shillings in English currency of the time. Even making allowance for the cheapness of food and services in Russia, this was far from enough to support a family. Furthermore, salaries were paid in paper money (assignats), which not long after their first emission in 1768 began to be discounted and in the reign of Alexander I circulated in terms of silver currency for as little as a fifth of their face value. The reforms of Peter and Catherine did not, therefore, alter either the economic situation of the bureaucracy, or the bureaucracy's relationship to society resulting from it. Like agents of the Mongol khans, chinovniki entrusted with provincial administration functioned primarily as collectors of taxes and recruits; they were not 'public servants' at all:

In consequence of the absence of an abstract, independent idea of the state, the officials did not serve 'the state', but took care first of themselves and then of the tsar; and in consequence of the identity of the bureaucracy and the state the officials lacked the capacity to distinguish private from governmental property.[5]

In old-regime Russia, therefore, corruption of public servants was not an aberration, a departure from prevailing norm, such as is common in most countries; it was part and parcel of the regular system of administration. Russian officials had been accustomed since the founding of the Kievan state to live off the land. The central government, hard as it tried, lacked the wherewithal to change this custom. And so it went on.

During the centuries over which it had been practised, bribery in Russia developed an elaborate etiquette. A distinction was drawn between 'innocent incomes' (*bezgreshnye dokhody*), and 'sinful incomes' (*greshnye dokhody*). The criterion used to separate one from the other was the nature of the victim. 'Sinful' were 'incomes' derived at the expense of the crown, such as embezzlement of government funds or deliberate falsification of some data required by a central office. 'Innocent incomes' were obtained at society's cost; they included proceeds of extortion, sums received by judges to settle a trial in favour of one person rather than another, and, most commonly, tips taken to expedite a citizen's business with the government. (The English word 'tip' is actually an acrostic formed of the first letters of the words 'To Insure Promptness', marked on bowls in eighteenth-century English coffee-houses.) It was not unusual for the recipient of a 'sinful' bribe to follow an unwritten tariff and return change. Government inspectors could be quite ruthless prosecuting officials guilty of damaging state interests, certainly under Peter and his followers. They rarely interceded where the injured party was an ordinary citizen.

The higher an official's rank, the greater were his opportunities of amassing a fortune at society's expense. The variety of devices used was so great that no more than a few can be mentioned by way of illustration. A Deputy Governor, among whose responsibilities lay certification of the vodka sold in his province, might attest – if suitably bribed by distillers – as unadulterated vodka which in fact had been mixed with water. Since the victim in this instance was the consumer, no prosecutions followed even if by some chance the deed was uncovered. Governors in the more remote provinces sometimes accused a wealthy local merchant of a fictitious crime and then ordered him to be arrested and held in jail until he paid up. Bribing was a subtle and even gracious art. It was considered in better taste to bribe indirectly. For example, one could offer a generous donation to a 'charitable' cause, chaired by the official's wife; or sell him a piece of property at a fraction of its actual value; or buy something from him (e.g. a painting) for a sum far in excess of its value. The novelist, M. E. Saltykov-Shchedrin, who held the post of Deputy Governor in the Tver and Riazan provinces early in the reign of Alexander II, wrote that money was better invested in bribes than in bank deposits, because in this form it guaranteed freedom from the harassment of the authorities which could be very costly.

The rank and file of provincial bureaucrats had to make ends meet from tips and petty extortions. To explain how the system worked, one can do no better than cite an incident from Saltykov-Shchedrin's *Provincial Sketches*, which describes in fictional form a perfectly real situation. The hero of this narrative, a minor provincial chinovnik of the old Nicholaevan school caught up in the reforms of Alexander II, reminisces nostalgically about the past:

Yes, we took, of course, we took – who is not a sinner in the eyes of the Lord, who is not guilty before the tsar? But tell me: is it better to accept no money and work badly? When you take money, work becomes easier, more exciting. Nowadays, I look around me, everybody is busy talking, especially about this thing 'disinterest', and nothing gets done; and as for the peasant who's supposed to be better off, he groans and moans worse than before.
In those days we chinovniki were very friendly with one another. There was no such thing as envy or backbiting: one could always turn to the others for advice and help. Suppose, for instance, that you have played cards all night and got cleaned out. What then? Well, you would go to the local police chief. 'Demian Ivanovich,' you would say to him, 'such and such happened. Please help.' Demian Ivanovich would hear out your story and laugh, the way bosses do. 'You sons of bitches,' he would say, 'you hold jobs and yet you won't ever learn how to make yourself a pile – everything you rake in you spend in taverns and at cards!' And then he would add: 'Well, what's done is done. Get yourself over to the Sharkovskii District and collect the taxes.' So you would proceed there, knowing you wouldn't collect any taxes but still get enough to pay for your kids' milk.
It was all so very simple. You never used torture or extortion of any kind. You'd just arrive and assemble the people together. 'All right fellows, we need your help: the tsar, our father, needs money. Hand over the taxes!'
And after saying this you'd step inside some cottage and look out of the window. The fellows would stand in place, scratching their heads. Then, all of a sudden, all would start talking at once and waving their arms. So they would cool off for an hour while you, of course, sat in the cottage as if nothing had happened and had yourself a good laugh. After an hour, you would send the village official over to them. 'Enough talk,' he would say, 'the master is getting angry.' Then the confusion would get worse and they'd start casting lots: a Russian muzhik can't do without lots. That meant things were moving along, they have decided to talk to the assessor and ask, wouldn't I, for heaven's sake, agree to wait until they had a chance to earn some money.
'Ah, my friends: but what about your father, the tsar? He needs the money. At least take pity on us, your officials!'
All this would be said in a kindly voice: no smacking in the teeth or pulling by the hair. No saying to them: 'I take no bribes, so you'd better know what kind

of a district official I am.' Nothing of the kind. You'd get right through to them by acting gently and appealing to pity.

'But, sire, couldn't you at least wait until the Feast of Intercession?'

And, of course, down on their knees they would go.

'One can wait, sure, why not, that depends only on us. But what am I going to say to my superiors? Judge for yourselves.'

So the fellows would return to the assembly. There they would talk some more and then scatter to their homes. A couple of hours later you would look out and see the village official bringing you, as a reward for your willingness to be patient with taxes, ten kopecks per soul. And since the district had some four thousand souls, you'd end up with 400 rubles, sometimes more ... And you'd head back home with a gayer heart.[6]

Chinovniki like this one populate the pages of Russian literature from Gogol to Chekhov, some good-natured and gentle, others overbearing and brutal, but both types living off the land as if they were foreign conquerors among a subjugated race. Their society resembled a closed order. They tended to associate only with their own kind, fawning on superiors (*nachal'stvo*) and bullying inferiors. They loved the hierarchical stratification of chiny, with its automatic promotions, of which they were part, and regarded all existence outside their system as wild anarchy. They instinctively ejected from their midst the overzealous and scrupulous because the system required all to be implicated in bribery so as to create a bond of mutual responsibility. Just as drunks do not like sober companions, thieves feel uncomfortable in the presence of honest men.

Like any self-contained, hierarchical order, the Russian civil service evolved an elaborate set of symbols to distinguish the ranks among each other. The symbolism was formalized in the reign of Nicholas I and spelled out in 869 solid paragraphs in Volume I of the Code of Laws. For ceremonial purposes, the ranks were grouped into several categories, each of which had to be addressed by an appropriate title, all translations from the German. The holders of the top two ranks had to be called 'Your High Excellency' (*Hohe Exzellenz* or *Vashe Vysokoe Prevoskhoditel'stvo*), those in Ranks 3 and 4, 'Your Excellency' (*Exzellenz* or *Vashe Prevoskhoditel'stvo*) and so down the scale, with holders of Rank 9 to 14 being addressed simply as 'Your Honour' (*Wohlgeboren* or *Vashe Blagorodie*). With each rank category went also an appropriate uniform, specified to the last sartorial detail: promotion from white to black trousers was an event of cataclysmic proportion in a chinovnik's life. Holders of medals and orders (St Vladimir, St Anne, St George, etc., with their several classes) were also entitled to elaborate distinctions.

Honest public officials were to be found almost exclusively in the centre, in ministerial offices or their equivalent. The idea of office-holding as a public service was entirely alien to the Russian bureaucracy; it was something imported from the west, mainly Germany. It was Baltic Germans who first demonstrated to the Russians that an official could use his power to serve society. The imperial government greatly valued these men and they acquired a disproportionate share of the topmost ranks; we have already noted the high proportion of foreigners, especially Lutherans, among the élite officials of the imperial bureaucracy (above, p. 182). Many of the best civil servants were graduates of two special schools, the Lyceum at Tsarskoe Selo and the Imperial School of Jurisprudence.

An almost unbridgeable gap separated bureaucrats employed in the central administrative offices in St Petersburg and Moscow from those serving in the provincial administration. The latter had little opportunity of ever advancing to posts in the capital cities, and, conversely, officials who by virtue of family background, education, or wealth began their career ascent up the ladder of the central administration, rarely ventured into the provinces unless to assume the position of Governor or Deputy Governor. This gap perpetuated the ancient cleavage between élite dvoriane inscribed in the service books of the city of Moscow and the ordinary provincial dvorianstvo. Secondly, and again in line with Muscovite traditions, the imperial bureaucracy displayed a distinct tendency to form a closed, hereditary caste. A large proportion of the chinovniki were sons of chinovniki; and those clergymen, merchants and other commoners who entered the civil service from the outside generally tended to push their children into bureaucratic careers as well. Dvoriane of any standing rarely joined the civil service, partly because of its low prestige, partly because the rigid ranking system forced them to compete with chinovniki far below them in education and social status. This situation began to change only towards the very end of the imperial regime when it became fashionable in upper circles to enter the civil service.

Because, by and large, the metropolitan and provincial bureaucracies did not mix, the public spirit which began to make its appearance among the former did not communicate itself to the country at large. For the overwhelming majority of officials, self-seeking and bribery were a way of life to which they could conceive of no alternative. The conservative historian Nicholas Karamzin had them in mind when he used to say that if one were to answer with one word the question: ' "what goes on in Russia?", one would have to reply "thieving".'[7]

Public corruption, ubiquitous in Russia of the Muscovite and imperial periods was a symptom of a deeper malaise, lawlessness, of which it is always a faithful companion.

Until the Judiciary Reform of 1864, but in some respects (which will be specified later) even after it, Russia knew nothing of independent justice. Justice was a branch of the administration, and as such its foremost concern was enforcing the government's will and protecting its interests. Nowhere is the undeveloped sense of the public order more evident in Russia than in the tradition which up to the very eve of the contemporary age treated crimes perpetrated by one private person against another or of an official against a private person as matters of no public concern.

In Rome, justice had been separated from administration by the second century BC. In countries with feudal traditions, that is in most of western Europe, this separation occurred in the late Middle Ages. In England, by the end of the thirteenth century the king's judicial councillors were distinguished from his administrative and fiscal agents. In France, too, the court known as the Parliament of Paris established itself by this time as an institution in its own right. Russia in this respect resembled rather the ancient oriental monarchies where royal officials typically dispensed justice as part of their administrative obligations. In Muscovy, each prikaz had its own judiciary section operating according to its private system of justice under whose authority came all within its administrative competence, exactly as had been the case earlier, during the appanage period, on large private domains. In addition, voevody dispensed justice on their territories. So did the church. Major cases of crimes against the state came before the tsar and his Council. As might be expected, efforts to establish a separate judiciary were made by Peter I and especially Catherine II, but they ran into insurmountable difficulties of all sorts, not the least of which was the absence of a law code. The only existing Code, that of 1649, had become largely irrelevant in post-Petrine Russia, and in any event it provided very little guidance as to how to deal with grievances of one subject against another. Even if by some remote chance he happened to care enough to look, an eighteenth-century judge could not put his hands on the laws applicable to the case before him. This situation continued until the reign of Nicholas I when the government at last published a collection of laws issued since 1649 and then followed it with a new Code. But since court procedure continued to follow tradition, Russians still avoided legal proceedings like the plague. Until the Reform of 1864, the government did not initiate legal proceedings except where its own interests were concerned; ordinary criminal and all civil trials began at the instigation of the injured party. They usually took the form of an auction at which he who offered the judge more money won the case. All of which had a very debilitating effect on the quality of life in Russia. There exists a fashionable theory, derived from Marx, which holds that law and courts are there to protect the interests of the ruling class. Historical experience indicates the contrary to be true. Those in power have no need of courts and laws to have their way; it is the poor and the weak who do. Anyone who doubts this proposition has only to compare the general condition and the sense of security of the lower orders in areas with weak legal traditions, as for example south-east Asia, with those like western Europe and the United States where they are deeply entrenched.

Until the 1860s Russian jurisprudence did not even recognize the distinction between laws, decrees, and administrative ordinances, all of which, once approved by the sovereign, were treated with equal solemnity and in 1830 entered in pitiless chronological order in the Full Collection of Laws. An edict introducing a new order of succession to the imperial throne or one permanently freeing dvoriane from compulsory state service was treated, from the formal legal point of view, on a par with an ukaz authorizing the construction of a manufacturing plant or granting the petition of some retired officer from the provinces. Indeed, most of the fundamental laws affecting Russia's system of government and the status of its citizens were never at all promulgated in any formal way. Among them were: the fixing of peasants to the soil and of urban inhabitants to the cities (i.e. serfdom); the principle that all secular land had to bear service; the introduction of the oprichnina; the authority of landlords over their peasants; the rule that civil servants were to be automatically promoted on the basis of seniority; the founding of the first centralized political police organ, the Preobrazhenskii Prikaz; and the introduction of limited residence rights (the 'Pale of Settlement') for Jewish inhabitants. Others were promulgated in highly casual fashion. For example, the legal basis of autocratic power exercised by Russia's rulers was formulated in an incidental phrase in Peter's Military Regulation, while the laws governing the persecution of political criminals until 1845 were for all practical purposes legally undefined. A corollary of this kind of disrespect for legal procedure was the lack of awareness of clear distinctions among the constitutional, criminal and civil branches of the law, such as had been common in the west since the Middle Ages. Failure to discriminate among types of legal acts as well as among the various branches of the law contributed greatly to the confusion which reigned in Russian jurisprudence until the 1860s. To make matters worse yet, until the 1860s Russian laws need not have been made public to go into effect; they were often promulgated in confidential memoranda known only to the officials charged with their execution. This practice outlived the 1864 Reform. As will be pointed out below, the Ministry of the Interior in the 1870s and 1880s often introduced measures affecting the life of every citizen by means of secret circulars, many of which remain unpublished to this day.

The underdevelopment of legal traditions and courts was, of course, greatly to the advantage of the bureaucracy. Some conservative Russian jurists even earnestly argued in favour of close links between justice and administration. Among these was a highly respected expert on constitutional law, Professor N.M.Korkunov, who worked out a theory of Russian jurisprudence according to which the main function of law in that country was not so much to enforce justice as to maintain order.[8] This view of law was expressed more crudely but also more honestly by Count Benckendorff, the Chief of the Secret Police under Nicholas I. Once, when the editor of a publication came to him to complain that he was being harassed by censors in violation of the law, Benckendorff exploded: 'Laws are written for subordinates, not for the authorities!'*

Until Nicholas I, political repression in Russia was practised in a haphazard manner. The Preobrazhenskii Prikaz of Peter the Great marked a major step forward towards the professionalization of political police functions, but the machinery which he had established was dismantled by Peter III and Catherine the Great who forbade the lodging of complaints of the 'word and deed' type. Neither Catherine II nor Alexander I, though not averse to giving political dissenters a lesson every now and then, cared much for police snooping. A Ministry of Police established in 1811 was disbanded eight years later. There existed in Russia since the second half of the eighteenth century a rural and an urban constabulary, but no special body responsible for ferreting out political opposition of the kind that existed then in many continental countries. There was also no censorship code. Nor were there specific statutes dealing with political subversion apart from some general and quite antiquated rulings in the 1649 Code and in certain of the regulations of Peter the Great. This amateurish manner of dealing with political opposition sufficed until the early nineteenth century; it was no longer adequate in the Restoration era when more sophisticated forms of dissent came into vogue in a Europe of which Russia, by its involvement in the campaigns of 1813–15, had become an intrinsic part.

The inadequacy of Russia's internal defences first became evident in connection with the Decembrist uprising. Implicated in this coup were over one hundred dvoriane, some of them members of the country's most distinguished families. This consideration of itself precluded a quiet disposal of the affair by administrative procedures such as ordinarily used with insubordinate commoners. Beyond this procedural difficulty, the revolt raised serious security questions: why should members of a class favoured by the crown with extraordinary privileges take

* '*Zakony pishutsia dlia podchinennykh a ne dlia nachal'stv*': *Zapiski Aleksandra Ivanovicha Kosheleva (1812–1883 gody)* (Berlin 1884), pp. 31–2.

up arms against it? How were they able to plot their conspiracy without being detected?

In 1826, Nicholas appointed a Supreme Criminal Commission to investigate the causes of the rebellion and to recommend punishments. The Commission faced an unusually difficult task because at the time Russia not only lacked a Criminal Code but even a precise legal definition of anti-state crimes. Anyone who takes the trouble to look at the Commission's final recommendations will find there, as legal grounds for the sentences given the Decembrists, a puzzling allusion to the 'first two points' (*po pervym dvum punktam*). This refers to a minor ukaz of Peter I, issued on 25 January 1715 (No. 2,877 in the Full Collection of Laws), the first two articles of which required every subject to denounce to the authorities actions harmful to state interests and, specifically, incitement to mutiny. Such were the tenuous legal grounds for prosecuting the Decembrists. Under the 'first two points' the mandatory punishment was death. But recognizing the broad range of guilt among the defendants, the Commission separated them into nine categories, for each of which it recommended a different punishment ranging from induction into the army as common soldier to death by quartering.

Nicholas, who liked order above all else, was not content with such a state of affairs. He wanted anti-state crimes to be precisely spelled out and matched with suitable punishments. The responsibility for this task lay with Speranskii who was heading a committee preparing a general Code of Russian Laws. But this work was of necessity slow, and in the meantime steps had to be taken to prevent the recurrence of the events of 14 December 1825.

The first move was to give the empire a regular political police. This Nicholas did in 1826 when he formed a Third Section of the Imperial Chancellery. The ostensible task of this bureau was to give protection to 'widows and orphans': its official emblem, a handkerchief, which Nicholas gave to its first director, was to symbolize the drying of tears. In fact, however, the Third Section was a regular secret police with tentacles spread through all the layers of society, and as such it indubitably caused more tears to flow than it ever dried up. Its staff was small, averaging thirty or forty full-time employees. But its effectives were more numerous than that. For one, the Third Section had on its payroll many informers who frequented salons, taverns, fairs, and other public gatherings and reported any specific information they had picked up as well as their general impressions of the public mood. Secondly, attached to the Third Section and serving under its Chief was a Corps of Gendarmes several thousand men strong. Its blue-tunicked and white-gloved troops had as their specific mission the safeguarding of state security; they constituted a special political police separate from the regular constabulary. The responsibilities of the Third Section and its Corps of Gendarmes were vaguely defined, but they did include, in addition to uncovering and forestalling subversive actions, surveillance of foreigners and religious dissenters, and a certain amount of censorship. Like its forerunner, the Preobrazhenskii Prikaz, it was exempt from supervision by other government agencies and reported directly to the emperor himself. The founders and early directors of the Third Section were Baltic Germans (A.Kh.Benckendorff, its first Chief, and M.Ia. von Vock, his assistant), but before long native specialists in work of this kind took over.

Another preventive measure taken at this time concerned censorship. Nicholas persuaded himself that the main cause of the Decembrist rising lay in the exposure of Russian youth to 'harmful', 'idle' ideas, and firmly decided to keep these out of the country. In Russia there has always been the presumption that the government had the right to determine what its subjects could publish or read. But prior to the reign of Nicholas there were few occasions to exercise this right: all the printing presses (until 1783) belonged either to the government or the church, and the literate population was so small that it was hardly worth the trouble to investigate its reading habits. In the seventeenth century, the authorities ordered the destruction of Old Believer books and of some religious works published in Kiev which the clergy considered polluted with Latinisms. In the eighteenth century, censorship was entrusted to the Academy of Sciences, which exercised its authority so sparingly that until the outbreak of the French Revolution Russians were free to read anything they chose. Censorship began in earnest in 1790, when Catherine impounded Radishchev's *Journey* and ordered its author to be imprisoned. Under Paul, many foreign books were prevented from entering Russia; thousands were burned. But with the accession of Alexander I censorship was once again reduced to the point where it hardly mattered. The Censorship Code which Nicholas approved in 1826 represented therefore a major innovation. As subsequently amended, it required that prior to their distribution all publications had to secure an imprimatur from one of the newly created 'censorship committees'. To qualify, printed matter published in Russia in the reign of Nicholas I had not only to be free of 'harmful' material, but also to make some positive contribution to public morals: an early hint of that 'positive censorship' which was to become prevalent in Russia in the 1930s. Subsequently, the rules of censorship were alternately tightened (e.g. 1848–55) and relaxed (e.g. 1855–63), but some form of censorship remained in force in Russia until the Revolution of 1905, when its most onerous features were done away with; it was reintroduced in full vigour thirteen years later. For all its formidable rules and large bureaucracy, however, imperial censorship was not strictly enforced. It is astonishing to a person familiar with more recent forms of repression to learn that between 1867 and 1894 – a period spanning the very conservative reign of Alexander III – only 158 books were forbidden to circulate in Russia. Some 2 per cent of the manuscripts passed on by preliminary censorship in one decade were turned down. Censorship of foreign publications was also rather lax. Of the 93,565,260 copies of books and periodicals sent to Russia from abroad in one late nineteenth-century decade only 9,386 were stopped.[9] All of which suggests that imperial censorship was more of a nuisance than a barrier to the free flow of ideas.

The Code of Laws, on which Speranskii had been working since the beginning of Nicholas's reign, came out in 1832. The Fifteenth Volume in this series contained the Criminal Code which embraced also offences against the state; but because it did nothing more than arrange in an orderly fashion the chaotic statutes issued until that date, including the 'two points' of 1715, it was immediately judged inadequate. Speranskii was asked to draft in its place a new systematic Criminal Code, but he died before completing the task which was taken over by D.N.Bludov. It finally came out in 1845. The new Criminal Code turned out to be a milestone in the historical evolution of the police state. Political crimes were dealt with in two chapters: No. 3 'Of felonies against the government', and No. 4 'Of felonies and misdemeanors against the system of administration'. These two sections, covering fifty-four printed pages, constitute a veritable constitutional charter of an authoritarian regime. Other continental countries also had on the statute books provisions, sometimes quite elaborate, for dealing with crimes against the state (a category of crime unknown to English and American jurisprudence); but none attached to them such importance or defined them as broadly and as loosely as did Russia. According to the 1845 Code:

1. All attempts to limit the authority of the sovereign, or to alter the prevailing system of government, as well as to persuade others to do so, or to give overt expression to such intentions, or to conceal, assist or fail to denounce anyone guilty of these offences, carried the death penalty and the confiscation of all property (Articles 263–65 and 271);

2. The spreading by word of mouth or by means of the written or printed word of ideas which, without actually inciting to sedition, as defined above, raised doubts about the authority of the sovereign or lessened respect for him of his office, were punishable by the loss of civil rights and terms of hard labour from four to twelve years, as well as corporal punishment and branding (Articles 267 and 274).

Chapters 3 and 4 of the Russian Criminal Code of 1845 are the founttainhead of all those misty generalizations which ever since have enabled the police of Russia and its dependencies, as well as countries which have emulated its system of government, perfectly lawfully to stifle all manifestations of political dissent. Since 1845, with but one interlude between the revolutions of 1905 and 1917, it has been a crime in Russia not only to seek changes in the existing system of government or administration, but even to raise questions about such issues. Politics has been declared by law a monopoly of those in power; the patrimonial spirit, for centuries a nebulous feeling, has here at long last been given flesh in neatly composed chapters, articles and paragraphs. Particularly innovative in these provisions is the failure to distinguish deed from intent – a blurring of degrees of guilt characteristic of modern police states. While the 'raising of doubts' about the existing political system was recognized as a lesser offence than efforts actually to change it, it was still treated as a very serious crime and penalized by hard labour, beating, and branding.

Since 1845, Russian Criminal Codes have each contained a political 'omnibus' clause worded with such imprecision that under its terms the organs of state security have been able to incarcerate citizens guilty of crimes no more specific than intent to 'weaken', 'undermine' or 'arouse doubts' or 'disrespect' for existing authority. A juxtaposition of such clauses from three consecutive Criminal Codes – 1845, 1927 and 1960 gives an instructive demonstration of the continuity of the police mentality in Russia irrespective of the nature of the regime:

Code of 1845, Articles 267 and 274:

Persons guilty of writing and spreading written or printed works or representations intended to arouse disrespect for Sovereign Authority, or for the personal qualities of the Sovereign, or for his government are on conviction sentenced, as offenders of Majesty, to the deprivation of all rights of property and exile for hard labour in fortified places from ten to twelve years ... Those who participate in the preparation of such works or representations or their distribution with criminal intent are subject to the same punishment. Those guilty of preparing works or images of such nature but not of their distribution with criminal intent are sentenced for this act, as one of criminal intent, to incarceration in a fortress from two to four years ... For the preparation and distribution of written or printed works or for public pronouncements in which, without there being direct and clear incitement to rebellion against Sovereign Authority, there is an effort to dispute or raise doubts about the inviolability of its rights or impudently to censure the system of administration established by state laws ... the guilty persons are sentenced to loss of all rights of property and exile for hard labour in factories from four to six years...[10]

Soviet (RSFSR) Code of 1927, Article 58, (1) and (10):

As counter-revolutionary are defined all actions directed at the overthrow, undermining or weakening [of the government] ... or the undermining or weakening ... of the basic economic, political, and national [policies of the Soviet state] ... Propaganda or agitation, containing appeals to the overthrow, undermining or weakening of Soviet authority ... and equally the spread or preparation or safeguarding of literature of such content carry the loss of freedom with strict isolation of no fewer than six months ... [11]

Soviet (RSFSR) Code of 1960, Article 70:

Agitation or propaganda carried on for the purpose of subverting or weakening Soviet authority or of committing particular, especially dangerous crimes against the state, or circulating for the same purpose slanderous fabrications which defame the Soviet state and social system, or circulating or preparing or keeping, for the same purpose, literature of such content, shall be punished by the deprivation of freedom for a term of six months to seven years, with or without additional exile for a term of two to five years, or by exile for a term of two to five years ... [12]

This type of legislation, and the police institutions created to enforce it, spread after the Revolution of 1917 by way of Fascist Italy and Nazi Germany to other authoritarian states in Europe and overseas. One is justified in saying, therefore, that Chapters Three and Four of the Russian Criminal Code of 1845 are to totalitarianism what the Magna Carta is to liberty.

Under Nicholas I the draconian laws against political dissent were much less strictly enforced than one might be inclined to imagine. The machinery of repression was still too primitive for the police authorities to function in a systematic fashion: for this to happen, railways, telegraphs and telephones were needed. For the time being, the rules were applied in a rough sort of way. Usually, people suspected from informers' reports of meddling in politics were detained and, after being questioned, either released with a warning or sent into the provinces for some specified period of time. Sometimes the interrogation was carried out by the Emperor himself. Between 1823 and 1861, 290,000 persons were sentenced to Siberian exile, 44,000 of them for terms of hard labour. But of these exiles more than nine-tenths were ordinary criminals, vagabonds, runaway serfs, etc. Perhaps only 5 per cent suffered for crimes of a political nature (among them, the Decembrists), but many of this number were Polish patriots. [13]

With the accession of Alexander II the government made an earnest effort to put an end to the arbitrary rule of the bureaucracy and police, and transform Russia into what the Germans called a *Rechtsstaat*, a state grounded in law. The slogans in the air in the 1860s were due process, open court proceedings, trial by jury and irremovable judges. The judiciary reform, completed in 1864, is by common consent the most successful of all the Great Reforms and the only one to have survived (with the notable exception described below) to the end of the old regime without being subjected to crippling restrictions. After 1864 all criminal offences, including those of a political nature, were to be tried in regular courts: the trials were to be public and their proceedings reported fully in the official *Government Messenger (Pravitel'stvennyi Vestnik)*. There is every reason to believe that the government of Alexander II wanted this reform to succeed; formal legality is the one feature of the liberal state that an authoritarian regime can adopt without necessarily subverting itself.

It was not long, however, before this effort was sabotaged – this time, for once, not by bureaucrats but by the radical intelligentsia and its sympathizers among the well-meaning, enlightened and liberal public. Defendants in political trials realized quickly what a superb opportunity had been handed to them to broadcast nationwide their views from the privileged tribune of the court and rather than defend themselves often used their trials as an occasion to make political speeches attacking the system. These speeches were duly reported the following day in the *Government Messenger*. Sometimes, as for instance in the so-called Trial of Fifty (1877), the defendants refused to recognize the competence of the court; at other times (e.g. the Trial of the 193 in 1877–8) they hurled insults at the judges. Notwithstanding such behaviour, the government kept on trying political offenders before regular courts, often with juries present. The results, from its point of view, were very disappointing. Most jurors had a very poor notion of legality and allowed their sympathy or pity for the young defendants to eclipse their duty of determining the issue of guilt. Even those who did not approve of the methods used by the radicals hesitated to render a verdict of guilty because to have done so seemed to range them on the side of the bureaucracy and gendarmes against youths who, though perhaps misguided, were at any rate idealistic and selfless. Defendants were often acquitted; and even on those charged guilty, the judges tended to impose perfunctory sentences for acts which by western European criminal codes would have made them liable to severe punishment. In retrospect, this 'politization' of justice by Russian radicals and their sympathizers was a great tragedy for Russia. For although the provisions of the Criminal Code dealing with political offences were outrageously broad and imprecise, and the punishments provided for them unusually harsh, still an attempt was being made – the very first in Russia's thousand-year-old history – to have the government submit its grievances against private citizens to the judgement of third parties. Out of this effort, in time, there might have emerged a genuine system of justice even for political offenders, and perhaps much more, a government subject to law. The exploitation of the opportunities provided by the 1864 Reform not for the strengthening of the court system but for the promotion of short-term political interests played right into the hands of arch-conservatives and those bureaucrats who had always regarded independent justice a misbegotten, 'un-Russian' idea. The most flagrant instance of subversion of justice by liberal circles occurred at the trial of Vera Zasulich, a terrorist who in January 1878 shot and gravely wounded the Police Chief of St Petersburg. On this occasion, the Public Prosecutor made every effort to treat the case as an ordinary rather than as a political crime. Yet, despite incontrovertible evidence that Vera Zasulich had been guilty as charged of an attempt at premeditated murder, the jury acquitted her. This verdict must have made every government employee feel that he had become fair game for the terrorists: shooting an official, if done for political reasons, was no longer a crime. Such miscarriage of justice outraged also Dostoevsky and the liberal theorist, Boris Chicherin, who seem to have realized better than most of their contemporaries the moral and political implications of a double standard of morality and justice adopted by the intelligentsia. It now became apparent even to officials of a more liberal persuasion that the government could not count on regular courts and juries to mete out impartial justice where politics were involved in any way. Steps were therefore taken to remove political cases from the competence of the courts and to dispose of them by administrative procedures. When courts were still resorted to, it was usually without a jury and sometimes without an audience. By 1890, the courts were given up altogether in anti-state crimes and from then on until the 1905 Revolution political offenders were dealt with by administrative means entrusted to the bureaucracy and gendarmerie. Thus on Russian 'progressive' opinion these rests a very heavy responsibility for sabotaging the only attempt made in the country's history to have the government confront its citizenry on equal terms.

Students of political sociology have observed that whereas political parties tend progressively to rid themselves of extremists and to gravitate towards centrist positions, unstructured 'movements', on the contrary, tend to come under the influence of their extreme elements. The 'going to the people' movement proved an unmitigated disaster. It was not just that the propagandists and agitators failed to arouse in the peasant and worker any interest for their ideas. The failure went deeper; the 'toiling masses' gave unmistakable evidence of an acquisitive spirit of the worst bourgeois type combined with moral cynicism and politically reactionary attitudes. The whole ideal of the Russian muzhik lay shattered. This disappointment forced many radicals out of the movement. But on its most dedicated members it had the opposite effect; disappointment made them even more determined to find a strategy which would bring the system to its knees.

The solution adopted in 1878–9 was terror. It was argued by radical theorists that a campaign of assassinations against high government officials would accomplish two aims: demoralize and hopefully grind to a halt the machinery of government, and at the same time demonstrate to the peasant the vulnerability of the monarchic system which he held in such awe. But once initiated, terror acquired a momentum of its own and its perpetrators quickly forgot their aims. Any sequence of daring suicidal acts, publicly committed – assassinations, bombings, self-immolations, hijackings – seems to produce a kind of resonance in some people who then become compulsively driven to re-enact it. The socialist-revolutionary terror, launched in 1878 and carried on for three years, kept on intensifying even after it had become apparent it would neither paralyse the government nor incite the peasants to rebel. In the end, it became terror for the sake of terror, carried out with impressive cunning and courage simply to prove that it could be done: a contest of wills between a tiny band of radicals and the whole imperial establishment.

As incidents of terror multiplied – and because of the very slight machinery for protecting government officials, they succeeded surprisingly often – the authorities were thrown into a state approaching panic. Although the actual number of terrorists at any one time was very small (the so-called Executive Committee of the People's Will, its whole effective force, had some thirty members), the psychology of an authoritarian regime is such that it tends wildly to over-react to direct challenges. In some respects, such a regime is like a commercial bank and its authority represents a form of credit. A bank keeps on hand only a small part of the capital entrusted to it by depositors – just enough to meet ordinary withdrawals – and the rest it invests. Depositors (those aware of the fact, at any rate) do not mind this practice as long as they are certain that whenever presented their claim will be fully honoured. But should a bank fail to meet even a single withdrawal demand, confidence in it is at once shattered, and depositors rush to reclaim their funds. The result is a bank run which forces the bank to suspend payments. An authoritarian state similarly succeeds in exacting universal obedience not because it has the forces required to meet all the possible challenges, but because it has enough of them to meet any anticipated ones. Failure to move decisively, producing a loss of prestige, invites multiple challenges and results in a kind of political bank run known as revolution.

In its eagerness to meet the threat posed by terrorism, the imperial government greatly over-reacted. It began to set in motion, sometimes overtly, sometimes secretly, all kinds of countermeasures, which in their totality strikingly anticipated the modern police state and even contained some seeds of totalitarianism. Betweeen 1878 and 1881 in Russia the legal and institutional bases were laid for a bureaucratic-police regime with totalitarian overtones that have not been dismantled since.

The roots of modern totalitarianism, one may well argue, are sought more properly here than in the ideas of a Rousseau or Hegel or Marx. For while ideas can always beget other ideas, they produce institutional changes only if they fall on a soil well conditioned to receive them.

The imperial government's initial response to terror was to turn for assistance to the military. On 4 August 1878, a terrorist striking in broad daylight on a St Petersburg street knifed to death the Chief of Gendarmes. Five days later, the government issued a 'temporary' ruling – one of the many destined to acquire permanence – that from that time on armed resistance to government organs or assaults on government personnel while in performance of their duties would be tried by courts martial in accord with military statutes operative in wartime. The sentences required only the confirmation of the Chief of the local Military District. Thus, as far as terrorist activities were concerned, Russia was to be treated by its government as if it were occupied enemy territory. Even more far-reaching was a secret circular issued on 1 September 1878 (unpublished so far) detailing stiff preventive measures.[14] These empowered members of the Corps of Gendarmes, and, in their absence, regular police officers, to detain and even exile administratively anyone *suspected* of political crimes. To exile someone under these provisions, the gendarmerie or police required only the approval of the Minister of the Interior and the Chief of Gendarmes; there was no need to request permission of the Procurator (Attorney General). The circular of 1 September marked in several important respects a major advance toward a police regime. Until that time, a Russian citizen actually had to commit a subversive act (verbal or written expression being included in that category) before being liable to exile. From now on, to suffer this fate it was enough for him merely to arouse suspicion. This measure put in place a second pillar of the police state; the first, set in 1845, had made it a criminal offence for a private individual to concern himself with politics; now he was treated as a criminal even if he only appeared likely to do so. Introduced here was the preventive element essential to the proper functioning of every police state. Secondly, the wide latitude granted to bureaucrats and policemen to sentence Russian citizens to exile entailed a diminution of the crown's authority. This was the first of several measures taken during this critical time which (unintentionally, of course) distributed prerogatives previously exercised exclusively by the monarch among his subordinate officials. Finally, the right of functionaries to exercise judiciary powers without consulting the Procurator marked the beginning of a shift of judiciary prerogatives from the Ministry of Justice to the Ministry of the Interior.*

* Already in February 1873 the administration of all civil prisons had been entrusted to this Ministry.

These extraordinary precautions did not inhibit the terrorists. In April 1879, yet another attempt was made on the life of the tsar, whereupon the government instituted in several major cities of the empire 'Temporary Governors General' whom it entrusted with wide discretionary powers over several contiguous provinces. These officials, usually drawn from the army, were authorized to turn over to military courts and to exile by administrative order not only persons suspected of harbouring designs against the government and its officials, but also those deemed prejudicial to 'peace and order' in general. In this manner another bit of authority was transferred from the crown to its subordinates.

Early in 1880, a revolutionary disguised as a carpenter succeeded in smuggling into the Winter Palace quantities of explosives which on 5 February he set off under the imperial dining room. Only the late arrival of the guest of honour saved Alexander II from being blown to bits. That terrorists should have been able to penetrate the imperial household demonstrated beyond doubt how inadequate were the existing precautions. Indeed, the Third Section was small, poorly subsidized, and ludicrously inefficient. In August 1880 it had on its payroll only seventy-two employees and even not all of those worked on political counter-intelligence. Much of its limited budget was used for counter-propaganda. There was gross confusion of competence between the Third Section, which functioned as part of the Imperial Chancellery, the Corps of Gendarmes which was under its jurisdiction as far as security operations were concerned but came under the Ministry of War in matters of military competence, and the regular police which served under the Ministry of the Interior.

In August 1880, on the recommendation of General Loris-Melikov, the Third Section was therefore abolished and replaced by a central political police called initially Department of State Police and after 1883, simply Department of Police. Administratively, the new organization formed part of the Ministry of the Interior which now became the chief guardian of state security in Russia. The instructions of the new Department as finally evolved were remarkably comprehensive. The Department was to be in charge of the preservation of public security and order, and the prevention of state crimes. In addition, it was made responsible for the guarding of state frontiers, the issuance of internal passports, supervision of foreigners resident in Russia and all Jews, as well as of taverns, fire-fighting equipment and explosives. It also had broad authority 'to approve the statutes of various associations and clubs and to grant permission for the holding of public lectures, readings, expositions, and conferences'.[15] It was organized into several sections, one of which dealt with 'secret' matters – that is, political counter-intelligence. Under the Department served three divisions of Gendarmes, headquartered in St Petersburg, Moscow and Warsaw, as well as many specialized detachments. The staff remained small; in 1895 the Police Department had only 161 full-time employees while the Corps of Gendarmes stayed under 10,000 men. However, in 1883 the regular police, numbering close to 100,000, were ordered to cooperate closely with the gendarmerie, which greatly increased the latter's effectives. The Minister of the Interior was *ex officio* Chief of Gendarmes but in time the actual responsibility was assumed by one of his deputies called Director of the Department of Police and Commander of the Corps of Gendarmes. On 9 June 1881, an order was issued exempting the gendarmerie from the authority of Governors and Governors General: their responsibility was exclusively to the Chief of Police. By this measure, the Corps of Gendarmes was set apart from the regular administrative apparatus and made law unto itself. The Department of Police and the Corps of Gendarmes continued to concern themselves exclusively with political offences; when their members chanced upon evidence of an ordinary crime, they turned it over to the regular police. Once a year, the Chief of Gendarmes submitted to the emperor a report on campaigns his organization had waged against subversives which read somewhat like a summary of military operations.

To cover up its arbitrary activities with the mantle of legality, the Ministry of the Interior attached to the Police Department a special '*Juridical Section*' (*Sudebnyi otdel*). This bureau handled the legal aspects of the cases which came within the purview of the Ministry of the Interior – that is, offences charged under the political clauses of the Criminal Code and withheld from regular courts, as well as those committed in violation of the numerous Extraordinary and Temporary laws issued during these years.

In 1898, when political life in Russia showed once again signs of stirring after many years of quiescence, and there were fears that terrorism might be revived, the 'Secret' Division of the Police Department detached a 'Special Section' *(Osobyi otdel),* a top-secret organization to serve as the nerve centre of the campaign against subversives. This Section kept close track of revolutionaries in Russia and abroad, and engineered elaborate provocations designed to flush them out. Its offices, located in St Petersburg on the fourth floor on Fontanka 16, were so isolated that none but its own employees had access to them.

Finally, on 14 August 1881, the government regularized the status of 'Protective Sections' (*Okhrannye otdeleniia,* or, for short, *Okhranki*), first established in the 1870s. These too fought revolutionaries, and they did so at a rather high professional level. Formally a branch of the Special Section, they seem to have operated independently of it.

The Police Department had several foreign branches to shadow

Russian *émigrés*, the principal of which was located in the Russian Embassy in Paris. In their work, these foreign agencies were often assisted by local police authorities, acting either out of political sympathy or greed.

The elaborate and rather flexible political police system established in Russia in the early 1880s was unique in at least two respects. Before the First World War no other country in the world had two kinds of police, one to protect the state and another to protect its citizens. Only a country with a deeply rooted patrimonial mentality could have devised such a dualism. Secondly, unlike other countries, where the police served as an arm of the law and was required to turn over all arrested persons to the judiciary, in imperial Russia and there alone police organs were exempt from this obligation. Where political offences were involved, after 1881 the Corps of Gendarmes was not subject to judiciary supervision; such controls as it had were strictly of a bureaucratic, in-house kind. Its members had the right to search, imprison and exile citizens on their own authority, without consulting the Public Prosecutor. In the 1880s, the whole broad range of crimes defined as political had become a matter largely disposed of administratively by security organs. These two features make the police institutions of late imperial Russia the forerunner, and, through the intermediacy of corresponding communist institutions, the prototype of all political police organs of the twentieth century.

The government of Alexander II did not confine its response to terror to repression. In its administration served several high functionaries perceptive enough to realize that unless accompanied by some constructive measures repression would be futile and possibly even harmful. At various times in Alexander's reign, serious thought was given to projects of political reform submitted either by government officials or influential public figures which in varying degrees and by different means sought to involve in the making of policy what were then known as 'trustworthy' elements of society. Some urged that the State Council be enlarged by the addition of elected representatives; others proposed to convoke consultative bodies resembling the Muscovite Land Assemblies; others yet called for reforms of local administration which would expand the competence of zemstva and provide additional outlets for public service to the landowning gentry. The hope was that by means such as these it would be possible to isolate the tiny band of terrorists, and gain sympathy for the government's predicament among educated society where so far it tended to encounter indifference spiked with malice. Among officials favouring such measures were P.A. Valuev, the Minister of the Interior, D.A. Miliutin, the Minister of War, and Loris-Melikov, an army

general who in the last year of the reign of Alexander II was given virtually dictatorial powers. The Emperor himself was not unattracted to
these proposals but he was slow to act on them because he faced the
solid opposition of the rank and file of the bureaucracy as well as that of
his son and heir apparent, the future Alexander III. The radicals unwit-
tingly assisted this conservative party; every time they made an attempt
on the life of the tsar or assassinated some high official, opponents of
political reform could press for yet more stringent police measures and
further postponement of basic reforms. The terrorists could not have
been more effective in scuttling political reform had they been on the
police payroll.

perhaps that's precisely what they had in mind

In resisting political reform the bureaucracy was fighting for its very
life. From its vantage point, zemstva were bad enough, disturbing as they
did the smooth flow of administrative directives from St Petersburg to the
most remote province. Had representatives of society been invited to
participate in legislation, even if only in a consultative capacity, the
bureaucracy would have found itself for the first time subject to some
form of public control; this certainly would have cramped its style and
could have ended up by undermining its power. Even the assurance that
only the most 'trustworthy' elements were to have been involved did not
calm its apprehensions. Russian monarchists of that time, while anti-
constitutionally disposed, by no means favoured the bureaucracy. Most
of them were influenced by Slavophile ideals and regarded the bureaucracy as an alien body which had improperly insinuated itself between
the tsar and his people.

Thanks to the archival researches of P.A.Zaionchkovskii, we are now
reasonably well informed about the deliberations of the government
during this critical period.[16] The arguments of the opponents of political
reform boiled themselves down to the following principal contentions:

1. The introduction of public representatives into government,
whether in the centre or the provinces, whether in a legislative or merely
a consultative capacity, would establish conflicting lines of responsibility
and disorganize the administration. In fact, to improve administrative
efficiency, zemstva should be abolished.

2. Because of its geographic and social characteristics, Russia requires
a system of administration subject to the least possible restraints and
controls. Russian functionaries should enjoy wide discretionary powers,
and police 'justice' should be separated from ordinary courts. This latter
point was expressed by the archetypal conservative bureaucrat, the
Minister of the Interior from 1882 to 1889, Dmitry A.Tolstoy:

The sparse population of Russia, distributed over an immense territory,
the unavoidable remoteness from courts which results from this, the low
economic level of the people and the patriarchal customs of our agrarian

class, all create conditions demanding the establishment of authority which in its activities *is not restrained by excessive formalism*, an authority able promptly to restore order and as quickly as possible to correct violations of the population's rights and interests.[17]

3. Political reforms granted under duress will be interpreted as a sign of weakness and contribute to the further deterioration of state authority. This argument was used even by a relatively liberal public servant like Loris-Melikov. Arguing against proposals to introduce into Russia representative institutions, he wrote:

I am deeply convinced that any reforms in the sense of these projects not only are not useful at present but, being utterly untimely, would cause harm ... The measure itself would appear as having been forced upon the government by circumstances, and would be so interpreted in Russia and abroad.[18]

4. The introduction of representative institutions in any form, even the most conservative, would mark the first step towards a constitutional regime; once taken, the others would inevitably have to follow.

5. Foreign experience with representative institutions indicates that they are not conducive to stability; if anything, parliaments interfere with efficient administration. This argument was particularly attractive to the heir-apparent.

To clinch the argument, opponents of political concessions greatly exaggerated the extent of sedition in the country, frightening the Emperor with the spectre of widespread conspiracy and unrest which bore little relation to the facts. As will be shown, the actual number of people involved in seditious activities was ludicrously small: even with their broad discretionary powers, the gendarmes could not put their hands on masses of subversives. But appeals to this sense of fear helped dissuade Alexander II from following the advice of his more liberal advisers.

The real rulers of Russia were ... Chief of Gendarmes Shuvalov and the St Petersburg Chief of Police Trepov. Alexander II carried out their will, was their instrument. They ruled by fear. Trepov had so scared Alexander with the spectre of revolution just about to break out in St. Petersburg that should the all-powerful police chief be a few minutes late in the palace with his daily report, the Emperor would make enquiry whether all was calm in the capital.[19]

The closest Alexander came to making political concessions was in 1880–1 when he agreed to a proposal submitted by Loris-Melikov. In addition to far-reaching changes in provincial administration, Loris-Melikov suggested the convocation in St Petersburg of several elected committees to discuss policy questions touching on questions of provincial administration, peasant economy, food supply and national finances.

Upon the completion of their work, these specialized commissions were to constitute a general commission to advise the government. This proposal, often incorrectly called the 'Loris-Melikov constitution' (the term was coined by Alexander III to discredit it) was modest enough, yet its implications were weighty. Russia was entering on unchartered waters, and no one could predict where the journey would lead. Even Alexander, while approving the proposal, muttered about Russian 'Estates General'. He was to have signed the decree calling for the convocation of Loris-Melikov's committees on 1 March 1881, but on that day he was killed by a terrorist bomb.

The murder of Alexander II saved the bureaucracy from that which it had dreaded the most: the participation of society in political decision-making. After momentary hesitation, Alexander III decided that order would be best restored not by further concessions but by more stringent measures of repression. Reform projects ceased; N.P.Ignatev, the new Minister of the Interior, who had the bad judgement to propose to Alexander III the convocation of estates on the model of Muscovite Land Assemblies was promptly dismissed from his post. The patrimonial principle, held in disfavour since the middle of the eighteenth century, surfaced once again. The 'state', as henceforth understood, meant the tsar and his officialdom; internal politics meant protecting both from the encroachments of society. A quick succession of emergency measures completed the subjection of society to the arbitrary power of the bureaucracy and police.

On 14 August 1881, Alexander III signed into law the most important piece of legislation in the history of imperial Russia between the abolition of serfdom in 1861 and the October Manifesto of 1905, and more durable than either. This document, which codified and systematized the repressive legislation issued in the preceding years, has been the real constitution under which – brief interludes apart – Russia has been ruled ever since. In a manner characteristic of Russian legislative practices, in the official Collection of Statutes and Ordinances this momentous piece of legislation is casually sandwiched between a directive approving minor alterations in the charter of the Russian Fire Insurance Company and one concerning the administration of a technical institute in the provincial town of Cherepovtsy.[20] Its full title reads 'Regulation concerning measures for the protection of the [established] system of government and of public tranquillity, and the placement of certain of the Empire's localities under a state of Reinforced Safeguard'. In its opening paragraphs, the decree asserted that ordinary laws had proved insufficient to preserve order in the empire so that it had become necessary to introduce certain 'extraordinary' procedures. In its operative parts, the decree fully concentrated the struggle against subversion in the hands of the Ministry of the Interior where it has largely remained since. Two kinds of special situations were provided for: 'Reinforced Safeguard' (*Usilennaia Okhrana*) and 'Extraordinary Safeguard' (*Chrezvychainaia Okhrana*), corresponding to what in western practice was known as Minor and Major States of Siege. The power to impose Reinforced Safeguard in any part of the empire was entrusted to the Minister of the Interior and Governors General acting with his concurrence. Extraordinary Safeguard required the approval of the tsar and cabinet. The conditions under which either state could be imposed were not clearly specified.

Under 'Reinforced Safeguard', the milder of the two states, Governors General, ordinary governors, and governors of cities could do any or all of the following: imprison any resident up to a period of three months and fine him up to 400 rubles; forbid all social, public, and private gatherings; close down all commercial and industrial enterprises either for a specified period or for the duration of the emergency; deny individuals the right to reside in their area; and hand over troublemakers to military justice. They were furthermore empowered to declare any person employed by the zemstva, city governments or courts as 'untrustworthy' (*neblagonadezhnyi*) and to order his instantaneous dismissal. Finally, organs of the local police and gendarmerie were authorized to detain for up to two weeks all persons 'inspiring substantial suspicion' from the point of view of state security. When it deemed it necessary to have recourse to Extraordinary Safeguard, the government appointed a Commander-in-Chief who, in addition to all the powers enumerated above, enjoyed the right to dismiss from their posts elected zemstvo deputies (as distinct from hired employees) or even to shut down the zemstva entirely, as well as to fire any civil servants below the highest three ranks. The latter provision was not casually inserted. Ignatev, the Minister of the Interior when this decree came out, considered bureaucrats and their children to harbour some of the most subversive elements in the country, and suggested periodic 'purges' of unreliable elements from the civil service. Under Extraordinary Safeguard, the Commander in Chief could also suspend periodical publications and close for up to one month institutions of higher learning. He could jail suspects for up to three months and impose fines of up to 3,000 rubles. The same edict also substantially increased the powers of the gendarmes in areas under either Reinforced or Extraordinary Safeguard.

The significance of this legislation can perhaps be best summarized in the words of a man who, as head of the Department of the Police from 1902 to 1905, had a great deal to do with its enforcement, namely A.A. Lopukhin. After his retirement he published a remarkable pamphlet in which he stated that the decree of 14 August 1881 caused the fate of the 'entire population of Russia to become dependent on the personal opinions of the functionaries of the political police'. Henceforth, in matters affecting state security there no longer were any objective criteria of guilt: guilt was determined by the subjective impression of police officials.[21] Ostensibly 'temporary', with a validity of three years, this law was regularly renewed every time it was about to expire until the very end of the imperial regime. Immediately upon the promulgation of the Decree of 14 August, ten provinces, including the two capital cities of St Petersburg and Moscow were placed under Reinforced Safeguard. The number was increased after 1900, and during the Revolution of 1905 some localities were placed under Extraordinary Safeguard. After the suppression of the revolution, under the prime ministership of P. Stolypin, in one form or another the provisions of this Decree were extended to all parts of the empire with the result that the laws pertaining to civil rights contained in the October Manifesto and in subsequent Duma legislation were effectively nullified.[22]

After 14 August 1881 Russia ceased to be an autocratic monarchy in any but the formal sense. As defined by Struve in 1903, the real difference between Russia of that time and the rest of the civilized world lay 'in the omnipotence of the political police' which had become the essence of the Russian monarchy; the instant this support were to be withdrawn, he predicted, it would collapse of its own weight no matter who controlled this autocratic power.[23] Lopukhin agreed: the police, he wrote, 'constitutes the entire might of a regime whose existence has come to and end'; adding prophetically: 'It is to the police that the regime will turn to first in the event it tries to resuscitate itself.[24] 'The paradox was that the steady encroachment on the rights of individual subjects carried out in the name of state security did not enhance the power of the crown; it was not the crown that benefited but the bureaucracy and police to whom ever greater latitude had to be given to cope with the revolutionary movement. And the absurdity of the situation lay in the fact that the challenge was entirely out of proportion to the measures taken to deal with it. In February 1880, at the height of terror, when Loris-Melikov was given dictatorial powers, the police knew of fewer than 1,000 active cases of anti-state crimes – this in an empire with nearly 100 million inhabitants![25]

The extent of police interference in everyday life of late imperial Russia is difficult to convey. One of the most powerful weapons in the hands of the police was its authority to issue certificates of 'trustworthiness' (*blagonadezhnost*') which every citizen was required to have before being allowed to enroll at the university or to assume a 'responsible' post. To have been refused such a certificate, condemned a Russian to the status of a second-rate citizen, and sometimes virtually forced him to join the revolutionaries. Furthermore, a vast range of activities was impossible without prior permission of the police. As listed in 1888–9 by a knowledgeable American observer, George Kennan (the great uncle of his namesake, the later Ambassador to Moscow), a Russian citizen of the late 1880s was subject to the following police restrictions:

If you are a Russian, and wish to establish a newspaper, you must ask the permission of the Minister of the Interior. If you wish to open a Sunday-school, or any other sort of school, whether in a neglected slum of St Petersburg or in a native village in Kamchatka, you must ask the permission of the Minister of Public Instruction. If you wish to give a concert or to get up tableaux for the benefit of an orphan asylum, you must ask permission of the nearest representative of the Minister of the Interior, then submit your programme of exercises to a censor for approval or revision, and finally hand over the proceeds of the entertainment to the police, to be embezzled or given to the orphan asylum, as it may happen. If you wish to sell newspapers on the street, you must get permission, be registered in the books of the police, and wear a numbered brass plate as big as a saucer around your neck. If you wish to open a drug-store, a printing-office, a photograph-gallery, or a book-store, you must get permission. If you are photographer and desire to change the location of your place of business, you must get permission. If you are a student and go to a public library to consult Lyell's *Principles of Geology* or Spencer's *Social Statics*, you will find that you cannot even look at such dangerous and incendiary volumes without special permission. If you are a physician, you must get permission before you can practice, and then, if you do not wish to respond to calls in the night, you must have permission to refuse to go; furthermore, if you wish to prescribe what are known in Russia as 'powerfully acting' medicines, you must have special permission, or the druggists will not dare to fill your prescriptions. If you are a peasant and wish to build a bath-house on your premises, you must get permission. If you wish to thresh out your grain in the evening by candle-light, you must get permission or bribe the police. If you wish to go more than fifteen miles away from your home, you must get permission. If you are a foreign traveler, you must get permission to come into the Empire, permission to go out of it, permission to stay in it longer than six months, and must notify the police every time you change your boarding-place. In short, you cannot live, move, or have your being in the Russian Empire without permission.

The police, with the Minister of the Interior at their head, control, by means of passports, the movements of all the inhabitants of the Empire; they keep thousands of suspects constantly under surveillance; they ascertain and certify to the courts the liabilities of bankrupts; they conduct pawnbrokers' sales of unredeemed pledges; they give certificates of identity to pensioners and all other persons who need them; they superintend repairs of roads and bridges; they exercise supervision over all theatrical performances, concerts, tableaux, theater programmes, posters, and street advertisements; they collect statistics, enforce sanitary regulations, make searches and seizures in private houses, read the correspondence of suspects, take charge of the bodies of persons found dead, 'admonish' church members who neglect too long to partake of the Holy Communion, and enforce obedience to thousands of multifarious orders and regulations intended to promote the welfare of the people or to insure the safety of the state. The legislation relating to the police fills more than five thousand sections in the Svod Zakonov, or collection of Russian laws, and it is hardly an exaggeration to say that in the peasant villages, away from the centers of education and enlightenment, the police are the omnipresent and omnipotent regulators of all human conduct – a sort of incompetent bureaucratic substitute for divine Providence.[26]

Another important source of police power was the right granted it by a decree of 12 March 1882 to declare any citizen subject to overt surveillance. An individual in this category, known as *podnadzornyi*, had to surrender his personal documents in exchange for special police papers. He was not allowed to move without police authorization and his quarters were liable to be searched at any time of day or night. He could not hold any government job or any public post, belong to private associations, or teach, deliver lectures, operate typographies, photographic laboratories or libraries, or deal in spirits; he could practise medicine, midwifery and pharmacology only under licence from the Ministry of the Interior. The same ministry decided whether or not he was to receive mail and telegrams.[27] Russians under overt surveillance constituted a special category of sub-citizens excluded from the operations of law and the regular administration and living under direct police rule.

The security measures outlined above were reinforced by criminal laws which tended to weigh Russian jurisprudence overwhelmingly in favour of the state. Kennan made the following observations, all of them readily verifiable, concerning the Criminal Code of 1885:

In order to appreciate the extraordinary severity of [the] laws for the protection of the Sacred Person, the Dignity, and the Supreme Authority of the Tsar it is only necessary to compare them with the laws contained in Title X. for the protection of the personal rights and honor of private citizens. From such a comparison it appears that to injure a portrait, statue, bust, or other representation of the Tsar set up in a public place is a more grievous crime than to so assault and injure a private citizen as to deprive him of eyes, tongue, an arm, a leg, or the sense of hearing. [Compare Section 246 with Section 1477.] To organise or take part in a society which has for its object the overthrow of the Government or a change in the form of the Government, even although such society does not contemplate a resort to violence nor immediate action, is a crime of greater gravity than to so beat, maltreat, or torture a human being as partly to deprive him of his mental faculties. [Compare Section 250 with Section 1490.] The making of a speech or the writing of a book which disputes or throws doubt upon the inviolability of the rights or privileges of the Supreme Authority is as serious an offense as the outraging of a woman. [Compare Section 252 with Section 1525.] The mere concealment of a person who has formed an evil design affecting the life, welfare, or honor of the Tsar, or the affording of refuge to a person who intends to bring about a restriction of the rights or privileges of the Supreme Authority, is a more serious matter than the premeditated murder of one's own mother. [Compare Section 243 with Section 1449.] Finally, in the estimation of the penal code, the private citizen who makes or circulates a caricature of the Sacred Person of the Tsar, for the purpose of creating disrespect for his personal characteristics or for his management of the empire, commits a more heinous crime than the jailer who outrages in a cell until she dies an imprisoned, helpless, and defenseless girl fifteen years of age. [Compare Section 245 with Sections 1525, 1526, and 1527.][28]

The system of political repression included exile. This could be imposed either by a court sentence or by administrative decision, and could take one of several forms ranging widely in severity. The mildest form was to be sent out of the country or into the provinces for a specified length of time to live under overt police surveillance. More severe was a sentence of exile for settlement to Siberia (western Siberia was considered a much milder place of punishment than eastern). Such 'settled exiles' (*ssylnoposelentsy*) were essentially free men allowed to work gainfully and have their families with them. If they had money to supplement the small government allowance, they could live in considerable comfort. The harshest form of exile was hard labour (*katorga*, from the Greek *katergon*, meaning galley). This type of penal servitude had been introduced by Peter the Great who used criminals to build ships, work mines, help construct St Petersburg and furnish free labour wherever else it was necessary. Hard labour convicts lived in prison barracks and performed menial work under guard. Dostoevsky, who spent time doing *katorga*, left an unforgettable picture of it in his *Notes from the House of the Dead*. After 1886, the exploitation of forced labour (including prison labour) was governed by special regulations designed to assure that the government made money on it. In 1887, for instance, it brought the Ministry of the Interior a gross income of 538,820 rubles out of which, after expenses, there remained a net profit of 166,440 rubles 82 kopeks.[29]

Because so many different officials had the power to impose sentences of exile, statistics on this type of punishment are hard to come by. The Encyclopedic Dictionary of Brockhaus and Ephron, usually a reliable source, estimates that in the 1890s there were in Siberia 300,000 exiles of all sorts, forming 5·2 per cent of the population, as well as 14,500 prisoners serving sentences of hard labour.[30] However, as had been the case in the first half of the century (p. 295), only a small fraction of these exiles were committed for political crimes. Zaionchkovskii, who had access to the pertinent archives, cites official reports to the effect that in 1880 there were in the whole Russian empire only about 1,200 people under sentences of exile for political crimes; of these, 230 resided in Siberia and the rest in European Russia; a mere 60 served terms of hard labour. (These figures do not include over 4,000 Poles exiled for participation in the 1863 uprising.) In 1901, the total number of political exiles of all sorts, both those sentenced by courts and administrative procedures, increased to 4,113, of which 3,838 were under overt police surveillance, and 180 on hard labour.[31]

To complete the picture of restrictive measures imposed by the government of Alexander III, mention must be made of policies subsumed under the term 'counter-reforms', whose avowed aim it was to emasculate the Great Reforms of Alexander II. Among them were limitations on the competence of zemstva, abolition of the office of justice of the peace, and introduction of 'Land Commandants', local officials with much discretionary authority over the peasants (p. 166). The Jews who were considered particularly prone to subversion were subjected in the reign of Alexander III to the full force of disabling laws which, though long on the statute books in the past, had not been strictly applied.

Thus, in the early 1880s, all the elements of the police state were present in imperial Russia. These may be summarized as follows:

1. Politics was declared the exclusive preserve of the government and its high functionaries; any meddling in them on the part of unauthorized personnel, which included all private citizens, was a crime punishable by law;

2. The enforcement of this principle was entrusted to a Department of Police and a Corps of Gendarmes whose exclusive concern was with crimes against the state;

3. These organs of state security had the power
   a. to search, arrest, interrogate, imprison, and exile persons either guilty of political activity or suspected of it;
   b. to refuse any citizen a certificate of 'trustworthiness', lacking which he was prevented from engaging in a great variety of activities, including attendance at institutions of higher learning and employment in public institutions, governmental or other;
   c. to supervise all kinds of cultural activities of citizens and to certify the statutes of public associations;

4. In the fulfilment of its duties, the Department of the Police and the Corps of Gendarmes were not subject to supervision by the organs of the judiciary; they were also exempt from the jurisdiction of the regular civil administration on whose territory they operated;

5. By a variety of means at its disposal, such as overt surveillance,

Siberian exile, and hard labour, the political police apparatus could partly or fully isolate dissidents from the rest of society;

6. No literature could be published in Russia or enter it from abroad without the censor's permission;

7. The Minister of the Interior had the authority to declare any region of the empire under Reinforced Safeguard, in which event normal laws and institutions were suspended and the entire population became subject to martial law; top provincial administrators likewise had the power, with the Minister's approval, to turn dissidents over to court martials.

Nor was this all. In the early years of the twentieth century, the imperial government carried out experimentally certain policies which overstepped the boundaries of police regime and moved into the even more sinister realm of totalitarianism. Under a police regime, political activity is outlawed and security organs are given practically unlimited powers to make sure the proscription is observed. The system is essentially defensive; it is created to beat back challenges. Totalitarianism is characterized by a more positive approach: while it includes also all the elements of police statehood, it goes beyond them, trying to reorganize society in such a manner that all public institutions and expressions of social life, even those with no political connotation, fall under the management of the bureaucracy, or, more specifically, its security apparatus. Everything is politicized and everything is directed.

The attempt referred to, linked with the name of Serge Zubatov, is usually treated as one of the more bizarre episodes in the running war between the imperial regime and the revolutionaries. However, from a broader historical perspective, Zubatov appears to have made a very major contribution to the techniques of authoritarian politics, and earned himself a prominent place in any list of political innovators.

Zubatov, who was born in 1866, seems in his youth to have been implicated in some kind of dissident activity. Solid biographical facts are lacking, but apparently some time in the mid-1880s he joined the Department of Police, rising to be the head first of the Moscow Okhrana and then of the Special Section. In intelligence and vision he towered above the run of the mill of policemen and gendarmes with whom his work brought him in contact. He was a true professional security officer, the first that Russia has ever had. With him he brought into the service dedicated young men, whom he appointed to run the branches of the Okhrana with which he covered the empire. He introduced such innovations as fingerprinting and photographing suspects. But he also had an ideology. A dedicated monarchist he felt it his duty to protect Russia from revolutionaries whom he feared would otherwise destroy his country. (In 1917, as soon as he had heard of the tsar's abdication, he put a bullet through his head.) Zubatov did not think the police should be used merely to forestall and suppress subversion; it ought actively to reach out into society. An admirer of Bismarck's, he envisaged for Russia some kind of social monarchism under which the crown would place itself at the head of the working class. Having from close observation of the nascent labour movement convinced himself (as did Lenin, with different conclusions) that Russian workers had no political aspirations, he began to experiment with police-sponsored trade unions. Between 1901 and 1903, with powerful backing in high circles, he launched his 'police socialism', setting up numerous trade-union organizations under police protection. The result surpassed all expectations. The workers, at last enabled to fight for their economic interests without fear of arrest, flocked to Zubatov's unions, the first legally operating labour associations in Russian history. He was especially popular with Jewish workers. All went well, but late in 1903 he fell from favour and was dismissed, a victim of bureaucratic intrigues and of protests from industrialists who objected to police agents backing their striking employees.[32]

The device which Zubatov introduced was infinitely expandable. If allowed to go on, he might have founded police-sponsored associations of every conceivable kind. Indeed, he did experiment for a while with police-sponsored student societies. Ultimately, one might have put together a parliament staffed exclusively with policemen or their appointees. In this manner, the security organs would have assumed a truly creative role in the nation's life. But intriguing as this subject is, it exceeds the chronological limits of our study.

Yet, when all is said and done, it would be difficult to maintain that imperial Russia was a full-blown police state; it was rather a forerunner, a rough prototype of such a regime, which fell far short of its full potential. The system had too many loopholes. Most of these resulted from the assimilation by the Russian ruling élite of western institutions and western values which, though incompatible with the patrimonial spirit, they were unwilling to give up. Such loopholes quite vitiated the elaborate set of repressive measures, introduced in the 1870s and 1880s.

Of these counterforces perhaps the most important was private property. The institution came late to Russia, but once introduced it soon made itself thoroughly at home. While harassing its subjects for the slightest political offences, the imperial regime was very careful not to violate their property rights. When publishing in London *The Bell*, that powerful irritant to the authorities, Alexander Herzen had his rents regularly forwarded to him from Russia by an international bank. Lenin's mother, even after one of her sons had been executed for an attempt on the tsar's life and two of her other children had been jailed for revolutionary activity, continued until her death to draw the government pension due to her as a civil servant's widow. The existence of private capital and private enterprise nullified the many police measures intended to cut off 'untrustworthy' elements from their means of livelihood. Political unreliables could almost always find employment with some private firm whose management was either unsympathetic to the government or politically neutral. Some of Russia's most radical journalists were subsidized by wealthy eccentrics. Zemstva openly engaged radical intellectuals as statisticians or teachers. The Union of Liberation, a clandestine society which played a critical role in sparking off the 1905 Revolution, was likewise supported from private resources. Private property created all over the empire enclaves which the police was powerless to trespass in so far as the existing laws, cavalier as they were with personal rights, strictly protected the rights of property. In the end, Zubatov's attempt at 'police socialism' could never have succeeded in imperial Russia because sooner or later it had to run afoul of private business interests.

Another loophole was foreign travel. Granted to dvoriane in 1785 it was gradually extended to the other estates. It survived even during the darkest periods of repression. Nicholas I tried to limit it by treatening to deprive dvoriane, who between the ages of ten and eighteen studied abroad, of the right to enter state service. In 1834 he required dvoriane to confine their foreign residence to five years, and in 1851 he reduced it further to two years. In the Criminal Code there were provisions requiring Russian citizens to return home from abroad when so ordered by the government. But none of these measures made much difference. Russians travelled in western Europe frequently and stayed there for long periods of time; in 1900, for instance, 200,000 Russian citizens spent abroad an average of 80 days. In Wilhelmian Germany, they constituted the largest contingent of foreign students. To obtain a passport valid for travel abroad one merely had to send an application with a small fee to the local governor. Passports were readily granted even to individuals with known subversive records, evidently on the assumption that they would cause less trouble abroad than at home. It is not in the least remarkable that the revolutionary party which in October 1917 took control of Russia had had its leader and operational headquarters for many years in western Europe.

Thirdly, there were powerful factors of a cultural nature inhibiting the full use of the existing machinery of repression. The élite ruling imperial Russia was brought up in the western spirit, and it dreaded disgrace. It hesitated to act too harshly for fear of being ridiculed by the civilized world. It was embarrassed to appear even in its own eyes as behaving in an 'Asiatic' manner. The imperial élite certainly was psychologically incapable of applying violence regardless of its consequences. There exists a touchingly prim note from Nicholas II, a kind of epitaph of his reign, which he sent late in 1916 to relatives who had interceded on behalf of a Grand Duke implicated in the assassination of Rasputin: 'No one is permitted to engage in murders.'[33] Such an ethic simply did not go with police rule.

The result of the conflict between the old patrimonial psychology and modern western influences, was to yield a police force that was ubiquitous, meddlesome, and often brutal, but on the whole inefficient. The powers given to the political police were entirely out of proportion to the results achieved. We have seen some statistics bearing on political offences: the small number of people under surveillance or in exile, and the insignificant proportion of books intercepted by censorship. In the decade of the 1880s, there were only seventeen persons executed for political crimes, all of them perpetrators of assassination or assassination attempts. During the reign of Alexander III – a period of severe repression – a total of four thousand persons were detained and interrogated in connection with political offences. These are very insignificant figures when one considers Russia's size and the massiveness of the machinery set up to deal with subversion.

The principal if unintended accomplishment of the proto-police regime was to radicalize Russian society. Its definition of political crimes was so comprehensive that the far-flung nets of security precautions caught and united people who had next to nothing in common with one another. From the legal point of view, hardly any distinction was drawn between conservative, nationalist, liberal, democratic, socialist and anarchist forms of discontent. A monarchist landlord outraged by the incompetence or corruption of the bureaucracy in his district became in the eyes of the law and the gendarmerie an ally of the anarchist assembling bombs to blow up the imperial palace. With its proscriptions, the government actually pushed its citizens into opposition ranks, where they became receptive to extremist appeals. For example, the laws in force in the 1880s forbade university students to form corporate organizations of any kind. Given the loneliness, poverty and natural social inclinations of young men it was inevitable that they would seek each other out and, in contravention of the law, form associations; these by their very existence acquired clandestine status and as such were easily infiltrated and taken over by radicals. It was the same with labour legislation. Stringent prohibitions against the formation of worker associations transformed even the most harmless labour activities into anti-state crimes. Workers whose sole interest might have lain in self-education or economic betterment were driven into the arms of radical students whom they actually mistrusted and disliked. Thus it was the government itself which helped accomplish the seemingly impossible, namely an alliance of all shades of public opinion, from the Slavophile right to the socialist-revolutionary left, which under the name 'Liberational Movement' (*Osvoboditel'noe Dvizhenie*) in 1902–5 at long last wrung a constitution out of the government.

That the existing legislation, far from stamping out revolution actually contributed to it did not escape perceptive contemporaries. Among those who foresaw the disastrous consequences of such policies was Lopukhin, the ex-Director of the Police Department, who has been cited before. In 1907 he wrote prophetically:

Given its lack of elementary scientific notions of law, given its acquaintance with public life only as it manifests itself within the walls of military academies and regimental barracks, the whole political outlook of the ranks of the Corps of Gendarmes boils itself down to the following propositions: that there are the people and there is state authority, that the latter is under constant threat from the former, for which reason it is subject to protective measures, and that to execute these measures any means may be used with impunity. When an outlook such as this happens to coincide with a poorly developed spirit of service responsibility and the lack of sufficient intelligence to make sense of complex public occurrences, then observations based on this outlook confine themselves to the external manifestations of these occurrences and fail to assimilate their inner meaning. Hence, every public occurrence assumes the character of a threat to state authority. As a result, the protection of the state as carried out by the Corps of Gendarmes turns into a war against all of society, and, in the final analysis, leads to a destruction also of state authority, whose inviolability can be assured only by a union with society. By widening the gulf between state authority and the people, it engenders a revolution. This is why the activity of the political police is inimical not only to the people; it is inimical to the state as well.[34]

In the theory, of course, the crown might have reverted to the Muscovite system, expropriating all private property, reharnessing the classes in service or tiaglo, hermetically sealing off Russia from the rest of the world, and declaring itself the Third Rome. Such a transformation would have enabled Russia to close the loopholes which made mockery of its police system. But to have done so required a veritable social and cultural revolution. Given their upbringing, the leaders of imperial Russia were not the men to carry out such an upheaval. This required entirely new people, with a different psyche and different values.

The system of repression just sketched is usually labelled in the historical literature as 'reactionary'. However, techniques are neutral. Methods of suppressing dissidence can be applied by regimes of a 'left' orientation as readily as by those considered 'right'. Once tried and proven successful, they are certain to be used by any government, which – on whatever grounds – regards itself as entitled to a monopoly in politics.

Just as the tactics of massive breakthrough by mechanized armour, inaugurated but not exploited in the First World War by the British at Cambrai were perfected by their enemies, the Germans, in the Second World War, so the techniques of police rule, introduced piecemeal by the Russian imperial regime, were first utilized to their fullest potential by their one-time victims, the revolutionaries. The people who came to power in Russia in October 1917 had grown up under the regime of 'Extraordinary' and 'Temporary' Laws: this was the only Russian constitution that they had ever known. All of them had been shadowed, searched, arrested, kept in jail, and sentenced to exile by the political police of the imperial government. They had battled with the censorship. They had had to contend with *agents provocateurs* planted in their midst. They knew the system intimately, from the inside, which meant that they also knew its shortcomings and loopholes. Their vision of a proper government was a mirror image of the imperial regime's to the extent that what the latter called 'subversion' (*kramola*) they labelled 'counter-revolution'. Long before they came to power, Social Democrats like Plekhanov and Lenin made no secret of the fact that they thought it proper to kill their ideological opponents.[35]

So it was not in the least surprising that almost the instant they took power, the Bolsheviks began to put together the pieces of the imperial proto-police apparatus which the short-lived and democratic Provisional Government had dismantled. A political police, Cheka, was formally founded in December 1917, but its functions had been informally exercised from the day of the coup by the Military-Revolutionary Committee. The Cheka enjoyed much vaster powers than the old Department of Police, Okhrana, or Corps of Gendarmes, being given complete licence to deal with whomever it chose to define as 'counter-revolutionaries'. In September 1918, with the proclamation of Red Terror, it executed in one day over five hundred 'enemies of the state', some of them hostages, others persons often guilty of nothing more criminal than having been born in the wrong social class. Within two months of the Bolshevik seizure of power, the opposition press was silenced and orders were issued for the apprehension of leading political opponents. There was already then talk of concentration camps for 'subversives' and soon forced labour was reintroduced. The Criminal Code of 1927, as has been noted (p. 294) contained provisions against anti-state crimes which neither in the breadth of definition nor in the severity of punishments differed substantially from those instituted by the imperial regime.

All this was done shortly after power had been seized. Then with each passing year the mechanism of repression was perfected until under Stalin's dictatorship it attained a level of wanton destructiveness never before experienced in human history.

Lenin and his fellow-revolutionaries who so quickly on taking power began the reconstruction of the police state certainly regarded these moves as emergency measures, exactly as in its day did the imperial government. The Cheka and its 'Revolutionary Tribunals', the mass executions, forced labour camps, exile, censorship and all the other repressive measures which they instituted were conceived by them as necessary to uproot what was still left of the old regime. This done, they were to be dissolved. But the same fate befell communist 'temporary' repressive measures as their predecessors: regularly renewed, the indiscriminate application of their violence came to overshadow the order they were meant to protect. Had they read more history and fewer polemical tracts the Bolshevik leaders might have been able to foresee this outcome. For the very idea that politics can be isolated from the vicissitudes of life and monopolized by one group or one ideology is under conditions of modern life unenforceable. Any government that persists in this notion must give ever wider berth to its police apparatus and eventually fall victim to it.

NOTES

NOTES

CHAPTER I: THE ENVIRONMENT AND ITS CONSEQUENCES

1 A good description of Russia's geography in its relationship to the country's past is W.H.Parker, *An Historical Geography of Russia* (London 1968).

2 B.H.Slicher van Bath, 'Yield ratios, 810–1820', in *Afdeling Agrarische Geschiedenis, Bijdragen* (Wageningen 1963), No. 10, p. 14. All my statistics on west European yields are drawn from this source.

3 A.L.Shapiro in Akademiia Nauk Estonskoi SSR, *Ezhegodnik po agrarnoi istorii Vostochnoi Evropy (1958)* (Tallin 1959), p. 221.

4 A.L.Shapiro, *Agrarnaia istoriia Severo-Zapada Rossii* (Leningrad 1971), pp. 366–7, 373 ('severo-zapad' – 'north-west' – is a common Soviet euphemism for the Novgorod state); also *Istoriia SSSR*, (1972), No. 1, p. 156.

5 For western Europe: *Entsiklopedicheskii Slovar' ob-a Brogkauz i Efron*, (St Petersburg 1902), XXIVa, pp. 930–1.

6 I.D.Kovalchenko, *Russkoe krepostnoe krest'ianstvo v pervoi polovine XIX Veka* (Moscow 1967), p. 77.

7 August von Haxthausen, *Studien über die innern Zustände ... Russlands* (Hanover 1847), I, pp. 174–7.

8 A.N.Engelgardt quoted in *Trudy Imperatorskogo Vol'nogo Ekonomicheskogo Obshchestva*, May 1866, Vol. II, Part 4, p. 410. I owe this reference to Mr Steven Grant.

9 H.Storch, *Tableau historique et statistique de l'Empire de Russie* (Paris 1801), cited in Parker, *Historical Geography*, p. 158.

10 V.O.Kliuchevskii, *Boiarskaia Duma drevnei Rusi* (Petersburg 1919), p. 307.

11 The population statistics cited above come from several sources, including S.V.Voznesenskii, *Ekonomika Rossii XIX–XX vv. v tsifrakh* (Leningrad 1924), I; A.I.Kopanev, 'Naselenie russkogo gosudarstva v XVI v.', in *Istoricheskie Zapiski* (1959), No. 64, p. 254; V.M.Kabuzan, *Narodonaseleniie Rossii v xviii – pervoi polovine xix v.* (Moscow 1963); and A.G. Rashin, *Naselenie Rossii za 100 let, (1811–1913 gg.)* (Moscow 1956).

12 S.M.Dubrovskii, *Stolypinskaia reforma*, 2nd ed. (Moscow 1930), p. 18.

13 V.O.Kliuchevskii, *Kurs russkoi istorii* (Moscow 1937), I, p. 20.

14 R.Dion, *Essai sur la formation du paysage rural français* (Tours 1934), p. 31, cited in Michael Confino, *Systèmes agraires et progrès agricole* (Paris–The Hague 1969), p. 415.

15 Karl A.Wittfogel, *Oriental Despotism* (New Haven, Conn. 1957).
16 I.P.Kozlovskii, *Pervye pochty i pervye pochmeistry v Moskovskom gosudarstve* 2 vols (Warsaw 1913), *passim*.
17 Thomas Hobbes, *The Elements of Law, Natural and Politic* (Cambridge 1928), pp. 81–2, 99–100.
18 Max Weber, *The Theory of Social and Economic Organization* (London 1947), p. 318.
19 Max Weber, *Wirtschaft und Gesellschaft* (Tübingen 1947), II, p. 684.
20 M.Rostovtzeff, *The Social and Economic History of the Hellenistic World*, 3 vols (Oxford 1941), and E.Bevan, *A History of Egypt under the Ptolomeic Dynasty* (London 1927).
21 *Geschichte des Hellenismus*, 2nd ed. (Leipzig-Berlin 1926), II, pp. 335–6.

CHAPTER 2: THE GENESIS OF THE PATRIMONIAL STATE IN RUSSIA

1 M.K.Liubavskii, *Obrazovanie osnovnoi gosudarstvennoi territorii velikorusskoi narodnosti* (Leningrad 1929).
2 P.Miliukov, *Glavnye techeniia russkoi istoricheskoi mysli* (Moscow 1898), pp. 192–204.
3 V.I.Lamanskii, ed., *Stat'i po slavianovedeniiu* (St Petersburg 1904), I, pp. 298–304; translated in the *Annals of the Ukrainian Academy of Sciences in the United States*, II, No. 4/6 (1952), pp. 355–64.
4 Alexandre Eck, *Le Moyen Age Russe* (Paris 1933), p. 43n.
5 V.O.Kliuchevskii, 'Podushnaia podat' i otmena kholopstva v Rossii', in *Opyty i issledovaniia: Pervyi sbornik statei* (Petrograd 1918), pp. 315–16.
6 S.V.Bakhrushin, 'Kniazheskoe khoziaistvo XV i pervoi poloviny XVI v.', in his *Nauchnye trudy* (Moscow 1954), II, p. 14.
7 Summarized in his *Feodalizm v drevnei Rusi* (St Petersburg 1907). An excellent critique of this position and analysis of the whole problem of Russian 'feudalism' is P.B.Struve's 'Nabliudeniia i issledovaniia iz oblasti khoziaistvennoi zhizni i prava drevnei Rusi', *Sbornik Russkogo Instituta v Prage* (1929), I, pp. 389–464 (reprinted in P.B.Struve, *Collected Works in Fifteen Volumes* Ann Arbor, Mich. 1970, XIII, No. 607).
8 Jean Touchard, *Histoire des idées politiques* (Paris 1959), I, p. 159.
9 *Feudal Society* (London 1961), p. 452.
10 *Feodal'noe zemlevladenie v Severo-Vostochnoi Rusi* (Moscow-Leningrad 1947), I, pp. 264, 283.
11 Struve, 'Nabliudeniia', p. 415. Struve uses 'vassalage' idiosyncratically to mean service voluntarily rendered rather than that performed under compulsion.
12 Feudalism's contribution to the formation of the modern state is the theme of Heinrich Mitteis's *Lehnrecht und Staatsgewalt* (Weimar 1933).

CHAPTER 3: THE TRIUMPH OF PATRIMONIALISM

1 A.N.Nasonov, *Mongoly i Rus'* (Moscow-Leningrad 1940), p. 110.

2 Karl Marx, *Secret Diplomatic History of the Eighteenth Century* (London 1969), p. 112.

3 S.M.Solovev, *Istoriia Rossii s drevneishikh vremen* (Moscow 1960), III, pp. 146–7.

4 Paul Vinogradoff in *The Legacy of the Middle Ages*, C.G.Crump and E.F.Jacob, eds. (Oxford 1926), p. 300.

5 M.Diakonov, *Vlast' moskovskikh gosudarei* (St Petersburg 1889), p. 133.

6 Paul Vinogradoff, *Roman Law in Medieval Europe* (Oxford 1929), p. 62.

7 Jean Bodin, *The Six Bookes of a Commonweale* (1606) (Cambridge, Mass. 1962), Book II, Ch. 2, pp. 197–204.

8 Jacques Ellul, *Histoire des Institutions* (Paris 1956), II, pp. 235–6, 296.

9 J.H.Elliott, *Imperial Spain, 1469–1716* (London 1963), p. 73.

10 Edward L. Keenan, *The Kurbskii-Groznyi Apocrypha* (Cambridge, Mass. 1971).

11 N.E.Nosov, *Ocherki po istorii mestnogo upravleniia russkogo gosudarstva pervoi poloviny XVI veka* (Moscow-Leningrad 1957), p. 322; see further A.A. Zimin in *Istoricheskie zapiski*, No. 63 (1958), p. 181.

12 P.Miliukov, *Ocherki po istorii russkoi kul'tury*, 6th ed. (St Petersburg 1909), Pt. 1, p. 197.

13 I here follow mainly A.K.Leontev, *Obrazovaniie prikaznoi sistemy upravleniia v russkom gosudarstve* (Moscow 1961).

14 V.Sergeevich, *Drevnosti russkogo prava* 2nd ed. (St Petersburg 1911), III, pp. 22–3.

15 G.E.Kochin, ed., *Materialy dlia terminologicheskogo slovaria drevnei Rossii* (Moscow-Leningrad 1937), p. 126.

16 Giles Fletcher, *Of the Russe Commonwealth* (London 1591), p. 41.

17 Cited in Helmut Neubauer, *Car und Selbstherrscher* (Wiesbaden 1964), pp. 39–40.

18 *Pamiatniki diplomaticheskikh snoshenii drevnei Rossii s derzhavami inostrannymi* (St Petersburg 1851), I, p. 12.

19 V.Sergeevich, *Drevnosti russkogo prava* 3rd ed. (St Petersburg 1908), II, p. 34.

20 A.Lappo-Danilevskii, *Organizatsiia priamogo oblozheniia v Moskovskom gosudarstve* (St Petersburg 1890), pp. 14–15.

21 V.Savva, *Moskovskie tsari i vizantiiskie vasilevsy* (Kharkov 1901), p. 400.

22 *O Rossii v tsarstvovanie Alekseia Mikhailovicha, sochinenie Grigor'ia Kotoshikhina* 4th ed. (St Petersburg 1906), p. 1.

23 Antonio Possevino, *Moscovia* (Antwerp 1587), pp. 55, 93.

24 Diakonov, *Vlast'*, pp. 146–62; and his *Ocherki obshchestvennogo i gosudastvennogo stroia drevnei Rusi*, 3rd ed. (St Petersburg 1910), pp. 419–20.

25 'v bratstve k nemu ne prikazal, potomu chto ne vedaet evo gosudarstva – nevedomo: on – gosudar' ili gosudarstvu tomu uriadnik,'; *Russko-indiiskie otnosheniia v XVII v.*; *Sbornik dokumentov* (Moscow 1958), p. 6.

26 J.Baly, *Eur-Aryan Roots* (London 1897), I, pp. 355–7.

27 Werner Philipp, 'Ein Anonymus der Tverer Publizistik im 15. Jahrhundert', *Festschrift für Dmytro Čyževskyj zum 60. Geburtstag* (Berlin 1954), pp. 230–7.

28 A.L.Shapiro, ed., *Agrarnaia istoriia Severo-Zapada Rossii* (Leningrad 1971), p. 332.

29 *Patriarshaia ili Nikonovskaia Letopis'*, *Polnoe Sobranie Russkikh Letopisei* (St Petersburg 1901), XII, p. 170 ff.

CHAPTER 4: THE ANATOMY OF THE PATRIMONIAL REGIME

1 S.Herberstein, *Rerum Moscoviticarum Commentarii* (Basle 1571), p. 49.

2 A.Eck, *Le Moyen Age Russe* (Paris 1933), pp. 89–92; M.Diakonov, *Ocherki obshchestvennogo i gosudarstvennogo stroia drevnei Rusi*, 3rd ed. (St Petersburg 1910), pp. 264–5.

3 V.Sergeevich, *Drevnosti russkogo prava*, 2nd ed. (St Petersburg 1911), III, pp. 17–18.

4 Jerome Blum, *Lord and Peasant in Russia* (Princeton, N.J. 1961), p. 169.

5 M.Iablochkov, *Istoriia dvorianskogo sosloviia v Rossii* (St Petersburg 1876), pp. 415–16.

6 A.L.Shapiro, ed., *Agrarnaia istoriia Severo-Zapada Rossii* (Leningrad 1971), p. 333.

7 Giles Fletcher, *Of the Russe Commonwealth* (London 1591), p. 31v–2.

8 V.O.Kliuchevskii, *Boiarskaia Duma drevnei Rusi* (St Petersburg 1919), p. 216.

9 P.Miliukov, *Gosudarstvennoe khoziaistvo Rossii v pervoi chetverti XVIII stoletiia i reforma Petra Velikogo*, 2nd ed. (St Petersburg 1905), p. 11.

10 S.B.Veselovskii, *K voprosu o proiskhozhdenii votchinnogo rezhima* (Moscow 1926).

11 Cited in Institut Istorii Akademii Nauk SSSR, *Istoriia SSSR* (Moscow 1948), I, p. 421.

12 M.M.Speranskii, *Proekty i zapiski* (Moscow–Leningrad 1961), p. 43.

13 N.Khlebnikov, *O vlianii obshchestva na organizatsiiu gosudarstva v tsarskii period russkoi istorii* (St Petersburg 1869), p. 273.

14 *Opyty i issledovaniia – pervyi sbornik statei* (Petrograd 1918), p. 406.

15 N.F.Demidova, 'Biurokratizatsiia gosudarstvennogo apparata absoliutizma v xvii–xviii vv.', Akademiia Nauk, Institut Istorii, *Absoliutizm v Rossii (XVII–XVIII vv.)* (Moscow 1964), pp. 206–42.

16 A.A.Kizevetter, *Mestnoe samoupravlenie v Rossii – IX–XIX St. – Istoricheskii ocherk*, 2nd ed. (Petrograd 1917), pp. 47–52.

17 S.M.Solovev, *Istoriia Rossii s drevneishikh vremen* (Moscow 1960), VII, p. 43.

18 Solovev, *Istoriia* (Moscow 1961), V, p. 340.

19 A.S.Muliukin, *Priezd inostrantsev v Moskovskoe gosudarstve* (St Petersburg 1909), p. 58.

CHAPTER 5: THE PARTIAL DISMANTLING OF THE PATRIMONIAL STATE

1 Cited in V.O.Kliuchevskii, *Kurs russkoi istorii* (Moscow 1937), IV, p. 225.

2 V.Semevskii, 'Razdacha naselennykh imenii pri Ekaterine II', *Otechestvennye zapiski*, Vol. CCXXXIII, No. 8 (August 1877), Section 'Sovremennoe obozrenie', pp. 204–27.

3 *Statesman's Yearbook ... for the Year 1939* (London 1939), pp. 874 and 1119; and, Tsentral'noe Statisticheskoe Upravlenie, *Itogi vsesoiuznoi perepisi naseleniia 1970 goda* (Moscow 1973), IV, pp. 14–15.

4 N.Ustrialov, *Istoriia tsarstvovaniia Petra Velikogo* (St Petersburg 1859), VI, pp. 346–8.

5 G.N.Clark, *The Seventeenth Century*, 2nd ed. (Oxford 1947), p. 100.

6 N[icholas] Tourgueneff, *La Russie et les Russes* (Paris 1847), II, p. 17.

7 Brenda Meehan-Waters, 'The Muscovite Noble Origins of the Russians in the Generalitet of 1730', *Cahiers du monde russe et soviétique*, Vol. XII, No. 1–2, (1971), p. 34.

8 The following account is based largely on S.P.Luppov, *Istoriia stroitel'stva Peterburga v pervoi chetverti XVIII veka* (Moscow-Leningrad 1957).

9 A.Romanovich-Slavatinskii, *Dvorianstvo v Rossii*, 2nd ed. (Kiev 1912), p. 151.

10 Reinhard Wittram, *Peter I; Czar und Kaiser* (Göttingen n.d.) II, pp. 121–2.

11 N.B.Golikova, *Politicheskie protsessy pri Petre I* (Moscow 1957), p. 9.

12 Figures for 1782 and 1858 from V.M.Kabuzan and S.M.Troitskii, 'Izmeneniia v chislennosti, udel'nom vese i razmeshchenii dvorianstva v Rossii v 1782–1858 gg.', *Istoriia SSSR*, No. 4 (1971), p. 158.

13 Pierre Dolgoroukov, *La vérité sur la Russie* (Paris 1860), pp. 83–6.

14 Romanovich-Slavatinskii, *Dvorianstvo v Rossii*, pp. 487–8.

15 A.I.Gertsen, *Sobranie sochinenii* (Moscow 1956), VIII, p. 236.

16 M.Bogoslovskii, *Byt i nravy russkogo dvorianstva v pervoi polovine xviii veka* (Moscow 1906), p. 50.

17 Robert E.Jones, *The Emancipation of the Russian Nobility, 1762–1785* (Princeton 1973), p. 80.

see p. 133

CHAPTER 6: THE PEASANTRY

1 On this subject see the superb study of Michael Confino, *Systèmes agraires et progrès agricole* (Paris-The Hague 1969).

2 V.Kliuchevskii, *Kurs russkoi istorii* (Moscow 1937), I, pp. 324–5.

3 A.Troinitskii, *Krepostnoe naselenie v Rossii po desiatoi narodnoi perepisi* (St Petersburg 1861).

4 I.D.Kovalchenko, *Russkoe krepostnoe krest'ianstvo v pervoi polovine XIX v.* (Moscow 1967), p. 86.

5 Kovalchenko, op. cit., pp. 68–9.

6 'Economic History as a Discipline', *Encyclopedia of the Social Sciences* (New York 1944), V, p. 328.

7 Alexander Pushkin, *Polnoe sobranie sochinenii v desiati tomakh* (Moscow-Leningrad 1949), VII, pp. 289–91. Pushkin's views of obrok and corvée in Russia are not entirely correct.

8 Captain John Dundas Cochrane, *Narrative of a Pedestrian Journey through Russia and Siberian Tartary* (London 1824), p. 68. It is Cochrane that Pushkin seems to have had in mind in the citation quoted above.

9 Robert Bremner, *Excursions in the Interior of Russia* (London 1839), I, pp. 154–5.

10 I.I.Ignatovich, *Pomeshchich'i krest'iane nakanune osvobozhdeniia* (St Petersburg 1902), p. 24.

11 A. von Haxthausen, *Studien über die innern Zustände ... Russlands* (Hanover 1847), II, p. 511.

12 Bremner, *Excursions*, I, p. 156.

13 Daniel Field in *Kritika* (Cambridge Mass.), Vol. I, No. 2 (Winter 1964–65) p. 20.

14 Cited in B.E.Nolde, *Iurii Samarin i ego vremia* (Paris 1926), p. 69.

15 Letter to D.I.Ivanov of 7 August 1837 in [V.G.] Belinskii, *Pis'ma* (St Petersburg 1914), I, p. 92.

16 S.V.Pakhman, *Obychnoe grazhdanskoe pravo v Rossii* (St Petersburg 1877), I, pp. 410–12.

17 Cited in N.L.Brodskii, ed. *Rannie slavianofily* (Moscow 1910), p. LIII.

18 A.N.Engelgardt, *Iz derevni: 12 pisem*, cited in R.Wortman, *The Crisis of Russian Populism* (Cambridge 1967), p. 58.

19 Maxim Gorkii, *O russkom krest'ianstve* (Berlin 1922), p. 23.

20 Ralph E.Matlaw, ed., *Belinsky, Chernyshevsky, and Dobrolyubov: Selected Criticism* (New York 1962), pp. 86–7.

21 O.V.Aptekman, *Obshchestvo 'Zemlia i volia '70-kh gg.* (Petrograd 1924), pp. 144–5.

22 This view, first advanced by Peter Struve in 1898, has since been confirmed by economic historians; see, for example, N.L.Rubinshtein, *Sel'skoe khoziastvo Rossii vo vtoroi polovine XVIII v.* (Moscow 1957), pp. 127–30, and Michael Confino, *Domaines et seigneurs en Russie vers la fin du XVIIIe siècle* (Paris 1963), pp. 194–201.

23 Iu.F.Samarin, 'O krepostnom sostoianii', in his *Sochineniia* (Moscow 1878) II, p. 19.

24 George Pavlovsky, *Agricultural Russia on the Eve of the Revolution* (London 1930), pp. 92, 94.

25 A.N.Chelintsev, *Russkoe sel'skoe khoziaistvo pered revoliutsei*, 2nd ed. (Moscow 1928), pp. 10–11.

CHAPTER 7: DVORIANSTVO

1 A.S.Pushkin, *Polnoe sobranie sochinenii v desiati tomakh* (Moscow-Leningrad 1949), VII, pp. 539–40.

2 N.Khlebnikov, *O vlianii obshchestva na organizatsiiu gosudarstva v tsarskii period russkoi istorii* (St Petersburg 1869), p. 13.

3 Alexandre Eck, *Le Moyen Age Russe* (Paris 1933), p. 232, and Iu.V.Gote, *Zamoskovnyi krai v XVIII veke* (Moscow 1937), p. 287.

4 Jerome Blum, *Lord and Peasant in Russia* (Princeton, N.J. 1961), p. 215; E.I.Indova, *Krepostnoe khoziaistvo v nachale XIX veka po materialam votchinnogo arkhiva Vorontsovykh* (Moscow 1955), pp. 28–9; and K.N. Shchepetov, *Krepostnoe pravo v votchinakh Sheremetevykh, 1708–1885* (Moscow 1947), p. 22.

5 A.T.Bolotov, cited by Michael Confino, *Systèmes agraires et progrès agricole* (Paris-The Hague 1969), pp. 104–5.

6 Eck, *Le Moyen Age*, p. 233. Khlebnikov (*O vlianii*, pp. 31–2) produces similar estimates.

7 E.D.Clarke, *Travels in Russia, Tartary and Turkey* (Edinburgh 1839), p. 15, cited by M. Confino in 'A propos de la noblesse russe au xviii siècle', *Annales*, No. 6 (1967), p. 1196. Confino's essay (pp. 1163–205) provides a convincing picture of the misery of most dvoriane.

8 'Zapiski Senatora Ia. A. Solov'eva', *Russkaia starina* Vol. XXX (April 1881), pp. 746–7.

9 V.M.Kabuzan and S.M.Troitskii,'Izmeneniia v chislennosti, udel'nom vese i razmeshchenii dvorianstva v Rossii v 1782–1858 gg.', *Istoriia SSSR*, No. 4 (1971), p. 158. See also the statistics given on p. 131 above from the same source.

10 S.B.Veselovskii, *Feodal'noe zemlevladenie v severo-vostochnoi Rusi* (Moscow-Leningrad 1947), I, pp. 165–202.

11 G.A.Holmes, *The Estates of the Higher Nobility in Fourteenth-Century England* (Cambridge 1957).

12 G.E.Mingay, *English Landed Society in the Eighteenth Century* (London-Toronto 1963), p. 26.

13 A.Romanovich-Slavatinskii, *Dvorianstvo v Rossii*, 2nd ed. (Kiev 1912), p. 535.

14 Figures for 1777 from V.I.Semevskii, *Krest'iane v tsarstvovanie Imperatritsy Ekateriny II* (St Petersburg 1903), I, p. 32. Those for 1858–9 are based on figures supplied by A.Troinitskii, *Krepostnoe naselenie v Rossii po 10-oi narodnoi perepisi* (St Petersburg 1861), Table D, p. 45. In addition to the 87,269 serf-owners listed in Table 1 there were in the 37 provinces considered, some 3,000 dvoriane who had serfs (on the average 3) but no land.

15 Romanovich-Slavatinskii, *Dvorianstvo*, p. 572.

16 N.Zagoskin, *Ocherki organizatsii i proiskhozhdeniia sluzhilogo sosloviia v do-Petrovskoi Rusi* (Kazan 1875), pp. 177–9.

17 Eric Amburger, *Geschichte der Behördenorganisation Russlands von Peter dem Grossen bis 1917* (Leiden 1966), p. 517; Walter M.Pinter in *Slavic Review*, Vol. 29, No. 3 (September 1970), p. 438.

18 M.M.Speranskii, 'Pis'ma Speranskogo k A.A. Stolypinu,' *Russkii arkhiv* (1869), VII, No. 9, p. 1977.

19 D.A.Korsakov, *Votsarenie Imperatritsy Anny Ioannovny* (Kazan 1880), p. 93.

20 Grand Duke Nikolai Mikhailovich, *Graf Pavel Aleksandrovich Stroganov, 1774–1817* (St Petersburg 1903), II, pp. 111–2.

21 Pushkin, *Polnoe sobranie sochinenii*, VII, pp. 229–30.

CHAPTER 8: THE MISSING BOURGEOISIE

1 B.G.Kurts, *Sostoianie Rossii v 1650–1655gg po doneseniiam Rodesa* (Moscow 1914), p. 148.

2.B.G.Kurts, *Sochinenie Kil'burgera o russkoi torgovle v tsarstvovanie Alekseia Mikhailovicha* (Kiev 1915), pp. 87–8.

3.'Puteshestvie v Moskoviiu Barona Avgustina Maierberga', *Chteniia v*

Imperatorskom Obshchestve Istorii i Drevnostei Rossiiskikh Book 3 (1873), Part 4, p. 92.

4 N.Khlebnikov, *O vlianii obshchestva na organizatsiiu gosudarstva v tsarskii period Russkoi istorii* (St Petersburg 1869), p. 284.

5 Max Weber, *Wirtschaft und Gesellschaft*, 3rd ed. (Tübingen 1947), II, p. 523.

6 Pavel Smirnov, *Goroda moskovskogo gosudarstva v pervoi polovine xvii veka*, Vol. I, Part 2 (Kiev 1919), pp. 351–2, and A.M.Sakharov, *Obrazovanie i razvitie rossiiskogo gosudarstva v xiv–xvii v.* (Moscow 1969), p. 77.

7 Smirnov, *Goroda*, I/2, Table XXVIII, pp. 346–7, 352.

8 A.A.Kizevetter, *Posadskaia obshchina v Rossii xviii st.* (Moscow 1903), pp. 171–4.

9 I.M.Kulisher, *Ocherk istorii russkoi torgovli* (St Petersburg 1923), pp. 154–5.

10 I.Ditiatin, *Ustroistvo i upravlenie gorodov Rossii* (St Petersburg 1875), I, p. 109.

11 These etymologies are based on Max Vasmer's *Russisches etymologisches Wörterbuch* 3 vols. (Heidelberg 1950–8).

12 Giles Fletcher, *Of the Russe Commonwealth* (London 1591), pp. 46v–7.

13 V.P.Riabushinskii, cited in P.A.Buryshkin, *Moskva kupecheskaia* (New York 1954), p. 110.

14 *Moskovskii sukonnyi dvor* (Leningrad 1934), pp. xxvi–xxvii and *passim*.

15 M.Tugan-Baranovskii, *Russkaia fabrika v proshlom i nastoiashchem*, 7th ed. (Moscow 1938), I, p. 29.

16 M.F.Zlotnikov, 'K voprosu ob izuchenii istorii rabochego klassa i promyshlennosti', *Katorga i ssylka*, No. 1/116 (1935), p. 59.

17 His story, told in *Russkaia starina* for May–September 1881, is summarized in I.I.Ignatovich, *Pomeshchich'i krest'iane nakanune osvobozhdeniia* (St Petersburg 1902), pp. 76–8.

18 *Istoricheskie zapiski*, No. 32 (1950), p. 133.

19 Ditiatin, *Ustroistvo*, pp. 374–5, and A.A.Kizevetter, *Istoricheskie ocherki* (Moscow 1912), p. 243.

20 Valentine T. Bill, *The Forgotten Class* (New York 1959), p. 153.

21 Buryshkin, *Moskva kupecheskaia*, p. 31.

22 Bertrand Gille, *Histoire économique et sociale de la Russie* (Paris 1949), p. 187, and P.A.Khromov, *Ekonomicheskoe razvitie Rossii v XIX–XX vekakh* (1800–1917), ([Moscow] 1950), p. 386.

CHAPTER 9: THE CHURCH AS SERVANT OF THE STATE

1 Anatole Leroy-Beaulieu, *L'Empire des Tsars et les Russes* (Paris 1889), III, p. 167.

2 Wilhelm Ensslin in Norman H.Baynes and H.St.L.B.Moss, *Byzantium* (Oxford 1949), p. 274.

3 Mitropolit Moskovskii Makarii, *Istoriia russkoi tserkvi* (St Petersburg 1886), V, Book II, pp. 480–81.

4 N.M.Nikolskii, *Istoriia russkoi tserkvi* (Moscow 1931), p. 62. Lest Nikolskii, whose book appeared under the auspices of 'The Union of Militant

Atheists of the USSR' be suspected of overstating his case, it may be added that respected pre-Revolutionary historians, sympathetic to the church, arrived at similar conclusions: L.P.Rushchinskii, *Religioznyi byt russkikh po svedeniiam inostrannykh pisatelei xvi–xvii vekov* (Moscow 1871), and S. Tregubov, *Religioznyi byt russkikh i sostoianie dukhoventstva v xviii v. po memuaram inostrantsev* (Kiev 1884).

5 Cited in A.Pavlov, *Istoricheskii ocherk sekiularizatsii tserkovnykh zemel' v Rossii*, (Odessa 1871), Pt. I, pp. 84n–85n.

6 Cited in N.F.Kapterev, *Patriarkh Nikon i tsar' Aleksei Mikhailovich*, (Sergiev Posad 1909), I, p. 34.

7 Ihor Ševčenko, 'A neglected Byzantine source of Muscovite Political Ideology', *Harvard Slavic Studies* (1954), II, pp. 141–79.

8 Vladimir Soloviev, *L'idée russe* (Paris 1888), p. 25, referring to the conservative historian M.P.Pogodin.

9 J.G.Korb, *Diary of an Austrian Secretary of Legation at the Court of Czar Peter the Great*, (London 1863), II, p. 161.

10 William Palmer, *The Patriarch and the Tsar*, I, 'The Replies of the Humble Nicon' (London 1871), pp. 189–90, 251–3. These texts are available only in English translation, never having been published in Russia.

11 Estimates from: P.I.Melnikov [Pecherskii], *Polnoe sobranie sochinenii* (St Petersburg-Moscow 1898), XIV, pp. 379–94; F.C.Conybeare, *Russian Dissenters* (Cambridge, Mass. 1921), pp. 245–9; and, P.Miliukov, *Ocherki po istorii russkoi kul'tury*, II, Pt 1 (Paris 1931), pp. 153–5.

12 Pierre Pascal, *Avvakum et les débuts du raskol* (Paris 1938), p. 574.

13 Alexander V.Muller, *The Spiritual Regulation of Peter the Great* (Seattle, Wash. 1972), p. [6].

14 James Cracraft, *The Church Reform of Peter the Great* (London 1971), pp. 238–9.

15 *O Rossii v tsarstvovanie Alekseia Mikhailovicha, sochinenie Grigor'ia Kotoshikhina*, 4th ed. (St Petersburg 1906), p. 147; William Coxe, *Travels into Poland, Russia, Sweden and Denmark* (Dublin 1784), II, p. 330.

16 *New York Times*, 23 March 1972, p. 6.

CHAPTER 10: THE INTELLIGENTSIA

1 P.A.Berlin, *Russkaia burzhuaziia v staroe i novoe vremia* (Moscow 1922), p. 169.

2 Otto Mueller, *Intelligentcija: Untersuchungen zur Geschichte eines politischen Schlagwortes* (Frankfurt 1971); Richard Pipes, '"Intelligentsia" from the German "Intelligenz"? a Note', *Slavic Review*, Vol. XXX, No. 3 (September 1971), pp. 615–18.

3 The 'worker intelligentsia' is described in my *Social Democracy and the St Petersburg Labor Movement, 1885–1897* (Cambridge, Mass. 1963); the 'peasant intelligentsia' (mostly ex-serfs who joined the free professions) in E.S.Kots, *Krepostnaia intelligentsiia* (Leningrad 1926).

4 S.M.Solovev, *Istoriia Rossii s drevneishikh vremen*, Vol. V (Moscow 1961), pp. 331–2.

5 G. Gukovskii, *Ocherki po istorii russkoi literatury XVIII veka* (Moscow-Leningrad 1936), p. 19.
6 Cited in V.Bogoliubov, *N.I. Novikov i ego vremia* (Moscow 1916), p. 38.
7 N.I.Novikov, *Izbrannye sochineniia* (Moscow-Leningrad 1951), p. 59.
8 V.P.Semennikov, *Radishchev: ocherki i issledovaniia* (Moscow-Petrograd 1923), pp. 268–9.
9 Cited in Abbot Gleason, *European and Muscovite: Ivan Kireevskii and the Origins of Slavophilism* (Canbridge, Mass. 1972), p. 38.
10 Cited in Martin Malia, *Alexander Hertzen and the Birth of Russian Socialism, 1825–1855* (Cambridge, Mass. 1961), p. 203.
11 A.N.Pypin, *Belinskii, ego zhizn' i perepiska*, 2nd ed., (St Petersburg 1908), p. 88.
12 L.V.Kamosko, 'Izmeneniia soslovnogo sostava uchashchikhsia srednei i vysshei shkoly Rossii (30–80e gody XIX v.)', *Voprosy isorii*, No. 10 (1970), p. 206.
13 V.R.Leikina-Svirskaia, *Intelligentsiia v Rossii vo vtoroi polovine XIX veka* (Moscow 1971), p. 70.
14 The First Letter on the Philosophy of History in M.Gershenzon, ed., *Sochineniia i pis'ma P.Ia. Chaadaeva*, Vol. I (Moscow 1913), p. 79.
15 P.Ia.Chaadaev, 'Neopublikovannaia Stat'ia', *Zven'ia*, Vol. III/IV (1934), p. 380.
16 *Dnevnik A.S.Suvorina* (Moscow-Petrograd 1923), cited in Isaiah Berlin, *Fathers and Children* (Oxford 1972), p. 62.
17 My views on Russian conservatism are explained at greater length in a paper delivered to the XIIIth International Congress of Historical Sciences, *Russian Conservatism in the Second Half of the Nineteenth Century* (Moscow 1970); it has been reprinted in the *Slavic Review*, Vol. 30, No. 1 (March 1971), pp. 121–8.
18 Ivan Aksakov, *Sochineniia*, 2nd ed. (St Petersburg 1891), II, pp. 3–4.
19 *Russkii vestnik*, Vol. 40 (July 1862), p. 411.
20 F.M.Dostoevskii, *Pis'ma*, Vol. III (Moscow-Leningrad, 1934), p. 50.
21 I.S.Turgenev, *Polnoe sobranie sochinenii i pisem*; *Sochineniia*, Vol. IX (Moscow-Leningrad 1965), p. 119.
22 N.G.Chernyshevskii, 'Ocherki gogolevskogo perioda.' in his *Estetika i literaturnaia kritika: izbrannye stat'i* (Moscow-Leningrad 1951), p. 338. Professor Donald Fanger kindly called my attention to this passage.
23 N.V.Gogol, 'Neskol'ko slov o Pushkine,' *Sobranie sochinenii*, (Moscow 1950), VI, p. 33.
24 Cited in S.Balukhatyi, ed., *Russkie pisateli o literature*, Vol. I (Leningrad 1939), p. 109.
25 Cited in [E.Solovev] Andreevich, *Opyt filosofii russkoi literatury*, 2nd ed. (St Petersburg 1909), p. 6.
26 D.I.Pisarev, *Sochineniia*, Vol. 3 (Moscow 1956), p. 399.
27 Letter to A.S.Suvorin (1 April 1890) in *Pis'ma A.P. Chekhova*, Vol. III (Moscow 1913), p. 44.
28 Letter to P.D.Boborykin (1865), cited in Balukhatyi, ed., *Russkie pisateli* Vol. II, p. 97.

CHAPTER 11: TOWARDS THE POLICE STATE

1 Iu.Gote, *Istoriia oblastnogo upravleniia v Rossii ot Petra I do Ekateriny II* (Moscow 1913), I, p. 449, and M.Bogoslovskii, *Oblastnaia reforma Petra Velikogo* (Moscow 1902), p. 263.

2 Bogoslovskii, *Oblastnaia reforma*, p. 262.

3 S.Frederick Starr, *Decentralization and Self-Government in Russia, 1830–1870* (Princeton 1972), p. 48.

4 M. Le Comte de Ségur, *Mémoirs* (Paris 1826), II, p. 297.

5 Hans-Joachim Torke, 'Das Russische Beamtentum in der ersten Hälfte des 19. Jahrhunderts', *Forschungen zur Osteuropäischen Geschichte*, Vol. 13 (Berlin 1967), p. 227.

6 N.Shchedrin (M.E.Saltykov), *Gubernskie ocherki*, in his *Sobranie Sochinenii* (Moscow 1951), I, pp. 59–60.

7 P.A.Viazemskii, 'Staraia zapisnaia knizhka', *Polnoe sobranie sochinenii Kniazia P.A.Viazemskogo* (St Petersburg 1883), VIII, p. 113.

8 N.M.Korkunov, *Russkoe gosudarstvennoe pravo* (St Petersburg 1909), I, pp. 215–22.

9 P.A.Zaionchkovskii, *Rossiiskoe samoderzhavie v kontse XIX stoletiia* (Moscow 1970), pp. 299–301.

10 *Ulozhenie o Nakazaniiakh Ugolovykh i Ispravitel'nykh* (St Petersburg 1845), pp. 65–6, 69. These articles were retained with minor modifications in the Criminal Code of 1885.

11 *Sobranie Kodeksov R.S.F.S.R.*, 4th ed. (Moscow 1927), pp. 665, 668.

12 Harold J.Berman, *Soviet Criminal Law and Procedure: The RSFSR Codes* (Cambridge, Mass. 1966), p. 180.

13 S.Maksimov, *Sibir' i katorga*, Pt 2 (St Petersburg 1871), pp. 229, 305.

14 It is summarized, on the basis of archival sources, in P.A. Zaionchkovskii, *Krisis samoderzhaviia na rubezhe 1870–1880–kh godov* (Moscow 1964), pp. 76–7.

15 *Svod Zakonov Rossiiskoi Imperii*, Vol. I, Pt 1, Book V (St Petersburg 1892), p. 40, Article 362.

16 His two major monographs on the subject are listed in notes 9 and 14 above.

17 Ministerstvo Vnutrennykh Del, *Istoricheskii ocherk* (St Petersburg 1902), p. 172. Document dated 1886. Emphasis supplied.

18 *Byloe*, No. 4/5 (1918), pp. 158–9.

19 A.Kropotkin, cited in Ronald Hingley, *The Russian Secret Police* (New York 1970), p. 55.

20 *Sobranie uzakonenii i rasporiazhenii pravitel'stva* (St Petersburg 1881), dated 4 September 1881, No. 616, pp. 1553–65.

21 A.A.Lopukhin, *Nastoiashchee i budushchee russkoi politsii* (Moscow 1907), pp. 26–7.

22 P.Miliukov, *Ocherki po istorii russkoi kul'tury*, 6th ed. (St Petersburg 1909), I, pp. 216–17.

23 P.B.Struve, 'Rossiia pod nadzorom politsii', *Osvobozhdeniie*, Vol. I, No. 20/21 (18 April/1 May 1903), p. 357.

24 Lopukhin, *Nastoiashchee i budushchee*, p. 5.
25 Zaionchkovskii, *Krizis samoderzhaviia*, p. 182.
26 George Kennan, 'The Russian Police', *The Century Illustrated Magazine*, Vol. XXXVII (1888–9), pp. 890–2.
27 *Sobranie uzakonenii i rasporiazhenii pravitel'stva* (St Petersburg 1882), dated 16 April 1882, No. 212.
28 George Kennan, 'The Russian Penal Code', *The Century Illustrated Magazine*, Vol. XXXV (1887–8), pp. 884–5.
29 Ministerstvo Vnutrennykh Del, *Istoricheskii ocherk*, p. 215.
30 *Entsiklopedicheskii Slovar' Ob-a Brokgauz i Efron*, 'Ssylka', Vol. XXXI (St Petersburg 1900), pp. 380–1 and 'Katorga', Vol. XIVa (St Petersburg 1895), p. 759.
31 Zaionchkovskii, *Krizis samoderzhaviia*, pp. 184, 296, and *Rossiiskoe samoderzhavie*, p. 168.
32 The fullest account of Zubatov's activities is Dimitry Pospielovsky's *Russian Police Trade Unionism* (London 1971).
33 Grand Duchess Marie, *Education of a Princess* (New York 1931), p. 279.
34 Lopukhin, *Nastoiashchee i budushchee*, pp. 32–3.
35 Richard Pipes, *Struve: Liberal on the Left, 1870–1905* (Cambridge, Mass. 1970), pp. 257 and 279.

CHRONOLOGY

CHRONOLOGY

Listed here are the principal events in Russian history mentioned in the text. Dates are 'Old Style', which until its abolition in 1918 was 13 days behind the western calendar in the twentieth century, 12 in the nineteenth, 11 in the eighteenth, and so on.

EARLY HISTORY

6–8th centuries Slavs migrate from central Europe into the forest zone of Russia.

7th century Turkic Khazars conquer Black Sea steppe and establish their kaganate; end of 8th century they convert to Judaism; 8–9th centuries, Slavs in south pay tribute to Khazars.

c. 800 Old Ladoga, first Norse settlement in Russia; 9th century, Norsemen spread out along Volga and Dnieper basins and raid Constantinople; c. 882, Prince Oleg unites Novgorod with Kiev to form one state.

966–7 Prince Sviatoslav attacks and destroys Khazar state.

970–1 Sviatoslav conquers Bulgaria.

c. 978–1015 Prince Vladimir.

987 Kiev converts to Christianity.

second half 10th century Pechenegs invade Black Sea steppe, followed in 11th century by Polovtsy (Cumans).

1019–54 Prince Iaroslav.

1097 Liubech meeting of princes, the first of several.

1113–25 Vladimir Monomakh; Rostov the Great: c. 1090–1157, Iurii Dolgorukii (1155–57 Great Prince of Kiev); c. 1157–74, Andrei Bogoliubskii Prince of Suzdal; 1169, Bogoliubskii takes Kiev but does not move there.

1126 First elected governor (*posadnik*) in Novgorod; 1156, first elected bishop.

c. 1200 Polovtsy cut Kiev-Constantinople trading route.

1204 Crusaders capture and sack Constantinople.

MONGOL DOMINATION

Mongols:

end 12th century Mongol tribes consolidate.

1206 Genghis Khan assumes command.

1215–80 Mongols conquer China.

1218–21 Conquest of central Asia.

1227 Death of Genghis Khan.

1236 Baty (Batu), Genghis Khan's grandson, begins conquest of western territories.

1237–8 Mongol armies under Baty conquer north-eastern Russia.

1240–2 Mongols attack southern Russia, Poland and Hungary and then withdraw to Mongolia.

c. 1243 Formation of Golden Horde of which north-eastern Russia and Novgorod become tributaries.

1256–9 Mongols conquer the Caucasus and Iran.

1257 Mongols conduct first census of Russia.

Novgorod:

1257–9 Anti-Mongol uprisings.

1265 Oldest surviving princely contract.

1348 By mutual agreement, Pskov separates itself and forms independent city-state.

c. 1350 Strigolnik heresy.

Lithuania-Poland:

13–14th centuries Lithuanians take over Dnieper basin.

1386 Dynastic union of Lithuania with Poland and conversion of Lithuanian dynasty to Catholicism.

North-eastern Russia:

c. 1150–c. 1450 So-called 'appanage period'.

1252–63 Alexander Nevskii, Great Prince of Vladimir.

c. 1276 Appanage principality of Moscow carved out for Nevskii's son, Danil, who rules c. 1276–1303.

1299 Metropolitan of Kiev transfers his see to Vladimir.

1303–25 Iurii Danilovich, prince of Moscow.

1325–40 Ivan I (Kalita or 'Moneybag'), prince of Moscow (Great Prince of Vladimir, 1328–40).

1327 Anti-Mongol uprising in Tver, suppressed by Ivan I with Mongol help.

1328 Metropolitan's see transferred from Vladimir to Moscow.

1359–89 Dmitrii (Donskoi), prince of Moscow (Great Prince after 1362).

mid–14th century Mongol power collapses in Iran.

1360s–70s Dynastic crises in Golden Horde.

1368 Collapse of Mongol power in China.

1370s Moscow begins to interfere with boyar departure rights.

1380 Dmitrii defeats one of the claimants to Golden Horde throne at Kulikovo.

1382 Moscow sacked by Mongols.

1389–95 Timur (Tamerlane) attacks Golden Horde and sacks Sarai, its capital.

MOSCOW'S RISE TO PREEMINENCE

1389–1425 Basil I.

1392 Acquisition of Nizhnii Novgorod.

1425–62 Basil II (with interruptions.)

1439 Florence Union of Greek and Roman churches; Russian hierarchy rejects it.

c. 1450 Golden Horde falls apart; formation of Kazan, Astrakhan, and Crimean principalities (khanates).

1453 Turks seize Constantinople.

1462–1505 Ivan III.

1470s Judaizer heresy spreads in Novgorod.

1471 Moscow attacks Novgorod and defeats its armies.

1472 Ivan III marries Sophia Paleologue.

1477 Moscow again attacks Novgorod and annexes it.

after 1477 Massive land expropriations carried out by Moscow in Novgorod; introduction of conditional land tenure (*pomest'e*).

1484, 1489 Massacres in Novgorod and deportation of its leading citizens to inland Russia.

1485 Tver annexed to Moscow.

1489 Viatka annexed to Moscow.

1494 Hansa depot in Novgorod shut down.

1497 First legal code (*Sudebnik*).

1503 Church Council turns down Nil Sorskii's appeal for voluntary renunciation of ecclesiastical properties; beginning of battle between pro- and anti-property parties in the Russian church.

THE SIXTEENTH CENTURY

1505–33 Basil III.

1510 Capture and annexation of Pskov, followed by mass deportations.

1521 Basil III deposes Metropolitan Varlaam.

1525 Metropolitan Danil authorizes Basil's divorce.

1533–84 Ivan IV (the Terrible).

1533–8 Regency of Ivan's mother, Elena.

1535 Edicts against further monastic acquisitions of land.

1547 Ivan IV crowned 'tsar'.

1549–56 Period of reforms; 1550: second law code (*Tsarskii Sudebnik*); 1550: 1,064 'boyars' sons' given pomestia in the environs of Moscow; 1551: 'Hundred-headed' (*Stoglavyi*) Synod; 1550s: first prikazy formed and reforms of local administration; 1555 or 56: attempt to regulate terms of state service.

1552 Capture and annexation of Khanate of Kazan.

1553 British discover northern maritime route to Russia.

1556 Capture and annexation of the khanate of Astrakhan.

1550s Moscow constructs chain of stockades along the southern border and Russian colonization of the steppe begins.

1558–83 Russian war against Livonia.

1564–72 Oprichnina terror.

1566 Land Assembly convened to discuss Livonian War.

1569 Union of Lublin resulting in the merger of Poland and Lithuania, formation of Commonwealth (*Rzeczpospolita*).

1570 Novgorod razed on orders of Ivan IV; massacres of inhabitants.

— 1581–92 New cadaster books drawn up which serve as basis of serfdom.
— 1584–98 Fedor I.
1588–9 Giles Fletcher in Russia.
1589 Russian Patriarchate created.
1596 Brest Union of Catholics and Orthodox, creating on Polish-Lithuanian territory an Uniate Church.
— 1598 With death of Fedor, Riurik dynasty expires; beginning of 'Time of Troubles' (*smutnoe vremia*), ended in 1613.
1598–1605 Boris Godunov.

THE SEVENTEENTH CENTURY

1581–1639 Russian conquest of Siberia.
1601–2 Edicts restricting further peasant mobility.
1606–10 Vasilii Shuiskii tsar.
1610 Russians offer throne to Polish Prince Wladyslaw.
— 1613–1917 Romanov dynasty.
1613–45 Michael tsar; between 1619 and 1633, his father, Patriarch Filaret, co-ruler.
1632–4 Russian attempt to capture Smolensk from the Poles.
1632 Winius and Marselis found Tula and Kashira iron foundries.
1645–76 Alexis.
1648 Urban rebellions.
1648–9 Important Assembly in session.
— 1649 New Code (*Ulozhenie*).
1649 British commercial privileges withdrawn.
1652 Nikon Patriarch.
1653 Last Assembly.
1654–67 Wars with Poland over the Ukraine.
— 1666 Synod condemns Nikon, retains his reforms; beginning of schism (*raskol*).
1667 New Trading Regulation (*Novotorgovyi ustav*).
1667 Andrussovo Treaty with Poland; Russia acquires Kiev.
— 1670–1 Peasant rebellion led by Stepan (Stenka) Razin.
1676–81 War with the Ottoman Empire and the Crimea.
1676–82 Fedor III.
1682–9 Regency of Sophia; V.V.Golitsyn actual ruler.
— 1682 *Mestnichestvo* abolished.
1687, 1689 Unsuccessful campaigns against the Crimean Tatars.

PETER I (1689–1725)

1689 Sophia's Regency overthrown, Peter takes over (until 1696 co-ruler with his brother, Ivan).
1697–8 Peter's trip to western Europe ('Great Embassy').
1697 Preobrazhenskii Prikaz given exclusive competence over political crimes.
1700 Patriarch Adrian dies, replaced by acting head of church.

1700 Russian defeat at Swedish hands in battle of Narva.

1701 Monasteries required to turn over revenues to state.

1702 Decision to construct St Petersburg; 1703, foundations of new city laid.

1703 *Vedomosti*, Russia's first newspaper.

1705 Recruitment obligation instituted.

1709 Russians defeat Swedes at Poltava. - result of scorched earth policy etc.

1709 Construction of St Petersburg begins; 1712, Russian capital transferred there.

1710 Russians take Livonia and Estonia.

1711 Peter abolishes most trading monopolies.

1711 Tsar's Council ('Boyar Duma') replaced by the Senate.

1711 Russian defeat in campaign against the Turks on the Prut River.

1714 Edict requiring landowners to bequeath estates intact to a single heir.

1714 Kormleniia abolished and civil servants placed on a salary.

1718 Beginning of first 'soul' census.

1718 Colleges replace prikazy.

1721 Merchants allowed to purchase villages in order to attach labouring force to industrial and mining enterprises.

1721 Senate proclaims Peter 'Emperor'.

1721 Ecclesiastical Regulation: Patriarchate abolished and replaced with Holy Synod.

1722 Table of Ranks.

1722 Succession law abolished: emperors free to choose successors.

1724 Soul tax introduced.

1724 First comprehensive protective tariff.

1725 Academy of Sciences founded.

PETER'S IMMEDIATE SUCCESSORS

1725–7 Catherine I.

1727–30 Peter II.

1730 Constitutional crisis; unsuccessful attempt by Supreme Privy Council to impose 'Conditions' on Anne.

1730–40 Anne.

1730 Inheritance law of 1714 repealed.

1731 Establishment of Noble Cadet Corps.

1736 Compulsory state service limited to 25 years and may begin at age of 20; one son of landlord may remain home.

1736 'Possessional' serfs attached in perpetuity to factories and mines.

1741–61 Elizabeth.

1753 Internal tariffs and tolls in Russian Empire abolished.

1755 University of Moscow.

PETER III AND CATHERINE II (1761–96)

1761–2 Peter III.

18 February 1762 'Manifesto of Dvorianstvo Liberty', exempting dvoriane from compulsory state service.

1762 Church and monastic properties sequestered; law goes into effect in 1764.

1762 Most commercial and manufacturing monopolies (regalia) abolished.

1762 Law of 1721, allowing merchants to buy villages revoked.

28 June 1762–1796 Catherine II.

1764 Automatic promotion for certain categories of civil servants.

1767 Automatic promotion rules for civil servants extended.

1767–8 Legislative Commission convoked to draft new code of laws.

1769 Russia's first satirical journals (*Vsiakaia vsiachina* and *Truten'*).

1772 First Partition of Poland. ; Smolny Institute (for girls) estab

1773–5 Peasant and Cossack uprising under Emelian Pugachev.

1775 Provincial reform.

1775 All manufacturing activity open to all estates.

see Rogger

1783 Dvoriane allowed to operate private printing presses. Estab of the Russian Acade

1784–91 Novikov leases Moscow University typography.

21 April 1785 Charter of Dvorianstvo and Charter of Cities.

1787–91 War with the Ottoman Empire.

1790 Publication of Radishchev's *Journey*, followed by his arrest.

1792 Novikov arrested.

1793 Second Partition of Poland.

1795 Third Partition of Poland.

FIRST HALF OF THE NINETEENTH CENTURY

1796–1801 Paul.

1797 Department of Appanages created.

1797 Paul restores succession law to the throne, abolished by Peter I in 1722.

1801–25 Alexander I.

1809 Abortive attempt to introduce civil service examinations.

1811 Ministry of the Police created; abolished in 1819.

1812 French invasion of Russia, followed by Russian entry into western Europe and occupation of Paris.

1825–55 Nicholas I.

14 December 1825 'Decembrist' uprising.

1826 Supreme Criminal Commission set up to try Decembrists.

1826 Third Department established.

1826 Censorship Code.

1830 Full Collection of Laws published.

1830–1 Polish uprising; abrogation of Polish Constitution.

1833 Code of Laws issued.

1835 Reform of University Statutes.

1836 Publication of Chaadaev's First Philosophical Letter.

1837 Ministry of State Domains established.

1839 Knoop settles in Russia.

1845 Hereditary dvorianstvo restricted to top five ranks.

1845 Revised version of Criminal Code.

1847 Haxthausen's book published.

1853–6 Crimean War.

[handwritten margin note: Florinshy p. 908 & S-W 386 / Say universal conscription = 1874]

ALEXANDER II (1855–81)

1856 Hereditary dvorianstvo restricted to top four ranks.
1860 Rural courts introduced.
19 February 1861 Emancipation of serfs.
1863 Polish uprising.
1864 Court Reform.
1864 Introduction of zemstva and city self-government.
1864–80 Russia conquers Turkestan.
1870 Compulsory military service.
1874 First 'going to the people' movement.
1877–8 Trials of 'Fifty' and '193'.
1878 Vera Zasulich shoots St Petersburg police chief.
4 August 1878 Terrorist assasinates Chief of Gendarmes.
9 August 1878 Temporary laws introducing courts-martial for terrorists.
1 September 1878 Secret circular authorizing arrest and exile of persons suspected of seditious intent.
April 1879 'Temporary Governors General' created.
5 February 1880 Terrorists succeed in planting bomb in Winter Palace.
February 1880 General Loris-Melikov dictator.
August 1880 Third Department abolished; establishment of new Department of State Police.
1 March 1881 Assassination of Alexander II.

ALEXANDER III (1881–94)

14 August 1881 Major edict concerning 'Temporary Laws'.
12 March 1882 Rules for overt surveillance.
1882–95 Dmitry Tolstoy, Minister of the Interior.
1883 Law requiring peasants to buy out their land allotment.
1885 New edition of Criminal Code.
1886 Special rules governing forced labour.
1887 Soul tax abolished.
1889 Land Commandants created.
1893 Clauses in Emancipation Edict permitting leaving of communes abrogated.

NICHOLAS II (1894–1917)

1901–3 Zubatov active.
November 1904 Zemstvo 'banquet' campaign demanding constitution.
January 1905 'Bloody Sunday' in St Petersburg.
October 1905 Manifesto promising civil liberties and representative institutions.
1906 Fundamental Laws (constitution) and First Duma.
November 1906 New legislation enabling peasants to consolidate holdings and leave commune.
1907 Redemption payments and arrears cancelled.
1909 *Vekhi*.

February 1917 Nicholas II abdicates; Provisional Government formed by Duma takes over.

SINCE 1917

October 1917 Bolshevik power seizure.

1918–21 Civil War and War Communism.

July 1918 Murder of ex-tsar and his family.

September 1918 Proclamation of 'Red Terror'.

1921 New Economic Policy (NEP) inaugurated.

1927 Soviet Criminal Code.

1928–32 'Collectivization': creation of kolkhozy.

1934 Clauses added to Criminal Code sections dealing with anti-state ('counter-revolutionary') crimes.

INDEX

In the index which follows, all Russian technical words and the names of all historical figures are given stress. The rules of Russian pronunciation can be roughly stated:
1. an unstressed 'o' is pronounced as if it were an 'a': thus, Godunóv is pronounced 'Gadunóv'; 2. 'ë' is spoken as if it were 'yo' and, unless otherwise indicated, it is stressed: 'Solovëv' should sound 'Salavyóv'; 3. the soft sign is transliterated with an apostrophe: it has no exact equivalent in English, but one can obtain a vague idea of its sound by putting an 'i' in its place (e.g. *strel'tsy*=*strelitsy*); with one exception (Rus'), the soft sign is used only in Italicized Russian words.

'Oblomovitis', 271
obrók (rent), 147, 149; and serf industry, 213
obshchéstvennoe dvizhénie ('social movement'), 256
óbshchestvo (society), 71, 127
óbshchina see mir
October Manifesto, 307
Octobrists, 219
Oder river, 1
odnodvórtsy ('single-householders'), 175
Odóevskii, Prince V.F.: response to idealism, 260–1
Office of Ambassadors, 111, 197
Office of the Heroldmeister, 123, 130
Office of Pomestia, 109
oikos, 21, 22, 43
oilfields: Caucasus, 218
Oka river, 29, 80
Oka-Volga region, 36
Okhrána, 301, 317
see also police, political police
okól'nichii (rank), 90
Old Believers, Old Ritualists, 213, 236–8, 239, 243, 292; numbers, 239
old Slavonic, see Church Slavonic
Olearius, Adam, 200, 228
Olonetsk, 177n
Onega, lake, 80
opera, 218
opríchniki, 95
opríchnina, 94, 101
Orel, 177n
Orenburg, 177n
'Oriental Despotism', 20–1, 112
Orthodox Church, 46, 158; anti-intellectualism, 243; art and ritual, 221; centred in Moscow, 234; church language, 227; conversion of Normans, 32; conversion of Russia, 223; conservatism as a feature in state-church relations, 225–6; doctrine, 221–2; failures, 244–5; fasts, 143; and magic elements in religion, 242; favoured treatment from Mongols, 226; land ownership, 226–7, 229–31, 234, 240–1, 242; low public esteem, 243–4; loses semi-autonomy under Peter the Great, 239–43; Nikon's reforms, 235; schism, 234ff; schools, 243; serf ownership, 240; support for monarchy and state, 62, 127–8, 222, 224–5, 232–4, 235–6, 239; taxation, 240–1; tiaglo households, 104; tradition, 225–6; wealth, 240
Otéchestvennye Zapíski (Annals of the Fatherland), 264
Ottoman Empire, 116, 148

overt surveillance (nadzór, podnadzórnyi), 309, 311

pai (share or security), 204
painting, 218
Pakhman, S.V., 326
Pale of Settlement, 250, 289
Palmer, William, (236), 329
paper mills, 196; ownership, 212
Parker, W. H., 321
Parliament of Paris, 288
Pascal, Pierre, (239), 329
passports, internal, 164n
patriarchate: abolition, 240, 241
Patrimonial Monarchy, xxii, 22–4, 64–6; anatomy, ch. 4; attitude to territory, 79–80, 84; classic examples, 23–4, 112; dangers of limited partnership with society, 129; military shortcomings, 112–13; origins, ch. 2; partial dismantling, ch. 5; politicization, 71ff; triumph, ch. 3
Paul I, Emperor, 135, 211n, 259
Pavlov, A., (230), 329
Pavlov-Silvanskii, N.P., 48, 322
Pavlovsky, George, (167), 326
Peasant Bank, 166
peasantry, ch. 6: absolutism preferred, 250; and abstract thought, 157–8; and appanage system, 48; attitude towards the tsar, 161–2; and 'black land', 47–8; character, 160, 168; classes, 144–8; communal institutions, see commune, mir; consciousness of rank, 159; dissimulation, 156; dominant element in population, 141; economic decline after Emancipation Edict, 165–6; indebtedness, 102–3; enserfment, 100–5; family structure, 16–17; foreign accounts, 151–2; Gorky's description, 159–60; hostile to authority, 155; inability to support itself from agriculture, 167–8; land ownership, 153, 155–6, 169; and landlords, 104–5, 153; legal position, 154; living conditions, 143–4; personal identity, 158–9; political attitudes, 161–2; and radical movement, 273–4, 297; religion, 160–1, 243; rural violence, 155–6; and serfdom, 154ff; social mobility through trade, 217; taxation see soul tax; trading, 210, 211–12; traditionalism 153, 155; uprisings, 155–6, 169–70
Pechenegs, 32, 34n, 35, 37
pedigree (rodoslóvnost'), 97
Penza, 177n
Pereieslavets, 34n